NON-LEAGUE FOOTBALL TABLES 1889-2007

EDITOR
Michael Robinson

British Library Cataloguing in Publication Data
A catalogue record for this book is available from the British Library

ISBN: 978-1-86223-162-7

Manufactured in the UK by LPPS Ltd, Wellingborough, NN8 3PJ

FOREWORD

In selecting the Leagues to be included in this fifth edition of Non-League Football Tables we have again chosen those forming the pinnacle of the Non-League Football Pyramid, i.e. The Football Conference and it's three direct feeders.

In addition we have once more included the briefly-lived Football Alliance which became, effectively, the 2nd Division of the Football League in 1892 together with The Midland Combination, The Hellenic League and The Devon County League which has closed down at the end of the 2006/2007 season and merged with the South-Western League to form a new South-West Peninsula League.

Furthermore, as league sponsors change frequently, we have not used sponsored names (eg. Rymans League) other than in an indicative way on the cover.

We have slightly modified the way in which the statistics are presented for the three additional Leagues covered in this edition of our Non-League Football Tables book. For these three Leagues, the names of clubs which have earned promotion from the lower divisions for the following season have been highlighted in bold text. Similarly, clubs who have been relegated are highlighted in bold italic text.

We believe that these changes will prove helpful in following the statistics from one season to the next.

We are indebted to Mick Blakeman for providing tables for the three new Leagues included in this edition of the book.

CONTENTS

FOOTBALL ALLIANCE

1889-90

Sheffield Wednesday	22	15	2	5	70	39	32
Bootle	22	13	2	7	66	39	28
Sunderland Albion	21	12	2	7	64	39	28
Grimsby Town	22	12	2	8	58	47	26
Crewe Alexandra	22	11	2	9	68	59	24
Darwen	22	10	2	10	70	75	22
Birmingham St George	21	9	3	9	62	49	21
Newton Heath	22	9	2	11	40	44	20
Walsall Town Swifts	22	8	3	11	44	59	19
Small Heath	22	6	5	11	44	67	17
Nottingham Forest	22	6	5	11	31	62	17
Long Eaton Rangers	22	4	2	16	35	73	10

Sunderland Albion record includes 2 points awarded when Birmingham St George refused to fulfil a fixture which the Alliance committee had ordered to be replayed.

1890-91

Stoke	22	13	7	2	57	39	33
Sunderland Albion	22	12	6	4	69	28	30
Grimsby Town	22	11	5	6	43	27	27
Birmingham St George	22	12	2	8	64	62	26
Nottingham Forest	22	9	7	6	66	39	25
Darwen	22	10	3	9	64	59	23
Walsall Town Swifts	22	9	3	10	34	61	21
Crewe Alexandra	22	8	4	10	59	67	20
Newton Heath	22	7	3	12	37	55	17
Small Heath	22	7	2	13	58	66	16
Bootle	22	3	7	12	40	61	13
Sheffield Wednesday	22	4	5	13	39	66	13

1891-92

Nottingham Forest	22	14	5	3	59	22	33
Newton Heath	22	12	7	3	69	33	31
Small Heath	22	12	5	5	53	36	29
Sheffield Wednesday	22	12	4	6	65	35	28
Burton Swifts	22	12	2	8	54	52	26
Grimsby Town	22	6	6	10	40	39	18
Crewe Alexandra	22	7	4	11	44	49	18
Ardwick	22	6	6	10	39	51	18
Bootle	22	8	2	12	42	64	18
Lincoln City	22	6	5	11	37	65	17
Walsall Town Swifts	22	6	3	13	33	59	15
Birmingham St George	22	5	3	14	34	64	13

SOUTHERN LEAGUE

1894-95

First Division

Millwall Athletic	16	12	4	0	68	19	28
Luton Town	16	9	4	3	36	22	22
Southampton St Mary's	16	9	2	5	34	25	20
Ilford	16	6	3	7	26	40	15
Reading	16	6	2	8	33	38	14
Chatham	16	4	5	7	22	25	13
Royal Ordnance Factories	16	3	6	7	20	30	12
Clapton	16	5	1	10	22	38	11
Swindon Town	16	4	1	11	24	48	9

Second Division

New Brompton	12	11	0	1	57	10	22
Sheppey United	12	6	1	5	25	23	13
Old St Stephen's	12	6	0	6	26	26	12
Uxbridge	12	4	3	5	14	20	11
Bromley	12	4	1	7	23	30	9
Chesham	12	3	3	6	20	42	9
Maidenhead	12	2	4	6	19	33	8

1895-96

First Division

Millwall Athletic	18	16	1	1	75	16	33
Luton Town	18	13	1	4	68	14	27
Southampton St Mary's	18	12	0	6	44	23	24
Reading	18	11	1	6	45	38	23
Chatham	18	9	2	7	43	45	20
New Brompton	18	7	4	7	30	37	18
Swindon Town	18	6	4	8	38	41	16
Clapton	18	4	2	12	30	67	10
Royal Ordnance Factories	18	3	3	12	23	44	9
Ilford	18	0	0	18	10	81	0

Second Division

Wolverton L & NW Railway	16	13	1	2	43	10	27
Sheppey United	16	11	3	2	60	19	25
1st Scots Guards	16	8	5	3	37	22	21
Uxbridge	16	9	1	6	28	23	19
Old St Stephen's	16	6	3	7	34	21	15
Guildford	16	7	1	8	29	41	15
Maidenhead	16	4	1	11	20	49	9
Chesham	16	2	3	11	15	48	7
Bromley	16	2	2	12	16	49	6

1896-97

First Division

Southampton St Mary's	20	15	5	0	63	18	35
Millwall Athletic	20	13	5	2	63	24	31
Chatham	20	13	1	6	54	29	27
Tottenham Hotspur	20	9	4	7	43	29	22
Gravesend United	20	9	4	7	35	34	22
Swindon Town	20	8	3	9	33	37	19
Reading	20	8	3	9	31	49	19
New Brompton	20	7	2	11	32	42	16
Northfleet	20	5	4	11	24	46	14
Sheppey United	20	5	1	14	34	47	11
Wolverton L & NW Railway	20	2	0	18	17	74	4

Second Division

Dartford	24	16	4	4	83	19	36
Royal Engineers Training Battalion	24	11	9	4	49	37	31
Freemantle	24	12	4	8	58	40	28
Uxbridge	24	11	5	8	62	37	27
Wycombe Wanderers	24	10	6	8	37	54	26
Chesham	24	11	3	10	41	55	25
Southall	24	9	6	9	55	52	24
1st Scot Guards	24	9	6	9	49	50	24
West Herts	24	11	1	12	41	49	23
Warmley (Bristol)	24	10	2	12	44	43	22
Old St Stephen's	24	5	7	12	36	52	17
Maidenhead	24	4	8	12	33	64	16
1st Coldstream Guards	24	3	6	15	30	66	12

1897-98

First Division

Southampton	22	18	1	3	53	18	37
Bristol City	22	13	7	2	67	33	33
Tottenham Hotspur	22	12	4	6	52	31	28
Chatham	22	12	4	6	50	34	28
Reading	22	8	7	7	39	31	23
New Brompton	22	9	4	9	37	37	22
Sheppey United	22	10	1	11	40	49	21
Gravesend United	22	7	6	9	28	39	20
Millwall Athletic	22	8	2	12	48	45	18
Swindon Town	22	7	2	13	36	48	16
Northfleet	22	4	3	15	29	60	11
Wolverton L & NW Railway	22	3	1	18	28	82	7

Second Division

Royal Artillery (Portsmouth)	22	19	1	2	75	22	39
Warmley (Bristol)	22	19	0	3	108	15	38
West Herts	22	11	6	5	50	48	28
Uxbridge	22	11	2	9	39	57	24
St Albans	22	9	5	8	47	41	23
Dartford	22	11	0	11	68	55	22
Southall	22	8	2	12	49	61	18
Chesham	22	8	2	12	38	48	18
Olsd St Stephen's	22	7	2	13	47	66	16
Wycombe Wanderers	22	7	2	13	37	55	16
Maidenhead	22	4	4	14	27	81	12
Royal Engineers Training Battalion	22	4	2	16	26	62	10

1898-99

First Division

Southampton	24	15	5	4	54	24	35
Bristol City	24	15	3	6	55	12	33
Millwall Athletic	24	12	6	6	59	35	30
Chatham	24	10	8	6	32	23	28
Reading	24	9	8	7	31	24	26
New Brompton	24	10	5	9	38	30	25
Tottenham Hotspur	24	10	4	10	40	36	24
Bedminster	24	10	4	10	35	39	24
Swindon Town	24	9	5	10	43	49	23
Brighton United	24	9	2	13	37	48	20
Gravesend United	24	7	5	12	42	52	19
Sheppey United	24	5	3	16	23	53	13
Royal Artillery (Portsmouth)	24	4	4	16	17	60	12

Second Division (London Section)

Thames Ironworks	22	19	1	2	64	16	39
Wolverton L & NW Railway	22	13	4	5	88	43	30
Watford	22	14	2	6	62	35	30
Brentford	22	11	3	8	59	39	25
Wycombe Wanderers	22	10	2	10	55	57	22
Southall	22	11	0	11	44	55	22
Chesham	22	9	2	11	45	62	20
St Albans	22	8	3	11	45	59	19
Shepherds Bush	22	7	3	12	37	53	17
Fulham	22	6	4	12	36	44	16
Uxbridge	22	7	2	13	29	48	16
Maidenhead	22	3	2	17	33	86	8

Second Division (South West Section)

Cowes	10	10	0	0	58	8	20
Ryde	10	7	0	3	30	11	14
Freemantle	10	4	1	5	18	31	9
Sandown	10	4	0	6	20	29	8
Eastleigh	10	2	1	7	17	37	5
Andover	10	2	0	8	14	41	4

1899-1900

First Division

Tottenham Hotspur	28	20	4	4	67	26	44
Portsmouth	28	20	1	7	58	27	41
Southampton	28	17	1	10	70	33	35
Reading	28	15	2	11	41	28	32
Swindon Town	28	15	2	11	50	42	32
Bedminster	28	13	2	13	44	45	28
Millwall Athletic	28	12	3	13	36	37	27
Queens Park Rangers	28	12	2	14	49	57	26
Bristol City	28	9	7	12	43	47	25
Bristol Rovers	28	11	3	14	46	55	25
New Brompton	28	9	6	13	39	49	24
Gravesend United	28	10	4	14	38	58	24
Chatham	28	10	3	15	38	58	23
Thames Ironworks	28	8	5	15	30	45	21
Sheppey United	28	3	7	18	24	66	13

Second Division

Watford	20	14	2	4	57	25	30
Fulham	20	10	4	6	44	23	24
Chesham Town	20	11	2	7	43	37	24
Wolverton L & NW Railway	20	9	6	5	46	36	24
Grays United	20	8	6	6	63	29	22
Shepherds Bush	20	9	4	7	45	37	22
Dartford	20	8	3	9	36	44	19
Wycombe Wanderers	20	8	3	9	35	50	19
Brentford	20	5	7	8	31	48	17
Southall	20	6	3	11	21	44	15
Maidenhead	20	1	2	17	16	64	4

1900-01

First Division

Southampton	28	18	5	5	58	26	41
Bristol City	28	17	5	6	54	27	39
Portsmouth	28	17	4	7	56	32	38
Millwall Athletic	28	17	2	9	55	32	36
Tottenham Hotspur	28	16	4	8	55	33	36
West Ham United	28	14	5	9	40	28	33
Bristol Rovers	28	14	4	10	46	35	32
Queens Park Rangers	28	11	4	13	43	48	26
Reading	28	8	8	12	24	25	24
Luton Town	28	11	2	15	43	49	24
Kettering	28	7	9	12	33	46	23
New Brompton	28	7	5	16	34	51	19
Gravesend United	28	6	7	15	32	85	19
Watford	28	6	4	18	24	52	16
Swindon Town	28	3	8	17	19	47	14

Second Division

Brentford	16	14	2	0	63	11	30
Grays United	16	12	2	2	62	12	26
Sheppey United	16	8	1	7	44	26	17
Shepherds Bush	16	8	1	7	30	30	17
Fulham	16	8	0	8	38	26	16
Chesham Town	16	5	1	10	26	39	11
Maidenhead	16	4	1	11	21	49	9
Wycombe Wanderers	16	4	1	11	23	68	9
Southall	16	4	1	11	22	68	9

1901-02

First Division

Portsmouth	30	20	7	3	67	24	47
Tottenham Hotspur	30	18	6	6	61	22	42
Southampton	30	18	6	6	71	28	42
West Ham United	30	17	6	7	45	28	40
Reading	30	16	7	7	57	24	39
Millwall Athletic	30	13	6	11	48	31	32
Luton Town	30	11	10	9	31	35	32
Kettering	30	12	5	13	44	39	29
Bristol Rovers	30	12	5	13	43	39	29
New Brompton	30	10	7	13	39	38	27
Northampton	30	11	5	14	53	64	27
Queens Park Rangers	30	8	7	15	34	56	23
Watford	30	9	4	17	36	60	22
Wellingborough	30	9	4	17	34	75	22
Brentford	30	7	6	17	34	61	20
Swindon Town	30	2	3	25	17	93	7

Second Division

Fulham	16	13	0	3	51	19	26
Grays United	16	12	1	3	49	14	25
Brighton & Hove Albion	16	11	0	5	34	17	22
Wycombe Wanderers	16	7	3	6	36	30	17
West Hampstead	16	6	4	6	39	29	16
Shepherds Bush	16	6	1	9	31	31	13
Southall	16	5	2	9	28	52	12
Maidenhead	16	3	1	12	23	59	7
Chesham Town	16	2	2	12	24	64	6

1902-03

First Division

Southampton	30	20	8	2	83	20	48
Reading	30	19	7	4	72	30	45
Portsmouth	30	17	7	6	69	32	41
Tottenham Hotspur	30	14	7	9	47	31	35
Bristol Rovers	30	13	8	9	46	34	34
New Brompton	30	11	11	8	37	35	33
Millwall Athletic	30	14	3	13	52	37	31
Northampton Town	30	12	6	12	39	48	30
Queens Park Rangers	30	11	6	13	34	42	28
West Ham United	30	9	10	11	35	49	28
Luton Town	30	10	7	13	43	44	27
Swindon Town	30	10	7	13	38	46	27
Kettering	30	8	11	11	33	40	27
Wellingborough	30	11	3	16	36	56	25
Watford	30	6	4	20	35	87	16
Brentford	30	2	1	27	16	84	5

Second Division

Fulham	10	7	1	2	27	7	15
Brighton & Hove Albion	10	7	1	2	34	11	15
Grays United	10	7	0	3	28	12	14
Wycombe Wanderers	10	3	3	4	13	19	9
Chesham Town	10	2	1	7	9	37	5
Southall	10	1	0	9	10	35	2

1903-04

First Division

Southampton	34	22	6	6	75	30	50
Tottenham Hotspur	34	16	11	7	54	37	43
Bristol Rovers	34	17	8	9	66	42	42
Portsmouth	34	17	8	9	41	38	42
Queens Park Rangers	34	15	11	8	53	37	41
Reading	34	14	13	7	48	35	41
Millwall	34	16	8	10	64	42	40
Luton Town	34	14	12	8	38	33	40
Plymouth Argyle	34	13	10	11	44	34	36
Swindon Town	34	10	11	13	30	42	31
Fulham	34	9	12	13	33	34	30
West Ham United	34	10	7	17	38	43	27
Brentford	34	9	9	16	34	48	27
Wellingborough	34	11	5	18	44	63	27
Northampton Town	34	10	7	17	36	69	27
New Brompton	34	6	13	15	26	43	25
Brighton & Hove Albion	34	6	12	16	45	79	24
Kettering	34	6	7	21	30	78	19

Second Division

Watford	20	18	2	0	70	15	38
Portsmouth Reserves	20	15	2	3	85	25	32
Millwall Reserves	20	9	4	7	35	39	22
Southampton Reserves	20	9	3	8	59	35	21
Grays United	20	9	3	8	25	55	21
Fulham Reserves	20	8	4	8	40	34	20
Swindon Town Reserves	20	8	3	9	50	44	19
Reading Reserves	20	8	2	10	43	42	18
Wycombe Wanderers	20	5	5	10	29	64	15
Southall	20	4	2	14	25	62	10
Chesham Town	20	1	2	17	19	65	4

1904-05

First Division

Bristol Rovers	34	20	8	6	74	36	48
Reading	34	18	7	9	57	38	43
Southampton	34	18	7	9	54	40	43
Plymouth Argyle	34	18	5	11	57	39	41
Tottenham Hotspur	34	15	8	11	53	34	38
Fulham	34	14	10	10	46	34	38
Queens Park Rangers	34	14	8	12	51	46	36
Portsmouth	34	16	4	14	61	56	36
New Brompton	34	11	11	12	40	41	33
West Ham United	34	12	8	14	48	42	32
Brighton & Hove Albion	34	13	6	15	44	45	32
Northampton Town	34	12	8	14	43	54	32
Watford	34	14	3	17	41	44	31
Brentford	34	10	9	15	33	38	29
Millwall	34	11	7	16	38	47	29
Swindon Town	34	12	5	17	41	59	29
Luton Town	34	12	3	19	45	54	27
Wellingborough	34	5	3	26	25	104	13

Second Division

Fulham Reserves	22	16	4	2	78	25	36
Portsmouth Reserves	22	14	2	6	75	28	30
Swindon Town Reserves	22	12	3	7	54	47	27
Grays United	22	11	3	8	61	40	25
Southampton Reserves	22	10	5	7	52	35	25
Brighton & Hove Albion	22	9	3	10	48	49	21
West Ham United Reserves	22	8	5	9	45	47	21
Clapton Orient	22	7	7	8	47	56	21
Watford Reserves	22	5	6	11	30	62	16
Southall	22	7	2	13	31	66	16
Wycombe Wanderers	22	6	2	14	37	70	14
Reading Reserves	22	4	4	14	24	57	12

1905-06

First Division

Fulham	34	19	12	3	44	15	50
Southampton	34	19	7	8	58	39	45
Portsmouth	34	17	9	8	61	35	43
Luton Town	34	17	7	10	64	40	41
Tottenham Hotspur	34	16	7	11	46	29	39
Plymouth Argyle	34	16	7	11	52	33	39
Norwich City	34	13	10	11	46	38	36
Bristol Rovers	34	15	5	14	56	56	35
Brentford	34	14	7	13	43	52	35
Reading	34	12	9	13	53	46	33
West Ham United	34	14	5	15	42	39	33
Millwall	34	11	11	12	38	41	33
Queens Park Rangers	34	12	7	15	58	44	31
Watford	34	8	10	16	38	57	26
Swindon Town	34	8	9	17	31	52	25
Brighton & Hove Albion	34	9	7	18	30	55	25
New Brompton	34	7	8	19	20	62	22
Northampton Town	34	8	5	21	32	79	21

Second Division

Crystal Palace	24	19	4	1	66	14	42
Leyton	24	16	6	2	61	18	38
Portsmouth Reserves	24	12	8	4	52	24	32
Fulham Reserves	24	11	6	7	52	39	28
Southampton Reserves	24	7	9	8	39	41	23
Southern United	24	8	7	9	45	49	23
St Leonard's United	24	9	4	11	54	50	22
Watford Reserves	24	8	5	11	43	47	21
West Ham United Reserves	24	7	5	12	46	48	19
Grays United	24	8	3	13	24	77	19
Reading Reserves	24	6	5	13	36	49	15
Swindon Town Reserves	24	5	5	14	36	51	15
Wycombe Wanderers	24	5	3	16	36	83	13

1906-07

First Division

Fulham	38	20	13	5	58	32	53
Portsmouth	38	22	7	9	64	36	51
Brighton & Hove Albion	38	18	9	11	53	43	45
Luton Town	38	18	9	11	52	52	45
West Ham United	38	15	14	9	60	41	44
Tottenham Hotspur	38	17	9	12	63	45	43
Millwall	38	18	6	14	71	50	42
Norwich City	38	15	12	11	57	48	42
Watford	38	13	16	9	46	43	42
Brentford	38	17	8	13	57	56	42
Southampton	38	13	9	16	49	56	35
Reading	38	14	6	18	57	47	34
Leyton	38	11	12	15	38	60	34
Bristol Rovers	38	12	9	17	55	54	33
Plymouth Argyle	38	10	13	15	43	50	33
New Brompton	38	12	9	17	47	59	33
Swindon Town	38	11	11	16	43	54	33
Queens Park Rangers	38	11	10	17	47	55	32
Crystal Palace	38	8	9	21	46	66	25
Northampton Town	38	5	9	24	29	88	19

Second Division

Southend United	22	14	5	3	58	23	33
West Ham United Reserves	22	14	3	5	64	30	31
Portsmouth Reserves	22	11	6	5	53	24	28
Fulham Reserves	22	11	4	7	47	32	26
Hastings & St Leonards	21	10	4	7	46	31	24
Tunbridge Wells Rangers	22	10	1	11	46	36	21
Salisbury City	22	9	2	11	40	42	20
Southampton Reserves	22	8	2	12	37	56	18
Swindon Town Reserves	22	7	3	12	35	43	17
Reading Reserves	22	6	4	12	32	47	16
Royal Engineers (Aldershot)	21	5	4	12	27	58	14
Wycombe Wanderers	22	4	6	12	28	68	14

The match between Tunbridge Wells Rangers and Royal Engineers (Aldershot) was not completed.

1907-08

First Division

Queens Park Rangers	38	21	9	8	82	57	51
Plymouth Argyle	38	19	11	8	50	31	49
Millwall	38	19	8	11	49	32	46
Crystal Palace	38	17	10	11	54	51	44
Swindon Town	38	16	10	12	55	40	42
Bristol Rovers	38	16	10	12	59	56	42
Tottenham Hotspur	38	17	7	14	59	48	41
Northampton Town	38	15	11	12	50	41	41
Portsmouth	38	17	6	15	63	52	40
West Ham United	38	15	10	13	47	48	40
Southampton	38	16	6	16	51	60	38
Reading	38	15	6	17	55	50	36
Bradford Park Avenue	38	12	12	14	53	54	36
Watford	38	12	10	16	47	49	34
Brentford	38	14	5	19	49	52	33
Norwich City	38	12	9	17	46	49	33
Brighton & Hove Albion	38	12	8	18	46	59	32
Luton Town	38	12	6	20	33	56	30
Leyton	38	8	11	19	51	73	27
New Brompton	38	9	7	22	44	75	25

Second Division

Southend	18	13	3	2	47	16	29
Portsmouth Reserves	18	10	5	3	39	22	25
Croydon Common	18	10	3	5	35	25	23
Hastings & St Leonard's	18	10	2	6	43	29	22
Southampton Reserves	18	7	4	7	54	46	18
Tunbridge Wells Rangers	18	7	3	8	42	38	17
Salisbury City	18	6	4	8	35	46	16
Swindon Town Reserves	18	5	5	8	36	40	15
Brighton & Hove Albion Reserves	18	4	4	10	34	47	12
Wycombe Wanderers	18	1	1	16	16	72	3

1908-09

First Division

Northampton Town	40	25	5	10	90	45	55
Swindon Town	40	22	5	13	96	55	49
Southampton	40	19	10	11	67	58	48
Portsmouth	40	18	10	12	68	60	46
Bristol Rovers	40	17	9	14	60	63	43
Exeter City	40	18	6	16	56	65	42
New Brompton	40	17	7	16	48	59	41
Reading	40	11	18	11	60	57	40
Luton Town	40	17	6	17	59	60	40
Plymouth Argyle	40	15	10	15	46	47	40
Millwall	40	16	6	18	59	61	38
Southend United	40	14	10	16	52	54	38
Leyton	40	15	8	17	52	55	38
Watford	40	14	9	17	51	64	37
Queens Park Rangers	40	12	12	16	52	50	36
Crystal Palace	40	12	12	16	62	62	36
West Ham United	40	16	4	20	56	60	36
Brighton & Hove Albion	40	14	7	19	60	61	35
Norwich City	40	12	11	17	59	75	35
Coventry City	40	15	4	21	64	91	34
Brentford	40	13	7	20	59	74	33

Second Division

Croydon Common	12	10	0	2	67	14	20
Hastings & St Leonard's	12	8	1	3	42	18	17
Depot Battalion Royal Engineers	12	8	1	3	23	22	17
2nd Grenadier Guards	12	5	0	7	21	33	10
South Farnborough Athletic	12	2	4	6	20	39	8
Salisbury City	12	3	1	8	24	36	7
Chesham Town	12	2	1	9	17	52	5

1909-10

First Division

Brighton & Hove Albion	42	23	13	6	69	28	59
Swindon Town	42	22	10	10	92	46	54
Queens Park Rangers	42	19	13	10	56	47	51
Northampton Town	42	22	4	16	90	44	48
Southampton	42	16	16	10	64	55	48
Portsmouth	42	20	7	15	70	63	47
Crystal Palace	42	20	6	16	69	50	46
Coventry City	42	19	8	15	71	60	46
West Ham United	42	15	15	12	69	56	45
Leyton	42	16	11	15	60	46	43
Plymouth Argyle	42	16	11	15	61	54	43
New Brompton	42	19	5	18	76	74	43
Bristol Rovers	42	16	10	16	37	48	42
Brentford	42	16	9	17	50	58	41
Luton Town	42	15	11	16	72	92	41
Millwall	42	15	7	20	45	59	37
Norwich City	42	13	9	20	59	78	35
Exeter City	42	14	6	22	60	69	34
Watford	42	10	13	19	51	76	33
Southend United	42	12	9	21	51	90	33
Croydon Common	42	13	5	24	52	96	31
Reading	42	7	10	25	38	73	24

Second Division - Section A

Stoke	10	10	0	0	48	9	20
Ton Pentre	10	4	2	4	17	21	10
Merthyr Town	9	4	1	4	16	21	9
Salisbury City	8	2	1	5	7	18	5
Burton United	6	2	0	4	8	21	4
Aberdare	7	1	0	6	6	11	2

Second Division - Section B

Hastings & St Leonard's	9	6	3	0	26	11	15
Kettering	10	6	0	4	34	19	12
Chesham Town	10	5	2	3	25	25	12
Peterborough City	10	4	2	4	16	23	10
South Farnborough Athletic	10	4	1	5	23	19	9
Romford	9	0	0	9	7	33	0

1910-11

First Divison

Swindon Town	38	24	5	9	80	31	53
Northampton Town	38	18	12	8	54	27	48
Brighton & Hove Albion	38	20	8	10	58	35	48
Crystal Palace	38	17	13	8	55	48	47
West Ham United	38	17	11	10	63	46	45
Queens Park Rangers	38	13	14	11	52	41	40
Leyton	38	16	8	14	57	52	40
Plymouth Argyle	38	15	9	14	54	55	39
Luton Town	38	15	8	15	67	63	38
Norwich City	38	15	8	15	46	48	38
Coventry City	38	16	6	16	65	68	38
Brentford	38	14	9	15	41	42	37
Exeter City	38	14	9	15	51	53	37
Watford	38	13	9	16	49	65	35
Millwall	38	11	9	18	42	54	31
Bristol Rovers	38	10	10	18	42	55	30
Southampton	38	11	8	19	42	67	30
New Brompton	38	11	8	19	34	65	30
Southend United	38	10	9	19	47	64	29
Portsmouth	38	8	11	19	34	53	27

Second Division

Reading	22	16	3	3	55	11	35
Stoke	22	17	1	4	72	21	35
Merthyr Town	22	15	3	4	52	22	33
Cardiff City	22	12	4	6	48	29	28
Croydon Common	22	11	3	8	61	26	25
Treharris	22	10	3	9	38	31	23
Aberdare	22	9	5	8	38	33	23
Ton Pentre	22	10	3	9	44	40	23
Walsall	22	7	4	11	37	41	18
Kettering	22	6	1	15	34	68	13
Chesham Town	22	1	3	18	16	93	5
Salisbury City	22	0	3	19	16	92	3

1911-12

First Division

Queens Park Rangers	38	21	11	6	59	35	53
Plymouth Argyle	38	23	6	9	63	31	52
Northampton Town	38	22	7	9	82	41	51
Swindon Town	38	21	6	11	82	50	48
Brighton & Hove Albion	38	19	9	10	73	35	47
Coventry City	38	17	8	13	66	54	42
Crystal Palace	38	15	10	13	70	46	40
Millwall	38	15	10	13	60	57	40
Watford	38	13	10	15	56	68	36
Stoke	38	13	10	15	51	63	36
Reading	38	11	14	13	43	69	36
Norwich City	38	10	14	14	40	60	34
West Ham United	38	13	7	18	64	69	33
Brentford	38	12	9	17	60	65	33
Exeter City	38	11	11	16	48	62	33
Southampton	38	10	11	17	46	63	31
Bristol Rovers	38	9	13	16	41	62	31
New Brompton	38	11	9	18	35	72	31
Luton Town	38	9	10	19	49	61	28
Leyton	38	7	11	20	27	62	25

Second Division

Merthyr Town	26	19	3	4	60	14	41
Portsmouth	26	19	3	4	73	20	41
Cardiff City	26	15	4	7	55	26	34
Southend United	26	16	1	9	73	24	33
Pontypridd	26	13	6	7	39	24	32
Ton Pentre	26	12	3	11	56	45	27
Walsall	26	13	1	11	44	41	27
Treharris	26	11	5	10	44	47	27
Aberdare	26	10	3	13	39	44	23
Kettering	26	11	0	15	37	62	22
Croydon Common	26	8	2	15	43	45	18
Mardy	26	6	6	12	37	51	18
Cwm Albion	26	5	1	16	27	70	11
Chesham Town	26	1	0	25	18	131	2

1912-13

First Division

Plymouth Argyle	38	22	6	10	77	36	50
Swindon Town	38	20	8	10	66	41	48
West Ham United	38	18	12	8	66	43	48
Queens Park Rangers	38	16	11	11	46	35	43
Crystal Palace	38	17	11	10	55	36	45
Millwall	38	19	7	12	62	43	45
Exeter City	38	18	8	12	48	44	44
Reading	38	17	8	13	59	55	42
Brighton & Hove Albion	38	13	12	13	48	47	38
Northampton Town	38	12	12	14	61	48	36
Portsmouth	38	14	8	16	41	49	36
Merthyr Town	38	12	12	14	42	60	36
Coventry City	38	13	8	17	53	59	34
Watford	38	12	10	16	43	50	34
Gillingham	38	12	10	16	36	53	34
Bristol Rovers	38	12	9	17	55	64	33
Southampton	38	10	11	17	40	72	31
Norwich City	38	10	9	19	39	50	29
Brentford	38	11	5	22	42	55	27
Stoke	38	10	4	24	39	75	24

Second Division

Cardiff City	24	18	5	1	54	15	41
Southend United	24	14	6	4	43	23	34
Swansea Town	24	12	7	5	29	23	31
Croydon Common	24	13	4	7	51	29	30
Luton Town	24	13	4	7	52	39	30
Llanelly	24	9	6	9	33	39	24
Pontypridd	24	6	11	7	30	28	23
Mid Rhondda	24	9	4	11	33	31	22
Aberdare	24	8	6	10	38	40	22
Newport County	24	7	5	12	29	36	19
Mardy	24	6	3	15	38	38	15
Treharris	24	5	2	17	18	60	12
Ton Pentre	24	3	3	18	22	69	9

1913-14

First Division

Swindon Town	38	21	8	9	81	41	50
Crystal Palace	38	17	16	5	60	32	50
Northampton Town	38	14	19	5	50	37	47
Reading	38	17	10	11	43	36	44
Plymouth Argyle	38	15	13	10	46	42	43
West Ham United	38	15	12	11	61	60	42
Brighton & Hove Albion	38	15	12	11	43	45	42
Queens Park Rangers	38	16	9	13	45	43	41
Portsmouth	38	14	12	12	57	48	40
Cardiff City	38	13	12	13	46	42	38
Southampton	38	15	7	16	55	54	37
Exeter City	38	10	16	12	39	38	36
Gillingham	38	13	9	16	48	49	35
Norwich City	38	9	17	12	49	51	35
Millwall	38	11	12	15	51	56	34
Southend Unied	38	10	12	16	41	66	32
Bristol Rovers	38	10	11	17	46	67	31
Watford	38	10	9	19	50	56	29
Merthyr Town	38	9	10	19	38	61	28
Coventry City	38	6	14	18	43	68	26

Second Division

Croydon Common	30	23	5	2	76	14	51
Luton Town	30	24	3	3	92	22	51
Brentford	30	20	4	6	80	18	44
Swansea Town	30	20	4	6	66	23	44
Stoke	30	19	2	9	71	34	40
Newport County	30	14	8	8	49	38	36
Mid Rhondda	30	13	7	10	55	37	33
Pontypridd	30	14	5	11	43	38	33
Llanelly	30	12	4	14	45	39	28
Barry	30	9	8	13	44	70	26
Abertillery	30	8	4	18	44	57	20
Ton Pentre	30	8	4	18	33	61	20
Mardy	30	6	6	18	30	60	18
Caerphilly	30	4	7	19	21	103	15
Aberdare	30	4	5	21	33	87	13
Treharris	30	2	4	24	19	106	8

1914-15

First Division

Watford	38	22	8	8	68	46	52
Reading	38	21	7	10	68	43	49
Cardiff City	38	22	4	12	72	38	48
West Ham United	38	18	9	11	58	47	45
Northampton Town	38	16	11	11	56	51	43
Southampton	38	19	5	14	78	74	43
Portsmouth	38	16	10	12	54	42	42
Millwall	38	16	10	12	50	51	42
Swindon Town	38	15	11	12	77	59	41
Brighton & Hove Albion	38	16	7	15	46	47	39
Exeter City	38	15	8	15	50	41	38
Queens Park Rangers	38	13	12	13	55	56	38
Norwich City	38	11	14	13	53	56	36
Luton Town	38	13	8	17	61	73	34
Crystal Palace	38	13	8	17	47	61	34
Bristol Rovers	38	14	3	21	53	75	31
Plymouth Argyle	38	8	14	16	51	61	30
Southend United	38	10	8	20	44	64	28
Croydon Common	38	9	9	20	47	63	27
Gillingham	38	6	8	24	43	82	20

Second Division

Stoke	24	17	4	3	62	15	38
Stalybridge Celtic	24	17	3	4	47	22	37
Merthyr Town	24	15	5	4	46	20	35
Swansea Town	24	16	1	7	48	21	33
Coventry City	24	13	2	9	56	33	28
Ton Pentre	24	11	6	7	42	43	28
Brentford	24	8	7	9	35	45	23
Llanelly	24	10	1	13	39	32	21
Barry	24	6	5	13	30	35	17
Newport County	24	7	3	14	27	42	17
Pontypridd	24	5	6	13	31	58	16
Mid Rhondda	24	3	6	15	17	40	12
Ebbw Vale	24	3	1	20	23	88	7

1919-20

First Division

Portsmouth	42	23	12	7	73	27	58
Watford	42	26	6	10	69	42	58
Crystal Palace	42	22	12	8	69	43	56
Cardiff City	42	18	17	7	70	43	53
Plymouth Argyle	42	20	10	12	57	29	50
Queens Park Rangers	42	18	10	14	62	50	46
Reading	42	16	13	13	51	43	45
Southampton	42	18	8	16	72	63	44
Swansea Town	42	16	11	15	53	45	43
Exeter City	42	17	9	16	57	51	43
Southend United	42	13	17	12	46	48	43
Norwich City	42	15	11	16	64	57	41
Swindon Town	42	17	7	18	65	68	41
Millwall	42	14	12	16	52	55	40
Brentford	42	15	10	17	52	59	40
Brighton & Hove Albion	42	14	8	20	60	72	36
Bristol Rovers	42	11	13	18	61	78	35
Newport County	42	13	7	22	45	70	33
Northampton Town	42	12	9	21	64	103	33
Luton Town	42	10	10	22	51	76	30
Merthyr Town	42	9	11	22	47	78	29
Gillingham	42	10	7	25	34	74	27

Second Division

Mid Rhondda	20	17	3	0	79	10	37
Ton Pentre	20	12	7	1	50	14	31
Llanelly	20	10	5	5	47	30	25
Pontypridd	20	10	3	7	33	29	23
Ebbw Vale	20	7	7	6	38	40	21
Barry	20	7	5	8	32	27	19
Mardy	20	7	5	8	29	30	19
Abertillery	20	6	5	9	29	40	17
Porth Athletic	20	4	4	12	30	74	12
Aberaman Athletic	20	4	3	13	28	48	11
Caerphilly	20	1	3	16	20	74	5

1920-21

English Section

Brighton & Hove Albion Reserves	24	16	3	5	65	29	35
Portsmouth Reserves	24	13	7	4	44	20	33
Millwall Reserves	24	12	4	8	46	24	28
Southampton Reserves	24	10	7	7	53	35	27
Boscombe	24	10	6	8	25	40	26
Reading Reserves	24	11	3	10	41	34	25
Luton Town Reserves	24	8	8	8	38	35	24
Charlton Athletic	24	8	8	8	41	41	24
Watford Reserves	24	9	4	11	43	45	22
Norwich City Reserves	24	7	7	10	31	39	21
Gillingham Reserves	24	6	5	13	32	47	17
Chatham	24	5	6	13	24	47	16
Thornycrofts	24	4	6	14	29	74	14

Welsh Section

Barry	20	13	4	3	35	12	30
Aberdare Athletic	20	12	3	5	29	23	27
Ebbw Vale	20	10	5	5	34	23	25
Pontypridd	20	10	3	7	34	23	23
Mid Rhondda	20	10	3	7	26	18	23
Abertillery Town	20	8	5	7	35	24	21
Ton Pentre	20	7	5	8	32	34	19
Aberaman Athletic	20	5	7	8	30	33	17
Llanelly	20	7	2	11	28	46	16
Mardy	20	2	6	12	18	39	10
Porth Athletic	20	3	3	14	28	54	9

1921-22

English Section

Plymouth Argyle Reserves	36	22	5	9	91	38	49
Bristol City Reserves	36	18	8	10	73	50	44
Portsmouth Reserves	36	17	10	9	63	41	44
Southampton Reserves	36	19	5	12	70	47	43
Gillingham Reserves	36	17	9	10	65	47	43
Charlton Athletic Reserves	36	18	6	12	69	54	42
Boscombe	36	17	5	14	58	55	39
Luton Town Reserves	36	17	4	15	50	54	38
Watford Reserves	36	15	7	14	65	53	37
Brighton & Hove Albion Reserves	36	12	13	11	60	52	37
Bath City	36	16	5	15	55	53	37
Swindon Town Reserves	36	14	7	15	59	46	35
Bristol Rovers Reserves	36	13	7	16	50	82	33
Millwall Reserves	36	13	4	19	49	53	30
Reading Reserves	36	11	7	18	46	59	29
Exeter City Reserves	36	10	9	17	42	63	29
Guildford United	36	11	6	19	44	56	28
Norwich City Reserves	36	10	6	20	47	86	26
Southend United Reserves	36	9	3	24	47	92	21

Welsh Section

Ebbw Vale	16	11	3	2	33	11	25
Ton Pentre	16	9	4	3	35	14	22
Aberaman Athletic	16	7	5	4	25	19	19
Porth Athletic	16	6	6	4	31	20	18
Pontypridd	16	7	4	5	28	19	18
Swansea Town Reserves	16	7	4	5	24	17	18
Barry	16	3	3	10	14	35	9
Abertillery Town	16	3	2	11	21	45	8
Mardy	16	2	3	11	14	43	7

1922-23

English Section

Bristol City Reserves	38	24	5	9	84	39	53
Boscombe	38	22	7	9	67	34	51
Portsmouth Reserves	38	23	3	12	93	51	49
Bristol Rovers Reserves	38	20	8	10	59	41	48
Plymouth Argyle Reserves	38	20	7	11	74	41	47
Torquay United	38	18	8	12	63	38	44
Brighton & Hove Albion Reserves	38	20	3	15	95	60	43
Luton Town Reserves	38	16	11	11	67	56	43
Southend United Reserves	38	18	6	14	69	68	42
Southampton Reserves	38	18	5	15	65	54	41
Millwall Reserves	38	15	10	13	61	55	40
Coventry City Reserves	38	15	8	15	56	61	38
Guildford Town Reserves	38	15	7	16	65	59	37
Swindon Town Reserves	38	13	6	19	54	73	32
Bath City	38	10	8	20	44	71	28
Watford Reserves	38	11	6	21	34	79	28
Yeovil & Petters United	38	10	6	22	56	104	26
Norwich City Reserves	38	9	7	22	42	68	25
Exeter City Reserves	38	10	5	23	43	81	25
Reading Reserves	38	7	6	25	43	95	20

Welsh Section

Ebbw Vale	12	6	5	1	22	15	17
Aberaman Athletic	12	7	2	3	30	19	16
Swansea Town Reserves	12	6	2	4	25	14	14
Pontypridd	12	6	2	4	18	18	14
Barry	12	4	3	5	15	11	11
Bridgend Town	12	4	2	6	15	21	10
Porth Athletic	12	0	2	10	18	24	2

1923-24

Eastern Section

Peterborough & Fletton United	30	20	2	8	54	31	42
Leicester City Reserves	30	19	3	8	72	30	41
Southampton Reserves	30	18	5	7	60	36	41
Millwall Reserves	30	18	3	9	56	38	39
Portsmouth Reserves	30	16	2	12	66	37	34
Brighton & Hove Albion Reserves	30	13	7	10	55	42	33
Norwich City Reserves	30	13	6	11	46	34	32
Folkestone	30	12	5	13	61	51	29
Coventry City Reserves	30	10	8	12	39	4	28
Watford Reserves	30	11	6	13	36	48	28
Reading Reserves	30	11	6	13	32	43	28
Northampton Town Reserves	30	9	10	11	32	47	28
Luton Town Reserves	30	10	7	13	40	49	27
Guildford United	30	7	5	18	38	72	19
Kettering	30	5	8	17	30	67	18
Bournemouth Reserves	30	4	5	21	40	85	13

Western Section

Yeovil & Petters United	34	25	3	6	71	30	53
Plymouth Argyle Reserves	34	21	5	8	74	37	47
Pontypridd	34	19	8	7	81	44	46
Torquay United	34	19	7	8	59	25	45
Bristol City Reserves	34	17	9	8	63	39	43
Swansea Town Reserves	34	19	5	10	62	38	43
Bristol Rovers Reserves	34	17	6	11	69	43	40
Cardiff City Reserves	34	15	4	15	55	31	34
Exeter City Reserves	34	11	11	12	48	47	33
Weymouth	34	15	3	16	48	60	33
Llanelly	34	14	5	15	47	62	33
Swindon Town Reserves	34	11	6	17	36	60	28
Bridgend Town	34	11	5	18	57	72	27
Newport County Reserves	34	10	7	17	57	79	27
Ebbw Vale	34	8	8	18	38	62	24
Bath City	34	6	9	19	32	71	21
Barry	34	6	7	21	36	74	19
Aberaman Athletic	34	6	4	24	41	87	16

1924-25

Eastern Section

Southampton Reserves	32	17	10	5	65	30	44
Kettering Town	32	17	6	9	67	39	40
Brighton & Hove Albion Reserves	32	15	10	7	68	42	40
Millwall Reserves	32	15	10	7	65	48	40
Peterborough & Fletton United	32	15	9	8	56	29	39
Bournemouth Reserves	32	15	9	8	66	48	39
Leicester City Reserves	32	15	7	10	61	45	37
Portsmouth Reserves	32	15	7	10	51	40	37
Folkestone	32	13	11	8	55	46	37
Norwich City Reserves	32	13	8	11	65	58	34
Coventry City Reserves	32	12	9	11	51	41	33
Luton Town Reserves	32	15	2	15	48	63	32
Northampton Town Reserves	32	10	5	17	38	59	25
Watford Reserves	32	7	7	18	44	71	21
Nuneaton Town	32	8	2	22	37	62	18
Reading Reserves	32	8	1	23	38	87	17
Guildford United	32	4	3	25	40	107	11

Western Section

Swansea Town Reserves	38	25	4	9	73	26	54
Plymouth Argyle Reserves	38	22	10	6	97	35	54
Pontypridd	38	24	4	10	81	39	52
Bridgend Town	38	20	11	7	74	52	51
Mid Rhondda United	38	21	6	11	79	48	48
Weymouth	38	21	4	13	77	50	46
Cardiff City Reserves	38	18	6	14	56	44	42
Newport County Reserves	38	17	8	13	71	60	42
Swindon Town Reserves	38	17	8	13	48	46	42
Bristol City Reserves	38	18	5	15	51	43	41
Yeovil & Petters United	38	15	10	13	49	50	40
Exeter City Reserves	38	16	6	16	78	55	38
Taunton United	38	15	6	17	55	51	36
Bristol Rovers Reserves	38	13	6	19	45	50	32
Torquay United	38	9	11	18	41	73	29
Llanelly	38	6	12	20	49	94	24
Ebbw Vale	38	9	6	23	40	91	24
Bath City	38	8	8	22	28	85	24
Barry	38	8	6	24	38	82	22
Aberaman Athletic	38	6	7	25	39	95	19

1925-26

Eastern Section

Millwall Reserves	34	24	6	4	106	37	54
Leicester City Reserves	34	23	2	9	105	60	48
Brighton & Hove Albion Reserves	34	21	4	9	105	69	46
Kettering Town	34	19	5	10	98	68	43
Peterborough & Fletton United	34	19	3	12	76	62	41
Portsmouth Reserves	34	17	5	12	76	67	39
Norwich City Reserves	34	17	4	13	85	90	38
Bournemouth Reserves	34	15	7	12	76	67	37
Southampton Reserves	34	14	7	13	65	72	35
Fulham Reserves	34	13	6	15	86	77	32
Grays Thurrock United	34	13	5	16	63	77	31
Guildford United	34	11	8	15	71	87	30
Watford Reserves	34	12	2	20	62	94	26
Luton Town Reserves	34	11	3	20	70	78	25
Folkestone	34	9	6	19	67	93	24
Reading Reserves	34	10	3	21	58	84	23
Coventry City Reserves	34	9	5	20	54	93	23
Nuneaton Town	34	7	3	24	61	113	17

Western Section

Plymouth Argyle Reserves	26	20	1	5	67	31	41
Bristol City Reserves	26	16	4	6	48	28	36
Bristol Rovers Reserves	26	13	4	9	51	35	30
Swindon Town Reserves	26	13	4	9	57	40	30
Ebbw Vale	26	13	3	10	60	46	29
Torquay United	26	12	5	9	59	46	29
Yeovil & Petters United	26	9	8	9	43	48	26
Mid Rhondda	26	12	1	13	47	49	25
Weymouth	26	10	3	13	64	60	23
Exeter City Reserves	26	8	5	13	40	49	21
Barry	26	8	4	14	47	55	20
Taunton United	26	9	2	15	44	60	20
Pontypridd	26	7	5	14	44	77	19
Bath City	26	7	1	18	38	86	15

1926-27

Eastern Section

Brighton & Hove Albion Reserves	32	21	6	5	86	47	48
Peterborough & Fletton United	32	18	9	5	80	39	45
Portsmouth Reserves	32	19	6	7	95	65	44
Kettering Town	32	15	10	7	66	41	40
Millwall Reserves	32	16	5	11	67	56	37
Bournemouth Reserves	32	14	6	12	69	64	34
Norwich City Reserves	32	14	5	13	79	74	33
Dartford	32	13	7	12	60	71	33
Reading Reserves	32	12	8	12	75	79	32
Luton Town Reserves	32	10	11	11	75	70	1
Leicester City Reserves	32	12	5	15	94	72	29
Watford Reserves	32	10	8	14	74	84	28
Southampton Reserves	32	10	6	16	57	77	26
Poole	32	9	6	17	55	86	24
Grays Thurrock United	32	10	3	19	49	66	23
Guildford United	32	6	7	19	57	106	19
Folkestone	32	7	4	21	57	98	18

Western Section

Torquay United	26	17	4	5	63	30	38
Bristol City Reserves	26	14	10	2	77	37	38
Plymouth Argyle Reserves	26	15	4	7	56	38	34
Ebbw Vale	26	14	2	10	67	45	30
Bristol Rovers Reserves	26	12	4	10	51	43	28
Swindon Town Reserves	26	11	5	10	60	57	27
Barry	26	11	4	11	65	50	26
Essex City Reserves	26	10	6	10	62	49	26
Weymouth	26	12	2	12	48	65	26
Newport County Reserves	26	9	6	11	57	53	24
Bath City	26	7	9	10	44	52	23
Yeovil & Petters United	26	9	5	12	49	66	23
Taunton United	26	4	4	18	36	83	12
Mid Rhondda United	26	2	5	19	22	89	9

1927-28

Easter Section

Kettering Town	34	23	6	5	90	39	52
Peterborough & Fletton United	34	21	3	10	73	43	45
Northfleet United	34	17	7	10	83	54	41
Brighton & Hove Albion Reserves	34	20	0	14	90	63	40
Norwich City Reserves	34	17	6	11	69	69	40
Southampton Reserves	34	16	7	11	92	70	39
Aldershot Town	34	17	5	12	85	66	39
Sittingbourne	34	16	5	13	64	70	37
Millwall Reserves	34	15	6	13	66	59	36
Poole	34	15	5	14	69	84	35
Folkestone	34	12	6	16	71	91	30
Guildford City	34	12	5	17	65	89	29
Dartford	34	12	4	18	46	49	28
Gillingham Reserves	34	10	7	17	72	84	27
Sheppey United	34	11	3	20	57	87	25
Chatham	34	10	4	20	49	70	24
Grays Thurrock United	34	10	3	21	48	88	23
Bournemouth Reserves	34	9	4	21	48	62	22

Western Section

Bristol City Reserves	30	20	3	7	95	51	43
Exeter City Reserves	30	18	4	8	104	56	40
Bristol Rovers Reserves	30	16	3	11	80	64	35
Plymouth Argyle Reserves	30	16	2	12	88	53	34
Newport County Reserves	30	13	8	9	99	70	34
Ebbw Vale	30	15	3	12	67	74	33
Swindon Town Reserves	30	13	4	13	80	74	30
Aberdare & Aberaman	30	12	6	12	62	68	30
Yeovil & Petters United	30	11	7	12	64	57	29
Torquay United Reserves	30	11	6	13	51	67	28
Bath City	30	12	3	15	64	68	27
Taunton Town	30	11	5	14	60	65	27
Weymouth	30	10	6	14	50	83	26
Merthyr Town Reserves	30	9	4	17	50	77	22
Barry	30	8	6	16	45	87	22
Mid Rhondda United	30	7	6	17	36	81	20

1928-29

Eastern Section

Kettering Town	36	24	4	8	96	46	52
Peterborough & Fletton United	36	21	5	10	86	44	47
Brighton & Hove Albion Reserves	36	19	9	8	91	56	47
Millwall Reserves	36	21	4	11	90	67	46
Bournemouth Reserves	36	20	5	11	82	58	45
Aldershot Town	36	18	5	13	68	52	41
Sheppey United	36	17	7	12	58	58	41
Folkestone	36	17	6	13	83	80	40
Northfleet United	36	17	4	15	87	65	38
Gillingham Reserves	36	15	8	13	68	70	38
Guildford City	36	13	11	12	85	78	37
Southampton Reserves	36	14	6	16	86	79	34
Poole	36	13	8	15	62	66	34
Thames Association	36	13	5	18	67	74	31
Dartford	36	10	6	20	55	106	26
Chatham	36	8	8	20	47	81	24
Sittingbourne	36	11	1	24	59	98	23
Norwich City Reserves	36	8	6	22	48	96	22
Grays Thurrock United	36	6	6	24	47	91	18

Western Section

Plymouth Argyle Reserves	26	15	6	5	69	27	36
Newport County Reserves	26	15	2	9	64	58	32
Bristol Rovers Reserves	26	14	3	9	54	45	31
Bristol City Reserves	26	14	2	10	70	46	30
Torquay United Reserves	26	13	4	9	52	42	30
Bath City	26	13	4	9	43	59	30
Exeter City Reserves	26	11	6	9	69	53	28
Lovells Athletic	26	11	6	9	54	48	28
Swindon Town Reserves	26	11	5	10	68	74	27
Yeovil & Petters United	26	11	2	13	49	57	24
Taunton Town	26	9	5	12	58	66	23
Ebbw Vale	26	9	5	12	56	66	23
Barry	26	6	3	17	38	66	15
Merthyr Town Reserves	26	3	1	22	37	92	7

1929-30

Eastern Section

Aldershot Town	32	21	6	5	84	39	48
Millwall Reserves	32	21	3	8	75	56	45
Thames Association	32	17	6	9	80	60	40
Peterborough & Fletton United	32	18	3	11	66	39	39
Northampton Town Reserves	32	17	4	11	86	60	38
Southampton Reserves	32	14	7	11	73	62	35
Sheppey United	32	15	5	12	76	69	35
Kettering Town	32	13	7	12	70	69	33
Dartford	32	14	5	13	57	59	33
Norwich City Reserves	32	14	3	15	69	69	31
Guildford City	32	13	2	17	65	97	28
Bournemouth Reserves	32	10	7	15	59	63	27
Brighton & Hove Albion Reserves	32	12	2	18	56	79	26
Folkestone	32	13	0	19	56	82	26
Sittingbourne	32	10	5	17	55	59	25
Northfleet United	32	6	7	19	53	77	19
Grays Thurrock United	32	7	2	23	54	101	16

Western Section

Bath City	28	16	6	6	85	52	38
Bristol Rovers Reserves	28	16	4	8	66	50	36
Taunton Town	28	14	7	7	50	40	35
Barry	28	15	3	10	65	55	33
Yeovil & Petters United	28	12	7	9	63	47	31
Plymouth Argyle Reserves	28	14	3	11	68	52	31
Newport County Reserves	28	13	4	11	68	76	30
Lovells Athletic	28	13	2	13	59	57	28
Exeter City Reserves	28	11	6	11	49	54	28
Bristol City Reserves	28	11	5	12	59	63	27
Swindon Town Reserves	28	10	6	12	69	67	26
Torquay United Reserves	28	10	6	12	76	77	26
Llanelly	28	10	4	14	55	52	24
Ebbw Vale	28	5	6	17	52	97	16
Merthyr Town Reserves	28	5	1	22	48	93	11

1930-31

Eastern Section

Dartford	16	9	5	2	39	18	23
Aldershot Town	16	10	3	3	50	28	23
Norwich City Reserves	16	9	1	6	47	38	19
Peterborough & Fletton United	16	6	5	5	35	29	17
Thames Association Reserves	16	7	2	7	38	31	16
Millwall Reserves	16	7	0	9	47	40	14
Folkestone	16	4	3	9	31	46	11
Guildford City	16	5	1	10	28	53	11
Sheppey United	16	4	2	10	31	63	10

Western Section

Exeter City Reserves	22	15	2	5	59	28	32
Llanelly	22	10	8	4	72	39	28
Merthyr Town	22	12	3	7	62	49	27
Plymouth Argyle Reserves	22	12	2	8	55	34	26
Bath City	22	10	6	6	47	39	26
Torquay United Reserves	22	9	5	8	66	49	23
Swindon Town Reserves	22	7	7	8	48	52	21
Bristol Rovers Reserves	22	7	6	9	58	64	20
Barry	22	7	5	10	29	39	19
Taunton Town	22	5	7	10	36	62	17
Newport County Reserves	22	6	2	14	36	66	14
Ebbw Vale	22	5	1	16	32	79	11

1931-32

Eastern Section

Dartford	18	12	3	3	53	18	27
Folkestone	18	12	2	4	58	27	26
Guildford City	18	11	1	6	33	24	23
Norwich City Reserves	18	9	2	7	46	33	20
Millwall Reserves	18	9	2	7	41	39	20
Tunbridge Wells Rangers	18	7	5	6	23	25	19
Bournemouth Reserves	18	6	4	8	43	61	16
Peterborough & Fletton United	18	4	5	9	28	29	13
Aldershot Town	18	3	5	10	17	30	11
Sheppey United	18	2	1	15	16	72	5

Western Section

Yeovil & Petters United	24	16	4	4	65	31	36
Plymouth Argyle Reserves	24	15	5	4	81	31	35
Bath City	24	12	7	5	50	33	31
Llanelly	24	12	4	8	65	46	28
Taunton Town	24	13	2	9	53	58	28
Newport County Reserves	24	10	6	8	70	51	26
Exeter City Reserves	24	9	7	8	59	43	25
Merthyr Town	24	9	4	11	66	73	22
Bristol Rovers Reserves	24	8	4	12	54	47	20
Swindon Town Reserves	24	8	4	12	54	95	20
Barry	24	7	3	14	58	76	17
Torquay United Reserves	24	5	6	13	43	66	16
Ebbw Vale	24	3	2	19	34	102	8

1932-33

Eastern Section

Norwich City Reserves	14	9	2	3	34	22	20
Dartford	14	8	2	4	26	23	18
Folkestone	14	7	1	6	35	32	15
Bournemouth Reserves	14	5	4	5	36	33	14
Tunbridge Wells Rangers	14	5	2	7	23	24	12
Guildford City	14	5	2	7	22	28	12
Millwall Reserves	14	5	1	8	27	31	11
Aldershot Reserves	14	3	4	7	24	34	10

Western Section

Bath City	20	13	4	3	62	34	30
Exeter City Reserves	20	12	3	5	62	46	27
Torquay United Reserves	20	12	1	7	56	37	25
Plymouth Argyle Reserves	20	11	2	7	68	38	24
Yeovil & Petters United	20	11	2	7	59	44	24
Llanelly	20	10	2	8	53	33	22
Bristol Rovers Reserves	20	7	3	10	53	65	17
Newport County Reserves	20	6	4	10	42	55	16
Merthyr Tydfil	20	7	1	12	39	58	15
Barry	20	3	4	13	30	72	10
Taunton Town	20	4	2	14	21	63	10

1933-34

Eastern Section

Norwich City Reserves	16	9	4	3	41	15	22
Margate	16	8	3	5	23	20	19
Millwall Reserves	16	7	4	5	28	28	18
Clapton Orient Reserves	16	8	1	7	33	34	17
Bournemouth Reserves	16	6	3	7	28	30	15
Tunbridge Wells Rangers	16	6	2	8	25	36	14
Folkestone	16	5	3	8	26	26	13
Guildford City	16	5	3	8	27	33	13
Dartford	16	4	5	7	15	24	13

Western Section

Plymouth Argyle Reserves	20	13	6	1	62	22	32
Bristol Rovers Reserves	20	14	3	3	56	27	31
Bath City	20	11	3	6	43	25	25
Torquay United Reserves	20	9	4	7	54	36	22
Yeovil & Petters United	20	10	1	9	35	39	21
Exeter City Reserves	20	8	3	9	54	47	19
Merthyr Town	20	8	2	10	39	50	18
Llanelly	20	8	1	11	25	39	17
Barry	20	4	5	11	37	64	13
Newport County Reserves	20	4	3	13	36	54	11
Taunton Town	20	5	1	14	27	65	11

Central Section

Plymouth Argyle Reserves	18	16	1	1	47	14	33
Clapton Orient Reserves	18	9	3	6	35	25	21
Norwich City Reserves	18	8	4	6	41	27	20
Yeovil & Petters United	18	7	4	7	34	38	18
Bath City	18	7	3	8	31	36	17
Dartford	18	6	4	8	28	26	16
Tunbridge Wells Rangers	18	7	1	10	26	37	15
Llanelly	18	6	2	10	28	39	14
Folkestone	18	6	1	11	30	41	13
Guildford City	18	6	1	11	28	45	13

1934-35

Eastern Section

Norwich City Reserves	18	12	1	5	52	21	25
Dartford	18	8	6	4	36	22	22
Margate	18	7	6	7	38	30	20
Bournemouth Reserves	18	8	3	8	34	26	19
Guildford City	18	7	5	6	41	34	19
Aldershot Reserves	18	7	3	8	29	43	17
Folkestone	18	5	6	7	30	39	16
Tunbridge Wells Rangers	18	6	4	8	32	56	16
Clapton Orient Reserves	18	5	4	9	33	35	14
Millwall Reserves	18	3	6	9	26	45	12

Western Section

Yeovil & Petters United	16	11	2	3	49	18	24
Newport County Reserves	16	8	5	3	45	29	21
Plymouth Argyle Reserves	16	7	5	4	40	24	19
Exeter City Reserves	16	7	2	7	38	32	16
Bath City	16	6	4	6	35	32	16
Bristol Rovers Reserves	16	5	5	6	33	37	15
Barry	16	6	3	7	30	40	15
Torquay United Reserves	16	5	3	8	24	29	13
Taunton Town	16	1	3	12	13	66	5

Central Section

Folkestone	20	11	4	5	43	31	26
Guildford City	20	11	4	5	43	39	26
Plymouth Argyle Reserves	20	6	9	5	40	28	21
Torquay United Reserves	20	7	6	7	34	35	20
Bristol Rovers Reserves	20	8	4	8	38	46	20
Margate	20	8	3	9	40	34	19
Dartford	20	8	3	9	43	38	19
Aldershot Reserves	20	8	3	9	33	44	19
Tunbridge Wells Rangers	20	6	10	4	33	37	18
Yeovil & Petters United	20	8	1	11	45	51	17
Bath City	20	6	3	11	34	43	15

1935-36

Eastern Section

Margate	18	13	2	3	49	16	28
Folkestone	18	11	3	4	46	23	25
Dartford	18	9	3	6	47	25	21
Tunbridge Wells Rangers	18	9	1	8	26	41	19
Clapton Orient Reserves	18	7	4	7	39	31	18
Millwall Reserves	18	7	3	8	42	39	17
Norwich City Reserves	18	8	0	10	39	38	16
Guildford City	18	6	3	9	32	52	15
Aldershot Reserves	18	6	1	11	24	45	13
Bournemouth Reserves	18	3	2	13	25	59	8

Western Section

Plymouth Argyle Reserves	16	12	3	1	51	18	27
Bristol Rovers Reserves	16	8	3	5	35	30	19
Newport County Reserves	16	8	3	5	29	30	19
Torquay United Reserves	16	7	1	8	25	28	15
Bath City	16	5	5	6	18	26	15
Cheltenham Town	16	6	2	8	32	28	14
Yeovil & Petters United	16	5	3	8	31	35	13
Barry	16	5	2	9	29	41	12
Exeter City Reserves	16	4	2	10	24	38	10

Central Section

Margate	20	14	3	3	57	18	31
Bristol Rovers Reserves	20	13	1	6	51	37	27
Plymouth Argyle Reserves	20	12	2	6	53	32	26
Aldershot Reserves	20	9	4	7	37	37	22
Folkestone	20	9	3	8	51	36	21
Tunbridge Wells Rangers	20	7	4	9	40	41	18
Dartford	20	7	3	10	34	42	17
Guildford City	20	7	3	10	33	47	17
Cheltenham Town	20	5	5	10	32	45	15
Bath City	20	5	5	10	34	52	15
Yeovil & Petters United	20	3	5	12	40	75	11

1936-37

Ipswich Town	30	19	8	3	68	35	46
Norwich City Reserves	30	18	5	7	70	35	41
Folkestone	30	17	4	9	71	62	38
Margate	30	15	4	11	64	49	34
Guildford City	30	15	4	11	54	60	34
Bath City	30	14	5	11	65	55	33
Yeovil & Petters United	30	15	3	12	77	69	33
Plymouth Argyle Reserves	30	11	8	11	64	58	30
Newport County Reserves	30	11	8	11	72	68	30
Barry	30	12	4	14	58	72	28
Cheltenham Town	30	10	4	16	61	70	24
Dartford	30	9	5	16	41	55	23
Exeter City Reserves	30	8	7	15	57	78	23
Tunbridge Wells Rangers	30	8	6	16	62	64	22
Torquay United Reserves	30	8	5	17	46	76	21
Aldershot Reserves	30	7	6	17	47	74	20

Midweek Section

Margate	18	12	1	5	48	24	25
Bath City	18	10	5	3	38	28	25
Norwich City Reserves	18	9	5	4	44	27	23
Folkestone	18	7	6	5	32	36	20
Millwall Reserves	18	8	3	7	44	47	19
Portsmouth Reserves	18	6	5	7	40	27	17
Tunbridge Wells Rangers	18	5	4	9	30	41	14
Aldershot Reserves	18	6	2	10	20	30	14
Guildford City	18	3	6	9	24	36	12
Dartford	18	4	3	11	19	43	11

1937-38

Guildford City	34	22	5	7	94	60	49
Plymouth Argyle Reserves	34	18	9	7	98	58	45
Ipswich Town	34	19	6	9	89	54	44
Yeovil & Petters United	34	14	14	6	72	45	42
Norwich City Reserves	34	15	11	8	77	55	41
Colchester United	34	15	8	11	90	58	38
Bristol Rovers Reserves	34	14	8	12	63	62	36
Swindon Town Reserves	34	14	7	13	70	76	35
Tunbridge Wells Rangers	34	14	6	14	68	74	34
Aldershot Reserves	34	10	12	12	42	55	32
Cheltenham Town	34	13	5	16	72	68	31
Exeter City Reserves	34	13	5	16	71	75	31
Dartford	34	9	11	14	51	70	29
Bath City	34	9	9	16	45	65	27
Folkestone	34	10	6	18	58	82	26
Newport County Reserves	34	10	6	18	56	86	26
Barry	34	8	7	19	50	88	23
Torquay United Reserves	34	8	7	19	46	81	23

Midweek Section

Millwall Reserves	18	13	3	2	59	21	29
Colchester United	18	13	1	4	42	23	27
Aldershot Reserves	18	11	3	4	38	29	25
Norwich City Reserves	18	9	1	8	45	39	19
Portsmouth Reserves	18	5	5	8	31	30	15
Dartford	18	6	3	9	32	35	15
Folkestone	18	6	3	9	34	38	15
Tunbridge Wells Rangers	18	5	4	9	28	36	14
Bath City	18	5	3	10	27	45	13
Guildford City	18	4	0	14	21	61	8

1938-39

Colchester United	44	31	5	8	110	37	67
Guildford City	44	30	6	8	126	52	66
Gillingham	44	29	6	9	104	57	64
Plymouth Argyle Reserves	44	26	5	13	128	63	57
Yeovil & Petters United	44	22	10	12	85	70	54
Arsenal Reserves	44	21	9	14	92	57	51
Cardiff City Reserves	44	24	3	17	105	72	51
Tunbridge Wells Rangers	44	22	6	16	93	76	50
Norwich City Reserves	44	23	4	17	86	76	50
Chelmsford City	44	18	8	18	74	73	44
Bath City	44	16	12	16	58	74	44
Barry	44	18	7	19	76	90	43
Cheltenham Town	44	16	9	19	76	105	41
Ipswich Town Reserves	44	14	12	18	64	76	40
Worcester City	44	13	14	17	72	90	40
Folkestone	44	16	6	22	74	85	38
Newport County Reserves	44	13	10	21	74	108	36
Exeter City Reserves	44	12	9	23	51	107	33
Torquay United Reserves	44	12	8	24	53	89	32
Swindon Town Reserves	44	11	9	24	66	101	31
Aldershot Reserves	44	12	6	26	69	92	30
Bristol Rovers Reserves	44	9	11	24	66	85	29
Dartford	44	8	5	31	53	119	21

Midweek Section

Tunbridge Wells Rangers	16	8	7	1	37	18	23
Colchester United	16	9	2	5	36	21	20
Norwich City Reserves	16	7	4	5	40	26	18
Millwall Reserves	16	7	4	5	33	23	18
Portsmouth Reserves	16	5	4	7	21	29	14
Guildford City	16	4	6	6	24	39	14
Aldershot Reserves	16	4	5	7	22	25	13
Folkestone	16	4	5	7	24	35	13
Dartford	16	4	3	9	24	45	11

1939-40

Eastern Section

Chelmsford City	7	5	0	2	29	9	10
Guildford City	8	4	1	3	26	13	9
Tunbridge Wells Rangers	7	2	3	2	21	16	7
Dartford	7	2	1	4	17	30	5
Norwich City Reserves	7	2	1	4	9	34	5

Western Section

Lovells Athletic	14	11	1	2	53	22	23
Worcester City	14	9	2	3	55	30	20
Hereford United	14	8	0	6	45	31	16
Yeovil & Petters United	14	7	2	5	30	24	16
Gloucester City	14	5	0	9	35	49	10
Barry	14	4	1	9	31	56	9
Cheltenham Town	13	3	2	8	21	38	8
Bath City	13	3	2	8	21	41	8

1945-46

Chelmsford City	18	15	1	2	66	23	34
Hereford United	20	13	3	4	59	31	29
Bath City	20	12	2	6	62	32	26
Cheltenham Town	18	9	1	8	35	54	22
Barry Town	20	8	4	8	42	42	20
Yeovil & Petters United	18	7	1	10	57	52	18
Worcester City	20	8	2	10	60	58	18
Colchester United	20	7	3	10	29	47	17
Bedford Town	16	4	1	11	30	49	15
Swindon Town Reserves	18	4	3	11	36	65	14
Cardiff City Reserves	20	4	5	11	39	60	13

1946-47

Gillingham	31	20	6	5	103	45	47
Guildford City	32	21	4	7	86	39	46
Merthyr Tydfil	31	21	2	8	104	37	45
Yeovil Town	32	19	6	7	100	49	44
Chelmsford City	31	17	3	11	90	60	38
Gravesend & Northfleet	32	17	4	11	82	58	38
Barry Town	30	14	6	10	89	61	36
Colchester United	31	15	4	12	65	60	35
Cheltenham Town	31	14	3	14	68	75	32
Millwall	24	8	5	11	59	57	29
Dartford	32	10	5	17	71	100	25
Bedford Town	32	8	8	16	63	98	24
Hereford United	32	8	7	17	37	85	23
Worcester City	31	8	5	18	55	90	22
Exeter City Reserves	32	10	2	20	69	126	22
Bath City	32	7	7	18	52	93	21
Gloucester City	32	8	1	23	57	120	17

1947-48

Merthyr Tydfil	34	23	7	4	84	38	53
Gillingham	34	21	5	8	81	43	47
Worcester City	34	21	3	10	74	45	45
Colchester United	34	17	10	7	88	41	44
Hereford United	34	16	10	8	77	53	42
Lovells Athletic	34	17	6	11	74	50	40
Exeter City Reserves	34	15	7	12	65	57	37
Yeovil Town	34	12	11	11	56	50	35
Chelmsford City	34	14	7	13	62	58	35
Cheltenham Town	34	13	9	12	71	71	35
Bath City	34	12	8	14	55	62	32
Barry Town	34	10	9	15	60	70	29
Gravesend & Northfleet	34	11	6	17	52	81	28
Guildford City	34	11	4	19	69	74	26
Dartford	34	10	6	18	35	62	26
Gloucester City	34	8	6	20	45	78	22
Torquay United Reserves	34	6	9	19	43	95	21
Bedford Town	34	6	3	25	41	104	15

1948-49

Gillingham	42	26	10	6	104	48	62
Chelmsford City	42	27	7	8	115	64	61
Merthyr Tydfil	42	26	8	8	133	54	60
Colchester United	42	21	10	11	94	61	52
Worcester City	42	22	7	13	87	56	51
Dartford	42	21	9	12	73	53	51
Gravesend & Northfleet	42	20	9	13	60	46	49
Yeovil Town	42	19	9	14	90	53	47
Cheltenham Town	42	19	9	14	71	64	47
Kidderminster Harriers	42	19	6	17	77	96	44
Exeter City Reserves	42	18	7	17	83	73	43
Hereford United	42	17	6	19	83	84	40
Bath City	42	15	8	19	72	87	38
Hastings United	42	14	10	18	69	93	38
Torquay United Reserves	42	15	7	20	73	93	37
Lovells Athletic	42	14	8	20	73	74	36
Guildford City	42	12	12	18	58	85	36
Gloucester City	42	12	10	20	78	100	34
Barry Town	42	12	10	20	55	95	34
Tonbridge	42	9	7	26	54	105	25
Chingford Town	42	6	9	27	43	94	21
Bedford Town	42	5	8	29	32	101	18

1949-50

Merthyr Tydfil	46	34	3	9	143	62	71
Colchester United	46	31	9	6	109	51	71
Yeovil Town	46	29	7	10	104	45	65
Chelmsford City	46	26	9	11	121	64	61
Gillingham	46	23	9	14	93	61	55
Dartford	46	20	9	17	70	65	49
Worcester City	46	21	7	18	85	80	49
Guildford City	46	18	11	17	79	73	47
Weymouth	46	19	9	18	80	82	47
Barry Town	46	18	10	18	78	72	46
Exeter City Reserves	46	16	14	16	73	83	46
Lovells Athletic	46	17	10	19	86	78	44
Tonbridge	46	16	12	18	65	76	44
Hastings United	46	17	8	21	92	140	42
Gravesend & Northfleet	46	16	9	21	88	82	41
Torquay United Reserves	46	14	12	20	80	89	40
Bath City	46	16	7	23	61	78	39
Gloucester City	46	14	11	21	72	101	39
Hereford United	46	15	8	23	74	76	38
Cheltenham Town	46	13	11	22	75	96	37
Headington United	46	15	7	24	72	97	37
Bedford Town	46	12	11	23	63	79	35
Kidderminster Harriers	46	12	11	23	65	108	35
Chingford Town	46	10	6	30	61	151	26

1950-51

Merthyr Tydfil	44	29	8	7	156	66	66
Hereford United	44	27	7	10	110	69	61
Guildford City	44	23	8	13	88	60	54
Chelmsford City	44	21	12	11	84	58	54
Llanelly	44	19	13	12	89	73	51
Cheltenham Town	44	21	8	15	91	61	50
Headington United	44	18	11	15	84	83	47
Torquay United Reserves	44	20	6	18	93	79	46
Exeter City Reserves	44	16	12	16	90	94	44
Weymouth	44	16	12	16	82	88	44
Tonbridge	44	16	12	16	79	87	44
Gloucester City	44	16	11	17	81	76	43
Yeovil Town	44	13	15	16	72	72	41
Worcester City	44	15	11	18	69	78	41
Bath City	44	15	10	19	66	73	40
Dartford	44	14	11	19	61	70	39
Bedford Town	44	15	9	20	64	94	39
Gravesend & Northfleet	44	12	14	18	65	83	38
Kettering Town	44	13	11	20	87	87	37
Lovells Athletic	44	12	13	19	81	93	37
Kidderminster Harriers	44	13	9	22	58	103	35
Barry Town	44	13	7	24	54	104	33
Hastings United	44	11	6	27	91	143	28

1951-52

	P	W	D	L	F	A	Pts
Merthyr Tydfil	42	27	6	9	128	60	60
Weymouth	42	22	13	7	81	42	57
Kidderminster Harriers	42	22	10	10	70	40	54
Guildford City	42	18	16	8	66	47	52
Hereford United	42	21	9	12	80	59	51
Worcester City	42	23	4	15	86	73	50
Kettering Town	42	18	10	14	83	56	46
Lovells Athletic	42	18	10	14	87	68	46
Gloucester City	42	19	8	15	68	55	46
Bath City	42	19	6	17	75	67	44
Headington United	42	16	11	15	55	53	43
Bedford Town	42	16	10	16	75	64	42
Barry Town	42	18	6	18	84	89	42
Chelmsford City	42	15	10	17	67	80	40
Dartford	42	15	9	18	63	65	39
Tonbridge	42	15	6	21	63	84	36
Yeovil Town	42	12	11	19	56	76	35
Cheltenham Town	42	15	4	23	59	85	34
Exeter City Reserves	42	13	7	22	76	106	33
Llanelly	42	13	6	23	70	111	32
Gravesend & Northfleet	42	12	7	23	68	88	31
Hastings United	42	3	5	34	41	131	11

1952-53

	P	W	D	L	F	A	Pts
Headington United	42	23	12	7	93	50	58
Merthyr Tydfil	42	25	8	9	117	66	58
Bedford Town	42	24	8	10	91	61	56
Kettering Town	42	23	8	11	88	50	54
Bath City	42	22	10	10	71	46	54
Worcester City	42	20	11	11	100	66	51
Llanelly	42	21	9	12	95	72	51
Barry Town	42	22	3	17	89	69	47
Gravesend & Northfleet	42	19	7	16	83	76	45
Gloucester City	42	17	9	16	50	78	43
Guildford City	42	17	8	17	64	60	42
Hastings United	42	18	5	19	75	66	41
Cheltenham Town	42	15	11	16	70	89	41
Weymouth	42	15	10	17	70	75	40
Hereford United	42	17	5	20	76	73	39
Tonbridge	42	12	9	21	62	88	33
Lovells Athletic	42	12	8	22	68	81	32
Yeovil Town	42	11	10	21	75	99	32
Chelmsford City	42	12	7	23	58	92	31
Exeter City Reserves	42	13	4	25	71	94	30
Kidderminster Harriers	42	12	5	25	54	85	29
Dartford	42	6	5	31	40	121	17

1953-54

	P	W	D	L	F	A	Pts
Merthyr Tydfil	42	27	8	7	97	55	62
Headington United	42	22	9	11	68	43	53
Yeovil Town	42	20	8	14	87	76	48
Bath City	42	17	12	13	73	67	46
Kidderminster Harriers	42	18	9	15	62	59	45
Weymouth	42	18	8	16	83	72	44
Barry Town	42	17	9	16	108	91	43
Bedford Town	42	19	5	18	80	84	43
Gloucester City	42	16	11	15	69	77	43
Hastings United	42	16	10	16	73	67	42
Kettering Town	42	15	12	15	65	63	42
Hereford United	42	16	9	17	66	62	41
Llanelly	42	16	9	17	80	85	41
Guildford City	42	15	11	16	56	60	41
Gravesend & Northfleet	42	16	8	18	76	77	40
Worcester City	42	17	6	19	66	71	40
Lovells Athletic	42	14	11	17	62	60	39
Tonbridge	42	15	9	18	85	91	39
Chelmsford City	42	14	10	18	67	71	38
Exeter City Reserves	42	11	13	18	61	72	35
Cheltenham Town	42	11	12	19	56	83	34
Dartford	42	6	13	23	42	89	25

1954-55

	P	W	D	L	F	A	Pts
Yeovil Town	42	23	9	10	105	66	55
Weymouth	42	24	7	11	105	84	55
Hastings United	42	21	9	12	94	60	51
Cheltenham Town	42	21	8	13	85	72	50
Guildford City	42	20	8	14	72	59	48
Worcester City	42	19	10	13	80	73	48
Barry Town	42	16	15	11	82	87	47
Gloucester City	42	16	13	13	66	54	45
Bath City	42	18	9	15	73	80	45
Headington Town	42	18	7	17	82	62	43
Kidderminster Harriers	42	18	7	17	84	86	43
Merthyr Tydfil	42	17	8	17	97	94	42
Exeter City Reserves	42	19	4	19	67	78	42
Lovells Athletic	42	15	11	16	71	68	41
Kettering Town	42	15	11	16	70	69	41
Hereford United	42	17	5	20	91	72	39
Llanelly	42	16	7	19	78	81	39
Bedford Town	42	16	3	23	75	103	35
Tonbridge	42	11	8	23	68	91	30
Dartford	42	9	12	21	55	76	30
Chelmsford City	42	11	6	25	73	111	28
Gravesend & Northfleet	42	9	9	24	62	97	27

1955-56

	P	W	D	L	F	A	Pts
Guildford City	42	26	8	8	74	34	60
Cheltenham Town	42	25	6	11	82	53	56
Yeovil Town	42	23	9	10	98	55	55
Bedford Town	42	21	9	12	99	69	51
Dartford	42	20	9	13	78	62	49
Weymouth	42	19	10	13	83	63	48
Gloucester City	42	19	9	14	72	60	47
Lovells Athletic	42	19	9	14	91	78	47
Chelmsford City	42	18	10	14	67	55	46
Kettering Town	42	16	11	15	105	86	43
Exeter City Reserves	42	17	9	16	75	76	43
Gravesend & Northfleet	42	17	8	17	79	75	42
Hereford United	42	17	7	18	90	90	41
Hastings United	42	15	10	17	90	76	40
Headington United	42	17	6	19	82	86	40
Kidderminster Harriers	42	14	7	21	86	108	35
Llanelly	42	14	6	22	64	98	34
Barry Town	42	11	11	20	91	108	33
Worcester City	42	12	9	21	66	83	33
Tonbridge	42	11	11	20	53	74	33
Merthyr Tydfil	42	7	10	25	52	127	24
Bath City	42	7	10	25	43	107	24

1956-57

	P	W	D	L	F	A	Pts
Kettering Town	42	28	10	4	106	47	66
Bedford Town	42	25	8	9	89	52	58
Weymouth	42	22	10	10	92	71	54
Cheltenham Town	42	19	15	8	73	46	53
Gravesend & Northfleet	42	21	11	10	74	58	53
Lovells Athletic	42	21	7	14	99	84	49
Guildford City	42	18	11	13	68	49	47
Hereford United	42	19	8	15	96	60	46
Headington United	42	19	7	16	64	61	45
Gloucester City	42	18	8	16	74	72	44
Hastings United	42	17	9	16	70	58	43
Worcester City	42	16	10	16	81	80	42
Dartford	42	16	10	16	79	88	42
Chelmsford City	42	16	9	17	73	85	41
Tonbridge	42	14	12	16	74	65	40
Yeovil Town	42	14	11	17	83	85	39
Bath City	42	15	8	19	56	78	38
Exeter City Reserves	42	10	10	22	52	89	30
Merthyr Tydfil	42	9	11	22	72	95	29
Barry Town	42	6	11	25	39	84	23
Kidderminster Harriers	42	7	10	25	60	83	20
Llanelly	42	5	8	29	39	123	18

1957-58

Gravesend & Northfleet	42	27	5	10	109	71	59
Bedford Town	42	25	7	10	112	64	57
Chelmsford City	42	24	9	9	93	57	57
Weymouth	42	25	5	12	90	61	55
Worcester City	42	23	7	12	95	59	53
Cheltenham Town	42	21	10	11	115	66	52
Hereford United	42	21	6	15	79	56	48
Kettering Town	42	18	9	15	99	76	45
Headington Town	42	18	7	17	90	83	43
Poole Town	42	17	9	16	82	81	43
Hasting United	42	13	15	14	78	77	41
Gloucester City	42	17	7	18	70	70	41
Yeovil Town	42	16	9	17	70	84	41
Dartford	42	14	9	19	66	92	37
Lovells Athletic	42	15	6	21	60	83	36
Bath City	42	13	9	20	65	64	35
Guildford City	42	12	10	20	58	92	34
Tonbridge	42	13	7	22	77	100	33
Exeter City Reserves	42	12	8	22	60	94	32
Barry Town	42	11	9	22	72	101	31
Kidderminster Harriers	42	10	10	22	60	101	30
Merthyr Tydfil	42	9	3	30	69	137	21

1958-59

North-Western Zone

Hereford United	34	22	5	7	80	37	49
Kettering Town	34	20	7	7	83	63	47
Boston United	34	18	8	8	73	47	44
Cheltenham Town	34	20	4	10	65	47	44
Worcester City	34	19	4	11	74	47	42
Bath City	34	17	5	12	89	62	39
Wellington Town	34	15	9	10	74	58	39
Nuneaton Borough	34	17	5	12	76	66	39
Wisbech Town	34	16	5	13	77	54	37
Headington United	34	16	3	15	76	61	35
Barry Town	34	15	5	14	64	67	35
Merthyr Tydfil	34	16	3	15	54	59	35
Gloucester City	34	12	6	16	50	65	30
Corby Town	34	10	8	16	59	79	28
Lovells Athletic	34	10	3	21	51	70	23
Rugby Town	34	7	6	21	45	93	20
Kidderminster Harriers	34	7	3	24	42	94	17
Burton Albion	34	3	3	28	41	104	9

South-Eastern Zone

Bedford Town	32	21	6	5	90	41	48
Gravesend & Northfleet	32	21	2	9	79	54	44
Dartford	32	20	3	9	77	41	43
Yeovil Town	32	17	8	7	60	41	42
Weymouth	32	13	11	8	61	43	37
Chelmsford City	32	12	12	8	74	53	36
King's Lynn	32	14	5	13	70	63	33
Poole Town	32	12	8	12	60	65	32
Cambridge City	32	12	7	13	61	54	31
Hastings United	32	13	5	14	60	59	31
Tonbridge	32	14	3	15	51	59	31
Cambridge United	32	11	8	13	55	77	30
Trowbridge Town	32	12	4	16	53	75	28
Exeter City Reserves	32	7	12	13	47	71	26
Guildford City	11	7	6	19	45	67	20
Clacton Town	32	6	7	19	44	81	19
Yiewsley	32	3	7	22	36	78	13

1959-60

Premier Division

Bath City	42	32	3	7	116	50	67
Headington United	42	23	8	11	78	61	54
Weymouth	42	22	9	11	93	69	53
Cheltenham Town	42	21	6	15	82	68	48
Cambridge City	42	18	11	13	81	72	47
Chelmsford Town	42	19	7	16	90	70	45
Bedford Town	42	21	3	18	97	85	45
King's Lynn	42	17	11	14	89	78	45
Boston United	42	17	10	15	83	80	44
Wisbech Town	42	17	10	15	81	84	44
Yeovil Town	42	17	8	17	81	73	42
Hereford United	42	15	12	15	70	74	42
Tonbridge	42	16	8	18	79	73	40
Hastings United	42	16	8	18	63	77	40
Wellington Town	42	13	11	18	63	78	37
Dartford	42	15	7	20	64	82	37
Gravesend & Northfleet	42	14	8	20	69	84	36
Worcester City	42	13	10	19	72	89	36
Nuneaton Borough	42	11	11	20	64	78	33
Barry Town	42	14	5	23	78	103	33
Poole Town	42	10	8	24	69	96	28
Kettering Town	42	9	10	23	60	90	28

First Division

Clacton Town	42	27	5	10	106	69	59
Romford	42	21	11	10	65	40	53
Folkestone Town	42	23	5	14	93	71	51
Exeter City Reserves	42	23	3	16	85	62	49
Guildford City	42	19	9	14	79	56	47
Sittingbourne	42	20	7	15	66	55	47
Margate	42	20	6	16	88	77	46
Trowbridge Town	42	18	9	15	90	78	45
Cambridge United	42	18	9	15	71	72	45
Yiewsley	42	17	10	15	83	69	44
Bexleyheath & Welling	42	16	11	15	85	77	43
Merthyr Tydfil	42	16	10	16	63	65	42
Ramsgate Athletic	42	16	8	18	83	84	40
Ashford Town	42	14	12	16	61	70	40
Tunbridge Wells United	42	17	5	20	77	73	39
Hinckley Athletic	42	14	8	20	62	75	36
Gloucester City	42	13	9	20	56	84	35
Dover	42	14	6	22	59	85	34
Kidderminster Harriers	42	14	6	22	59	97	34
Corby Town	42	15	3	24	75	91	33
Burton Albion	42	11	10	21	52	79	32
Rugby Town	42	10	11	21	67	91	31

1960-61

Premier Division

Oxford United	42	27	10	5	104	43	64
Chelmsford City	42	23	11	8	91	55	57
Yeovil Town	42	23	9	10	109	54	55
Hereford United	42	21	10	11	83	67	52
Weymouth	42	21	9	12	78	63	51
Bath City	42	18	14	10	74	52	50
Cambridge City	42	16	12	14	101	71	44
Wellington Town	42	17	9	16	66	68	43
Bedford Town	42	18	7	17	94	97	43
Folkestone Town	42	18	7	17	75	86	43
King's Lynn	42	13	16	13	68	66	42
Worcester City	42	15	11	16	69	69	41
Clacton Town	42	15	11	16	82	83	41
Romford	42	13	15	14	66	69	41
Guildford City	42	14	11	17	65	62	39
Tonbridge	42	16	6	20	79	85	38
Cheltenham Town	42	15	7	20	81	81	37
Gravesend & Northfleet	42	15	7	20	75	101	37
Dartford	42	13	11	18	57	90	37
Hastings United	42	8	9	25	60	100	25
Wisbech Town	42	9	6	27	58	112	24
Boston United	42	6	8	28	62	123	20

Oxford United were previously known as Headington United.

First Division

Kettering Town	40	26	7	7	100	55	59
Cambridge United	40	25	5	10	100	53	55
Bexleyheath & Welling	40	22	8	10	93	46	52
Merthyr Tydfil	40	23	6	11	88	65	52
Sittingbourne	40	21	10	9	77	63	52
Hinckley Athletic	40	17	13	10	74	59	47
Ramsgate Athletic	40	19	7	14	77	56	45
Rugby Town	40	18	9	13	89	71	45
Corby Town	40	16	10	14	82	73	42
Poole Town	40	18	5	17	71	65	41
Barry Town	40	16	9	15	65	74	41
Yiewsley	40	17	7	16	65	76	41
Trowbridge Town	40	14	10	16	71	73	38
Ashford Town	40	14	8	18	61	67	36
Margate	40	11	12	17	62	75	34
Dover	40	12	7	21	67	74	31
Canterbury City	40	10	10	20	52	75	30
Nuneaton Borough	40	11	7	22	60	91	29
Burton Albion	40	12	4	24	63	85	28
Tunbridge Wells United	40	8	5	27	56	115	21
Gloucester City	40	7	7	26	40	102	21

1961-62

Premier Division

Oxford United	42	28	5	9	118	46	61
Bath City	42	25	7	10	102	70	57
Guildford City	42	24	8	10	79	49	56
Yeovil Town	42	23	8	11	97	59	54
Chelmsford City	42	19	12	11	74	60	50
Weymouth	42	20	7	15	80	64	47
Kettering Town	42	21	5	16	90	84	47
Hereford United	42	21	2	19	81	68	44
Cambridge City	42	18	8	16	70	71	44
Bexleyheath & Welling	42	19	5	18	69	75	43
Romford	42	15	9	18	63	70	39
Cambridge United	42	13	12	17	76	78	38
Wellington United	42	14	10	18	75	78	38
Gravesend & Northfleet	42	17	4	21	59	92	38
Bedford Town	42	16	5	21	73	79	37
Worcester City	42	15	7	20	51	64	37
Merthyr Tydfil	42	13	11	18	62	80	37
Clacton Town	42	13	10	19	74	91	36
Tonbridge	42	10	14	18	71	92	34
King's Lynn	42	12	8	22	59	74	32
Folkestone Town	42	12	6	24	64	103	30
Cheltenham	42	9	7	26	48	86	25

First Division

Wisbech Town	38	21	11	6	76	42	53
Poole Town	38	23	6	9	81	47	52
Dartford	38	21	8	9	89	50	50
Rugby Town	38	20	9	9	82	49	49
Margate	38	20	6	12	73	55	46
Corby Town	38	19	6	13	82	60	44
Sittingbourne	38	16	12	10	69	51	44
Dover	38	19	6	13	66	55	44
Yiewsley	38	18	6	14	64	51	42
Barry Town	38	14	11	13	55	51	39
Ashford Town	38	14	11	13	66	70	39
Hinckley Athletic	38	15	8	15	75	65	38
Burton Albion	38	16	5	17	70	79	37
Nuneaton Borough	38	12	12	14	63	69	36
Tunbridge Wells United	38	12	7	19	60	85	31
Canterbury City	38	11	8	19	60	82	30
Ramsgate Athletic	38	10	9	19	48	70	29
Trowbridge Town	38	9	9	20	45	69	27
Gloucester City	38	6	4	28	46	104	16
Hastings United	38	5	4	29	45	115	14

1962-63

Premier Division

Cambridge City	40	25	6	9	99	64	56
Cambridge United	40	23	7	10	74	50	53
Weymouth	40	20	11	9	82	43	51
Guildford City	40	20	11	9	70	50	51
Kettering Town	40	22	7	11	66	49	51
Wellington Town	40	19	9	12	71	49	47
Dartford	40	19	9	12	61	54	47
Chelmsford City	40	18	10	12	63	50	46
Bedford Town	40	18	8	14	61	45	44
Bath City	40	18	6	16	58	56	42
Yeovil Town	40	15	10	15	64	54	40
Romford	40	14	11	15	73	68	39
Bexleyheath & Welling	40	13	11	16	55	63	37
Hereford United	40	14	7	19	56	66	35
Merthyr Tydfil	40	15	4	21	54	71	34
Rugby Town	40	14	5	21	65	76	33
Wisbech Town	40	15	3	22	64	84	33
Worcester City	40	12	9	19	47	65	33
Poole Town	40	10	12	18	54	66	32
Gravesend & Northfleet	40	10	3	27	62	91	23
Clacton Town	40	3	7	30	50	135	13

First Division

Margate	38	21	13	4	86	47	55
Hinckley Athletic	38	22	9	7	66	38	53
Hastings United	38	22	8	8	86	36	52
Nuneaton Borough	38	21	10	7	82	41	52
Tonbridge	38	22	8	8	81	51	52
Dover	38	22	7	9	78	56	51
Corby Town	38	19	8	11	79	50	46
King's Lynn	38	19	7	15	76	66	45
Cheltenham Town	38	18	7	13	83	52	43
Folkestone Town	38	15	10	13	79	57	40
Canterbury City	38	14	8	16	42	56	36
Yiewsley	38	11	10	17	63	71	32
Ramsgate Athletic	38	12	7	19	58	82	31
Trowbridge Town	38	11	9	18	50	81	31
Burton Albion	38	10	10	18	48	76	30
Gloucester City	38	9	11	18	42	78	29
Sittingbourne	38	12	3	23	56	75	27
Ashford Town	38	9	6	23	58	76	24
Barry Town	38	6	5	27	35	75	17
Tunbridge Wells United	38	6	2	30	43	118	14

1963-64

Premier Division

Yeovil Town	42	29	5	8	93	36	63
Chelmsford City	42	26	7	9	99	55	59
Bath City	42	24	9	9	88	51	57
Guildford City	42	21	9	12	90	55	51
Romford	42	20	9	13	71	58	49
Hastings United	42	20	8	14	75	61	48
Weymouth	42	20	7	15	65	53	47
Bedford Town	42	19	9	14	71	68	47
Cambridge United	42	17	9	16	92	77	43
Cambridge City	42	17	9	16	76	70	43
Wisbech Town	42	17	8	17	64	68	42
Bexley United	42	16	10	16	70	77	42
Dartford	42	16	8	18	56	71	40
Worcester City	42	12	15	15	70	74	39
Nuneaton Borough	42	15	8	19	58	61	38
Rugby Town	42	15	8	19	68	86	38
Margate	42	12	13	17	68	81	37
Wellington Town	42	12	9	21	73	85	33
Merthyr Tydfil	42	12	8	22	69	108	32
Hereford United	42	12	7	23	58	86	31
Kettering Town	42	10	5	27	49	89	25
Hinckley Athletic	42	7	6	29	51	104	20

First Division

Folkstone Town	42	28	7	7	82	38	63
King's Lynn	42	28	5	9	94	44	61
Cheltenham Town	42	25	10	7	92	49	60
Tonbridge	42	24	11	7	98	54	59
Corby town	42	24	7	11	114	56	55
Stevenage Town	42	21	6	15	70	59	48
Ashford Town	42	19	9	14	73	57	47
Burton Albion	42	19	8	15	76	70	46
Poole Town	42	17	11	14	75	61	45
Dover	42	18	9	15	86	75	45
Canterbury City	42	16	12	14	66	66	44
Crawley Town	42	20	2	20	81	71	42
Trowbridge Town	42	16	9	17	71	78	41
Clacton Town	42	19	1	22	76	88	39
Gloucester City	42	17	4	21	88	89	38
Yiewsley	42	15	8	19	63	77	38
Sittingbourne	42	15	8	19	52	70	38
Ramsgate Athletic	42	13	9	20	57	55	35
Tunbridge Wells Rangers	42	10	8	24	47	89	28
Gravesend & Northfleet	42	7	9	26	43	96	23
Deal Town	42	5	7	30	48	106	17
Barry Town	42	3	6	33	33	137	12

1964-65

Premier Division

Weymouth	42	24	8	10	99	50	56
Guildford City	42	21	12	9	73	49	54
Worcester City	42	22	6	14	100	62	50
Yeovil Town	42	18	14	10	76	55	50
Chelmsford City	42	21	8	13	86	77	50
Margate	42	20	9	13	88	79	49
Dartford	42	17	11	14	74	64	45
Nuneaton Borough	42	19	7	16	57	55	45
Cambridge United	42	16	11	15	78	66	43
Bedford Town	42	17	9	16	66	70	43
Cambridge City	42	16	9	17	72	69	41
Cheltenham Town	42	15	11	16	72	78	41
Folkestone Town	42	17	7	18	72	79	41
Romford	42	17	7	18	61	70	41
King's Lynn	42	13	13	16	56	79	39
Tonbridge	42	10	16	16	66	75	36
Wellington Town	42	13	10	19	63	78	36
Rugby Town	42	15	6	21	71	98	36
Wisbech Town	42	14	6	22	75	91	34
Bexley United	42	14	5	23	67	74	33
Hastings United	42	9	14	19	58	86	32
Bath City	42	13	3	26	60	86	29

First Division

Hereford United	42	34	4	4	124	39	72
Wimbledon	42	24	13	5	108	52	61
Poole Town	42	26	6	10	92	56	58
Corby Town	42	24	7	11	88	55	55
Stevenage Town	42	19	13	10	83	43	51
Hillingdon Borough	42	21	7	14	105	63	49
Crawley Town	42	22	5	15	83	52	49
Merthyr Tydfil	42	20	9	13	75	59	49
Gloucester City	42	19	10	13	68	65	48
Burton Albion	42	20	7	15	83	75	47
Canterbury City	42	13	16	13	73	53	42
Kettering Town	42	14	13	15	74	64	41
Ramsgate Athletic	42	16	8	18	51	59	40
Dover	42	14	10	18	54	59	38
Hinckley Athletic	42	13	9	20	56	81	35
Trowbridge Town	42	13	5	24	68	106	31
Ashford Town	42	11	8	23	60	98	30
Barry Town	42	11	7	24	47	103	29
Deal Town	42	7	13	22	61	127	27
Tunbridge Wells Rangers	42	10	6	26	51	107	26
Gravesend & Northfleet	42	9	7	26	57	101	25
Sittingbourne	42	8	5	29	58	103	21

1965-66

Premier Division

Weymouth	42	22	13	7	70	35	57
Chelmsford City	42	21	12	9	74	50	54
Hereford United	42	21	10	11	81	49	52
Bedford Town	42	23	6	13	80	57	52
Wimbledon	42	20	10	12	80	47	50
Cambridge City	42	19	11	12	67	52	49
Romford	42	21	7	14	87	72	49
Worcester City	42	20	8	14	69	54	48
Yeovil Town	42	17	11	14	91	70	45
Cambridge United	42	18	9	15	72	64	45
King's Lynn	42	18	7	17	75	72	43
Corby Town	42	16	9	17	66	73	41
Wellington Town	42	13	13	16	65	70	39
Nuneaton Borough	42	15	8	19	60	74	38
Folkestone Town	42	14	9	19	53	75	37
Guildford City	42	14	8	20	70	84	36
Poole Town	42	14	7	21	61	75	35
Cheltenham Town	42	13	9	20	69	99	35
Dartford	42	13	7	22	62	69	33
Rugby Town	42	11	10	21	67	95	32
Tonbridge	42	11	6	25	63	101	28
Margate	42	8	10	24	66	111	26

First Division

Barnet	46	30	9	7	114	49	69
Hillingdon Borough	46	27	10	9	101	46	64
Burton Albion	46	28	8	10	121	60	64
Bath City	46	25	13	8	88	50	63
Hastings United	46	25	10	11	104	59	60
Wisbech Town	46	25	9	12	98	54	59
Canterbury City	46	25	8	13	89	66	58
Stevenage Town	46	23	9	14	86	49	55
Kettering Town	46	22	9	15	77	74	53
Merthyr Tydfil	46	22	6	18	95	68	50
Dunstable Town	46	15	14	17	76	72	44
Crawley Town	46	17	10	19	72	71	44
Bexley United	46	20	4	22	65	71	44
Trowbridge Town	46	16	11	19	79	81	43
Dover	46	17	8	21	59	62	42
Barry Town	46	16	10	20	72	94	42
Gravesend & Northfleet	46	16	9	21	84	86	41
Gloucester City	46	14	12	20	75	98	40
Sittingbourne	46	11	12	23	77	121	34
Ramsgate Athletic	46	9	15	22	35	76	33
Hinckley Athletic	46	10	12	24	59	93	32
Tunbridge Wells Rangers	46	12	8	26	47	88	32
Ashford Town	46	9	10	27	44	92	28
Deal Town	46	3	4	39	29	165	10

1966-67

Premier Division

Romford	42	22	8	12	80	60	52
Nuneaton Borough	42	21	9	12	82	54	51
Weymouth	42	18	14	10	64	40	50
Wimbledon	42	19	11	12	88	60	49
Barnet	42	18	13	11	86	66	49
Guildford City	42	19	10	13	65	51	48
Wellington Town	42	20	7	15	70	67	47
Cambridge United	42	16	13	13	75	67	45
Chelmsford City	42	15	15	12	66	59	45
Hereford United	42	16	12	14	79	61	44
King's Lynn	42	15	14	13	78	72	44
Cambridge City	42	15	13	14	66	70	43
Cheltenham Town	42	16	11	15	60	71	43
Yeovil Town	42	14	14	14	66	72	42
Burton Albion	42	17	5	20	63	71	39
Corby Town	42	15	9	18	60	75	39
Poole Town	42	14	11	17	52	65	39
Hillingdon Borough	42	11	13	18	49	70	35
Bath City	42	11	12	19	51	74	34
Worcester City	42	11	8	23	59	79	30
Bedford Town	42	8	13	21	54	72	29
Folkestone Town	42	6	15	21	44	81	27

First Division

Team	P	W	D	L	F	A	Pts
Dover	46	29	12	5	92	35	70
Margate	46	31	7	8	127	54	69
Stevenage Town	46	29	8	9	90	32	66
Hastings United	46	25	16	5	89	45	66
Kettering Town	46	27	9	10	105	62	63
Crawley Town	46	26	8	12	81	48	60
Ramsgate Athletic	46	23	8	15	79	62	54
Dartford	46	19	15	12	92	67	53
Tonbridge	46	21	10	15	91	69	52
Trowbridge Town	46	20	12	14	73	60	52
Ashford Town	46	18	8	20	74	68	44
Merthyr Tydfil	46	17	9	20	81	71	43
Gloucester City	46	18	6	22	69	83	42
Canterbury City	46	17	8	21	57	75	42
Wisbech Town	46	16	9	21	87	93	41
Bexley United	46	13	15	18	53	69	41
Banbury United	46	13	14	19	88	100	40
Rugby Town	46	15	7	24	57	77	37
Dunstable Town	46	14	6	26	55	87	34
Barry Town	46	11	11	24	62	89	33
Gravesend & Northfleet	46	11	9	26	63	106	31
Hinckley Athletic	46	10	8	28	44	100	28
Tunbridge Wells Rangers	46	4	15	27	31	96	23
Sittingbourne	46	5	10	31	44	136	20

1967-68

Premier Division

Team	P	W	D	L	F	A	Pts
Chelmsford City	42	25	7	10	85	50	57
Wimbledon	42	24	7	11	85	47	55
Cambridge United	42	20	13	9	73	42	53
Cheltenham Town	42	23	7	12	97	67	53
Guildford City	42	18	13	11	56	43	49
Romford	42	20	8	14	72	60	48
Barnet	42	20	8	14	81	71	48
Margate	42	19	8	15	80	71	46
Wellington Town	42	16	13	13	70	66	45
Hillingdon Borough	42	18	9	15	53	54	45
King's Lynn	42	18	8	16	66	57	44
Yeovil Town	42	16	12	14	45	43	44
Weymouth	42	17	8	17	65	62	42
Hereford United	42	17	7	18	58	62	41
Nuneaton Borough	42	13	14	15	62	64	40
Dover	42	17	6	19	54	56	40
Poole Town	42	13	10	19	55	74	36
Stevenage Town	42	13	9	20	57	75	35
Burton Albion	42	14	6	22	51	73	34
Corby Town	42	7	13	22	40	77	27
Cambridge City	42	10	6	26	51	81	26
Hastings United	42	4	8	30	33	94	16

First Division

Team	P	W	D	L	F	A	Pts
Worcester City	42	23	14	5	92	35	60
Kettering Town	42	24	10	8	88	40	58
Bedford Town	42	24	7	11	101	40	55
Rugby Town	42	20	15	7	72	44	55
Dartford	42	23	9	10	70	48	55
Bath City	42	21	12	9	78	51	54
Banbury United	42	22	9	11	79	59	53
Ramsgate Athletic	42	17	7	8	70	37	51
Merthyr Tydfil	42	18	13	11	80	66	49
Tonbridge	42	18	9	15	76	71	45
Canterbury City	42	16	11	15	66	63	43
Ashford Town	42	18	6	18	73	78	42
Brentwood Town	42	16	9	17	63	73	41
Bexley United	42	12	13	17	56	64	37
Trowbridge Town	42	12	11	19	64	70	35
Gloucester City	42	12	9	21	54	68	33
Wisbech Town	42	11	10	21	43	78	32
Crawley Town	42	10	8	24	54	85	28
Folkestone Town	42	10	7	25	49	80	27
Dunstable Town	42	8	10	24	44	94	26
Barry Town	42	7	12	23	36	81	26
Gravesend & Northfleet	42	6	7	29	28	112	19

1968-69

Premier Division

Team	P	W	D	L	F	A	Pts
Cambridge United	42	27	5	10	72	39	59
Hillingdon Borough	42	24	10	8	68	47	58
Wimbledon	42	21	12	9	66	48	54
King's Lynn	42	20	9	13	68	60	49
Worcester City	42	19	11	12	53	47	49
Romford	42	18	12	12	58	52	48
Weymouth	42	16	15	11	52	41	47
Yeovil Town	42	16	13	13	52	50	45
Kettering Town	42	18	8	16	51	55	44
Dover	42	17	9	16	66	61	43
Nuneaton Borough	42	17	7	18	74	58	41
Barnet	42	15	10	17	72	66	40
Chelmsford City	42	17	6	19	56	58	40
Hereford United	42	15	9	18	66	62	39
Telford United	42	14	10	18	62	61	38
Poole Town	42	16	6	20	75	76	38
Burton Albion	42	16	5	21	55	71	37
Margate	42	14	7	21	79	90	35
Cheltenham Town	42	15	5	22	55	64	35
Bedford Town	42	11	12	19	46	63	34
Rugby Town	42	10	6	26	38	83	26
Guildford City	42	7	11	24	41	73	25

First Division

Team	P	W	D	L	F	A	Pts
Brentwood Town	42	26	12	4	44	37	64
Bath City	42	26	10	6	96	40	62
Gloucester City	42	25	9	8	100	53	59
Crawley Town	42	21	13	8	65	32	55
Corby Town	42	22	6	14	81	65	50
Dartford	42	20	8	14	79	51	48
Ramsgate Athletic	42	19	9	14	72	57	47
Salisbury	42	20	6	16	69	52	46
Cambridge City	42	18	10	14	73	63	46
Banbury United	42	16	12	14	67	72	44
Trowbridge Town	42	15	8	19	70	60	44
Folkestone Town	42	19	5	18	53	59	43
Canterbury City	42	17	7	18	67	63	41
Ashford Town	42	16	8	18	72	73	40
Bexley United	42	15	9	18	62	75	39
Hastings United	42	15	9	18	58	69	39
Wisbech Town	42	11	13	18	57	70	35
Dunstable Town	42	14	6	22	73	99	34
Merthyr Tydfil	42	10	7	25	49	101	27
Barry Town	42	8	10	24	39	78	26
Gravesend & Northfleet	42	8	9	25	51	79	25
Tonbridge	42	2	6	34	36	137	10

1969-70

Premier Division

Team	P	W	D	L	F	A	Pts
Cambridge United	42	26	6	10	86	49	58
Yeovil Town	42	25	7	10	78	48	57
Chelmsford City	42	20	11	11	76	58	51
Weymouth	42	18	14	10	59	37	50
Wimbledon	42	19	12	11	64	52	50
Hillingdon Borough	42	19	12	11	56	50	50
Barnet	42	16	15	11	71	54	47
Telford United	42	18	10	14	61	62	46
Brentwood Town	42	16	13	13	61	38	45
Hereford United	42	18	9	15	74	65	45
Bath City	42	18	8	16	63	55	44
King's Lynn	42	16	11	15	72	68	43
Margate	42	17	8	17	70	64	42
Dover	42	15	10	17	51	50	40
Kettering Town	42	18	3	21	64	75	39
Worcester City	42	14	10	18	35	44	38
Romford	42	13	11	18	50	62	37
Poole Town	42	8	19	15	48	57	35
Gloucester City	42	12	9	21	53	73	33
Nuneaton Borough	42	11	10	21	52	74	32
Crawley Town	42	6	15	21	53	101	27
Burton Albion	42	3	9	30	24	82	15

First Division

Bedford Town	42	26	9	7	93	37	61
Cambridge City	42	26	8	8	104	43	60
Dartford	42	24	11	7	33	46	58
Ashford Town	42	19	15	8	71	43	53
Rugby Town	42	20	10	12	82	66	50
Trowbridge Town	42	20	8	14	72	65	48
Hastings United	42	18	11	13	67	51	47
Guildford City	42	19	9	14	68	58	47
Banbury United	42	19	8	15	86	72	46
Cheltenham Town	42	20	5	17	78	81	45
Canterbury City	42	15	13	14	61	57	43
Corby Town	42	14	15	13	58	53	43
Folkestone Town	42	19	5	18	57	55	43
Ramsgate Athletic	42	14	13	15	53	57	41
Salisbury	42	13	13	16	48	53	39
Gravesend & Northfleet	42	13	11	18	62	71	37
Bexley United	42	10	11	21	58	76	31
Dunstable Town	42	11	9	22	52	82	31
Merthyr Tydfil	42	9	11	22	40	80	29
Barry Town	42	11	6	25	39	76	28
Wisbech Town	42	8	9	25	58	116	25
Tonbridge	42	4	10	28	46	101	18

1971-72

Premier Division

Chelmsford City	42	28	6	8	109	46	62
Hereford United	42	24	12	6	68	30	60
Dover	42	20	11	11	67	45	51
Barnet	42	21	7	14	80	57	49
Dartford	42	20	8	14	75	68	48
Weymouth	42	21	5	16	69	43	47
Yeovil Town	42	18	11	13	67	51	47
Hillingdon Borough	42	20	6	16	64	58	46
Margate	42	19	8	15	74	68	46
Wimbledon	42	19	7	16	75	64	45
Romford	42	16	13	13	54	49	45
Guildford City	42	20	5	17	71	65	45
Telford United	42	18	7	17	83	68	43
Nuneaton Borough	42	16	10	16	46	47	42
Bedford Town	42	16	9	17	59	66	41
Worcester City	42	17	7	18	46	57	41
Cambridge City	42	12	14	16	68	71	38
Folkestone	42	14	7	21	58	64	35
Poole Town	42	9	11	22	43	72	29
Bath City	42	11	4	27	45	86	26
Merthyr Tydfil	42	7	8	27	29	93	22
Gravesend & Northfleet	42	5	6	31	30	110	16

1970-71

Premier Division

Yeovil Town	42	25	7	10	66	31	57
Cambridge City	42	22	11	9	67	38	55
Romford	42	23	9	10	63	42	55
Hereford United	42	23	8	11	71	53	54
Chelmsford City	42	20	11	11	61	32	51
Barnet	42	18	14	10	69	49	50
Bedford Town	42	20	10	12	62	46	50
Wimbledon	42	20	8	14	72	54	48
Worcester City	42	20	8	14	61	46	48
Weymouth	42	14	16	12	64	48	44
Dartford	42	15	12	15	53	51	42
Dover	42	16	9	17	64	63	41
Margate	42	15	10	17	64	70	40
Hillingdon Borough	42	17	6	19	61	68	40
Bath City	42	13	12	17	48	68	38
Nuneaton Borough	42	12	12	18	43	66	36
Telford United	42	13	8	21	64	70	34
Poole Town	42	14	6	22	57	75	34
King's Lynn	42	11	7	24	44	67	29
Ashford Town	42	8	13	21	52	86	29
Kettering Town	42	8	11	23	48	84	27
Gloucester City	42	6	10	26	34	81	21

First Division

Guildford City	38	22	10	6	76	36	54
Merthyr Tydfil	38	19	12	7	52	33	50
Gravesend & Northfleet	38	19	10	9	74	42	48
Folkestone	38	20	8	10	83	53	48
Burton Albion	38	19	10	9	56	37	48
Rugby Town	38	17	14	7	58	40	48
Ramsgate Athletic	38	20	5	13	83	54	45
Trowbridge Town	38	19	7	12	78	55	45
Bexley United	38	17	11	10	57	45	45
Crawley Town	38	15	11	12	84	68	41
Hastings United	38	13	12	13	51	50	38
Banbury United	38	13	11	14	58	53	37
Corby Town	38	14	8	16	57	60	36
Salisbury	38	13	7	18	56	60	33
Cheltenham Town	38	8	15	15	44	58	31
Stevenage Athletic	38	12	7	19	55	79	21
Tonbridge	38	8	8	22	48	83	24
Barry Town	38	9	6	23	35	82	24
Dunstable Town	38	8	4	26	32	81	20
Canterbury City	38	5	4	29	37	105	14

First Division (North)

Kettering Town	34	23	6	5	70	27	52
Burton Albion	34	18	13	3	58	27	49
Cheltenham Town	34	20	4	10	72	51	44
Rugby Town	34	18	7	9	52	36	43
Wellingborough Town	34	15	10	9	73	44	40
Stourbridge	34	13	14	7	59	42	40
King's Lynn	34	14	11	9	62	45	39
Corby Town	34	15	9	10	47	35	39
Ilkeston Town	34	14	11	9	44	38	39
Banbury United	34	14	5	15	54	46	33
Bury Town	34	14	5	15	47	44	33
Wealdstone	34	14	5	15	51	58	33
Lockheed Leamington	34	15	3	16	41	52	33
Gloucester City	34	8	8	18	46	61	24
Stevenage Athletic	34	8	8	18	41	69	24
Bletchley	34	7	7	20	36	70	21
Dunstable Town	34	5	7	22	29	75	17
Barry Town	34	1	7	26	22	84	9

First Division (South)

Waterlooville	30	15	9	6	40	22	39
Ramsgate Athletic	30	14	11	5	42	27	39
Maidstone United	30	14	10	6	48	28	38
Crawley Town	30	15	5	10	67	55	35
Metropolitan Police	30	15	3	12	48	41	33
Tonbridge	30	12	9	9	37	34	33
Bexley United	30	14	4	12	52	46	32
Basingstoke Town	30	14	4	12	37	36	32
Andover	30	11	9	10	32	34	31
Ashford Town	30	12	4	14	43	48	28
Salisbury	30	10	7	13	45	44	27
Winchester City	30	10	7	13	40	47	27
Hastings United	30	10	7	13	28	42	27
Trowbridge Town	30	8	7	15	41	49	23
Canterbury City	30	7	8	15	39	56	22
Woodford Town	30	4	6	20	22	52	14

1972-73

Premier Division

Kettering Town	42	20	17	5	74	44	57
Yeovil Town	42	21	14	7	67	61	56
Dover	42	23	9	10	61	68	55
Chelmsford City	42	23	7	12	75	43	53
Worcester City	42	20	13	9	68	47	53
Weymouth	42	20	12	10	72	51	52
Margate	42	17	15	10	80	60	49
Bedford Town	42	16	15	11	43	36	47
Nuneaton Borough	42	16	14	12	51	41	46
Telford United	42	12	20	10	57	47	44
Cambridge City	42	14	15	13	64	53	43
Wimbledon	42	14	14	14	50	50	42
Barnet	42	15	11	16	60	59	41
Romford	42	17	5	20	51	65	39
Hillingdon Borough	42	16	6	20	52	58	38
Dartford	42	12	11	19	49	63	35
Folkestone	42	11	11	20	41	72	33
Guildford City	42	10	11	21	59	84	31
Ramsgate	42	9	13	20	35	61	31
Poole Town	42	10	10	22	50	88	30
Burton Albion	42	9	7	26	43	81	25
Waterlooville	42	4	16	22	33	63	24

First Division (North)

Grantham	42	29	8	5	113	41	66
Atherstone Town	42	23	11	8	82	48	57
Cheltenham Town	42	24	8	10	87	47	56
Rugby Town	42	20	10	12	60	47	50
Kidderminster Harriers	42	19	12	11	67	56	50
Merthyr Tydfil	42	17	12	13	51	40	46
Corby Town	42	14	16	12	62	56	44
Stourbridge	42	16	11	15	70	64	43
Gloucester City	42	18	7	17	55	64	43
Bromsgrove Rovers	42	17	8	17	63	54	42
Redditch United	42	18	6	18	58	59	42
Banbury United	42	18	5	19	60	53	41
Wellingborough Town	42	17	7	18	58	71	41
King's Lynn	42	14	12	16	45	49	40
Lockheed Leamington	42	13	12	17	51	58	38
Enderby Town	42	12	14	16	50	61	38
Stevenage Athletic	42	12	13	17	50	63	37
Tamworth	42	14	8	20	45	65	36
Bury Town	42	13	9	20	52	69	35
Barry Town	42	11	10	21	45	71	32
Ilkeston Town	42	9	6	27	35	68	24
Bedworth United	42	10	3	29	42	94	23

First Division (South)

Maidstone United	42	25	12	5	90	38	62
Tonbridge	42	26	7	9	70	44	59
Ashford Town	42	24	7	11	90	40	55
Bideford	42	19	14	9	70	43	52
Minehead	42	20	12	10	65	47	52
Gravesend & Northfleet	42	22	7	13	81	55	51
Bath City	42	18	11	13	56	54	47
Wealdstone	42	16	12	14	81	61	44
Bletchley Town	42	14	13	15	54	51	41
Hastings United	42	14	13	15	53	53	41
Andover	42	15	11	16	62	70	41
Canterbury City	42	14	12	16	51	59	40
Basingstoke Town	42	14	12	16	48	57	40
Crawley Town	42	14	11	17	59	76	39
Metropolitan Police	42	15	8	19	82	75	38
Trowbridge Town	42	15	8	19	65	77	38
Bexley United	42	12	14	16	54	64	38
Salisbury	42	14	10	18	49	60	38
Bognor Regis Town	42	12	9	21	41	66	33
Dorchester Town	42	10	12	20	47	73	32
Winchester City	42	7	11	24	41	79	25
Dunstable Town	42	4	10	28	38	105	18

1973-74

Dartford	42	22	13	7	67	37	57
Grantham	42	18	13	11	70	49	49
Chelmsford City	42	19	10	13	62	49	48
Kettering Town	42	16	16	10	62	51	48
Maidstone United	42	16	14	12	54	43	46
Yeovil Town	42	13	20	9	45	39	46
Weymouth	42	19	7	16	60	41	45
Barnet	42	18	9	15	55	46	45
Nuneaton Borough	42	13	19	10	54	47	45
Cambridge City	42	15	12	15	45	54	42
Atherstone Town	42	16	9	17	61	59	41
Wimbledon	42	15	11	16	50	56	41
Telford United	42	12	16	14	51	57	40
Dover	42	11	17	14	41	46	39
Tonbridge	42	12	15	15	38	45	39
Romford	42	11	17	14	39	52	39
Margate	42	15	8	19	56	63	38
Guildford City	42	13	11	18	48	67	37
Worcester City	42	11	14	17	53	67	36
Bedford Town	42	11	14	17	38	51	36
Folkestone	42	11	12	19	56	65	34
Hillingdon Borough	42	9	15	18	44	65	33

First Division (North)

Stourbridge	42	29	11	2	103	36	69
Burton Albion	42	27	9	6	88	32	63
Cheltenham Town	42	24	8	10	75	51	56
AP Leamington	42	21	12	9	82	45	54
Enderby Town	42	19	14	9	60	36	52
Witney Town	42	20	10	12	69	55	50
Stevenage Athletic	42	19	11	12	65	46	49
Banbury United	42	19	11	12	69	57	49
King's Lynn	42	19	10	13	65	50	48
Kidderminster Harriers	42	15	14	13	67	53	44
Merthyr Tydfil	42	16	12	14	70	61	44
Redditch United	42	14	11	17	56	73	39
Bromsgrove Rovers	42	14	10	18	54	61	38
Bedworth United	42	14	10	18	50	77	38
Tamworth	42	13	11	18	42	51	37
Corby Town	42	12	11	19	40	57	35
Bletchley Town	42	10	15	17	47	71	35
Barry Town	42	10	8	24	53	85	29
Bury Town	42	10	6	26	57	84	26
Gloucester City	42	10	6	26	52	81	26
Wellingborough Town	42	7	9	26	42	87	23
Dunstable Town	42	5	11	26	26	83	21

First Division (South)

Wealdstone	38	26	7	5	75	35	59
Bath City	38	20	8	10	55	34	48
Waterlooville	38	16	15	7	55	38	47
Minehead	38	16	15	7	69	52	47
Bideford	38	17	12	9	61	51	46
Poole Town	38	18	9	11	67	47	45
Bexley United	38	18	7	13	50	42	43
Hastings United	38	16	9	13	45	36	41
Basingstoke Town	38	14	11	13	55	44	39
Gravesend & Northfleet	38	13	13	12	58	52	39
Bognor Regis Town	38	13	12	13	48	54	38
Ashford Town	38	14	8	16	41	42	36
Ramsgate	38	13	9	16	46	44	35
Dorchester Town	38	10	13	15	40	48	33
Canterbury City	38	9	12	17	37	46	30
Trowbridge Town	38	8	14	16	44	61	30
Salisbury	38	10	9	19	40	60	29
Metropolitan Police	38	9	11	18	37	61	29
Andover	38	11	3	24	38	70	25
Crawley Town	38	6	9	23	35	79	21

1974-75

Premier Division

Team	P	W	D	L	F	A	Pts
Wimbledon	42	25	7	10	63	33	57
Nuneaton Borough	42	23	8	11	56	37	54
Yeovil Town	42	21	9	12	64	34	51
Kettering Town	42	20	10	12	73	41	50
Burton Albion	42	18	13	11	54	48	49
Bath City	42	20	8	14	63	50	48
Margate	42	17	12	13	64	64	46
Wealdstone	42	17	11	14	62	61	45
Telford United	42	16	13	13	55	56	45
Chelmsford City	42	16	12	14	62	51	44
Grantham	42	16	11	15	70	62	43
Dover	42	15	13	14	43	53	43
Maidstone United	42	15	13	15	52	50	42
Atherstone Town	42	14	14	14	48	53	42
Weymouth	42	13	13	16	66	58	39
Stourbridge	42	13	12	17	56	70	38
Cambridge	42	11	14	17	51	56	36
Tonbridge	42	11	12	19	44	66	34
Romford	42	10	13	19	46	62	33
Dartford	42	9	13	20	52	70	31
Barnet	42	10	9	23	44	76	29
Guildford & Dorking United	42	10	5	27	45	82	25

First Division (North)

Team	P	W	D	L	F	A	Pts
Bedford Town	42	28	9	5	85	33	65
Dunstable Town	42	25	8	9	105	61	58
AP Leamington	42	25	7	10	68	48	57
Redditch United	42	22	12	8	76	40	56
Worcester City	42	24	8	10	84	50	56
Cheltenham Town	42	21	9	12	72	53	51
Tamworth	42	21	8	13	74	53	50
King's Lynn	42	19	10	13	71	64	48
Enderby Town	42	17	12	13	61	48	46
Banbury United	42	18	10	14	52	51	46
Stevenage Athletic	42	16	13	13	62	48	45
Bromsgrove Rovers	42	18	9	15	63	52	45
Merthyr Tydfil	42	11	15	16	53	64	37
Witney Town	42	16	4	22	57	76	36
Corby Town	42	11	13	18	60	57	35
Kidderminster Harriers	42	12	11	19	50	66	35
Gloucester City	42	13	8	21	55	75	34
Wellingborough Town	42	9	13	20	42	61	31
Barry Town	42	10	10	22	49	73	30
Bedworth United	42	9	9	24	60	91	27
Milton Keynes City	42	7	5	30	48	100	19
Bury Town	42	5	7	30	36	119	17

First Division (South)

Team	P	W	D	L	F	A	Pts
Gravesend & Northfleet	38	24	12	2	70	30	60
Hillingdon Borough	38	22	8	8	87	45	52
Minehead	38	21	9	8	74	33	51
Ramsgate	38	19	11	8	70	37	49
Bexley United	38	19	7	12	61	44	45
Waterlooville	38	17	11	10	67	49	45
Ashford Town	38	16	12	10	64	55	44
Basingstoke Town	38	16	11	11	64	50	43
Canterbury City	38	16	9	13	54	43	41
Hastings United	38	13	14	11	54	45	40
Poole Town	38	11	13	14	50	60	35
Metropolitan Police	38	11	13	14	54	66	35
Folkestone & Shepway	38	10	14	14	53	57	34
Andover	38	12	8	18	52	71	32
Bognor Regis Town	38	10	11	17	49	64	31
Salisbury	38	9	11	18	45	66	29
Trowbridge Town	38	10	9	19	48	76	29
Bideford	38	10	8	20	40	71	28
Dorchester Town	38	8	10	20	40	63	26
Crawley Town	38	3	5	30	31	102	11

1975-76

Premier Division

Team	P	W	D	L	F	A	Pts
Wimbledon	42	26	10	6	74	29	62
Yeovil Town	42	21	12	9	68	35	54
Atherstone Town	42	18	15	9	56	55	51
Maidstone United	42	17	16	9	52	39	50
Nuneaton Borough	42	16	18	8	41	33	50
Gravesend & Northfleet	42	16	18	8	49	47	50
Grantham	42	15	14	13	56	47	44
Dunstable Town	42	17	9	16	52	43	43
Bedford Town	42	13	17	12	55	51	43
Burton Albion	42	17	9	16	52	53	43
Margate	42	15	12	15	62	60	42
Hillingdon Borough	42	13	14	15	61	54	40
Telford United	42	14	12	16	54	51	40
Chelmsford City	42	13	14	15	52	57	40
Kettering Town	42	11	17	14	48	52	39
Bath City	42	11	16	15	62	57	38
Weymouth	42	13	9	20	51	67	35
Dover	42	8	18	16	51	60	34
Wealdstone	42	12	9	21	61	82	33
Tonbridge AFC	42	11	11	20	45	70	33
Cambridge City	42	8	15	19	41	67	31
Stourbridge	42	10	9	23	38	72	29

First Division (North)

Team	P	W	D	L	F	A	Pts
Redditch United	42	29	11	2	101	39	69
AP Leamington	42	27	10	5	85	31	64
Witney Town	42	24	9	9	66	40	57
Worcester City	42	24	8	10	90	49	56
Cheltenham Town	42	20	10	12	87	55	50
Barry Town	42	19	10	13	52	47	48
King's Lynn	42	17	14	11	52	48	48
Tamworth	42	18	11	13	65	43	47
Barnet	42	15	12	15	56	56	42
Oswestry Town	42	16	8	18	63	71	40
Enderby Town	42	16	6	20	48	51	38
Banbury United	42	15	8	19	58	67	38
Merthyr Tydfil	42	11	15	16	59	67	37
Bromsgrove Rovers	42	13	11	18	49	65	37
Milton Keynes City	42	15	6	21	51	63	36
Bury Town	42	12	11	19	52	72	35
Gloucester City	42	13	9	20	49	78	35
Kidderminster Harriers	42	13	8	21	54	70	34
Bedworth United	42	8	18	16	41	66	34
Corby Town	42	11	10	21	50	65	32
Wellingborough Town	42	9	11	22	42	68	29
Stevenage Athletic	42	6	6	30	46	105	18

First Division (South)

Team	P	W	D	L	F	A	Pts
Minehead	38	27	8	3	102	35	62
Dartford	38	26	4	8	84	46	56
Romford	38	21	9	8	66	37	51
Salisbury	38	17	11	10	73	53	45
Hastings United	38	15	15	8	67	51	45
Poole United	38	20	2	16	57	57	42
Bexley United	38	14	13	11	62	53	41
Waterlooville	38	13	13	12	62	54	39
Basingstoke Town	38	13	12	13	69	71	38
Ashford Town	38	14	8	16	67	73	36
Canterbury City	38	11	13	14	53	60	35
Folkestone & Shepway	38	9	14	15	36	51	34
Metropolitan Police	38	9	14	15	46	58	32
Trowbridge Town	38	11	10	17	48	75	32
Guildford & Dorking United	38	9	13	16	43	50	31
Bognor Regis Town	38	6	17	15	44	72	29
Ramsgate	38	9	10	19	57	76	28
Crawley Town	38	9	10	19	46	66	28
Andover	38	9	10	19	42	62	28
Dorchester Town	38	11	6	21	45	69	28

1976-77

Premier Division

Wimbledon	42	28	7	7	64	22	63
Minehead	42	23	12	7	73	39	58
Kettering Town	42	20	16	6	66	46	56
Bath City	42	20	15	7	51	30	55
Nuneaton Borough	42	20	11	11	52	35	51
Bedford Town	42	17	14	11	54	47	48
Yeovil Town	42	15	16	11	54	42	46
Dover	42	13	16	13	46	43	42
Grantham	42	14	12	16	55	50	40
Maidstone United	42	13	14	15	46	50	40
Gravesend & Northfleet	42	13	13	16	38	43	39
AP Leamington	42	12	15	15	44	53	39
Redditch United	42	12	14	16	45	54	38
Wealdstone	42	13	12	17	54	66	38
Hillingdon Borough	42	14	10	18	45	59	38
Atherstone Town	42	14	9	19	41	49	37
Weymouth	42	16	5	21	53	73	37
Dartford	42	13	10	19	52	57	36
Telford United	42	11	12	19	36	50	34
Chelmsford City	42	9	13	20	56	68	31
Burton Albion	42	10	10	22	41	52	30
Margate	42	9	10	23	47	85	28

First Division (North)

Worcester City	38	32	5	1	97	22	69
Cheltenham Town	38	23	8	7	85	35	54
Witney Town	38	21	8	9	48	31	50
Bromsgrove Rovers	38	20	8	10	61	37	48
Barry Town	38	19	8	11	62	45	46
Cambridge City	38	17	10	11	68	43	44
Stourbridge	38	17	9	12	48	35	43
Kidderminster Harriers	38	17	6	15	74	65	40
Banbury United	38	15	10	13	51	47	40
Gloucester City	38	18	4	16	70	81	40
Enderby Town	38	15	9	14	50	44	39
King's Lynn	38	13	11	14	47	53	37
Corby Town	38	11	13	14	56	64	35
Tamworth	38	11	13	14	49	58	35
Merthyr Tydfil	38	12	6	20	60	69	30
Oswestry Town	38	8	10	20	30	60	26
Wellingborough Town	38	8	7	23	37	73	23
Dunstable	38	7	7	24	38	84	21
Bedworth United	38	5	10	23	28	68	20
Milton Keynes City	38	7	6	25	31	76	20

First Division (South)

Barnet	34	23	8	3	65	25	54
Hastings United	34	18	11	5	47	18	47
Waterlooville	34	19	6	9	50	25	44
Dorchester Town	34	16	11	7	48	30	43
Salisbury	34	15	11	8	57	39	41
Romford	34	18	5	11	47	32	41
Poole Town	34	17	7	10	40	35	41
Trowbridge Town	34	15	8	11	47	39	38
Crawley Town	34	14	9	11	53	42	37
Folkestone & Shepway	34	12	11	11	39	42	35
Basingstoke Town	34	12	10	12	51	43	34
Canterbury City	34	6	16	12	36	46	28
Bognor Regis Town	34	9	9	16	33	50	27
Tonbridge AFC	34	9	9	16	33	50	27
Metropolitan Police	34	5	12	17	37	61	22
Andover	34	4	11	19	17	49	19
Ashford Town	34	5	8	21	32	65	18
Aylesbury United	34	5	6	23	27	68	16

1977-78

Premier Division

Bath City	42	22	18	2	83	32	62
Weymouth	42	21	16	5	64	36	58
Maidstone United	42	20	11	11	59	41	51
Worcester City	42	20	11	11	67	50	51
Gravesend & Northfleet	42	19	11	12	57	42	49
Kettering Town	42	18	11	13	58	48	47
Barnet	42	18	11	13	63	58	47
Wealdstone	42	16	14	12	54	48	46
Telford United	42	17	11	14	52	45	45
Nuneaton Borough	42	15	14	13	38	36	44
Dartford	42	14	15	13	57	65	43
Yeovil Town	42	14	14	14	57	49	42
Hastings United	42	15	9	18	49	60	39
Cheltenham Town	42	12	14	16	43	52	38
Hillingdon Borough	42	13	9	20	45	54	35
Atherstone Town	42	10	15	17	41	56	35
Redditch United	42	15	5	22	40	55	35
AP Leamington	42	11	13	18	34	57	35
Minehead	42	11	12	19	43	48	34
Dover	42	9	13	20	41	63	31
Bedford Town	42	8	13	21	51	75	29
Grantham	42	11	6	25	40	66	28

First Division (North)

Witney Town	38	20	15	3	54	27	55
Bridgend Town	38	20	9	9	59	45	49
Burton Albion	38	17	11	10	48	32	45
Enderby Town	38	17	10	11	59	44	44
Bromsgrove Rovers	38	16	12	10	56	41	44
Banbury United	38	17	10	11	52	47	44
Kidderminster Harriers	38	16	11	11	58	41	43
Merthyr Tydfil	38	18	6	14	85	62	42
Cambridge City	38	14	12	12	56	45	40
Barry Town	38	14	11	13	58	48	39
Wellingborough Town	38	11	15	12	47	43	37
King's Lynn	38	12	13	13	55	55	37
Gloucester City	38	14	8	16	68	75	36
Corby Town	38	9	17	12	46	48	35
Dunstable Town	38	11	13	14	49	59	35
Stourbridge	38	9	15	14	52	53	33
Tamworth	38	10	11	17	37	48	31
Bedworth United	38	8	14	16	36	58	30
Milton Keynes City	38	5	11	22	26	74	21
Oswestry Town	38	6	8	24	29	85	20

First Division (South)

Margate	38	24	10	4	92	32	58
Dorchester Town	38	23	10	5	67	31	56
Salisbury	38	21	10	7	60	27	52
Waterlooville	38	19	13	6	66	36	51
Romford	38	17	15	6	58	37	49
Aylesbury United	38	20	7	11	56	42	47
Trowbridge Town	38	16	11	11	65	59	43
Chelmsford City	38	15	11	12	58	46	41
Folkestone & Shepway	38	16	9	13	64	56	41
Taunton Town	38	15	10	13	57	54	40
Addlestone	38	14	10	14	57	60	38
Crawley Town	38	14	9	15	61	60	37
Basingstoke Town	38	11	11	16	44	50	33
Tonbridge AFC	38	13	5	20	64	77	31
Ashford Town	38	9	13	16	39	60	31
Hounslow	38	10	10	18	43	62	30
Bognor Regis Town	38	9	8	21	52	69	26
Poole Town	38	8	10	20	43	68	26
Andover	38	4	12	22	30	68	20
Canterbury City	38	2	6	30	31	113	10

1978-79

Premier Division

Worcester City	42	27	11	4	92	33	65
Kettering Town	42	27	7	8	109	43	61
Telford United	42	22	10	10	60	39	54
Maidstone United	42	18	18	6	55	35	54
Bath City	42	17	19	6	59	41	53
Weymouth	42	18	15	9	71	51	51
AP Leamington	42	19	11	12	65	53	49
Redditch United	42	19	10	13	70	57	48
Yeovil Town	42	15	16	11	59	49	46
Witney Town	42	17	10	15	53	52	44
Nuneaton Borough	42	13	17	12	59	50	43
Gravesend & Northfleet	42	15	12	15	56	55	42
Barnet	42	16	10	16	52	64	42
Hillingdon Borough	42	12	16	14	50	41	40
Wealdstone	42	12	12	18	51	59	36
Atherstone Town	42	9	17	16	46	65	35
Dartford	42	10	14	18	40	56	34
Cheltenham Town	42	11	10	21	38	72	32
Margate	42	10	9	23	44	75	29
Dorchester Town	42	7	11	24	46	86	25
Hastings United	42	5	13	24	37	85	23
Bridgend Town	42	6	6	30	39	90	18

First Division (North)

Grantham	38	21	10	7	70	45	52
Merthyr Tydfil	38	22	7	9	90	53	51
Alvechurch	38	20	10	8	70	42	50
Bedford Town	38	19	9	10	74	49	47
King's Lynn	38	17	11	10	57	46	45
Oswestry Town	38	18	8	12	63	43	44
Gloucester City	38	18	8	12	76	59	44
Burton Albion	38	16	10	12	51	40	42
Kidderminster Harriers	38	13	14	11	70	60	40
Bedworth United	38	13	14	11	41	34	40
Tamworth	38	15	8	15	47	45	38
Stourbridge	38	15	7	16	64	61	37
Barry Town	38	14	9	15	51	53	37
Enderby Town	38	14	8	16	46	55	36
Banbury United	38	10	13	15	42	58	33
Wellingborough Town	38	13	6	19	50	71	32
Cambridge City	38	9	9	20	37	62	27
Bromsgrove Rovers	38	6	14	18	33	61	26
Milton Keynes City	38	7	9	22	37	87	23
Corby Town	38	5	6	27	40	85	16

First Division (South)

Dover	40	28	9	3	88	20	65
Folkestone & Shepway	40	22	6	12	84	50	50
Gosport Borough	40	19	11	10	62	47	49
Chelmsford City	40	20	7	13	65	61	47
Minehead	40	16	13	11	58	39	45
Poole Town	40	15	15	10	48	44	45
Hounslow	40	16	12	12	56	45	44
Waterlooville	40	17	10	13	52	43	44
Trowbridge Town	40	15	12	13	65	61	42
Aylesbury United	40	16	9	15	54	52	41
Taunton Town	40	16	9	15	53	51	41
Bognor Regis Town	40	17	7	16	58	58	41
Dunstable	40	18	4	18	57	55	40
Tonbridge AFC	40	15	10	15	43	47	40
Salisbury	40	13	10	17	47	51	36
Basingstoke Town	40	12	11	17	49	62	35
Addlestone	40	12	9	19	56	64	33
Andover	40	12	6	22	47	69	30
Ashford Town	40	10	10	20	28	53	30
Crawley Town	40	9	9	22	44	75	27
Canterbury City	40	6	3	31	31	98	15

1979-80

Midland Division

Bridgend Town	42	28	6	8	85	39	62
Minehead	42	22	15	5	70	42	59
Bedford Town	42	20	12	10	71	42	52
Kidderminster Harriers	42	23	6	13	81	59	52
Merthyr Tydfil	42	20	11	11	70	47	51
Enderby Town	42	21	8	13	62	50	50
Stourbridge	42	19	11	12	67	49	49
Alvechurch	42	17	14	11	78	60	48
Trowbridge Town	42	19	9	14	62	61	47
Bromsgrove Rovers	42	18	10	14	67	56	46
Barry Town	42	15	12	15	64	58	42
King's Lynn	42	15	11	16	48	55	41
Banbury United	42	13	14	15	56	56	40
Taunton Town	42	16	8	18	55	62	40
Witney Town	42	10	19	13	43	45	39
Bedworth United	42	12	15	15	40	42	39
Milton Keynes City	42	15	7	20	46	59	37
Gloucester City	42	10	14	18	55	68	32
Cheltenham Town	42	13	5	24	49	70	31
Wellingborough Town	42	9	7	26	54	106	25
Cambridge City	42	6	9	27	30	73	21
Corby Town	42	5	9	28	40	94	19

Gloucester City had points deducted

Southern Division

Dorchester Town	46	25	12	9	81	53	62
Aylesbury United	46	25	11	10	73	40	61
Dover	46	22	13	11	78	47	57
Gosport Borough	46	21	15	10	70	50	57
Dartford	46	21	14	11	66	45	56
Bognor Regis Town	46	20	15	11	66	38	55
Hillingdon Borough	46	19	16	11	64	41	54
Dunstable	46	17	19	10	93	64	53
Addlestone	46	20	13	13	72	57	53
Hastings United	46	19	15	12	74	65	53
Fareham Town	46	16	16	14	61	53	48
Waterlooville	46	17	12	17	67	64	46
Andover	46	16	13	17	65	65	45
Poole Town	46	16	13	17	49	64	45
Canterbury City	46	15	15	15	56	60	44
Hounslow	46	14	14	17	44	57	43
Margate	46	17	8	21	51	62	42
Folkestone & Shepway	46	14	11	21	54	63	39
Ashford Town	46	12	14	20	54	71	38
Crawley Town	46	13	11	22	55	72	37
Chelmsford City	46	9	18	19	47	69	36
Basingstoke Town	46	9	15	22	48	79	33
Salisbury	46	10	12	24	47	59	32
Tonbridge AFC	46	3	9	34	30	128	15

1980-81

Midland Division

Alvechurch	42	26	9	7	76	40	61
Bedford Town	42	25	11	6	63	32	61
Trowbridge Town	42	24	9	9	69	39	57
Kidderminster Harriers	42	23	9	10	67	41	55
Barry Town	42	21	9	12	60	40	51
Stourbridge	42	17	16	9	75	49	50
Enderby Town	42	21	8	13	71	47	50
Cheltenham Town	42	18	12	12	70	59	48
Bromsgrove Rovers	42	19	9	14	65	50	47
Corby Town	42	19	7	16	69	58	45
Bridgend Town	42	19	7	16	74	64	45
Minehead	42	19	7	16	54	60	45
Gloucester City	42	19	6	17	82	72	44
Merthyr Tydfil	42	15	12	15	60	50	42
Bedworth United	42	14	12	16	49	46	40
Banbury United	42	11	11	20	51	65	33
Taunton Town	42	10	9	23	48	68	29
Cambridge City	42	8	12	22	46	87	28
Witney Town	42	9	9	24	44	65	27
Wellingborough Town	42	10	7	25	43	91	27
Redditch United	42	11	4	27	54	92	26
Milton Keynes City	42	3	7	32	28	103	13

Southern Division

Dartford	46	26	14	6	76	39	66
Bognor Regis Town	46	25	13	8	95	43	63
Hastings United	46	24	14	8	87	43	62
Gosport Borough	46	24	12	10	84	52	60
Waterlooville	46	19	21	6	67	50	59
Dorchester Town	46	21	13	12	84	56	55
Dover	46	22	10	14	70	50	54
Poole Town	46	19	14	13	70	56	52
Addlestone & Weybridge	46	21	9	16	66	57	51
Dunstable	46	19	13	14	73	68	51
Aylesbury United	46	20	10	16	66	60	50
Hounslow	46	17	13	16	65	55	47
Hillingdon Borough	46	16	15	15	50	49	47
Basingstoke Town	46	16	14	16	69	58	46
Crawley Town	46	18	4	24	64	78	40
Ashford Town	46	12	15	19	55	76	39
Tonbridge AFC	46	12	15	19	44	68	39
Chelmsford City	46	13	12	21	54	78	38
Canterbury City	46	12	13	21	40	59	37
Salisbury	46	14	8	24	57	76	36
Folkestone	46	11	11	24	47	65	33
Margate	46	11	7	28	65	117	29
Fareham Town	46	5	18	23	31	73	28
Andover	46	6	10	30	41	94	22

1982-83

Premier Division

AP Leamington	38	25	4	9	78	50	79
Kidderminster Harriers	38	23	7	8	69	40	76
Welling United	38	21	6	11	63	40	69
Chelmsford City	38	16	11	11	57	40	59
Bedworth United	38	16	11	11	47	39	59
Dartford	38	16	8	14	48	38	56
Gosport Borough	38	14	13	11	47	43	55
Fareham Town	38	16	7	15	73	82	55
Dorchester Town	38	14	12	12	52	50	54
Gravesend & Northfleet	38	14	12	12	49	50	54
Gloucester City	38	13	12	13	61	57	51
Witney Town	38	12	13	13	60	48	47
Alvechurch	38	13	8	17	60	66	47
Stourbridge	38	12	11	15	48	54	47
Corby Town	38	12	11	15	58	67	47
Hastings United	38	11	11	16	48	61	44
Enderby Town	38	11	9	18	44	62	42
Waterlooville	38	10	9	19	62	83	39
Poole Town	38	9	9	20	57	73	36
Addlestone & Weybridge	38	5	10	23	24	62	25

Witney Town had 2 points deducted for fielding an ineligible player

1981-82

Midland Division

Nuneaton Borough	42	27	11	4	88	32	65
Alvechurch	42	26	10	6	79	34	62
Kidderminster Harriers	42	22	12	8	71	40	56
Stourbridge	42	21	10	11	69	47	52
Gloucester City	42	21	9	12	64	48	51
Bedworth United	42	20	10	12	59	40	50
Enderby Town	42	20	10	12	79	66	50
Witney Town	42	19	8	15	71	49	46
Barry Town	42	16	14	12	59	46	46
Corby Town	42	19	8	15	70	59	46
Merthyr Tydfil	42	16	12	14	63	54	44
Wellingborough Town	42	15	12	15	50	45	42
Bridgend Town	42	13	13	16	50	62	39
Bromsgrove Rovers	42	15	8	19	57	63	38
Bedford Town	42	12	13	17	45	54	37
Cheltenham Town	42	11	14	17	65	68	36
Taunton Town	42	12	8	22	46	76	32
Banbury United	42	11	8	23	63	91	30
Minehead	42	12	6	24	38	69	30
Cambridge City	42	10	8	24	38	80	28
Milton Keynes City	42	6	11	25	34	70	23
Redditch United	42	8	5	29	37	103	21

Midland Division

Cheltenham Town	32	22	5	5	65	29	71
Sutton Coldfield Town	32	21	7	4	62	24	70
Forest Green Rovers	32	21	3	8	68	32	66
Merthyr Tydfil	32	17	7	8	64	45	58
Willenhall Town	32	17	6	9	74	49	57
Oldbury United	32	16	6	10	52	49	54
Banbury United	32	15	3	14	59	55	48
Bridgend Town	32	12	11	9	46	37	47
Wellingborough Town	32	13	7	12	49	37	46
Bromsgrove Rovers	32	13	5	14	47	47	44
Dudley Town	32	12	7	13	40	45	43
Bridgwater Town	32	12	6	14	42	43	42
Aylesbury United	32	12	5	15	37	51	41
Redditch United	32	8	6	18	51	73	30
Taunton Town	32	5	7	20	30	64	22
Minehead	32	5	7	20	24	62	22
Milton Keynes City	32	0	4	28	22	90	4

Southern Division

Wealdstone	46	32	8	6	100	32	72
Hastings United	46	31	9	6	79	34	71
Dorchester Town	46	21	18	7	76	41	60
Gosport Borough	46	26	8	12	76	45	60
Fareham Town	46	20	14	12	58	48	54
Poole Town	46	19	15	12	92	63	53
Waterlooville	46	22	9	15	75	53	53
Welling United	46	19	13	14	70	48	51
Addlestone & Weybridge	46	17	17	12	71	53	51
Chelmsford City	46	20	11	15	64	53	51
Aylesbury United	46	19	12	15	79	61	50
Basingstoke Town	46	18	12	16	75	61	48
Dover	46	19	8	19	61	63	46
Ashford Town	46	16	14	16	52	56	46
Tonbridge AFC	46	19	7	20	62	70	45
Dunstable	46	18	8	20	63	68	44
Salisbury	46	16	10	20	64	81	42
Hounslow	46	15	11	20	59	83	41
Hillingdon Borough	46	14	10	22	46	58	38
Canterbury City	46	10	16	20	49	78	36
Crawley Town	46	9	12	25	46	81	30
Folkestone	46	10	6	30	49	101	26
Andover	46	4	11	31	39	100	19
Thanet United	46	5	7	34	37	110	17

Southern Division

Fisher Athletic	34	23	5	6	79	34	74
Folkestone	34	22	6	6	79	41	72
RS Southampton	34	21	7	6	66	30	70
Dunstable	34	19	5	10	57	39	62
Hillingdon Borough	34	14	11	9	41	30	53
Salisbury	34	14	10	10	59	49	52
Crawley Town	34	14	9	11	51	43	51
Ashford Town	34	13	10	11	51	41	49
Tonbridge AFC	34	14	5	15	57	57	47
Hounslow	34	11	12	11	46	47	45
Canterbury City	34	12	9	13	52	63	45
Cambridge City	34	12	5	17	56	63	41
Dover	34	11	7	16	35	52	40
Thanet United	34	10	5	19	30	61	35
Basingstoke Town	34	8	10	16	37	56	34
Woodford Town	34	6	9	19	29	57	27
Andover	34	6	8	20	28	53	26
Erith & Belvedere	34	5	9	20	26	62	24

1983-84

Premier Division

	P	W	D	L	F	A	Pts
Dartford	38	23	9	6	67	32	78
Fisher Athletic	38	22	9	7	80	42	75
Chelmsford City	38	19	9	10	67	45	66
Gravesend & Northfleet	38	18	9	11	50	38	63
Witney Town	38	18	6	14	75	50	60
King's Lynn	38	18	6	14	42	45	60
Folkestone	38	16	9	13	60	56	57
Cheltenham Town	38	16	7	15	63	56	55
Gloucester City	38	13	15	10	55	50	54
Hastings United	38	15	9	14	55	57	54
Bedworth United	38	15	9	14	51	55	54
Welling United	38	15	7	16	61	61	52
AP Leamington	38	14	9	15	73	83	51
Corby Town	38	12	14	12	55	54	50
Fareham Town	38	13	11	14	65	70	50
Alvechurch	38	12	12	14	56	62	48
Sutton Coldfield Town	38	10	14	14	49	53	44
Gosport Borough	38	6	15	17	31	64	33
Dorchester Town	38	4	8	26	40	69	20
Stourbridge	38	4	7	27	30	82	19

Midland Division

	P	W	D	L	F	A	Pts
Willenhall Town	38	27	4	7	100	44	85
Shepshed Charterhouse	38	25	5	8	88	37	80
Bromsgrove Rovers	38	20	8	10	73	43	68
Dudley Town	38	18	13	7	71	43	67
Aylesbury United	38	17	15	6	62	35	66
Moor Green	38	18	12	8	63	44	66
Rushden Town	38	17	12	9	68	42	63
Merthyr Tydfil	38	18	8	12	63	44	62
Redditch United	38	17	9	12	67	67	60
VS Rugby	38	15	12	11	68	51	57
Forest Green Rovers	38	15	12	11	67	51	57
Bridgnorth Town	38	16	9	13	64	52	57
Leicester United	38	12	9	17	58	58	45
Oldbury United	38	10	13	15	53	51	43
Coventry Sporting	38	11	7	20	40	67	40
Bridgwater Town	38	10	8	20	39	65	38
Wellingborough Town	38	7	9	22	43	80	30
Banbury United	38	6	11	21	37	78	29
Milton Keynes City	38	3	9	26	31	110	18
Tamworth	38	2	7	29	25	118	13

Southern Division

	P	W	D	L	F	A	Pts
RS Southampton	38	26	6	6	83	35	84
Crawley Town	38	22	9	7	68	28	75
Basingstoke Town	38	20	9	9	54	36	69
Tonbridge AFC	38	20	9	9	61	44	69
Addlestone & Weybridge	38	19	11	8	58	34	68
Poole Town	38	20	7	11	68	42	67
Hillingdon Borough	38	18	11	9	43	20	65
Ashford Town	38	19	5	14	65	47	62
Salisbury	38	17	8	13	61	48	59
Cambridge City	38	13	9	16	43	53	48
Canterbury City	38	12	9	17	44	52	45
Waterlooville	38	12	9	17	56	69	45
Dover Athletic	38	12	9	17	51	74	45
Chatham Town	38	11	10	17	46	56	43
Andover	38	12	6	20	35	54	42
Erith & Belvedere	38	11	9	18	43	68	42
Dunstable	38	10	8	20	38	65	38
Thanet United	38	9	8	21	40	65	35
Woodford Town	38	7	8	23	30	69	29
Hounslow	38	4	12	22	30	58	24

1984-85

Premier Division

	P	W	D	L	F	A	Pts
Cheltenham Town	38	24	5	9	83	41	77
King's Lynn	38	23	6	9	73	48	75
Crawley Town	38	22	8	8	76	52	74
Willenhall Town	38	20	8	10	57	38	68
RS Southampton	38	21	4	13	76	52	67
Welling United	38	18	11	9	55	38	65
Folkestone	38	19	6	13	70	54	63
Fisher Athletic	38	19	5	14	67	57	62
Chelmsford City	38	17	10	11	52	50	61
Shepshed Charterhouse	38	18	5	15	67	50	59
Corby Town	38	15	6	17	56	54	51
Bedworth United	38	14	8	16	48	52	50
Gravesend & Northfleet	38	12	12	14	46	46	48
Fareham Town	38	13	8	17	52	55	47
Alvechurch	38	11	7	20	53	59	40
Hastings United	38	11	7	20	46	71	40
Witney Town	38	9	12	17	51	58	39
Gloucester City	38	10	6	22	49	74	36
Trowbridge	38	10	5	23	45	83	35
AP Leamington	38	2	5	31	22	112	11

Midland Division

	P	W	D	L	F	A	Pts
Dudley Town	34	21	8	5	70	36	71
Aylesbury United	34	20	7	7	62	30	67
Hednesford Town	34	18	7	9	58	42	61
Moor Green	34	17	9	8	63	43	60
VS Rugby	34	17	9	8	59	41	60
Bromsgrove Rovers	34	16	10	8	53	42	58
Stourbridge	34	15	11	8	52	45	56
Redditch United	34	12	11	11	68	57	47
Sutton Coldfield Town	34	13	6	15	50	56	45
Bridgnorth Town	34	13	5	16	67	65	44
Coventry Sporting	34	11	9	14	45	52	42
Merthyr Tydfil	34	10	11	13	43	46	41
Rushden Town	34	10	7	17	42	52	37
Forest Green Rovers	34	9	10	15	49	65	37
Wellingborough Town	34	10	7	17	39	63	37
Oldbury United	34	10	6	18	52	66	36
Banbury United	34	9	5	20	33	59	32
Leicester United	34	3	6	25	17	62	15

Southern Division

	P	W	D	L	F	A	Pts
Basingstoke Town	38	24	9	5	61	22	81
Gosport Borough	38	22	6	10	78	41	72
Poole Town	38	20	12	6	69	38	72
Hillingdon	38	19	10	9	51	23	67
Thanet United	38	19	9	10	63	47	66
Salisbury	38	19	5	14	55	54	62
Sheppey United	38	18	6	14	49	45	60
Addlestone & Weybridge	38	16	9	13	68	54	57
Waterlooville	38	15	10	13	71	63	55
Canterbury City	38	15	7	16	61	64	52
Woodford Town	38	13	13	12	46	53	52
Tonbridge AFC	38	16	3	19	59	62	51
Andover	38	15	5	18	42	54	50
Dorchester Town	38	13	7	18	45	60	46
Cambridge City	38	11	11	16	59	71	44
Chatham Town	38	12	8	18	44	66	44
Ashford Town	38	10	9	19	54	69	39
Dunstable	38	8	10	20	35	56	34
Dover Athletic	38	7	7	24	39	78	28
Erith & Belvedere	38	6	8	24	36	65	26

1985-86

Premier Division

Welling United	38	29	6	3	95	31	93
Chelmsford City	38	20	10	8	68	41	70
Fisher Athletic	38	20	7	11	67	45	67
Alvechurch	38	19	9	10	71	56	66
Worcester City	38	19	9	10	64	50	66
Crawley Town	38	18	5	15	76	59	59
Shepshed Charterhouse	38	19	1	18	51	52	58
Aylesbury United	38	14	10	14	52	49	52
Folkestone	38	14	10	14	56	56	52
Bedworth United	38	14	8	16	44	49	50
Willenhall Town	38	12	13	13	51	44	49
Dudley Town	38	15	4	19	58	62	49
Corby Town	38	14	7	17	61	67	49
King's Lynn	38	12	10	16	39	42	46
Basingstoke Town	38	13	4	21	36	67	43
RS Southampton	38	11	9	18	44	61	42
Witney Town	38	11	6	21	44	74	39
Gosport Borough	38	10	8	20	42	66	38
Fareham Town	38	8	13	17	40	62	37
Gravesend & Northfleet	38	9	9	20	29	55	36

Midland Division

Bromsgrove Rovers	40	29	5	6	95	44	92
Redditch United	40	23	6	11	70	42	75
Merthyr Tydfil	40	21	10	9	60	40	73
VS Rugby	40	17	14	9	41	31	65
Stourbridge	40	15	14	11	62	49	59
Rusden Town	40	17	7	16	69	74	58
Bilston Town	40	15	12	13	60	48	57
Bridgnorth Town	40	13	18	9	56	45	57
Gloucester City	40	15	12	13	61	57	57
Grantham	40	16	7	17	46	59	55
Wellingborough Town	40	15	9	16	56	56	54
Sutton Coldfield Town	40	13	14	13	60	45	53
Hednesford Town	40	14	9	17	67	70	51
Forest Green Rovers	40	14	9	17	52	56	51
Mile Oak Rovers	40	14	8	18	56	73	50
Leicester United	40	13	10	17	41	48	49
Banbury United	40	13	8	19	38	55	47
Coventry Sporting	40	10	15	15	42	48	45
Moor Green	40	12	6	22	63	91	42
Leamington	40	10	6	24	40	77	36
Oldbury United	40	8	7	25	50	87	31

Southern Division

Cambridge City	40	23	11	6	87	41	80
Salisbury	40	24	8	8	84	51	80
Hastings Town	40	23	9	8	83	51	78
Dover Athletic	40	23	6	11	89	53	75
Corinthian	40	20	9	11	79	45	69
Tonbridge AFC	40	17	13	10	65	51	64
Dunstable	40	17	11	12	70	61	62
Ruislip	40	17	6	17	67	66	57
Erith & Belvedere	40	14	12	14	35	40	54
Waterlooville	40	16	6	18	52	58	54
Burnham & Hillingdon	40	16	6	18	44	59	54
Canterbury City	40	13	13	14	58	58	52
Trowbridge Town	40	13	13	14	57	63	52
Sheppey United	40	14	10	16	43	53	52
Thanet United	40	13	7	20	58	63	46
Woodford Town	40	12	10	18	49	62	46
Poole Town	40	12	7	21	55	63	43
Ashford Town	40	10	12	18	45	65	42
Chatham Town	40	8	15	17	53	70	39
Andover	40	10	8	22	52	92	38
Dorchester Town	40	5	8	27	35	94	23

1986-87

Premier Division

Fisher Athletic	42	25	11	6	72	29	86
Bromsgrove Rovers	42	24	11	7	82	41	83
Aylesbury United	42	24	11	7	72	40	83
Dartford	42	19	12	11	76	43	69
Chelmsford City	42	17	13	12	48	45	64
Cambridge City	42	14	20	8	68	52	62
Redditch United	42	16	14	12	59	54	62
Alvechurch	42	18	8	16	66	62	62
Corby Town	42	14	17	11	65	51	59
Worcester City	42	16	11	15	62	55	59
Shepshed Charterhouse	42	16	10	16	59	59	58
Bedworth United	42	15	12	15	55	51	57
Crawley Town	42	14	11	17	59	60	53
Fareham Town	42	11	17	14	58	49	50
Willenhall Town	42	13	11	18	48	57	50
Basingstoke Town	42	12	12	18	53	78	48
Witney Town	42	12	12	18	29	56	48
Gosport Borough	42	11	13	18	42	57	46
Salisbury	42	12	7	23	52	82	43
King's Lynn	42	9	13	20	48	72	40
Dudley Town	42	9	9	24	39	76	36
Folkestone	42	8	11	23	36	79	35

Midland Division

VS Rugby	38	25	5	8	81	43	80
Leicester United	38	26	1	11	89	49	79
Merthyr Tydfil	38	23	6	9	95	54	75
Moor Green	38	22	6	10	73	55	72
Halesowen Town	38	19	12	7	72	50	69
Hednesford Town	38	21	5	12	84	56	68
Gloucester City	38	19	5	14	77	59	62
Coventry Sporting	38	17	8	13	55	54	59
Forest Green Rovers	38	16	9	13	65	53	57
Stourbridge	38	16	7	15	56	56	55
Grantham	38	15	9	14	74	54	54
Banbury United	38	14	7	17	55	65	49
Buckingham Town	38	13	9	16	55	59	48
Bridgnorth Town	38	12	9	17	59	63	45
Wellingborough Town	38	13	6	19	55	76	45
Mile Oak Rovers	38	11	10	17	50	63	43
Sutton Coldfield Town	38	8	10	20	56	78	34
Bilston Town	38	8	7	23	37	76	31
Leamington	38	4	13	21	37	80	25
Rushden Town	38	1	10	27	42	124	13

Southern Division

Dorchester Town	38	23	8	7	83	42	77
Ashford Town	38	23	7	8	63	32	76
Woodford Town	38	22	6	10	72	44	72
Hastings Town	38	20	10	8	74	54	70
Dover Athletic	38	20	6	12	66	43	66
Gravesend & Northfleet	38	18	7	13	67	46	61
Tonbridge AFC	38	16	10	12	73	67	58
Erith & Belvedere	38	15	12	11	57	50	57
Chatham Town	38	16	9	13	53	46	57
Thanet United	38	14	14	10	56	50	56
Waterlooville	38	16	8	14	66	65	56
Trowbridge Town	38	15	9	14	77	65	54
Dunstable	38	13	9	16	60	57	48
Corinthian	38	11	12	15	56	65	45
Sheppey United	38	9	12	17	43	65	39
Andover	38	9	9	20	51	80	36
Burnham & Hillingdon	38	7	11	20	32	62	32
Poole Town	38	8	6	24	50	90	30
Ruislip	38	6	12	20	35	75	30
Canterbury City	38	8	5	25	46	82	29

1987-88

Premier Division

Aylesbury United	42	27	8	7	79	35	89
Dartford	42	27	8	7	79	39	89
Cambridge City	42	24	8	10	84	43	80
Bromsgrove Rovers	42	22	11	9	65	39	77
Worcester City	42	22	6	14	58	48	72
Crawley Town	42	17	14	11	73	63	65
Alvechurch	42	17	13	12	54	52	64
Leicester United	42	15	14	13	68	59	59
Fareham Town	42	16	11	15	51	59	59
Corby Town	42	16	8	18	61	64	56
Dorchester Town	42	14	14	14	51	57	56
Ashford Town	42	12	16	14	45	54	52
Shepshed Charterhouse	42	13	11	18	53	62	50
Bedworth United	42	12	14	16	49	64	50
Gosport Borough	42	10	17	15	39	49	47
Burton Albion	42	11	14	17	62	74	47
VS Rugby	42	10	16	16	52	57	46
Redditch United	42	10	13	19	55	63	43
Chelmsford City	42	11	10	21	60	75	43
Willenhall Town	42	9	12	21	39	76	39
Nuneaton Borough	42	8	13	21	58	77	37
Witney Town	42	8	11	23	45	71	35

Midland Division

Merthyr Tydfil	42	30	4	8	102	40	94
Moor Green	42	26	8	8	91	49	86
Grantham Town	42	27	4	11	97	53	85
Atherstone United	42	22	10	10	93	56	76
Sutton Coldfield Town	42	22	6	14	71	47	72
Halesowen Town	42	18	15	9	75	59	69
Gloucester City	42	18	14	10	86	62	68
Dudley Town	42	20	5	17	64	55	65
Forest Green Rovers	42	14	16	12	67	54	58
Banbury United	42	17	7	18	48	46	58
Bridgnorth Town	42	16	7	19	59	75	55
Buckingham Town	42	15	9	18	74	75	54
King's Lynn	42	16	6	20	53	63	54
Wellingborough Town	42	14	10	18	67	70	52
Rushden Town	42	14	9	19	69	85	51
Trowbridge Town	42	14	3	25	53	82	45
Bilston Town	42	12	8	22	52	87	44
Hednesford Town	42	11	10	21	50	81	43
Mile Oak Rovers	42	9	14	19	43	65	41
Coventry Sporting	42	11	8	23	46	83	41
Stourbridge	42	10	10	22	46	79	40
Paget Rangers	42	10	9	23	49	89	39

Southern Division

Dover Athletic	40	28	10	2	81	28	94
Waterlooville	40	27	10	3	88	33	91
Salisbury	40	24	11	5	71	33	83
Gravesend & Northfleet	40	20	12	8	60	32	72
Thanet United	40	17	13	10	60	38	64
Andover	40	17	13	10	64	58	64
Dunstable	40	17	12	11	78	56	63
Burnham	40	17	10	13	61	45	61
Bury Town	40	17	7	16	80	67	58
Erith & Belvedere	40	16	9	15	52	56	57
Sheppey United	40	14	10	16	58	52	52
Hastings Town	40	14	10	16	62	70	52
Tonbridge AFC	40	14	8	18	51	56	50
Poole Town	40	13	10	17	69	70	49
Baldock Town	40	12	12	16	44	53	48
Hounslow	40	11	8	21	41	76	41
Folkestone	40	9	11	20	47	76	38
Corinthian	40	9	10	21	49	67	37
Ruislip	40	5	13	22	33	80	28
Canterbury City	40	7	6	27	33	87	27
Chatham Town	40	7	5	28	39	88	26

1988-89

Premier Division

Merthyr Tydfil	42	26	7	9	104	58	85
Dartford	42	25	7	10	79	33	82
VS Rugby	42	24	7	11	64	43	79
Worcester City	42	20	13	9	72	49	73
Cambridge City	42	20	10	12	72	51	70
Dover Athletic	42	19	12	11	65	47	69
Gosport Borough	42	18	12	12	73	57	66
Burton Albion	42	18	10	14	79	68	64
Bath City	42	15	13	14	66	51	59
Bromsgrove Rovers	42	14	16	12	68	56	59
Wealdstone	42	16	10	16	60	53	59
Crawley Town	42	14	16	12	61	56	59
Dorchester Town	42	14	16	12	56	61	59
Alvechurch	42	16	8	18	56	59	56
Moor Green	42	14	13	15	58	70	55
Corby Town	42	14	11	17	55	59	53
Waterlooville	42	13	13	16	61	63	52
Ashford Town	42	13	13	16	59	76	52
Fareham Town	42	15	6	21	43	68	51
Leicester United	42	6	11	25	46	84	29
Redditch United	42	5	7	30	36	105	22
Bedworth United	42	4	7	31	36	102	19

Midland Division

Gloucester City	42	28	8	6	95	37	92
Atherstone United	42	26	9	7	85	38	87
Tamworth	42	26	9	7	85	45	87
Halesowen Town	42	25	10	7	85	42	85
Grantham Town	42	23	11	8	66	37	80
Nuneaton Borough	42	19	9	14	71	58	66
Rushden Town	42	19	8	15	71	50	65
Spalding United	42	17	13	12	72	64	64
Dudley Town	42	16	13	13	73	62	61
Sutton Coldfield Town	42	18	7	17	56	56	61
Willenhall Town	42	16	12	14	65	71	60
Forest Green Rovers	42	12	16	14	64	67	52
Bilston Town	42	15	7	20	63	71	52
Ashtree Highfield	42	12	15	15	57	62	51
Hednesford Town	42	12	15	15	49	57	51
Banbury United	42	10	14	18	53	74	44
Bridgnorth Town	42	12	7	23	59	77	43
Stourbridge	42	11	10	21	37	65	43
King's Lynn	42	7	13	22	31	67	34
Coventry Sporting	42	6	13	23	39	91	31
Wellingborough Town	42	5	15	22	39	72	30
Mile Oak Rovers	42	5	10	27	46	98	25

Southern Division

Chelmsford City	42	30	5	7	106	38	95
Gravesend & Northfleet	42	27	6	9	70	40	87
Poole Town	42	24	11	7	98	48	83
Bury Town	42	25	7	10	75	34	82
Burnham	42	22	13	7	78	47	79
Baldock Town	42	23	5	14	69	40	74
Hastings Town	42	21	11	10	75	48	74
Hounslow	42	21	6	15	75	60	69
Salisbury	42	20	5	17	79	58	65
Trowbridge Town	42	19	7	16	59	52	64
Folkestone	42	17	8	17	62	65	59
Corinthian	42	13	13	16	59	69	52
Canterbury City	42	14	8	20	52	60	50
Witney Town	42	13	11	18	61	71	50
Dunstable	42	11	14	17	42	57	47
Buckingham Town	42	12	10	20	56	79	46
Erith & Belvedere	42	11	10	21	48	63	43
Andover	42	11	9	22	56	90	42
Sheppey United	42	10	8	24	50	90	38
Thanet United	42	7	15	20	47	95	36
Tonbridge AFC	42	7	6	29	50	98	27
Ruislip	42	6	8	28	47	112	26

1989-90

Premier Division

Dover Athletic	42	32	6	4	87	27	102
Bath City	42	30	8	4	81	28	98
Dartford	42	26	9	7	80	35	87
Burton Albion	42	20	12	10	64	40	72
VS Rugby	42	19	12	11	51	35	69
Atherstone United	42	19	10	13	60	52	67
Gravesend & Northfleet	42	18	12	12	44	50	66
Cambridge City	42	17	11	14	76	56	62
Gloucester City	42	17	11	14	80	68	62
Bromsgrove Rovers	42	17	10	15	56	48	61
Moor Green	42	18	7	17	62	59	61
Wealdstone	42	16	9	17	55	54	57
Dorchester Town	42	16	7	19	52	67	55
Worcester City	42	15	10	17	62	63	54
Crawley Town	42	13	12	17	53	57	51
Waterlooville	42	13	10	19	63	81	49
Weymouth	42	11	13	18	50	70	46
Chelmsford City	42	11	10	21	52	72	43
Ashford Town	42	10	7	25	43	75	37
Corby Town	42	10	6	26	57	77	36
Alvechurch	42	7	5	30	46	95	26
Gosport Borough	42	6	5	31	28	93	23

Midland Division

Halesowen Town	42	28	8	6	100	49	92
Rushden Town	42	28	5	9	82	39	89
Nuneaton Borough	42	26	7	9	81	47	85
Tamworth	42	22	8	12	82	70	74
Barry Town	42	21	8	13	67	53	71
Spalding United	42	20	7	15	73	63	67
Sutton Coldfield Town	42	18	10	14	72	69	64
Stourbridge	42	17	12	13	73	61	63
Dudley Town	42	18	9	15	69	64	63
Stroud	42	16	13	13	75	62	61
Leicester United	42	17	5	20	66	77	56
Bridgnorth Town	42	13	14	15	68	73	53
King's Lynn	42	16	5	21	57	69	53
Grantham Town	42	14	10	18	57	63	52
Bedworth United	42	14	9	19	50	60	51
Hednesford Town	42	11	14	17	50	62	47
Bilston Town	42	11	14	17	40	54	47
Redditch United	42	11	13	18	57	64	46
Racing Club Warwick	42	11	11	20	45	66	44
Willenhall Town	42	9	9	24	37	66	36
Banbury United	42	9	9	24	46	83	34
Sandwell Borough	42	6	12	24	46	79	30

Southern Division

Bashley	42	25	7	10	80	47	82
Poole Town	42	23	8	11	85	60	77
Buckingham Town	42	22	10	10	67	46	76
Dunstable	42	20	14	8	56	38	74
Salisbury	42	21	9	12	72	50	72
Hythe Town	42	20	12	10	69	48	72
Trowbridge Town	42	20	9	13	79	64	69
Hastings Town	42	20	9	13	64	54	69
Bury Town	42	18	12	12	76	62	66
Baldock Town	42	18	11	13	69	52	65
Burnham	42	17	11	14	77	52	62
Fareham Town	42	14	14	14	49	53	56
Yate Town	42	16	6	20	53	52	54
Witney Town	42	16	6	20	54	56	54
Canterbury City	42	14	10	18	52	52	52
Margate	42	12	15	15	46	45	51
Folkestone	42	14	9	19	61	83	51
Andover	42	13	11	18	54	70	50
Hounslow	42	11	5	26	39	82	38
Erith & Belvedere	42	8	11	23	34	73	35
Corinthian	42	6	10	26	44	93	28
Sheppey United	42	6	7	29	35	83	25

1990-91

Premier Division

Farnborough Town	42	26	7	9	79	43	85
Gloucester City	42	23	14	5	86	49	83
Cambridge City	42	21	14	7	63	43	77
Dover Athletic	42	21	11	10	56	37	74
Bromsgrove Rovers	42	20	11	11	68	49	71
Worcester City	42	18	12	12	55	42	66
Burton Albion	42	15	15	12	59	48	60
Halesowen Town	42	17	9	16	73	67	60
VS Rugby	42	16	11	15	56	46	59
Bashley	42	15	12	15	56	52	57
Dorchester Town	42	15	12	15	47	54	57
Wealdstone	42	16	8	18	57	58	56
Dartford	42	15	9	18	61	64	54
Rushden Town	42	14	11	17	64	66	53
Atherstone United	42	14	10	18	55	58	52
Moor Green	42	15	6	21	64	75	51
Poole Town	42	12	13	17	56	69	49
Chelmsford City	42	11	15	16	37	68	48
Crawley Town	42	12	12	18	45	67	48
Waterlooville	42	11	13	18	51	70	46
Gravesend & Northfleet	42	9	7	26	46	91	34
Weymouth	42	4	12	26	50	88	24

Midland Division

Stourbridge	42	28	6	8	80	48	90
Corby Town	42	27	4	11	99	48	85
Hednesford Town	42	25	7	10	79	47	82
Tamworth	42	25	5	12	84	45	80
Nuneaton Borough	42	21	11	10	74	51	70
Barry Town	42	20	7	15	61	48	67
Newport AFC	42	19	6	17	54	46	63
King's Lynn	42	17	9	16	53	62	60
Grantham Town	42	17	7	18	62	56	58
Redditch United	42	16	10	16	66	75	58
Hinckley Town	42	16	9	17	72	68	57
Sutton Coldfield Town	42	15	11	16	56	65	56
Bedworth United	42	15	9	18	57	73	54
Bilston Town	42	14	9	19	69	79	51
Leicester United	42	14	10	18	65	77	51
Racing Club Warwick	42	12	13	17	56	65	49
Bridgnorth Town	42	13	9	20	62	74	48
Stroud	42	11	14	17	51	64	47
Dudley Town	42	11	13	18	48	73	46
Alvechurch	42	10	8	24	54	92	38
Willenhall Town	42	10	10	22	58	69	37
Spalding United	42	8	9	25	35	70	33

Southern Division

Buckingham Town	40	25	8	7	73	38	83
Trowbridge Town	40	22	12	6	67	31	78
Salisbury	40	22	11	7	63	39	77
Baldock Town	40	21	9	10	66	52	72
Ashford Town	40	22	5	13	82	52	71
Yate Town	40	21	8	11	76	48	71
Hastings Town	40	18	11	11	66	46	65
Hythe Town	40	17	9	14	55	44	59
Andover	40	16	6	18	69	76	54
Margate	40	14	11	15	52	55	53
Burnham	40	12	16	12	57	49	52
Bury Town	40	15	5	20	58	74	50
Sudbury Town	40	13	0	17	60	68	49
Newport IOW	40	13	9	18	56	62	48
Gosport Borough	40	12	11	17	47	58	47
Witney Town	40	12	11	17	57	75	47
Dunstable	40	9	15	16	48	63	42
Canterbury City	40	12	6	22	60	83	42
Erith & Belvedere	40	10	0	24	46	73	36
Fareham Town	40	9	9	22	46	74	36
Corinthian	40	5	12	23	34	78	27

1991-92

Premier Division

Bromsgrove Rovers	42	27	9	6	78	34	90
Dover Athletic	42	23	15	4	66	30	84
VS Rugby	42	23	11	8	70	44	80
Bashley	42	22	8	12	70	44	74
Cambridge City	42	18	14	10	71	53	68
Dartford	42	17	15	10	62	45	66
Trowbridge Town	42	17	10	15	69	51	61
Halesowen Town	42	15	15	12	61	49	60
Moor Green	42	15	11	16	61	59	56
Burton Albion	42	15	10	17	59	61	55
Dorchester Town	42	14	13	15	66	73	55
Gloucester City	42	15	9	18	67	70	54
Atherstone United	42	15	8	19	54	66	53
Corby Town	42	13	12	17	66	81	51
Waterlooville	42	13	11	18	43	56	50
Worcester City	42	12	13	17	56	59	49
Crawley Town	42	12	12	18	62	67	48
Chelmsford City	42	12	12	18	49	56	48
Wealdstone	42	13	7	22	52	69	46
Poole Town	42	10	13	19	46	77	43
Fisher Athletic	42	9	11	22	53	89	38
Gravesend & Northfleet	42	8	9	25	39	87	33

Midland Division

Solihull Borough	42	29	10	3	92	40	97
Hednesford Town	42	26	13	3	81	37	91
Sutton Coldfield Town	42	21	11	10	71	51	74
Barry Town	42	21	6	15	88	56	69
Bedworth United	42	16	15	11	67	63	63
Nuneaton Borough	42	17	11	14	68	53	62
Tamworth	42	16	12	14	66	52	60
Rushden Town	42	16	12	14	69	63	60
Stourbridge	42	17	8	17	85	62	59
Newport AFC	42	15	13	14	72	60	58
Yate Town	42	14	15	13	65	64	57
Bilston Town	42	15	10	17	56	67	55
Grantham Town	42	11	17	14	59	55	50
King's Lynn	42	13	11	18	61	68	50
Hinckley Town	42	14	8	20	61	87	50
Leicester United	42	12	13	17	56	63	49
Bridgnorth Town	42	12	12	18	61	74	48
Racing Club Warwick	42	11	14	17	45	61	47
Stroud	42	14	4	24	66	88	46
Redditch United	42	12	8	22	52	92	44
Alvechurch	42	11	10	21	54	88	43
Dudley Town	42	8	9	25	41	92	33

Southern Division

Hastings Town	42	28	7	7	80	37	91
Weymouth	42	22	12	8	64	35	78
Havant Town	42	21	12	9	67	46	75
Braintree Town	42	21	8	13	77	58	71
Buckingham Town	42	19	15	8	57	26	69
Andover	42	18	10	14	73	68	64
Ashford Town	42	17	12	13	66	57	63
Sudbury Town	42	18	9	15	70	66	63
Sittingbourne	42	19	10	13	63	41	61
Burnham	42	15	14	13	57	55	59
Baldock Town	42	16	10	16	62	67	58
Salisbury	42	13	16	13	67	51	55
Hythe Town	42	15	10	17	61	62	55
Margate	42	13	16	13	49	56	55
Newport IOW	42	13	10	19	58	63	49
Dunstable	42	12	12	18	55	67	48
Bury Town	42	14	4	24	52	94	46
Witney Town	42	11	12	19	55	76	45
Fareham Town	42	12	8	22	45	71	44
Erith & Belvedere	42	11	10	21	44	67	43
Canterbury City	42	8	14	20	43	69	38
Gosport Borough	42	6	9	27	32	65	27

1992-93

Premier Division

Dover Athletic	40	25	11	4	65	23	86
Cheltenham Town	40	21	10	9	76	40	73
Corby Town	40	20	12	8	68	43	72
Hednesford Town	40	21	7	12	72	52	70
Trowbridge Town	40	18	8	14	70	66	62
Crawley Town	40	16	12	12	68	59	60
Solihull Borough	40	17	9	14	68	59	60
Burton Albion	40	16	11	13	53	50	59
Bashley	40	18	8	14	60	60	59
Halesowen Town	40	15	11	14	67	54	56
Waterlooville	40	15	9	16	59	62	54
Chelmsford City	40	15	9	16	59	69	54
Gloucester City	40	14	11	15	66	68	53
Cambridge City	40	14	10	16	62	73	52
Atherstone United	40	13	14	13	56	60	50
Hastings Town	40	13	11	16	50	55	50
Worcester City	40	12	9	19	45	62	45
Dorchester Town	40	12	6	22	52	74	42
Moor Green	40	10	6	24	58	79	36
VS Rugby	40	10	6	24	40	63	36
Weymouth	40	5	10	25	39	82	23

Bashley had 3 points deducted

Midland Division

Nuneaton Borough	42	29	5	8	102	45	92
Gresley Rovers	42	27	6	9	94	55	87
Rushden & Diamonds	42	25	10	7	85	41	85
Barri	42	26	5	11	82	49	83
Newport AFC	42	23	8	11	73	58	77
Bedworth United	42	22	8	12	72	55	74
Stourbridge	42	17	9	16	93	79	60
Sutton Coldfield Town	42	17	9	16	82	78	60
Redditch United	42	18	6	18	75	79	60
Tamworth	42	16	11	15	65	51	59
Weston-super-Mare	42	17	7	18	79	86	58
Leicester United	42	16	9	17	67	67	57
Grantham Town	42	16	9	17	60	73	57
Bilston Town	42	15	10	17	74	69	55
Evesham United	42	15	8	19	67	83	53
Bridgnorth Town	42	15	7	20	61	68	52
Dudley Town	42	14	8	20	60	75	50
Yate Town	42	15	5	22	63	81	50
Forest Green Rovers	42	12	6	24	61	97	42
Hinckley Athletic	42	9	11	22	56	89	37
King's Lynn	42	10	6	26	45	90	36
Racing Club Warwick	42	3	7	32	40	88	16

Southern Division

Sittingbourne	42	26	12	4	102	43	90
Salisbury	42	27	7	8	87	50	88
Witney Town	42	25	9	8	77	37	84
Gravesend & Northfleet	42	25	4	13	99	63	79
Havant Town	42	23	6	13	78	55	75
Sudbury Town	42	20	11	11	89	54	71
Erith & Belvedere	42	22	5	15	73	66	71
Ashford Town	42	20	8	14	91	66	68
Braintree Town	42	20	6	16	95	65	66
Margate	42	19	7	16	65	58	64
Wealdstone	42	18	7	17	75	69	61
Buckingham Town	42	16	11	15	61	58	59
Baldock Town	42	15	9	18	59	63	54
Poole Town	42	15	7	20	61	69	52
Fareham Town	42	14	8	20	67	65	50
Burnham	42	14	8	20	53	77	50
Canterbury City	42	12	10	20	54	76	46
Newport IOW	42	9	16	17	44	56	43
Fisher Athletic	42	8	9	25	38	98	33
Andover	42	7	9	26	42	99	30
Dunstable	42	5	14	23	42	92	29
Bury Town	42	8	5	29	46	119	29

1993-94

Premier Division

	P	W	D	L	F	A	Pts
Farnborough Town	42	25	7	10	74	44	82
Cheltenham Town	42	21	12	9	67	38	75
Halesowen Town	42	21	11	10	69	46	74
Atherstone United	42	22	7	13	57	43	73
Crawley Town	42	21	10	11	56	42	73
Chelmsford City	42	21	7	14	74	59	70
Trowbridge Town	42	16	17	9	52	41	65
Sittingbourne	42	17	13	12	65	48	64
Corby Town	42	17	8	17	52	56	59
Gloucester City	42	17	6	19	55	60	57
Burton Albion	42	15	11	10	57	49	56
Hastings Town	42	16	7	19	51	60	55
Hednesford Town	42	15	9	18	67	66	54
Gresley Rovers	42	14	11	17	61	72	53
Worcester City	42	14	9	19	61	70	51
Solihull Borough	42	13	11	18	52	57	50
Cambridge City	42	13	11	18	50	60	50
Dorchester Town	42	12	11	19	38	51	47
Moor Green	42	11	10	21	49	66	43
Waterlooville	42	11	10	21	47	69	43
Bashley	42	11	10	21	47	80	43
Nuneaton Borough	42	11	8	23	42	66	41

Midland Division

	P	W	D	L	F	A	Pts
Rushden & Diamonds	42	29	11	2	109	37	98
VS Rugby	42	28	8	6	98	41	92
Weston-super-Mare	42	27	10	5	94	39	91
Newport AFC	42	26	9	7	84	37	87
Clevedon Town	42	24	10	8	75	46	82
Redditch United	42	19	11	12	79	62	68
Tamworth	42	19	7	16	82	68	64
Bilston Town	42	16	10	16	65	73	58
Stourbridge	42	17	6	19	71	75	57
Evesham United	42	16	8	18	50	60	56
Grantham Town	42	16	6	20	77	73	54
Bridgnorth Town	42	15	6	21	56	68	51
Racing Club Warwick	42	13	12	17	53	66	51
Dudley Town	42	13	10	19	64	61	49
Forest Green Rangers	42	12	12	18	61	84	48
Sutton Coldfield Town	42	12	8	22	53	75	44
Bedworth United	42	12	7	23	62	81	43
Hinckley Town	42	11	10	21	44	71	43
Leicester United	42	11	9	22	34	73	42
King's Lynn	42	9	11	22	47	72	38
Yate Town	42	10	6	26	48	86	36
Armitage	42	8	11	23	45	103	35

Southern Division

	P	W	D	L	F	A	Pts
Gravesend & Northfleet	42	27	11	4	87	24	92
Sudbury Town	42	27	8	7	98	47	89
Witney Town	42	27	8	7	69	36	89
Salisbury City	42	26	10	6	90	39	88
Havant Town	42	27	4	11	101	41	85
Ashford Town	42	24	13	5	93	46	85
Baldock Town	42	26	7	9	76	40	85
Newport IOW	42	22	8	12	74	51	74
Margate	42	20	8	14	76	58	68
Weymouth	42	18	9	15	71	65	63
Tonbridge	42	19	5	18	59	62	62
Buckingham Town	42	14	14	14	43	42	56
Braintree Town	42	16	7	19	72	84	55
Fareham Town	42	12	12	18	54	75	48
Poole Town	42	13	6	23	54	86	45
Burnham	42	10	9	23	53	92	39
Fisher 93	42	9	10	23	52	81	37
Dunstable	42	9	7	26	50	91	34
Erith & Belvedere	42	9	5	28	40	72	32
Canterbury City	42	8	7	27	35	80	31
Wealdstone	42	6	7	29	45	95	25
Bury Town	42	3	5	34	36	121	14

1994-95

Premier Division

	P	W	D	L	F	A	Pts
Hednesford Town	42	28	9	5	99	49	93
Cheltenham Town	42	25	11	6	87	39	86
Burton Albion	42	20	15	7	55	39	75
Gloucester City	42	22	8	12	76	48	74
Rushden & Diamonds	42	19	11	12	99	65	68
Dorchester Town	42	19	10	13	84	61	67
Leek Town	42	19	10	13	72	60	67
Gresley Rovers	42	17	12	13	70	63	63
Cambridge City	42	18	8	16	60	55	62
Worcester City	42	14	15	13	46	34	57
Crawley Town	42	15	10	17	64	71	55
Hastings Town	42	13	14	15	55	57	53
Halesowen Town	42	14	10	18	81	80	52
Gravesend & Northfleet	42	16	13	16	38	55	52
Chelmsford City	42	14	6	22	56	60	48
Atherstone United	42	12	12	18	51	67	48
VS Rugby	42	11	14	17	49	61	47
Sudbury Town	42	12	10	20	50	77	46
Solihull Borough	42	10	15	17	39	65	45
Sittingbourne	42	11	10	21	51	73	43
Trowbridge Town	42	9	13	20	43	69	40
Corby Town	42	4	10	28	36	113	21

Corby Town had 1 point deducted for fielding ineligible players

Midland Division

	P	W	D	L	F	A	Pts
Newport AFC	42	29	8	5	106	39	95
Ilkeston Town	42	25	6	11	101	75	81
Tamworth	42	24	8	10	98	70	80
Moor Green	42	23	8	11	105	63	77
Bridgnorth Town	42	22	10	10	75	49	76
Buckingham Town	42	20	14	8	55	37	74
Nuneaton Borough	42	19	11	12	76	55	68
Rothwell Town	42	19	7	16	71	71	64
King's Lynn	42	18	8	16	76	64	62
Racing Club Warwick	42	17	11	14	68	63	62
Dudley Town	42	17	10	15	65	69	61
Bilston Town	42	17	8	17	73	64	59
Bedworth United	42	17	7	18	64	68	58
Evesham United	42	14	10	18	57	56	52
Hinckley Town	42	14	0	18	61	76	52
Stourbridge	42	15	7	20	59	77	52
Sutton Coldfield Town	42	12	10	20	62	72	46
Forest Green Rovers	42	11	13	18	56	76	46
Redditch United	42	8	14	20	47	64	38
Leicester United	42	10	8	24	51	99	38
Grantham Town	42	8	9	25	55	93	33
Armitage	42	2	5	35	35	116	11

Southern Division

	P	W	D	L	F	A	Pts
Salisbury City	42	30	7	5	88	37	97
Baldock Town	42	28	10	4	92	44	94
Havant Town	42	25	10	7	81	34	85
Waterlooville	42	24	8	10	77	36	80
Ashford Town	42	21	12	9	106	72	75
Weston-super-Mare	42	18	13	11	82	54	67
Bashley	42	18	11	13	62	49	65
Weymouth	42	16	13	13	60	55	61
Newport IOW	42	17	10	15	67	67	61
Witney Town	42	14	14	14	57	57	56
Clevedon Town	42	14	13	15	73	64	55
Tonbridge Angels	42	14	12	16	74	87	54
Margate	42	15	7	20	60	72	52
Braintree Town	42	12	13	17	64	71	49
Wealdstone	42	13	8	21	76	94	47
Yate Town	42	11	13	18	57	75	46
Fisher 93	42	9	16	17	54	70	43
Bury Town	42	11	8	23	59	86	41
Erith & Belvedere	42	10	9	23	49	94	39
Poole Town	42	10	8	24	53	79	38
Fareham Town	42	10	8	24	46	91	38
Burnham	42	7	7	28	40	89	28

1995-96

Premier Division

Rushden & Diamonds	42	29	7	6	99	41	94
Halesowen Town	42	27	11	4	70	36	92
Cheltenham Town	42	21	11	10	76	57	74
Gloucester City	42	21	8	13	65	47	71
Gresley Rovers	42	20	10	12	70	58	70
Worcester City	42	19	12	11	61	43	69
Merthyr Tydfil	42	19	6	17	67	59	63
Hastings Town	42	16	13	13	68	56	61
Crawley Town	42	15	13	14	57	56	58
Sudbury Town	42	15	10	17	69	71	55
Gravesend & Northfleet	42	15	10	17	60	62	55
Chelmsford City	42	13	16	13	46	53	55
Dorchester Town	42	15	8	19	62	57	53
Newport AFC	42	13	13	16	53	59	52
Salisbury City	42	14	10	18	57	69	52
Burton Albion	42	13	12	17	55	56	51
Atherstone United	42	12	12	18	58	75	48
Baldock Town	42	11	14	17	51	56	47
Cambridge City	42	12	10	20	56	68	46
Ilkeston Town	42	11	10	21	53	87	43
Stafford Rangers	42	11	4	27	58	90	37
VS Rugby	42	5	10	27	37	92	25

Midland Division

Nuneaton Borough	42	30	5	7	82	35	95
King's Lynn	42	27	5	10	85	43	84
Bedworth United	42	24	10	8	76	42	81
Moor Green	42	22	8	12	81	47	74
Paget Rangers	42	21	9	12	70	45	72
Tamworth	42	22	3	17	97	64	69
Solihull Borough	42	19	9	14	77	64	66
Rothwell Town	42	17	14	11	79	62	65
Buckingham Town	42	18	9	15	74	62	63
Dudley Town	42	15	16	11	83	66	61
Stourbridge	42	17	8	17	60	63	59
Bilston Town	42	16	9	17	61	62	57
Sutton Coldfield Town	42	16	9	17	62	67	57
Grantham Town	42	17	5	20	71	83	56
Redditch United	42	14	11	17	57	77	53
Leicester United	42	13	13	16	58	72	52
Hinckley Town	42	14	7	21	62	83	49
Racing Club Warwick	42	10	13	19	67	90	43
Evesham United	42	11	6	25	59	94	39
Corby Town	42	9	7	26	52	95	34
Bury Town	42	8	8	26	57	95	32
Bridgnorth Town	42	7	6	29	53	112	27

Bedworth United 1 point deducted, King's Lynn had 2 points deducted

Southern Division

Sittingbourne	42	28	4	10	102	44	88
Ashford Town	42	25	9	8	75	44	84
Waterlooville	42	24	8	10	87	44	80
Newport IOW	42	24	6	12	75	58	78
Braintree Town	42	24	8	10	93	70	77
Weymouth	42	24	4	14	75	55	76
Havant Town	42	23	11	8	73	42	74
Forest Green Rovers	42	22	8	12	85	55	74
Trowbridge Town	42	18	8	16	86	51	62
Yate Town	42	17	8	17	85	71	59
Margate	42	18	5	19	68	62	59
Witney Town	42	16	11	15	60	54	59
Weston-super-Mare	42	16	9	17	78	68	57
Cinderford Town	42	16	8	18	74	77	56
Fisher 93	42	14	13	15	58	59	55
Bashley	42	14	11	17	63	61	53
Clevedon Town	42	15	6	21	70	80	51
Tonbridge Angels	42	13	10	19	58	79	49
Fleet Town	42	14	5	23	58	79	47
Fareham Town	42	12	5	25	71	97	41
Erith & Belvedere	42	4	4	34	38	111	16
Poole Town	42	0	1	41	17	188	1

Braintree Town 3 points deducted, Havant Town had 6 points deducted

1996-97

Premier Division

Gresley Rovers	42	25	10	7	75	40	85
Cheltenham Town	42	21	11	10	76	44	74
Gloucester City	42	21	10	11	81	56	73
Halesowen Town	42	21	10	11	77	54	73
King's Lynn	42	20	8	14	65	61	68
Burton Albion	42	18	12	12	70	53	66
Nuneaton Borough	42	19	9	14	61	52	66
Sittingbourne	42	19	7	16	76	65	64
Merthyr Tydfil	42	17	9	16	69	61	60
Worcester City	42	15	14	13	52	50	59
Atherstone United	42	15	13	14	46	47	58
Salisbury City	42	15	13	14	57	66	58
Sudbury Town	42	16	7	19	72	72	55
Gravesend & Northfleet	42	16	7	19	63	73	55
Dorchester Town	42	14	9	19	62	66	51
Hastings Town	42	12	15	15	49	60	51
Crawley Town	42	13	8	21	49	67	47
Cambridge City	42	11	13	18	57	65	46
Ashford Town	42	9	18	15	53	79	45
Baldock Town	42	11	8	23	52	90	41
Newport AFC	42	9	13	20	40	60	40
Chelmsford City	42	6	14	22	49	70	32

Midland Division

Tamworth	40	30	7	3	90	28	97
Rothwell Town	40	20	11	9	82	54	71
Ilkeston Town	40	19	13	8	76	50	70
Grantham Town	40	22	4	14	65	46	70
Bedworth United	40	18	11	11	77	41	65
Solihull Borough	40	19	8	13	84	62	65
Bilston Town	40	18	10	12	74	57	64
Moor Green	40	18	7	15	88	68	61
Stafford Rangers	40	17	9	14	68	62	60
Raunds Town	40	16	11	13	61	66	59
Racing Club Warwick	40	16	10	14	70	72	58
Shepshed Dynamo	40	14	12	14	64	65	54
Redditch United	40	15	8	17	56	59	53
Paget Rangers	40	13	9	18	42	55	48
Dudley Town	40	12	10	18	70	89	46
Hinckley Town	40	11	11	18	39	63	44
Stourbridge	40	10	9	21	61	81	39
Evesham United	40	9	12	19	55	77	39
VS Rugby	40	9	9	22	49	81	36
Corby Town	40	8	8	24	49	88	32
Sutton Coldfield Town	40	7	9	24	29	85	30

Leicester United FC closed down and their record was expunged from the League table.

Southern Division

Forest Green Rovers	42	27	10	5	87	40	91
St Leonards Stamcroft	42	26	9	7	95	48	87
Havant Town	42	23	10	9	81	49	79
Weston-super-Mare	42	21	13	8	82	43	76
Margate	42	21	9	12	70	47	72
Witney Town	42	20	11	11	71	42	71
Weymouth	42	20	10	12	82	51	70
Tonbridge Angels	42	17	15	10	56	44	66
Newport IOW	42	15	15	12	73	58	60
Fisher Athletic (London)	42	18	6	18	77	77	60
Clevedon Town	42	17	9	16	75	76	60
Fareham Town	42	14	12	16	53	70	54
Bashley	42	15	8	19	73	84	53
Dartford	42	14	10	18	59	64	52
Waterlooville	42	14	9	19	58	67	51
Cirencester Town	42	12	12	18	50	68	48
Cinderford Town	42	13	7	22	64	76	46
Trowbridge Town	42	11	11	20	50	61	44
Yate Town	42	12	8	22	55	87	44
Fleet Town	42	12	6	24	47	91	42
Erith & Belvedere	42	9	10	23	60	95	37
Buckingham Town	42	2	8	32	27	107	14

1997-98

Premier Division

Team	P	W	D	L	F	A	Pts
Forest Green Rovers	42	27	8	7	93	55	89
Merthyr Tydfil	42	24	12	6	80	42	84
Burton Albion	42	21	8	13	64	43	71
Dorchester Town	42	19	13	10	63	38	70
Halesowen Town	42	18	15	9	70	38	69
Bath City	42	19	12	11	72	51	69
Worcester City	42	19	12	11	54	44	69
King's Lynn	42	18	11	13	64	65	65
Atherstone United	42	17	12	13	55	49	63
Crawley Town	42	17	8	17	63	60	59
Gloucester City	42	16	11	15	57	57	59
Nuneaton Borough	42	17	6	19	68	61	57
Cambridge City	42	16	8	18	62	70	56
Hastings Town	42	14	12	16	67	70	54
Tamworth	42	14	11	17	68	65	53
Rothwell Town	42	11	16	15	55	73	49
Gresley Rovers	42	14	6	22	59	77	48
Salisbury City	42	12	12	18	53	72	48
Bromsgrove Rovers	42	13	6	23	67	85	45
Sittingbourne	42	12	8	22	47	66	44
Ashford Town	42	8	5	29	34	85	29
St Leonards Stamcroft	42	5	10	27	48	97	25

Midland Division

Team	P	W	D	L	F	A	Pts
Grantham Town	40	30	4	6	87	39	94
Ilkeston Town	40	29	6	5	123	39	93
Solihull Borough	40	22	9	9	81	48	75
Raunds Town	40	20	8	12	73	44	68
Wisbech Town	40	20	7	13	79	57	67
Moor Green	40	20	7	13	72	55	67
Bilston Town	40	20	5	15	69	57	65
Blakenall	40	17	13	10	66	55	64
Stafford Rangers	40	18	6	16	57	56	60
Redditch United	40	16	11	13	59	41	59
Stourbridge	40	16	9	15	57	55	57
Hinckley United	40	15	11	14	59	56	56
Brackley Town	40	15	7	18	45	57	52
Bedworth United	40	15	5	20	50	73	50
Racing Club Warwick	40	11	9	20	49	56	42
Shepshed Dynamo	40	9	14	17	55	74	41
Sutton Coldfield Town	40	9	12	19	42	68	39
Paget Rangers	40	9	12	19	40	75	39
VS Rugby	40	8	12	20	53	93	36
Evesham United	40	7	9	24	47	94	30
Corby Town	40	2	8	30	41	112	14

Southern Division

Team	P	W	D	L	F	A	Pts
Weymouth	42	32	2	8	107	48	98
Chelmsford City	42	29	8	5	86	39	95
Bashley	42	29	4	9	101	59	91
Newport IOW	42	25	9	8	72	34	84
Fisher Athletic (London)	42	25	5	12	87	50	80
Margate	42	23	8	11	71	42	77
Newport AFC	42	21	6	15	83	65	69
Witney Town	42	20	9	13	74	58	69
Clevedon Town	42	20	7	15	57	55	67
Waterlooville	42	17	7	18	69	64	58
Dartford	42	17	7	18	60	60	58
Havant Town	42	13	14	16	65	70	53
Fleet Town	42	16	5	21	63	83	53
Tonbridge Angels	42	14	10	18	49	55	52
Trowbridge Town	42	14	6	22	55	69	48
Erith & Belvedere	42	11	13	18	47	68	46
Fareham Town	42	12	9	21	75	87	45
Cirencester Town	42	12	7	23	63	88	43
Weston-super-Mare	42	12	5	25	49	86	41
Baldock Town	42	10	5	27	53	81	35
Cinderford Town	42	6	5	31	40	112	23
Yate Town	42	5	7	30	44	97	22

1998-99

Premier Division

Team	P	W	D	L	F	A	Pts
Nuneaton Borough	42	27	9	6	91	33	90
Boston United	42	17	16	9	69	51	67
Ilkeston Town	42	18	13	11	72	59	67
Bath City	42	18	11	13	70	44	65
Hastings Town	42	18	11	13	57	49	65
Gloucester City	42	18	11	13	57	52	65
Worcester City	42	18	9	15	58	54	63
Halesowen Town	42	17	11	14	72	60	62
Tamworth	42	19	5	18	62	67	62
King's Lynn	42	17	10	15	53	46	61
Crawley Town	42	17	10	15	57	58	61
Salisbury City	42	16	12	14	56	61	60
Burton Albion	42	17	7	18	58	52	58
Weymouth	42	14	14	14	56	55	56
Merthyr Tydfil	42	15	8	19	52	62	53
Atherstone United	42	12	14	16	47	52	50
Grantham Town	42	14	8	20	51	58	50
Dorchester Town	42	11	15	16	49	63	48
Rothwell Town	42	13	9	20	47	67	48
Cambridge City	42	11	12	19	47	68	45
Gresley Rovers	42	12	8	22	49	73	44
Bromsgrove Rovers	42	8	7	27	38	84	31

Hastings Town resigned from the League

Midland Division

Team	P	W	D	L	F	A	Pts
Clevedon Town	42	28	8	6	83	35	92
Newport AFC	42	26	7	9	92	51	85
Redditch United	42	22	12	8	81	45	75
Hinckley United	42	20	12	10	58	40	72
Stafford Rangers	42	21	8	13	92	60	71
Bilston Town	42	20	11	11	79	69	71
Solihull Borough	42	19	12	11	76	53	69
Moor Green	42	20	7	15	71	61	67
Blakenall	42	17	14	11	65	54	65
Shepshed Dynamo	42	17	12	13	62	54	63
Sutton Coldfield Town	42	17	8	17	46	57	59
Stourbridge	42	16	10	16	60	55	58
Evesham United	42	16	9	17	63	63	57
Wisbech Town	42	16	9	17	59	66	57
Weston-super-Mare	42	15	10	17	59	56	55
Bedworth United	42	15	9	18	63	52	54
Cinderford Town	42	13	8	21	61	74	47
Stamford AFC	42	13	7	22	60	75	46
Paget Rangers	42	11	12	19	49	58	45
VS Rugby	42	12	9	21	53	74	45
Racing Club Warwick	42	5	8	29	38	93	23
Bloxwich Town	42	1	2	39	26	151	5

Southern Division

Team	P	W	D	L	F	A	Pts
Havant & Waterlooville	42	29	7	6	86	32	94
Margate	42	27	8	7	84	33	89
Folkestone Invicta	42	26	8	8	92	47	86
Newport IOW	42	23	7	12	68	40	76
Chelmsford City	42	20	12	10	91	51	72
Raunds Town	42	19	13	10	87	50	70
Ashford Town	42	17	12	13	59	54	63
Baldock Town	42	17	9	16	60	59	60
Fisher Athletic (London)	42	16	11	15	58	54	59
Bashley	42	17	7	18	74	77	58
Witney Town	42	15	12	15	56	48	57
Cirencester Town	42	16	8	18	61	66	56
Sittingbourne	42	11	18	12	53	56	54
Dartford	42	14	10	18	48	53	52
Erith & Belvedere	42	15	7	20	48	64	52
Tonbridge Angels	42	12	15	15	48	59	51
St Leonards	42	14	8	20	57	72	50
Fleet Town	42	11	11	19	54	72	47
Corby Town	42	10	10	22	48	73	40
Yate Town	42	10	7	25	37	79	37
Andover	42	6	10	26	50	115	28
Brackley Town	42	6	8	28	41	105	26

1999-2000

Premier Division

Boston United	42	27	11	4	102	39	92
Burton Albion	42	23	9	10	73	43	78
Margate	42	23	8	11	64	43	77
Bath City	42	19	15	8	70	49	72
King's Lynn	42	19	14	9	59	43	71
Tamworth	42	20	10	12	80	51	70
Newport County	42	16	18	8	67	50	66
Clevedon Town	42	18	9	15	52	52	63
Ilkeston Town	42	16	12	14	77	69	60
Weymouth	42	14	16	12	60	51	58
Halesowen Town	42	14	14	14	52	54	56
Crawley Town	42	15	8	19	68	82	53
Havant & Waterlooville	42	13	13	16	63	68	52
Cambridge City	42	14	10	18	52	66	52
Worcester City	42	13	13	16	60	66	50
Salisbury City	42	14	8	20	70	84	50
Merthyr Tydfil	42	13	9	20	51	63	48
Dorchester Town	42	10	17	15	56	65	47
Grantham Town	42	14	5	23	63	76	47
Gloucester City	42	8	14	20	40	82	38
Rothwell Town	42	5	14	23	48	85	29
Atherstone United	42	5	13	24	30	76	28

Eastern Division

Fisher Athletic (London)	42	31	5	6	107	42	98
Folkestone Invicta	42	30	7	5	101	39	97
Newport IOW	42	25	7	10	74	40	82
Chelmsford City	42	24	8	10	74	38	80
Hastings Town	42	22	9	11	76	56	75
Ashford Town	42	21	9	12	70	49	72
Tonbridge Angels	42	20	10	12	82	60	70
Dartford	42	17	6	19	52	58	57
Burnham	42	15	9	18	55	64	54
Baldock Town	42	14	10	18	57	69	52
Erith & Belvedere	42	14	9	19	62	68	51
Witney Town	42	13	11	18	48	60	50
VS Rugby	42	13	11	18	58	79	50
Wisbech Town	42	14	7	21	58	66	49
Spalding United	42	14	6	22	52	71	48
Sittingbourne	42	13	7	22	48	75	46
Stamford	42	9	18	15	50	62	45
St Leonards	42	11	12	19	67	81	45
Raunds Town	42	11	12	19	44	63	45
Bashley	42	12	7	23	56	95	43
Corby Town	42	11	12	19	56	62	42
Fleet Town	42	8	8	26	54	104	32

Corby Town had 3 points deducted for fielding an ineligible player
Raunds Town gave notice to withdraw and take the place of the 2nd
relegated Club. They then unsuccessfully sought re-election

Western Division

Stafford Rangers	42	29	6	7	107	47	93
Moor Green	42	26	12	4	85	33	90
Hinckley United	42	25	12	5	89	47	87
Tiverton Town	42	26	7	9	91	44	85
Solihull Borough	42	20	11	11	85	66	71
Blakenall	42	19	12	11	70	46	69
Cirencester Town	42	20	8	14	72	64	68
Bilston Town	42	16	18	8	66	52	66
Cinderford Town	42	17	11	14	62	64	62
Redditch United	42	17	10	15	73	65	61
Gresley Rovers	42	14	15	13	54	49	57
Weston-super-Mare	42	16	9	17	55	55	57
Sutton Coldfield Town	42	13	17	12	49	52	56
Evesham Town	42	13	12	17	69	61	51
Bedworth Town	42	13	10	19	52	71	49
Rocester	42	12	12	18	63	78	48
Bromsgrove Rovers	42	13	7	22	59	72	46
Shepshed Dynamo	42	12	7	23	46	66	43
Paget Rangers	42	11	4	27	44	82	37
Racing Club Warwick	42	7	14	21	41	82	35
Stourbridge	42	10	3	29	45	101	33
Yate Town	42	3	3	36	28	108	12

2000-2001

Premier Division

Margate	42	28	7	7	75	27	91
Burton Albion	42	25	13	4	76	36	88
King's Lynn	42	18	11	13	67	58	65
Welling United	42	17	13	12	59	55	64
Weymouth	42	17	12	13	69	51	63
Havant & Waterlooville	42	18	9	15	65	53	63
Stafford Rangers	42	18	9	15	70	59	63
Worcester City	42	18	8	16	52	53	62
Moor Green	42	18	8	16	49	53	62
Newport County	42	17	10	15	70	61	61
Crawley Town	42	17	10	15	61	54	61
Tamworth	42	17	8	17	58	55	59
Salisbury City	42	17	8	17	64	69	59
Ilkeston Town	42	16	11	15	51	61	59
Bath City	42	15	13	14	67	68	55
Cambridge City	42	13	11	18	56	59	50
Folkestone Invicta	42	14	6	22	49	74	48
Merthyr Tydfil	42	11	13	18	49	62	46
Clevedon Town	42	11	7	24	61	74	40
Fisher Athletic (London)	42	12	6	24	51	85	39
Dorchester Town	42	10	8	24	40	70	38
Halesowen Town	42	8	13	21	47	69	37

Bath City and Fisher Athletic (London) both had 3 points deducted

Eastern Division

Newport IOW	42	28	10	4	91	30	94
Chelmsford City	42	27	9	6	102	45	90
Grantham Town	42	25	11	6	100	47	86
Histon	42	23	11	8	84	53	80
Baldock Town	42	23	10	9	81	44	79
Hastings Town	42	22	10	10	72	50	76
Stamford	42	20	11	11	69	59	71
Tonbridge Angels	42	18	11	13	79	58	65
Langney Sports	42	19	8	15	75	55	65
Rothwell Town	42	20	5	17	86	74	62
Corby Town	42	14	10	18	64	92	52
Ashford Town	42	15	4	23	53	83	49
Banbury United	42	12	11	19	57	54	47
Witney Town	42	12	11	19	55	71	47
Bashley	42	10	14	18	57	71	44
Dartford	42	11	11	20	49	67	44
Burnham	42	10	14	18	39	65	43
Wisbech Town	42	10	9	23	45	89	39
St Leonards	42	9	10	23	55	87	37
Erith & Belvedere	42	10	7	25	49	92	37
Sittingbourne	42	8	9	25	41	79	33
Spalding United	42	7	12	23	35	73	33

Burnham had 1 point deducted, Rothwell Town had 3 points deducted

Western Division

Hinckley United	42	30	8	4	102	38	98
Tiverton Town	42	28	7	7	97	36	91
Bilston Town	42	27	9	6	88	48	90
Evesham United	42	27	5	10	86	46	86
Mangotsfield United	42	25	9	8	91	45	84
Solihull Borough	42	22	12	8	73	43	78
Redditch United	42	17	13	12	76	69	64
Weston-super-Mare	42	17	10	15	68	58	61
Atherstone United	42	16	11	15	64	58	59
Rochester	42	18	5	19	57	77	59
Cirencester Town	42	14	15	13	65	74	57
Rugby United	42	13	10	19	51	68	49
Gloucester City	42	12	11	19	76	86	47
Blakenall	42	13	10	19	54	64	46
Shepshed Dynamo	42	12	9	21	56	73	45
Bedworth United	42	12	9	21	38	60	45
Racing Club Warwick	42	13	6	23	46	77	45
Gresley Rovers	42	11	8	23	46	65	41
Cinderford Town	42	11	8	23	56	84	41
Sutton Coldfield Town	42	7	14	21	45	66	35
Paget Rovers	42	9	4	29	38	93	31
Bromsgrove Rovers	42	7	9	26	47	92	30

Blakenall had 3 points deducted

2001-2002

Premier Division

Kettering Town	42	27	6	9	80	41	87
Tamworth	42	24	13	5	81	41	85
Havant & Waterlooville	42	22	9	11	74	50	75
Crawley Town	42	21	10	11	67	48	73
Newport County	42	19	9	14	61	48	66
Tiverton Town	42	17	10	15	70	63	61
Moor Green	42	18	7	17	64	62	61
Worcester City	42	16	12	14	65	54	60
Stafford Rangers	42	17	9	16	70	62	60
Ilkeston Town	42	14	16	12	58	61	58
Weymouth United	42	15	11	16	59	67	56
Hinckley Town	42	14	13	15	64	62	55
Folkestone Invicta	42	14	12	16	51	61	54
Cambridge City	42	12	16	14	60	70	52
Welling United	42	13	12	17	69	66	51
Hednesford Town	42	15	6	21	59	70	51
Bath City	42	13	11	18	56	65	50
Chelmsford City	42	13	11	18	63	75	50
Newport IOW	42	12	12	18	38	61	48
King's Lynn	42	11	13	18	44	57	46
Merthyr Tydfil	42	12	8	22	53	71	44
Salisbury City	42	6	8	28	36	87	26

Eastern Division

Hastings Town	42	29	8	5	85	38	95
Grantham Town	42	29	6	7	99	43	93
Dorchester Town	42	26	10	6	81	36	88
Histon	42	23	8	11	83	49	77
Stamford	42	24	4	14	76	61	76
Fisher Athletic (London)	42	20	10	12	83	56	70
Eastbourne Borough	42	21	6	15	63	46	69
Dartford	42	18	5	19	62	66	59
Erith & Belvedere	42	18	3	21	75	79	57
Bashley	42	15	11	16	71	63	56
Burnham	42	15	10	17	52	54	55
Rugby United	42	16	6	20	55	67	54
Rothwell Town	42	14	8	20	46	66	50
Ashford Town	42	14	6	22	58	78	48
Banbury United	42	13	9	20	53	66	47
Chatham Town	42	13	8	21	56	87	47
Sittingbourne	42	14	4	24	46	69	46
Spalding	42	13	6	23	72	84	45
Tonbridge Angels	42	13	6	23	65	80	45
St Leonards	42	14	3	25	52	88	45
Corby Town	42	10	13	19	54	82	43
Wisbech Town	42	11	8	23	56	84	41

Western Division

Halesowen Town	40	27	9	4	85	24	90
Chippenham Town	40	26	9	5	81	28	87
Weston-super-Mare	40	22	10	8	70	38	76
Solihull Borough	40	20	11	9	75	42	71
Gresley Rovers	40	19	9	12	59	50	66
Sutton Coldfield Town	40	17	11	12	53	46	62
Mangotsfield United	40	17	10	13	74	54	61
Stourport Swifts	40	18	6	16	59	59	60
Atherstone United	40	16	8	16	61	59	56
Clevedon Town	40	15	11	14	57	58	56
Bedworth United	40	16	7	17	59	63	55
Evesham United	40	16	7	17	54	70	55
Cirencester Town	40	17	3	20	64	69	54
Gloucester City	40	14	10	16	48	63	52
Cinderford Town	40	14	9	17	54	67	51
Shepshed Dynamo	40	10	10	20	64	84	40
Bilston Town	40	11	7	22	50	72	40
Redditch United	40	11	6	23	47	77	39
Swindon Supermarine	40	11	4	25	52	76	37
Racing Club Warwick	40	8	11	21	38	63	35
Rocester	40	5	12	23	33	75	27

2002-2003

Premier Division

Tamworth	42	26	10	6	73	32	88
Stafford Rangers	42	21	12	9	76	40	75
Dover Athletic	42	19	14	9	42	35	71
Tiverton Town	42	19	12	11	60	43	69
Chippenham Town	42	17	17	8	59	37	68
Worcester City	42	18	13	11	60	39	67
Crawley Town	42	17	13	12	64	51	64
Havant & Waterlooville	42	15	15	12	67	64	60
Chelmsford City	42	15	12	15	65	63	57
Newport County	42	15	11	16	53	52	56
Hednesford Town	42	14	13	15	59	60	55
Moor Green	42	13	14	15	49	58	53
Hinckley Town	42	12	16	14	61	64	52
Bath City	42	13	13	16	50	61	52
Welling United	42	13	12	17	55	58	51
Grantham Town	42	14	9	19	59	65	51
Weymouth	42	12	15	15	44	62	51
Cambridge City	42	13	10	19	54	56	49
Halesowen Town	42	12	13	17	52	63	49
Hastings United	42	10	13	19	44	57	43
Ilkeston Town	42	10	10	22	54	92	40
Folkestone Invicta	42	7	7	28	57	105	28

Eastern Division

Dorchester Town	42	28	9	5	114	40	93
Eastbourne Borough	42	29	6	7	92	33	93
Stamford	42	27	6	9	80	39	87
Salisbury City	42	27	8	7	81	42	86
Bashley	42	23	12	7	90	44	81
King's Lynn	42	24	7	11	98	62	79
Rothwell Town	42	22	10	10	77	52	76
Banbury United	42	21	11	10	75	50	74
Tonbridge Angels	42	20	11	11	71	55	71
Histon	42	20	7	15	99	62	67
Ashford Town	42	18	9	15	63	57	63
Sittingbourne	42	15	8	19	57	69	53
Burnham	42	15	7	20	62	79	52
Fisher Athletic	42	15	5	22	57	80	50
Chatham Town	42	14	5	23	54	84	47
Newport IOW	42	12	6	24	53	87	42
Dartford	42	11	8	23	48	78	41
Erith & Belvedere	42	11	6	25	65	96	39
Corby Town	42	9	11	22	49	84	38
Fleet Town	42	8	8	26	34	80	32
Spalding United	42	4	6	32	40	108	18
St. Leonards	42	4	4	34	38	116	16

Western Division

Merthyr Tydfil	42	28	8	6	78	32	92
Weston-super-Mare	42	26	7	9	77	42	85
Bromsgrove Rovers	42	23	7	12	73	41	76
Solihull Borough	42	21	13	8	77	48	76
Gloucester City	42	22	9	11	87	58	75
Mangotsfield United	42	21	10	11	106	53	73
Redditch United	42	22	6	14	76	42	72
Rugby United	42	20	9	13	58	43	69
Gresley Rovers	42	19	10	13	63	54	67
Taunton Town	42	20	7	15	76	78	67
Sutton Coldfield Town	42	18	10	14	63	54	64
Evesham United	42	19	6	17	76	72	63
Clevedon Town	42	14	13	15	54	60	55
Cirencester Town	42	15	7	20	62	82	52
Cinderford Town	42	13	12	17	50	67	51
Shepshed Dynamo	42	12	6	24	48	76	42
Stourport Swifts	42	10	11	21	48	66	41
Bedworth United	42	11	7	24	46	74	40
Swindon Supermarine	42	11	5	26	52	85	38
Atherstone United	42	9	10	23	45	78	37
Rocester	42	9	10	23	34	74	37
Racing Club Warwick	42	3	9	30	33	104	18

2003-2004

Premier Division

Crawley Town	42	25	9	8	77	43	84
Weymouth	42	20	12	10	76	47	72
Stafford Rangers	42	19	11	12	55	43	68
Nuneaton Borough	42	17	15	10	65	49	66
Worcester City	42	18	9	15	71	50	63
Hinckley United	42	15	14	13	55	46	59
Newport County	42	15	14	13	52	50	59
Cambridge City	42	14	15	13	54	53	57
Welling United	42	16	8	18	56	58	56
Weston-super-Mare	42	14	13	15	52	52	55
Eastbourne Borough	42	14	13	15	48	56	55
Havant & Waterlooville	42	15	10	17	59	70	55
Moor Green	42	14	12	16	42	54	54
Merthyr Tydfil	42	13	14	15	60	66	53
Tiverton Town	42	12	15	15	63	64	51
Bath City	42	13	12	17	49	57	51
Dorchester Town	42	14	9	19	56	69	51
Chelmsford City	42	11	16	15	46	53	49
Dover Athletic	42	12	13	17	50	59	49
Hednesford Town	42	12	12	18	56	69	48
Chippenham Town	42	10	17	15	51	63	47
Grantham Town	42	10	15	17	45	67	45

Eastern Division

King's Lynn	42	28	7	7	90	35	91
Histon	42	26	10	6	96	41	88
Tonbridge Angels	42	27	7	8	82	46	88
* Eastleigh	42	27	4	11	88	40	82
Folkestone Invicta	42	20	15	7	91	45	75
Salisbury City	42	21	11	10	73	45	74
Stamford	42	20	11	11	63	45	71
Banbury United	42	19	10	13	65	57	67
Burgess Hill Town	42	19	7	16	67	54	64
Sittingbourne	42	18	8	16	61	55	62
Bashley	42	18	7	17	66	58	61
Ashford Town	42	15	9	18	51	53	54
Chatham Town	42	13	10	19	49	67	49
Fisher Athletic	42	13	10	19	61	81	49
Corby Town	42	12	9	21	44	75	45
Dartford	42	13	6	23	48	81	45
* Burnham	42	12	11	19	52	76	44
Hastings United	42	12	7	23	60	91	43
Newport IOW	42	11	7	24	42	69	40
Rothwell Town	42	9	11	22	30	47	38
Erith & Belvedere	42	7	10	25	45	84	31
Fleet Town	42	5	7	30	35	114	22

* Eastleigh and Burnham both had 3 points deducted.

Western Division

Redditch United	40	25	9	6	75	30	84
Gloucester City	40	24	7	9	77	46	79
Cirencester Town	40	24	4	12	73	40	76
Halesowen Town	40	20	13	7	64	40	73
Rugby United	40	21	8	11	57	40	71
Team Bath	40	21	6	13	62	41	69
Solihull Borough	40	19	9	12	50	31	66
Sutton Coldfield	40	16	15	9	52	38	63
Bromsgrove Rovers	40	16	11	13	60	48	59
Ilkeston Town	40	16	10	14	58	59	58
Clevedon Town	40	16	5	19	55	59	53
Gresley Rovers	40	15	7	18	52	60	52
Mangotsfield United	40	14	8	18	70	70	50
Evesham United	40	15	5	20	56	57	50
Taunton Town	40	14	8	18	50	55	50
Yate Town	40	11	9	20	51	79	42
Swindon Supermarine	40	10	9	21	41	69	39
Stourport Swifts	40	9	11	20	43	62	38
Bedworth United	40	8	12	20	39	61	36
Cinderford Town	40	7	9	24	50	94	30
Shepshed Dynamo	40	5	13	22	31	87	28

2004-2005

Premier Division

Histon	42	24	6	12	93	57	78
Chippenham Town	42	22	9	11	81	55	75
Merthyr Tydfil	42	19	14	9	62	47	71
Hednesford Town	42	20	10	12	68	40	70
Bedford Town	42	19	12	11	70	52	69
Bath City	42	19	12	11	57	43	69
Cirencester Town	42	19	11	12	63	52	68
Tiverton Town	42	18	13	11	70	55	67
Halesowen Town	42	19	9	14	64	52	66
Aylesbury United	42	20	3	19	67	66	63
King's Lynn	42	19	4	19	78	69	61
Chesham United	42	18	5	19	84	82	59
Grantham Town	42	17	7	18	57	55	58
Team Bath	42	14	12	16	54	68	54
Gloucester City	42	12	17	13	63	61	53
Rugby United	42	13	12	17	48	60	51
Banbury United	42	13	9	20	56	69	48
Hitchin Town	42	13	9	20	55	77	48
Hemel Hempstead Town	42	11	10	21	60	88	43
Dunstable Town	42	11	6	25	56	98	39
Stamford	42	6	18	18	40	60	36
Solihull Borough	42	10	4	28	45	85	34

Eastern Division

Fisher Athletic	42	30	6	6	96	41	96
East Thurrock United	42	25	12	5	92	38	87
Maldon Town	42	27	6	9	92	51	87
Uxbridge	42	26	7	9	87	37	85
Wivenhoe Town	42	21	11	10	74	49	74
Barking & East Ham United	42	20	10	12	63	37	70
Boreham Wood	42	19	9	14	80	61	66
Barton Rovers	42	20	4	18	76	72	64
Waltham Forest	42	16	9	17	68	61	57
Leighton Town	42	13	15	14	57	59	54
Chatham Town	42	15	9	18	53	63	54
Wingate & Finchley	42	15	8	19	60	75	53
Arlesey Town	42	14	10	18	53	67	52
Beaconsfield SYCOB	42	12	12	18	54	65	48
Harlow Town	42	13	8	21	53	65	47
Dartford	42	11	13	18	58	75	46
Aveley	42	12	9	21	57	69	45
Berkhamsted Town	42	15	7	20	66	101	45
Sittingbourne	42	10	12	20	53	70	42
Great Wakering Rovers	42	9	11	22	45	78	38
Erith & Belvedere	42	11	7	24	56	92	37
Tilbury	42	6	9	27	41	108	27

Berkhamsted Town had 7 points deducted.
Erith & Belvedere had 3 points deducted.

Western Division

Mangotsfield United	42	24	11	7	89	49	83
Yate Town	42	24	9	9	83	40	81
Evesham United	42	23	10	9	66	31	79
Clevedon Town	42	24	6	12	82	49	78
Bromsgrove Rovers	42	19	15	8	60	42	72
Ashford Town (Middlesex)	42	17	13	12	63	46	64
Brackley Town	42	18	10	14	69	53	64
Paulton Rovers	42	18	7	17	62	61	61
Burnham	42	17	7	18	64	64	58
Rothwell Town	42	16	10	16	57	57	58
Thame United	42	17	6	19	58	69	57
Corby Town	42	14	12	16	52	62	54
Marlow	42	13	14	15	58	67	53
Stourport Swifts	42	15	7	20	62	63	52
Bedworth United	42	15	7	20	51	60	52
Cinderford Town	42	13	12	17	50	64	51
Taunton Town	42	14	8	20	66	75	50
Sutton Coldfield	42	16	11	15	54	61	48
Swindon Supermarine	42	12	12	18	43	60	48
Bracknell Town	42	10	13	19	53	75	43
Oxford City	42	11	8	23	49	71	41
Egham Town	42	6	4	32	25	97	22

Sutton Coldfield had 11 points deducted.

2005-2006

Premier Division

Salisbury City	42	30	5	7	83	27	95
Bath City	42	25	8	9	66	33	83
King's Lynn	42	25	7	10	73	41	82
Chippenham Town	42	22	11	9	69	45	77
Bedford Town	42	22	10	10	69	53	76
Yate Town	42	21	5	16	78	74	68
Banbury United	42	17	11	14	66	61	62
Halesowen Town	42	15	15	12	54	45	60
Merthyr Tydfil	42	17	9	16	62	58	60
Mangotsfield United	42	15	13	14	67	67	58
Grantham Town	42	15	11	16	49	49	56
Tiverton Town	42	14	10	18	69	65	52
Gloucester City	42	14	10	18	57	60	52
Hitchin Town	42	13	12	17	59	76	51
Rugby Town	42	13	11	18	58	66	50
Cheshunt	42	13	9	20	57	70	48
Team Bath	42	14	6	22	55	68	48
Cirencester Town	42	14	4	24	49	68	46
Northwood	42	12	6	24	53	88	42
Evesham United	42	9	14	19	46	58	41
Aylesbury United	42	9	12	21	43	69	39
Chesham United	42	9	9	24	43	84	36

Eastern Division

Boreham Wood	42	24	12	6	84	41	84
Corby Town	42	25	9	8	63	33	84
Enfield Town	42	24	9	9	75	43	81
Stamford	42	20	10	12	73	53	70
Barking & East Ham United	42	20	10	12	63	47	70
Wivenhoe Town	42	17	11	14	56	54	62
Dartford	42	16	13	13	65	57	61
Waltham Forest	42	17	8	17	64	66	59
Harlow Town	42	14	16	12	57	56	58
Arlesey Town	42	15	11	16	58	65	56
Rothwell Town	42	13	14	15	48	53	53
Wingate & Finchley	42	13	14	15	57	64	53
Great Wakering Rovers	42	13	12	17	65	67	51
Uxbridge	42	13	11	18	62	64	50
Potters Bar Town	42	13	11	18	60	66	50
Enfield	42	13	11	18	52	64	50
Chatham Town	42	13	10	19	51	57	49
Sittingbourne	42	12	12	18	53	69	48
Barton Rovers	42	13	8	21	59	73	47
Aveley	42	11	13	18	51	70	46
Ilford	42	8	17	17	35	59	41
Berkhamsted Town	42	8	12	22	51	81	36

Western Division

Clevedon Town	42	28	6	8	86	45	90
Ashford Town (Middlesex)	42	24	8	10	84	50	80
Brackley Town	42	23	9	10	71	34	78
Hemel Hempstead Town	42	22	9	11	86	47	75
Swindon Supermarine	42	22	9	11	70	47	75
Marlow	42	22	6	14	62	59	72
Sutton Coldfield Town	42	21	6	15	91	62	69
Leighton Town	42	19	8	15	55	48	65
Willenhall Town	42	17	12	13	78	61	63
Rushall Olympic	42	17	11	14	73	57	62
Bromsgrove Rovers	42	17	11	14	65	50	62
Solihull Borough	42	15	13	14	50	51	58
Beaconsfield SYCOB	42	14	13	15	60	66	55
Burnham	42	16	5	21	58	71	53
Cinderford Town	42	14	9	19	71	79	51
Bedworth United	42	14	9	19	46	57	51
Paulton Rovers	42	12	10	20	55	76	46
Taunton Town	42	12	9	21	67	81	45
Bracknell Town	42	12	6	24	53	77	42
Stourport Swifts	42	9	14	19	55	80	41
Dunstable Town	42	8	12	22	45	91	36
Thame United	42	4	5	33	30	122	17

2006-2007

Premier Division

Bath City	42	27	10	5	84	29	91
Team Bath	42	23	9	10	66	42	78
King's Lynn	42	22	10	10	69	40	76
Maidenhead United	42	20	10	12	58	36	70
Hemel Hempstead Town	42	19	12	11	79	60	69
Halesowen Town	42	18	13	11	66	53	67
Chippenham Town	42	19	9	14	61	56	66
Stamford	42	16	11	15	65	62	59
Mangotsfield United	42	13	19	10	44	45	58
Gloucester City	42	15	13	14	67	70	58
Hitchin Town	42	16	9	17	55	68	57
Merthyr Tydfil	42	14	14	14	47	46	56
Banbury United	42	15	10	17	60	64	55
Yate Town	42	14	12	16	59	71	54
Tiverton Town	42	14	8	20	56	67	50
Cheshunt	42	14	7	21	56	71	49
Rugby Town	42	15	4	23	58	79	49
Clevedon Town	42	12	12	18	60	61	48
Wealdstone	42	13	9	20	69	82	48
Corby Town	42	10	9	23	52	69	39
Cirencester Town	42	9	12	21	46	76	39
Northwood	42	8	10	24	44	74	34

Division One Midlands

Brackley Town	42	29	4	9	95	53	91
Bromsgrove Rovers	42	23	7	12	86	62	76
Chasetown	42	23	6	13	59	39	75
Willenhall Town	42	20	12	10	67	47	72
Evesham United	42	19	15	8	66	51	72
Aylesbury United	42	20	11	11	58	42	71
Stourbridge	42	17	15	10	70	53	66
Woodford United	42	18	11	13	71	54	65
Cinderford Town	42	18	10	14	70	60	64
Rothwell Town	42	18	7	17	72	61	61
Dunstable Town	42	16	12	14	64	53	60
Sutton Coldfield Town	42	16	9	17	62	63	57
Bishops Cleeve	42	17	5	20	68	66	56
Solihull Borough	42	17	5	20	72	84	56
Rushall Olympic	42	15	9	18	56	55	54
Bedworth United	42	13	8	21	73	83	47
Malvern Town	42	12	11	19	46	66	47
Leighton Town	42	12	8	22	44	60	44
Spalding United	42	12	6	24	45	62	42
Barton Rovers	42	11	9	22	51	93	42
Berkhamsted Town	42	10	7	25	53	97	37
Stourport Swifts	42	9	7	26	43	87	34

Division One South & West

Bashley	42	32	6	4	111	35	102
Paulton Rovers	42	20	14	8	66	42	74
Burnham	42	23	4	15	74	60	73
Swindon Supermarine	42	20	11	11	68	40	71
Taunton Town	42	19	14	9	68	50	71
Thatcham Town	42	21	7	14	70	60	70
Marlow	42	19	12	11	74	49	69
Uxbridge	42	20	8	14	68	58	68
Andover	42	19	9	14	70	59	66
Didcot Town	42	16	13	13	86	67	61
Abingdon United	42	16	11	15	68	67	59
Oxford City	42	17	8	17	62	75	59
Winchester City	42	16	10	16	67	65	58
Windsor & Eton	42	16	10	16	76	75	58
Chesham United	42	17	6	19	68	79	57
Hillingdon Borough	42	13	13	16	80	85	52
Lymington & New Milton	42	16	3	23	81	79	51
Brook House	42	14	6	22	71	92	48
Bracknell Town	42	11	13	18	51	62	46
Newport IOW	42	9	3	30	44	106	30
Hanwell Town	42	6	7	29	52	102	24
Beaconsfield SYCOB	42	5	6	31	36	104	21

Hanwell Town had one point deducted.

FOOTBALL CONFERENCE

1979-80

Altrincham	38	24	8	6	79	35	56
Weymouth	38	22	10	6	73	37	54
Worcester City	38	19	11	8	53	36	49
Boston United	38	16	13	9	52	43	45
Gravesend & Northfleet	38	17	10	11	49	44	44
Maidstone United	38	16	11	11	54	37	43
Kettering Town	38	15	13	10	55	50	43
Northwich Victoria	38	16	10	12	50	38	42
Bangor City	38	14	14	10	41	46	42
Nuneaton Borough	38	13	13	12	58	44	39
Scarborough	38	12	15	11	47	38	39
Yeovil Town	38	13	10	15	46	49	36
Telford United	38	13	8	17	52	60	34
Barrow	38	14	6	18	47	55	34
Wealdstone	38	9	15	14	42	54	33
Bath City	38	10	12	16	43	69	32
Barnet	38	10	10	18	32	48	30
AP Leamington	38	7	11	20	32	63	25
Stafford Rangers	38	6	10	22	41	57	22
Redditch United	38	5	8	25	26	69	18

1980-81

Altrincham	38	23	8	7	72	41	54
Kettering Town	38	21	9	8	66	37	51
Scarborough	38	17	13	8	49	29	47
Northwich Victoria	38	17	11	10	53	40	45
Weymouth	38	19	6	13	54	40	44
Bath City	38	16	10	12	51	32	42
Maidstone United	38	16	9	13	64	53	41
Boston United	38	16	9	13	63	58	41
Barrow	38	15	8	15	50	49	38
Frickley Athletic	38	15	8	15	61	62	38
Stafford Rangers	38	11	15	12	56	56	37
Worcester City	38	14	7	17	47	54	35
Telford United	38	13	9	16	47	59	35
Yeovil Town	38	14	6	18	60	64	34
Gravesend & Northfleet	38	13	8	17	48	55	34
AP Leamington	38	10	11	17	47	66	31
Barnet	38	12	7	19	39	64	31
Nuneaton Borough	38	10	9	19	49	65	29
Wealdstone	38	9	11	18	37	56	29
Bangor City	38	6	12	20	35	68	24

1981-82

Runcorn	42	28	9	5	75	37	93
Enfield	42	26	8	8	90	46	86
Telford United	42	23	8	11	70	51	77
Worcester City	42	21	8	13	70	60	71
Dagenham	42	19	12	11	69	51	69
Northwich Victoria	42	20	9	13	56	46	69
Scarborough	42	19	11	12	65	52	68
Barrow	42	18	11	13	59	50	65
Weymouth	42	18	9	15	56	47	63
Boston United	42	17	11	14	61	57	62
Altrincham	42	14	13	15	66	56	55
Bath City	42	15	10	17	50	57	55
Yeovil Town	42	14	11	17	56	68	53
Stafford Rangers	42	12	16	14	48	47	52
Frickley Athletic	42	14	10	18	47	60	52
Maidstone United	42	11	15	16	55	59	48
Trowbridge Town	42	12	11	19	38	54	47
Barnet	42	9	14	19	36	52	41
Kettering Town	42	9	13	20	64	76	40
Gravesend & Northfleet	42	10	10	22	51	69	40
Dartford	42	10	9	23	47	69	39
AP Leamington	42	4	10	28	40	105	22

1982-83

Enfield	42	25	9	8	95	48	84
Maidstone United	42	25	8	9	83	34	83
Wealdstone	42	22	13	7	80	41	79
Runcorn	42	22	8	12	73	53	74
Boston United	42	20	12	10	77	57	72
Telford United	42	20	11	11	69	48	71
Weymouth	42	20	10	12	63	48	70
Northwich Victoria	42	18	10	14	68	63	64
Scarborough	42	17	12	13	71	58	63
Bath City	42	17	9	16	58	55	60
Nuneaton Borough	42	15	13	14	57	60	58
Altrincham	42	15	10	17	62	56	55
Bangor City	42	14	13	15	71	77	55
Dagenham	42	12	15	15	60	65	51
Barnet	42	16	3	23	55	78	51
Frickley Athletic	42	12	13	17	66	77	49
Worcester City	42	12	10	20	58	87	46
Trowbridge Town	42	12	7	23	56	88	43
Kettering Town	42	11	7	24	69	99	40
Yeovil Town	42	11	7	24	63	99	40
Barrow	42	8	12	22	46	74	36
Stafford Rangers	42	5	14	23	40	75	29

1983-84

Maidstone United	42	23	13	6	71	34	70
Nuneaton Borough	42	24	11	7	70	40	69
Altrincham	42	23	9	10	64	39	65
Wealdstone	42	21	14	7	75	36	62
Runcorn	42	20	13	9	61	45	62
Bath City	42	17	12	13	60	48	53
Northwich Victoria	42	16	14	12	54	47	51
Worcester City	42	15	13	14	64	55	49
Barnet	42	16	10	16	55	58	49
Kidderminster Harriers	42	14	14	14	54	61	49
Telford United	42	17	11	14	50	58	49
Frickley Athletic	42	17	10	15	68	56	48
Scarborough	42	14	16	12	52	55	48
Enfield	42	14	9	19	61	58	43
Weymouth	42	13	8	21	54	65	42
Gateshead	42	12	13	17	59	73	42
Boston United	42	13	12	17	66	80	41
Dagenham	42	14	8	20	57	69	40
Kettering Town	42	12	9	21	53	67	37
Yeovil Town	42	12	8	22	55	77	35
Bangor City	42	10	6	26	54	82	29
Trowbridge Town	42	5	7	30	33	87	19

2 points awarded for a Home win, 3 points awarded for an Away win,
1 point awarded for any Draw

1984-85

Wealdstone	42	20	10	12	64	54	62
Nuneaton Borough	42	19	14	9	85	53	58
Dartford	42	17	13	12	57	48	57
Bath City	42	21	9	12	52	49	57
Altrincham	42	21	6	15	63	47	56
Scarborough	42	17	13	12	69	62	54
Enfield	42	17	13	12	84	61	53
Kidderminster Harriers	42	17	8	17	79	77	51
Northwich Victoria	42	16	11	15	50	46	50
Telford United	42	15	14	13	59	54	49
Frickley Athletic	42	18	7	17	65	71	49
Kettering Town	42	15	12	15	68	59	48
Maidstone United	42	15	13	14	58	51	48
Runcorn	42	13	15	14	48	47	48
Barnet	42	15	11	16	59	52	47
Weymouth	42	15	13	14	70	66	45
Boston United	42	15	10	17	69	69	45
Barrow	42	11	16	15	47	57	43
Dagenham	42	13	10	19	47	67	41
Worcester City	42	12	9	21	55	84	38
Gateshead	42	9	12	21	51	82	33
Yeovil Town	42	6	11	25	44	87	25

2 points awarded for a Home win, 3 points awarded for an Away win,
1 point awarded for any Draw.   Gateshead had 1 point deducted

1985-86

Enfield	42	27	10	5	94	47	76
Frickley Athletic	42	25	10	7	78	50	69
Kidderminster Harriers	42	24	7	11	99	62	67
Altrincham	42	22	11	9	70	49	63
Weymouth	42	19	15	8	75	60	61
Runcorn	42	19	14	9	70	44	60
Stafford Rangers	42	19	13	10	61	54	60
Telford United	42	18	10	14	68	66	51
Kettering Town	42	15	15	12	55	53	49
Wealdstone	42	16	9	17	57	56	47
Cheltenham Town	42	16	11	15	69	69	46
Bath City	42	13	11	18	53	54	45
Boston United	42	16	7	19	66	76	44
Barnet	42	13	11	18	56	60	41
Scarborough	42	13	11	18	54	66	40
Northwich Victoria	42	10	12	20	42	54	37
Maidstone United	42	9	16	17	57	66	36
Nuneaton Borough	42	13	5	24	58	73	36
Dagenham	42	10	12	20	48	66	36
Wycombe Wanderers	42	10	13	19	55	84	36
Dartford	42	8	9	25	51	82	26
Barrow	42	7	8	27	41	86	24

2 points awarded for a Home win; 3 points awarded for an Away win; 1 point awarded for any Draw

1986-87

Scarborough	42	27	10	5	64	33	91
Barnet	42	25	10	7	86	39	85
Maidstone United	42	21	10	11	71	48	73
Enfield	42	21	7	14	66	47	70
Altrincham	42	18	15	9	66	53	69
Boston United	42	21	6	15	82	74	69
Sutton United	42	19	11	12	81	51	68
Runcorn	42	18	13	11	71	58	67
Telford United	42	18	10	14	69	59	64
Bath City	42	17	12	13	63	62	63
Cheltenham Town	42	16	13	13	64	50	61
Kidderminster Harriers	42	17	4	21	77	81	55
Stafford Rangers	42	14	11	17	58	60	53
Weymouth	42	13	12	17	68	77	51
Dagenham	42	14	7	21	56	72	49
Kettering Town	42	12	11	19	54	66	47
Northwich Victoria	42	10	14	18	53	69	44
Nuneaton Borough	42	10	14	18	48	73	44
Wealdstone	42	11	10	21	50	70	43
Welling United	42	10	10	22	61	84	40
Frickley Athletic	42	7	11	24	47	82	32
Gateshead	42	6	13	23	48	95	31

1987-88

Lincoln City	42	24	10	8	86	48	82
Barnet	42	23	11	8	93	45	80
Kettering Town	42	22	9	11	68	48	75
Runcorn	42	21	11	10	68	47	74
Telford United	42	20	10	12	65	50	70
Stafford Rangers	42	20	9	13	79	58	69
Kidderminster Harriers	42	18	15	9	75	66	69
Sutton United	42	16	18	8	77	54	66
Maidstone United	42	18	9	15	79	64	63
Weymouth	42	18	9	15	53	43	63
Macclesfield Town	42	18	9	15	64	62	63
Enfield	42	15	10	17	68	78	55
Cheltenham Town	42	11	20	11	64	67	53
Altrincham	42	14	10	18	59	59	52
Fisher Athletic	42	13	13	16	58	61	52
Boston United	42	14	7	21	60	75	49
Northwich Victoria	42	10	17	15	46	57	47
Wycombe Wanderers	42	11	13	18	50	76	46
Welling United	42	11	9	22	50	72	42
Bath City	42	9	10	23	48	76	37
Wealdstone	42	5	17	20	39	76	32
Dagenham	42	5	6	31	37	104	21

1988-89

Maidstone United	40	25	9	6	92	46	84
Kettering Town	40	23	7	10	56	39	76
Boston United	40	22	8	10	61	51	74
Wycombe Wanderers	40	20	11	9	68	52	71
Kidderminster Harriers	40	21	6	13	68	57	69
Runcorn	40	19	8	13	77	53	65
Macclesfield Town	40	17	10	13	63	57	61
Barnet	40	18	7	15	64	69	61
Yeovil Town	40	15	11	14	68	67	56
Northwich Victoria	40	14	11	15	64	65	53
Welling United	40	14	11	15	45	46	53
Sutton United	40	12	15	13	64	54	51
Enfield	40	14	8	18	62	67	50
Altrincham	40	13	10	17	51	61	49
Cheltenham Town	40	12	12	16	55	58	48
Telford United	40	13	9	18	37	43	48
Chorley	40	13	6	21	57	71	45
Fisher Athletic	40	10	11	19	55	65	41
Stafford Rangers	40	11	7	22	49	74	40
Aylesbury United	40	9	9	22	43	71	36
Weymouth	40	7	10	23	37	70	31
Newport County	29	4	7	18	31	62	19

Newport County expelled from League – their record was deleted.

1989-90

Darlington	42	26	9	7	76	25	87
Barnet	42	26	7	9	81	41	85
Runcorn	42	19	13	10	79	62	70
Macclesfield Town	42	17	15	10	56	41	66
Kettering Town	42	18	12	12	66	53	66
Welling United	42	18	10	14	62	50	64
Yeovil Town	42	17	12	13	62	54	63
Sutton United	42	19	6	17	68	64	63
Merthyr Tydfil	42	16	14	12	67	63	62
Wycombe Wanderers	42	17	10	15	64	56	61
Cheltenham Town	42	16	11	15	58	60	59
Telford United	42	15	13	14	56	63	58
Kidderminster Harriers	42	15	9	18	64	67	54
Barrow	42	12	16	14	51	67	52
Northwich Victoria	42	15	5	22	51	67	50
Altrincham	42	12	13	17	49	48	49
Stafford Rangers	42	12	12	18	50	62	48
Boston United	42	13	8	21	48	67	47
Fisher Athletic	42	13	7	22	55	78	46
Chorley	42	13	6	23	42	67	45
Farnborough Town	42	10	12	20	60	73	42
Enfield	42	10	6	26	52	89	36

1990-91

Barnet	42	26	9	7	103	52	87
Colchester United	42	25	10	7	68	35	85
Altrincham	42	23	13	6	87	46	82
Kettering Town	42	23	11	8	67	45	80
Wycombe Wanderers	42	21	11	10	75	46	74
Telford United	42	20	7	15	62	52	67
Macclesfield Town	42	17	12	13	63	52	63
Runcorn	42	16	10	16	69	67	58
Merthyr Tydfil	42	16	9	17	62	61	57
Barrow	42	15	12	15	59	65	57
Welling United	42	13	15	14	55	57	54
Northwich Victoria	42	13	13	16	65	75	52
Kidderminster Harrier	42	14	10	18	56	67	52
Yeovil Town	42	13	11	18	58	58	50
Stafford Rangers	42	12	14	16	48	51	50
Cheltenham Town	42	12	12	18	54	72	48
Gateshead	42	14	6	22	52	92	48
Boston United	42	12	11	19	55	69	47
Slough Town	42	13	6	23	51	80	45
Bath City	42	10	12	20	55	61	42
Sutton United	42	10	9	23	62	82	39
Fisher Athletic	42	5	15	22	38	79	30

1991-92

Team							
Colchester United	42	28	10	4	98	40	94
Wycombe Wanderers	42	30	4	8	84	35	94
Kettering Town	42	20	13	9	72	50	73
Merthyr Tydfil	42	18	14	10	59	56	68
Farnborough Town	42	18	13	12	68	53	66
Telford United	42	19	7	16	62	66	64
Redbridge Forest	42	18	9	15	69	56	63
Boston United	42	18	9	15	71	66	63
Bath City	42	16	12	14	54	51	60
Witton Albion	42	16	10	16	63	60	58
Northwich Victoria	42	16	6	20	63	58	54
Welling United	42	14	12	16	69	79	54
Macclesfield Town	42	13	13	16	50	50	52
Gateshead	42	12	13	18	49	57	48
Yeovil Town	42	11	14	17	40	49	47
Runcorn	42	11	13	18	50	63	46
Stafford Rangers	42	10	16	16	41	59	46
Altrincham	42	11	12	19	61	82	45
Kidderminster Harriers	42	12	9	21	56	77	45
Slough Town	42	13	6	23	56	82	45
Cheltenham Town	42	10	13	19	56	83	43
Barrow	42	8	14	20	52	72	38

1992-93

Team							
Wycombe Wanderers	42	24	11	7	84	37	83
Bromsgrove Rovers	42	18	14	10	67	49	68
Dagenham & Redbridge	42	19	11	12	75	47	67
Yeovil Town	42	18	12	12	59	49	66
Slough Town	42	18	11	13	60	55	65
Stafford Rangers	42	18	10	14	55	47	64
Bath City	42	15	14	13	53	46	59
Woking	42	17	8	17	58	62	59
Kidderminster Harriers	42	14	16	12	60	60	58
Altrincham	42	15	13	14	49	52	58
Northwich Victoria	42	16	8	18	68	55	56
Stalybridge Celtic	42	13	17	12	48	55	56
Kettering Town	42	14	13	15	61	63	55
Gateshead	42	14	10	18	53	56	52
Telford United	42	14	10	18	55	60	52
Merthyr Tydfil	42	14	10	18	51	79	52
Witton Albion	42	11	17	14	62	65	50
Macclesfield	42	12	13	17	40	50	49
Runcorn	42	13	10	19	58	76	49
Welling United	42	12	12	18	57	72	48
Farnborough Town	42	12	11	19	68	87	47
Boston United	42	9	13	20	50	69	40

Dagenham & Redbridge had 1 point deducted

1993-94

Team							
Kidderminster Harriers	42	22	9	11	63	35	75
Kettering Town	42	18	15	8	46	24	72
Woking	42	18	13	11	58	58	67
Southport	42	18	12	12	57	51	66
Runcorn	42	14	19	9	63	57	61
Dagenham & Redbridge	42	15	14	13	62	54	59
Macclesfield Town	42	16	11	15	48	49	59
Dover Athletic	42	17	7	18	48	49	58
Stafford Rangers	42	14	15	13	56	52	57
Altrincham	42	16	9	17	41	42	57
Gateshead	42	15	12	15	45	53	57
Bath City	42	13	17	12	47	38	56
Halifax Town	42	13	16	13	55	49	55
Stalybridge Celtic	42	14	12	16	54	55	54
Northwich Victoria	42	11	19	12	44	45	52
Welling United	42	13	12	17	47	49	51
Telford United	42	13	12	17	41	49	51
Bromsgrove Rovers	42	12	15	15	54	66	51
Yeovil Town	42	14	9	19	49	62	51
Merthyr Tydfil	42	12	15	15	60	61	49
Slough Town	42	11	14	17	44	58	47
Witton Albion	42	7	13	22	37	63	44

Merthyr Tydfil had 2 points deducted

1994-95

Team							
Macclesfield Town	42	24	8	10	70	40	80
Woking	42	21	12	9	76	54	75
Southport	42	21	9	12	68	50	72
Altrincham Town	42	20	8	14	77	60	68
Stevenage Borough	42	20	7	15	68	49	67
Kettering Town	42	19	10	13	73	56	67
Gateshead	42	19	10	13	61	53	67
Halifax Town	42	17	12	13	68	54	63
Runcorn	42	16	10	16	59	71	58
Northwich Victoria	42	14	15	13	77	66	57
Kidderminster Harriers	42	16	9	17	63	61	57
Bath City	42	15	12	15	55	56	57
Bromsgrove Rovers	42	14	3	15	66	69	55
Farnborough Town	42	15	10	17	45	64	55
Dagenham & Redbridge	42	13	13	16	56	69	52
Dover Athletic	42	11	16	15	48	55	49
Welling United	42	13	10	19	57	74	49
Stalybridge Celtic	42	11	14	17	52	72	47
Telford United	42	10	16	16	53	62	46
Merthyr Tydfil	42	11	11	20	53	63	44
Stafford Rangers	42	9	11	22	53	79	38
Yeovil Town	42	8	14	20	50	71	37

Yeovil Town had 1 point deducted for fielding an ineligible player

1995-96

Team							
Stevenage Borough	42	27	10	5	101	44	91
Woking	42	25	8	9	83	54	83
Hednesford Town	42	23	7	12	71	46	76
Macclesfield Town	42	22	9	11	66	49	75
Gateshead	42	18	13	11	58	46	67
Southport	42	18	12	12	77	64	66
Kidderminster Harriers	42	18	10	14	78	66	64
Northwich Victoria	42	16	12	14	72	64	60
Morecambe	42	17	8	17	78	72	59
Farnborough Town	42	15	14	13	63	58	59
Bromsgrove Rovers	42	15	14	13	59	57	59
Altrincham	42	15	13	14	59	64	58
Telford United	42	15	10	17	51	56	55
Stalybridge Celtic	42	16	7	19	59	68	55
Halifax Town	42	13	13	16	49	63	52
Kettering Town	42	13	9	20	68	84	48
Slough Town	42	13	8	21	63	76	47
Bath City	42	13	7	22	45	66	46
Welling United	42	10	15	17	42	53	45
Dover Athletic	42	11	7	24	51	74	40
Runcorn	42	9	8	25	48	87	35
Dagenham & Redbridge	42	7	12	23	43	73	33

1996-97

Team							
Macclesfield Town	42	27	9	6	80	30	90
Kidderminster Harriers	42	26	7	9	84	42	85
Stevenage Borough	42	24	10	8	87	53	82
Morecambe	42	19	9	14	69	56	66
Woking	42	18	10	14	71	63	64
Northwich Victoria	42	17	12	13	61	54	63
Farnborough Town	42	16	13	13	58	53	61
Hednesford Town	42	16	12	14	52	50	60
Telford United	42	16	10	16	46	56	58
Gateshead	42	15	11	16	59	63	56
Southport	42	15	10	17	51	61	55
Rushden & Diamonds	42	14	11	17	61	63	53
Stalybridge Celtic	42	14	10	18	53	58	52
Kettering Town	42	14	9	19	53	62	51
Hayes	42	12	14	16	54	55	50
Slough Town	42	12	14	16	62	65	50
Dover Athletic	42	12	14	16	57	68	50
Welling United	42	13	9	20	50	60	48
Halifax Town	42	12	12	18	55	74	48
Bath City	42	12	11	19	53	80	47
Bromsgrove Rovers	42	12	5	25	41	67	41
Altrincham	42	9	12	21	49	73	39

1997-98

Team	P	W	D	L	F	A	Pts
Halifax Town	42	25	12	5	74	43	87
Cheltenham Town	42	23	9	10	63	43	78
Woking	42	22	8	12	72	46	74
Rushden & Diamonds	42	23	5	14	79	57	74
Morecambe	42	21	10	11	77	64	73
Hereford United	42	18	13	11	56	49	67
Hednesford Town	42	18	12	12	59	50	66
Slough Town	42	18	10	14	58	49	64
Northwich Victoria	42	15	15	12	63	59	60
Welling United	42	17	9	16	64	62	60
Yeovil Town	42	17	8	17	73	63	59
Hayes	42	16	10	16	62	52	58
Dover Athletic	42	15	10	17	60	70	55
Kettering Town	42	13	13	16	53	60	52
Stevenage Borough	42	13	12	17	59	63	51
Southport	42	13	11	18	56	58	50
Kidderminster Harriers	42	11	14	17	56	63	49
Farnborough Town	42	12	8	22	56	70	44
Leek Town	42	10	14	18	52	67	44
Telford United	42	10	12	20	53	76	42
Gateshead	42	8	11	23	51	87	35
Stalybridge Celtic	42	7	8	27	48	93	29

1998-99

Team	P	W	D	L	F	A	Pts
Cheltenham Town	42	22	14	6	71	36	80
Kettering Town	42	22	10	10	58	37	76
Hayes	42	22	8	12	63	50	74
Rushden & Diamonds	42	20	12	10	71	42	72
Yeovil Town	42	20	11	11	68	54	71
Stevenage Borough	42	17	17	8	62	45	68
Northwich Victoria	42	19	9	14	60	51	66
Kingstonian	42	17	13	12	50	49	64
Woking	42	18	9	15	51	45	62
Hednesford Town	42	15	16	11	49	44	61
Dover Athletic	42	15	13	14	54	48	58
Forest Green Rovers	42	15	13	14	55	50	58
Hereford United	42	15	10	17	49	46	55
Morecambe	42	15	8	19	60	76	53
Kidderminster Harriers	42	14	9	19	56	52	51
Doncaster Rovers	42	12	12	18	51	55	48
Telford United	42	10	16	16	44	60	46
Southport	42	10	15	17	47	59	45
Barrow	42	11	10	21	40	63	43
Welling United	42	9	14	19	44	65	41
Leek Town	42	8	8	26	48	76	32
Farnborough United	42	7	11	24	41	89	32

1999-2000

Team	P	W	D	L	F	A	Pts
Kidderminster Harriers	42	26	7	9	75	40	85
Rushden & Diamonds	42	21	13	8	71	42	76
Morecambe	42	18	16	8	70	48	70
Scarborough	42	19	12	11	60	35	69
Kingstonian	42	20	7	15	58	44	67
Dover Athletic	42	18	12	12	65	56	66
Yeovil Town	42	18	10	14	60	63	64
Hereford United	42	15	14	13	61	52	59
Southport	42	15	13	14	55	56	58
Stevenage Borough	42	16	9	17	60	54	57
Hayes	42	16	8	18	57	58	56
Doncaster Rovers	42	15	9	18	46	48	54
Kettering Town	42	12	16	14	44	50	52
Woking	42	13	13	16	45	53	52
Nuneaton Borough	42	12	15	15	49	53	51
Telford United	42	14	9	19	56	66	51
Hednesford Town	42	15	6	21	45	68	51
Northwich Victoria	42	13	12	17	53	78	51
Forest Green Rovers	42	13	8	21	54	63	47
Welling United	42	13	8	21	54	66	47
Altrincham	42	9	19	14	51	60	46
Sutton United	42	8	10	24	39	75	34

2000-2001

Team	P	W	D	L	F	A	Pts
Rushden & Diamonds	42	25	11	6	78	36	86
Yeovil Town	42	24	8	10	73	50	80
Dagenham & Redbridge	42	23	8	11	71	54	77
Southport	42	20	9	13	58	46	69
Leigh RMI	42	19	11	12	63	57	68
Telford United	42	19	8	15	51	51	65
Stevenage Borough	42	15	18	9	71	61	63
Chester City	42	16	14	12	49	43	62
Doncaster Rovers	42	15	13	14	47	43	58
Scarborough	42	14	16	12	56	54	58
Hereford United	42	14	15	13	60	46	57
Boston United	42	13	17	12	74	63	56
Nuneaton Borough	42	13	15	14	60	60	54
Woking	42	13	15	14	52	57	54
Dover Athletic	42	14	11	17	54	56	53
Forest Green Rovers	42	11	15	16	43	54	48
Northwich Victoria	42	11	13	18	49	67	46
Hayes	42	12	10	20	44	71	46
Morecambe	42	11	12	19	64	66	45
Kettering Town	42	11	10	21	46	62	43
Kingstonian	42	8	10	24	47	73	34
Hednesford Town	42	5	13	24	46	86	28

2001-2002

Team	P	W	D	L	F	A	Pts
Boston United	42	25	9	8	84	42	84
Dagenham & Redbridge	42	24	12	6	70	47	84
Yeovil Town	42	19	13	10	66	53	70
Doncaster Rovers	42	18	13	11	68	46	67
Barnet	42	19	10	13	64	48	67
Morecambe	42	17	11	14	63	67	62
Farnborough Town	42	18	7	17	66	54	61
Margate	42	14	16	12	59	53	58
Telford United	42	14	15	13	63	58	57
Nuneaton Borough	42	16	9	17	57	57	57
Stevenage Borough	42	15	10	17	57	60	55
Scarborough	42	14	14	14	55	63	55
Northwich Victoria	42	16	7	19	57	70	55
Chester City	42	15	9	18	54	51	54
Southport	42	13	14	15	53	49	53
Leigh RMI	42	15	8	19	56	58	53
Hereford United	42	14	10	18	50	53	52
Forest Green Rovers	42	12	15	15	54	76	51
Woking	42	13	9	20	59	70	48
Hayes	42	13	5	24	53	80	44
Stalybridge Celtic	42	11	10	21	40	69	43
Dover Athletic	42	11	6	25	41	65	39

2002-2003

Team	P	W	D	L	F	A	Pts
Yeovil Town	42	28	11	3	100	37	95
Morecambe	42	23	9	10	86	42	78
Doncaster Rovers	42	22	12	8	73	47	78
Chester City	42	21	12	9	59	31	75
Dagenham & Redbridge	42	21	9	12	71	59	72
Hereford United	42	19	7	16	64	51	64
Scarborough	42	18	10	14	63	54	64
Halifax Town	42	18	10	14	50	51	64
Forest Green Rovers	42	17	8	17	61	62	59
Margate	42	15	11	16	60	66	56
Barnet	42	13	14	15	65	68	53
Stevenage Borough	42	14	10	18	61	55	52
Farnborough Town	42	13	12	17	57	56	51
Northwich Victoria	42	13	12	17	66	72	51
Telford United	42	14	7	21	54	69	49
Burton Albion	42	13	10	19	52	77	49
Gravesend & Northfleet	42	12	12	18	62	73	48
Leigh RMI	42	14	6	22	44	71	48
Woking	42	11	14	17	52	81	47
Nuneaton Borough	42	13	7	22	51	78	46
Southport	42	11	12	19	54	69	45
Kettering Town	42	8	7	27	37	73	31

2003-2004

Chester City	42	27	11	4	85	34	92
Hereford United	42	28	7	7	103	44	91
Shrewsbury Town	42	20	14	8	67	42	74
Barnet	42	19	14	9	60	46	71
Aldershot Town	42	20	10	12	80	67	70
Exeter City	42	19	12	11	71	57	69
Morecambe	42	20	7	15	66	66	67
Stevenage Borough	42	18	9	15	58	52	63
Woking	42	15	16	11	65	52	61
Accrington Stanley	42	15	13	14	68	61	58
Gravesend & Northfleet	42	14	15	13	69	66	57
Telford United	42	15	10	17	49	51	55
Dagenham & Redbridge	42	15	9	18	59	64	54
Burton Albion	42	15	7	20	57	59	51
Scarborough	42	12	15	15	51	54	51
Margate	42	14	9	19	56	64	51
Tamworth	42	13	10	19	49	68	49
Forest Green Rovers	42	12	12	18	58	80	48
Halifax Town	42	12	8	22	43	65	44
Farnborough Town	42	10	9	23	53	74	39
Leigh RMI	42	7	8	27	46	97	29
Northwich Victoria	42	4	11	27	30	80	23

Burton Albion had 1 point deducted.

2004-2005

Conference National

Barnet	42	26	8	8	90	44	86
Hereford United	42	21	11	10	68	41	74
Carlisle United	42	20	13	9	74	37	73
Aldershot Town	42	21	10	11	68	52	73
Stevenage Borough	42	22	6	14	65	52	72
Exeter City	42	20	11	11	71	50	71
Morecambe	42	19	14	9	69	50	71
Woking	42	18	14	10	58	45	68
Halifax Town	42	19	9	14	74	56	66
Accrington Stanley	42	18	11	13	72	58	65
Dagenham & Redbridge	42	19	8	15	68	60	65
Crawley Town	42	16	9	17	50	50	57
Scarborough	42	14	14	14	60	46	56
Gravesend & Northfleet	42	13	11	18	58	64	50
Tamworth	42	14	11	17	53	63	50
Burton Albion	42	13	11	18	50	66	50
York City	42	11	10	21	39	66	43
Canvey Island	42	9	15	18	53	65	42
Northwich Victoria	42	14	10	18	58	72	42
Forest Green Rovers	42	6	15	21	41	81	33
Farnborough Town	42	6	11	25	35	89	29
Leigh RMI	42	4	6	32	31	98	18

Northwich Victoria had 10 points deducted.
Tamworth had 3 points deducted.

Conference North

Southport	42	25	9	8	83	45	84
Nuneaton Borough	42	25	6	11	68	45	81
Droylsden	42	24	7	11	82	52	79
Kettering Town	42	21	7	14	56	50	70
Altrincham	42	19	12	11	66	49	69
Harrogate Town	42	19	11	12	62	49	68
Worcester City	42	16	12	14	59	53	60
Stafford Rangers	42	14	17	11	52	44	59
Redditch United	42	18	8	16	65	59	59
Hucknall Town	42	15	14	13	59	57	59
Gainsborough Trinity	42	16	9	17	55	55	57
Hinckley United	42	15	11	16	55	62	56
Lancaster City	42	14	12	16	51	59	54
Alfreton Town	42	15	8	19	53	55	53
Vauxhall Motors	42	14	11	17	48	57	53
Barrow	42	14	10	18	50	64	52
Worksop Town	42	16	12	14	59	59	50
Moor Green	42	13	10	19	55	64	49
Stalybridge Celtic	42	12	12	18	52	70	48
Runcorn FC Halton	42	10	12	20	44	63	42
Ashton United	42	8	9	25	46	79	33
Bradford Park Avenue	42	5	9	28	37	70	24

Worksop Town had 10 points deducted.
Redditch United had 3 points deducted.

Conference South

Grays Athletic	42	30	8	4	118	31	98
Cambridge City	42	23	6	13	60	44	75
Thurrock	42	21	6	15	61	56	69
Lewes	42	18	11	13	73	64	65
Eastbourne Borough	42	18	10	14	65	47	64
Basingstoke Town	42	19	6	17	57	52	63
Weymouth	42	17	11	14	62	59	62
Dorchester Town	42	17	11	14	77	81	62
Bognor Regis Town	42	17	9	16	70	65	60
Bishop's Stortford	42	17	8	17	70	66	59
Weston-super-Mare	42	15	13	14	55	60	58
Hayes	42	15	11	16	55	57	56
Havant & Waterlooville	42	16	7	19	64	69	55
St. Albans City	42	16	6	20	64	76	54
Sutton United	42	14	11	17	60	71	53
Welling United	42	15	7	20	64	68	52
Hornchurch	42	17	10	15	71	63	51
Newport County	42	13	11	18	56	61	50
Carshalton Athletic	42	13	9	20	44	72	48
Maidenhead United	42	12	10	20	54	81	46
Margate	42	12	8	22	54	75	34
Redbridge	42	11	3	28	50	86	33

Horchurch and Margate had 10 points deducted.
Redbridge had 3 points deducted.

2005-2006

Conference National

Accrington Stanley	42	28	7	7	76	45	91
Hereford United	42	22	14	6	59	33	80
Grays Athletic	42	21	13	8	94	55	76
Halifax Town	42	21	12	9	55	40	75
Morecambe	42	22	8	12	68	41	74
Stevenage Borough	42	19	12	11	62	47	69
Exeter City	42	18	9	15	65	48	63
York City	42	17	12	13	63	48	63
Burton Albion	42	16	12	14	50	52	60
Dagenham & Redbridge	42	16	10	16	63	59	58
Woking	42	14	14	14	58	47	56
Cambridge United	42	15	10	17	51	57	55
Aldershot Town	42	16	6	20	61	74	54
Canvey Island	42	13	12	17	47	58	51
Kidderminster Harriers	42	13	11	18	39	55	50
Gravesend & Northfleet	42	13	10	19	45	57	49
Crawley Town	42	12	11	19	48	55	47
Southport	42	10	10	22	36	68	40
Forest Green Rovers	42	8	14	20	49	62	38
Tamworth	42	8	14	20	32	63	38
Scarborough	42	9	10	23	40	66	37
Altrincham	42	10	11	21	40	71	23

Altrincham had 18 points deducted for fielding an ineligible player but were not relegated after Canvey Island withdrew from the League and Scarborough were relegated for a breach of the rules.

Conference North

Northwich Victoria	42	29	5	8	97	49	92
Stafford Rangers	42	25	10	7	68	34	85
Nuneaton Borough	42	22	11	9	68	43	77
Droylsden	42	20	12	10	80	56	72
Harrogate Town	42	22	5	15	66	56	71
Kettering Town	42	19	10	13	63	49	67
Stalybridge Celtic	42	19	9	14	74	54	66
Worcester City	42	16	14	12	58	46	62
Moor Green	42	15	16	11	67	64	61
Hinckley United	42	14	16	12	60	55	58
Hyde United (P)	42	15	11	16	68	61	56
Hucknall Town	42	14	13	15	56	55	55
Workington (P)	42	14	13	15	60	62	55
Barrow	42	12	11	19	62	67	47
Lancaster City	42	12	11	19	52	66	47
Gainsborough Trinity	42	11	13	18	45	65	46
Alfreton Town	42	10	15	17	46	58	45
Vauxhall Motors	42	12	7	23	50	71	43
Worksop Town	42	10	11	21	46	71	41
Redditch United	42	9	12	21	53	78	39
Leigh RMI	42	9	13	20	45	79	39
Hednesford Town	42	7	14	21	42	87	35

Leigh RMI had 1 point deducted.

Conference South

Weymouth	42	30	4	8	80	34	90
St. Albans City	42	27	5	10	94	47	86
Farnborough Town	42	23	9	10	65	41	78
Lewes	42	21	10	11	78	57	73
Histon	42	21	8	13	70	56	71
Havant & Waterlooville	42	21	10	11	64	48	70
Cambridge City	42	20	10	12	78	46	67
Eastleigh	42	21	3	18	65	58	66
Welling United	42	16	17	9	58	44	65
Thurrock	42	16	10	16	60	60	58
Dorchester Town	42	16	7	19	60	72	55
Bognor Regis Town	42	12	13	17	54	55	49
Sutton United	42	13	10	19	48	61	49
Weston-super-Mare	42	14	7	21	57	88	49
Bishop's Stortford	42	11	15	16	55	63	48
Yeading	42	13	8	21	47	62	47
Eastbourne Borough	42	10	16	16	51	61	46
Newport County	42	12	8	22	50	67	44
Basingstoke Town	42	12	8	22	47	72	44
Hayes	42	11	9	22	47	60	42
Carshalton Athletic	42	8	16	18	42	68	40
Maidenhead United	42	8	9	25	49	99	31

Weymouth had 4 points deducted.
Havant & Waterlooville and Cambridge City had 3 points deducted.
Maidenhead United had 2 points deducted.

Conference South

Histon	42	30	4	8	85	44	94
Salisbury City	42	21	12	9	65	37	75
Braintree Town	42	21	11	10	51	38	74
Havant & Waterlooville	42	20	13	9	75	46	73
Bishop's Stortford	42	21	10	11	72	61	73
Newport County	42	21	7	14	83	57	70
Eastbourne Borough	42	18	15	9	58	42	69
Welling United	42	21	6	15	65	51	69
Lewes	42	15	17	10	67	52	62
Fisher Athletic	42	15	11	16	77	77	56
Farnborough Town	42	19	8	15	59	52	55
Bognor Regis Town	42	13	13	16	56	62	52
Cambridge City	42	15	7	20	44	52	52
Sutton United	42	14	9	19	58	63	51
Eastleigh	42	11	15	16	48	53	48
Yeading	42	12	9	21	56	78	45
Dorchester Town	42	11	12	19	49	77	45
Thurrock	42	11	11	20	58	79	44
Basingstoke Town	42	9	16	17	46	58	43
Hayes	42	11	10	21	47	73	43
Weston-super-Mare	42	8	11	23	49	77	35
Bedford Town	42	8	7	27	43	82	31

Farnborough Town had 10 points deducted.

2006-2007

Conference National

Dagenham & Redbridge	46	28	11	7	93	48	95
Oxford United	46	22	15	9	66	33	81
Morecambe	46	23	12	11	64	46	81
York City	46	23	11	12	65	45	80
Exeter City	46	22	12	12	67	48	78
Burton Albion	46	22	9	15	52	47	75
Gravesend & Northfleet	46	21	11	14	63	56	74
Stevenage Borough	46	20	10	16	76	66	70
Aldershot Town	46	18	11	17	64	62	65
Kidderminster Harriers	46	17	12	17	43	50	63
Weymouth	46	18	9	19	56	73	63
Rushden & Diamonds	46	17	11	18	58	54	62
Northwich Victoria	46	18	4	24	51	69	58
Forest Green Rovers	46	13	18	15	59	64	57
Woking	46	15	12	19	56	61	57
Halifax Town	46	15	10	21	55	62	55
Cambridge United	46	15	10	21	57	66	55
Crawley Town	46	17	12	17	52	52	53
Grays Athletic	46	13	13	20	56	55	52
Stafford Rangers	46	14	10	22	49	71	52
Altrincham	46	13	12	21	53	67	51
Tamworth	46	13	9	24	43	61	48
Southport	46	11	14	21	57	67	47
St. Alban's City	46	10	10	26	57	89	40

Crawley Town had 10 points deducted.

Conference North

Droylsden	42	23	9	10	85	55	78
Kettering Town	42	20	13	9	75	58	73
Workington	42	20	10	12	61	46	70
Hinckley United	42	19	12	11	68	54	69
Farsley Celtic	42	19	11	12	58	51	68
Harrogate Town	42	18	13	11	58	41	67
Blyth Spartans	42	19	9	14	57	49	66
Hyde United	42	18	11	13	79	62	65
Worcester City	42	16	14	12	67	54	62
Nuneaton Borough	42	15	15	12	54	45	60
Moor Green	42	16	11	15	53	51	59
Gainsborough Trinity	42	15	11	16	51	57	56
Hucknall Town	42	15	9	18	69	69	54
Alfreton Town	42	14	12	16	44	50	54
Vauxhall Motors	42	12	15	15	62	64	51
Barrow	42	12	14	16	47	48	50
Leigh RMI	42	13	10	19	47	61	49
Stalybridge Celtic	42	13	10	19	64	81	49
Redditch United	42	11	15	16	61	68	48
Scarborough	42	13	16	13	50	45	45
Worksop Town	42	12	9	21	44	62	45
Lancaster City	42	2	5	35	27	110	1

Scarborough and Lancaster City each had 10 points deducted.

ISTHMIAN LEAGUE

1905-06

London Caledonians	10	7	1	2	25	8	15
Clapton	10	6	1	3	11	13	13
Casuals	10	3	4	3	14	14	10
Civil Service	10	4	1	5	16	20	9
Ealing Association	10	3	2	5	15	19	8
Ilford	10	1	3	6	5	12	5

1906-07

Ilford	10	8	2	0	26	9	18
London Caledonians	10	6	0	4	19	14	12
Clapton	10	4	3	3	18	11	11
Civil Service	10	3	1	6	11	19	7
Ealing Association	10	3	1	6	12	22	7
Casuals	10	2	1	7	15	26	5

1907-08

London Caledonians	10	5	2	3	20	15	12
Clapton	10	4	3	3	24	14	11
Ilford	10	5	1	4	28	22	11
Oxford City	10	5	1	4	20	20	11
Dulwich Hamlet	10	3	2	5	15	18	8
West Norwood	10	3	1	6	13	31	7

1908-09

Bromley	18	11	1	6	42	29	23
Leytonstone	18	9	4	5	43	31	22
Ilford	18	9	4	5	37	36	22
Dulwich Hamlet	18	9	2	7	39	30	20
Clapton	18	8	4	6	34	32	20
Oxford City	18	6	4	8	29	32	16
Nunhead	18	7	2	9	31	35	16
Shepherd's Bush	18	6	3	9	26	44	15
London Caledonians	18	4	6	8	25	34	14
West Norwood	18	5	2	11	40	43	12

1909-10

Bromley	18	11	4	3	32	10	26
Clapton	18	10	4	4	56	19	24
Nunhead	18	10	4	4	49	26	24
Ilford	18	10	3	5	31	17	23
Dulwich Hamlet	18	8	4	6	26	26	20
Leytonstone	18	7	3	8	44	46	17
Oxford City	18	5	4	9	28	45	14
London Caledonians	18	5	3	10	19	40	13
West Norwood	18	5	2	11	28	54	12
Shepherd's Bush	18	2	3	13	23	55	7

1910-11

Clapton	18	11	4	3	39	19	26
Leytonstone	18	12	1	5	47	30	25
Dulwich Hamlet	18	8	5	5	28	22	21
Oxford City	18	7	4	7	32	43	18
Ilford	18	8	1	9	41	32	17
Shepherd's Bush	18	7	3	8	31	27	17
Bromley	18	8	4	6	32	27	16
Nunhead	18	5	4	9	32	36	14
West Norwood	18	4	5	9	24	43	13
London Caledonians	18	3	3	12	18	45	9

Bromley had 4 points deducted

1911-12

London Caledonians	20	11	7	2	39	25	29
Ilford	20	11	3	6	37	24	25
Nunhead	20	10	5	5	36	30	25
Dulwich Hamlet	20	8	5	7	33	23	21
West Norwood	20	9	3	8	38	38	21
Clapton	20	7	5	8	37	37	19
Woking	20	7	5	8	38	41	19
Shepherd's Bush	20	5	6	9	39	49	16
Leytonstone	20	5	6	9	28	38	16
Oxford City	20	5	5	10	33	36	15
Tunbridge Wells	20	5	4	11	23	40	14

1912-13

London Caledonians	20	14	5	1	38	12	33
Leytonstone	20	12	3	5	45	20	27
Nunhead	20	12	3	5	36	23	27
Clapton	20	7	7	6	23	20	21
Dulwich Hamlet	20	8	4	8	34	28	20
Woking	20	7	5	8	33	40	19
Oxford City	20	6	6	8	23	39	18
Ilford	20	6	5	9	27	37	17
Shepherd's Bush	20	5	5	10	26	38	15
Tunbridge Wells	20	5	4	11	22	36	14
West Norwood	20	3	3	14	23	37	9

1913-14

London Caledonians	20	12	6	2	55	23	30
Nunhead	20	11	6	3	49	27	28
Ilford	20	11	4	5	52	35	26
Dulwich Hamlet	20	10	4	6	34	22	24
New Crusaders	20	10	3	7	40	30	23
Oxford City	20	10	0	10	42	42	20
Leytonstone	20	8	4	8	29	32	20
Clapton	20	8	3	9	29	27	19
Shepherd's Bush	20	7	2	11	24	46	16
West Norwood	20	4	3	13	27	47	11
Woking	20	1	1	18	11	61	3

1919

Leytonstone	8	5	1	2	21	7	11
Ilford	8	4	2	2	22	16	10
Dulwich Hamlet	8	3	2	3	19	17	8
Nunhead	8	3	2	3	18	19	8
Clapton	8	0	3	5	14	35	3

1919-20

Dulwich Hamlet	22	15	3	4	58	16	33
Nunhead	22	14	5	3	48	26	33
Tufnell Park	22	12	4	6	45	32	28
Ilford	22	13	1	8	63	42	27
Oxford City	22	12	3	7	63	51	27
London Caledonians	22	10	3	9	32	30	23
Leytonstone	22	8	3	11	50	43	19
Clapton	22	8	3	11	38	44	19
Civil Service	22	7	4	11	35	40	18
Woking	22	6	3	13	36	42	15
West Norwood	22	5	4	13	19	53	14
Casuals	22	3	2	17	20	88	8

1920-21

Ilford	22	16	4	2	70	24	36
London Caledonians	22	13	5	4	45	17	31
Tufnell Park	22	14	3	5	43	24	31
Nunhead	22	12	5	5	53	33	29
Dulwich Hamlet	22	11	6	5	60	30	28
Oxford City	22	12	3	7	56	38	27
Leytonstone	22	8	6	8	36	29	22
Clapton	22	7	7	8	33	52	21
Civil Service	22	3	7	12	28	45	13
Woking	22	3	5	14	16	43	11
Casuals	22	3	3	16	31	87	9
West Norwood	22	2	2	18	18	67	6

1921-22

Ilford	26	17	4	5	66	34	38
Dulwich Hamlet	26	14	8	4	65	24	36
London Caledonians	26	16	4	6	41	21	36
Nunhead	26	12	5	9	65	41	29
Clapton	26	13	3	10	51	46	29
Tufnell Park	26	10	7	9	44	39	27
Oxford City	26	18	2	12	48	47	26
Wycombe Wanderers	26	18	2	12	61	64	26
Civil Service	26	9	8	9	60	48	26
Woking	26	10	6	10	39	49	26
Leytonstone	26	9	6	11	41	48	24
West Norwood	26	8	5	13	43	57	21
Wimbledon	26	7	4	15	52	56	18
Casuals	26	0	2	24	25	107	2

1922-23

Clapton	26	15	7	4	51	33	37
Nunhead	26	15	5	6	52	32	35
London Caledonians	26	13	7	6	43	26	33
Ilford	26	11	7	8	57	38	29
Casuals	26	12	5	9	68	51	29
Civil Service	26	9	10	7	39	36	28
Wycombe Wanderers	26	11	4	11	61	61	26
Dulwich Hamlet	26	9	7	10	60	44	25
Leytonstone	26	9	7	10	45	56	25
Tufnell Park	26	9	5	12	41	45	23
Wimbledon	26	10	2	14	49	50	22
Woking	26	7	6	13	42	67	20
Oxford City	26	6	5	15	45	68	17
West Norwood	26	5	5	16	25	71	15

1923-24

St Albans City	26	17	5	4	72	38	39
Dulwich Hamlet	26	15	6	5	49	28	36
Clapton	26	14	5	7	73	50	33
Wycombe Wanderers	26	14	5	7	88	65	33
London Caledonians	26	14	3	9	53	49	31
Civil Service	26	12	5	9	52	47	29
Casuals	26	13	1	12	65	54	27
Ilford	26	9	6	11	56	59	24
Nunhead	26	8	8	10	41	46	24
Wimbledon	26	8	4	14	43	62	20
Tufnell Park	26	8	2	16	38	53	18
Woking	26	5	8	13	31	62	18
Oxford City	26	7	2	17	53	74	16
Leytonstone	26	6	4	16	41	68	16

1924-25

London Caledonians	26	18	5	3	76	36	41
Clapton	26	19	1	6	64	34	39
St Albans City	26	16	2	8	69	39	34
Tufnell Park	26	11	4	11	47	41	26
Ilford	26	11	4	11	46	42	26
Leytonstone	26	12	2	12	55	63	26
The Casuals	26	12	1	13	55	58	25
Wycombe Wanderers	26	11	2	13	58	61	24
Civil Service	26	10	4	12	52	64	24
Nunhead	26	9	5	12	45	43	23
Wimbledon	26	10	2	14	50	54	22
Dulwich Hamlet	26	8	5	13	42	57	21
Oxford City	26	9	2	15	38	71	20
Woking	26	5	3	18	33	67	13

1925-26

Dulwich Hamlet	26	20	1	5	80	49	41
London Caledonians	26	18	1	7	81	44	37
Clapton	26	14	4	8	64	50	32
Wycombe Wanderers	26	14	3	9	97	83	31
St Albans City	26	12	6	8	76	54	30
Nunhead	26	13	4	9	49	43	30
Ilford	26	13	2	11	81	70	28
Leytonstone	26	12	1	13	75	63	25
Woking	26	8	6	12	56	73	22
Tufnell Park	26	8	5	13	36	53	21
The Casuals	26	8	4	14	48	61	20
Wimbledon	26	9	1	16	61	77	19
Oxford City	26	8	1	17	48	76	17
Civil Service	26	5	1	20	43	99	11

1926-27

St Albans City	26	20	1	5	96	34	41
Ilford	26	18	0	9	76	57	34
Wimbledon	26	15	3	8	72	45	33
Nunhead	26	11	8	7	51	33	30
Woking	26	12	6	8	68	60	30
London Caledonians	26	11	7	8	58	47	29
Clapton	26	11	4	11	58	60	26
Leytonstone	26	11	1	14	54	78	23
Dulwich Hamlet	26	9	4	13	60	58	22
Wycombe Wanderers	26	10	2	14	59	86	22
Tufnell Park	26	8	4	14	45	55	20
Oxford City	26	7	5	14	46	72	19
The Casuals	26	8	3	15	37	78	19
Civil Service	26	6	4	16	48	65	16

1927-28

St Albans City	26	15	5	6	86	50	35
London Caledonians	26	12	9	5	63	38	33
Ilford	26	14	4	8	72	54	32
Woking	26	13	5	8	72	56	31
Nunhead	26	13	2	11	57	54	28
Wimbledon	26	12	3	11	57	48	27
Leytonstone	26	13	1	12	53	56	27
Clapton	26	8	10	8	52	47	26
Dulwich Hamlet	26	8	9	9	56	49	25
The Casuals	26	8	8	10	54	58	24
Wycombe Wanderers	26	9	5	12	60	69	23
Oxford City	26	7	7	12	36	57	21
Civil Service	26	8	4	14	38	76	20
Tufnell Park	26	4	4	18	38	82	12

1928-29

Nunhead	26	15	6	5	47	35	36
London Caledonians	26	15	4	7	65	33	34
Dulwich Hamlet	26	14	6	6	65	34	34
Wimbledon	26	9	10	7	66	54	28
Ilford	26	12	3	11	67	52	27
Clapton	26	11	5	10	60	55	27
Tufnell Park	26	11	5	10	58	55	27
St Albans City	26	12	3	11	63	69	27
Leytonstone	26	11	3	12	56	79	25
Wycombe Wanderers	26	10	3	13	58	60	23
Oxford City	26	10	3	13	61	71	23
The Casuals	26	8	5	13	49	60	21
Woking	26	8	3	15	39	65	19
Civil Service	26	4	5	17	39	71	13

1929-30

Nunhead	26	19	3	4	69	36	41
Dulwich Hamlet	26	15	6	5	74	39	36
Kingstonian	26	15	4	7	57	37	34
Ilford	26	16	1	9	84	60	33
Woking	26	11	5	10	66	65	27
Wimbledon	26	11	2	13	64	66	24
Wycombe Wanderers	26	10	4	12	49	52	24
The Casuals	26	8	7	11	50	51	23
Oxford City	26	10	3	13	45	60	23
St Albans City	26	9	4	13	54	77	22
Clapton	26	8	4	14	47	57	20
London Caledonians	26	8	3	15	49	69	19
Leytonstone	26	8	3	15	48	68	19
Tufnell Park	26	6	7	13	35	54	19

1930-31

Wimbledon	26	18	6	2	69	37	42
Dulwich Hamlet	26	12	9	5	51	39	33
Wycombe Wanderers	26	12	6	8	67	45	30
The Casuals	26	12	6	8	71	56	30
St Albans City	26	11	7	8	67	66	29
Ilford	26	10	6	10	70	62	26
Oxford City	26	10	5	11	43	48	25
London Caledonians	26	8	8	10	43	53	24
Kingstonian	26	10	4	12	49	64	24
Tufnell Park	26	9	5	12	45	61	23
Nunhead	26	9	4	13	49	54	22
Woking	26	9	4	13	56	63	22
Clapton	26	7	4	15	62	75	18
Leytonstone	26	6	4	16	46	65	16

1931-32

Wimbledon	26	17	2	7	60	35	36
Ilford	26	13	9	4	71	45	35
Dulwich Hamlet	26	15	3	8	69	43	33
Wycombe Wanderers	26	14	5	7	72	50	33
Oxford City	26	15	2	9	63	49	32
Kingstonian	26	13	3	10	71	50	29
Tufnell Park	26	9	7	10	50	48	25
Nunhead	26	9	7	10	54	61	25
The Casuals	26	10	4	12	59	65	24
Clapton	26	9	5	12	50	57	23
Leytonstone	26	9	3	14	36	61	21
St Albans City	26	8	4	14	57	78	20
Woking	26	6	5	15	44	64	17
London Caledonians	26	2	7	17	24	74	11

1932-33

Dulwich Hamlet	26	15	6	5	71	45	36
Leytonstone	26	16	4	6	66	43	36
Kingstonian	26	15	2	9	77	49	32
Ilford	26	14	0	12	60	58	28
The Casuals	26	12	2	12	48	36	26
Tufnell Park	26	11	3	12	51	51	25
St Albans City	26	12	1	13	57	63	25
Clapton	26	10	5	11	51	65	25
Oxford City	26	9	6	11	49	54	24
Woking	26	10	4	12	53	61	24
Wycombe Wanderers	26	10	4	12	47	56	24
Nunhead	26	8	6	12	42	50	22
Wimbledon	26	8	5	13	55	67	21
London Caledonians	26	5	6	15	35	64	16

1933-34

Kingstonian	26	15	7	4	80	42	37
Dulwich Hamlet	26	15	5	6	68	36	35
Wimbledon	26	13	7	6	62	35	33
Tufnell Park	26	14	5	7	55	50	33
Ilford	26	15	2	9	60	56	32
The Casuals	26	13	5	8	47	32	31
Leytonstone	26	13	3	10	55	48	29
Nunhead	26	10	5	11	48	44	25
London Caledonians	26	7	8	11	29	51	22
Wycombe Wanderers	26	9	2	15	57	60	20
St Albans City	26	8	4	14	44	75	20
Oxford City	26	7	4	15	45	57	18
Clapton	26	5	6	15	35	62	16
Woking	26	6	1	19	43	81	13

1934-35

Wimbledon	26	14	7	5	63	30	35
Oxford City	26	14	4	8	69	50	32
Leytonstone	26	15	2	9	49	36	32
Dulwich Hamlet	26	11	7	8	66	45	29
Tufnell Park	26	11	7	8	53	44	29
Kingstonian	26	11	6	9	44	40	28
Nunhead	26	10	7	9	35	34	27
London Caledonians	26	9	7	10	40	41	25
St Albans City	26	9	6	11	61	80	24
Ilford	26	9	6	11	40	56	24
Clapton	26	7	7	12	46	48	21
Woking	26	9	3	14	44	68	21
Wycombe Wanderers	26	7	6	13	51	69	20
The Casuals	26	6	5	15	37	57	17

1935-36

Wimbledon	26	19	2	5	82	29	40
The Casuals	26	14	5	7	60	45	33
Ilford	26	13	3	10	67	47	29
Dulwich Hamlet	26	10	8	8	64	47	28
Nunhead	26	11	6	9	51	40	28
Wycombe Wanderers	26	13	2	11	60	68	28
Clapton	26	11	5	10	42	46	27
Oxford City	26	11	4	11	60	58	26
St Albans City	26	11	2	13	59	64	24
Woking	26	9	4	13	43	62	22
Tufnell Park	26	9	3	14	42	61	21
London Caledonians	26	9	3	14	35	52	21
Kingstonian	26	9	2	15	43	56	20
Leytonstone	26	7	3	16	34	67	17

1936-37

Kingstonian	26	18	3	5	63	43	39
Nunhead	26	17	3	6	77	32	37
Leytonstone	26	16	4	6	71	42	36
Ilford	26	14	5	7	86	39	33
Dulwich Hamlet	26	12	6	8	64	48	30
Wycombe Wanderers	26	10	5	11	55	52	25
Wimbledon	26	9	7	10	52	53	25
Clapton	26	10	5	11	42	51	25
The Casuals	26	10	3	13	46	58	23
Woking	26	9	4	13	53	69	22
Oxford City	26	8	5	13	56	89	21
St Albans City	26	7	5	14	44	62	19
Tufnell Park	26	4	7	15	43	74	15
London Caledonians	26	5	4	17	26	66	14

1937-38

Leytonstone	26	17	6	3	72	34	40
Ilford	26	17	3	6	70	39	37
Tufnell Park	26	15	2	9	62	47	32
Nunhead	26	14	3	9	52	44	31
Wycombe Wanderers	26	12	5	9	69	55	29
Dulwich Hamlet	26	13	3	10	57	46	29
Kingstonian	26	12	4	10	51	48	28
Clapton	26	9	6	11	49	53	24
Wimbledon	26	10	3	13	62	49	23
London Caledonians	26	9	4	13	44	55	22
Oxford City	26	7	7	12	35	71	21
The Casuals	26	8	3	15	51	74	19
Woking	26	7	2	17	41	72	16
St Albans City	26	4	5	17	31	60	13

1938-39

Leytonstone	26	18	4	4	68	32	40
Ilford	26	17	4	5	68	32	38
Kingstonian	26	17	3	6	62	39	37
Dulwich Hamlet	26	15	5	6	60	32	35
Wimbledon	26	14	3	9	88	56	31
Nunhead	26	11	6	9	54	44	28
The Casuals	26	11	6	9	54	51	28
Clapton	26	12	2	12	69	61	26
Wycombe Wanderers	26	10	6	10	62	62	26
St Albans City	26	8	5	13	44	50	21
Woking	26	9	2	15	35	56	20
Oxford City	26	4	4	18	44	84	12
Tufnell Park	26	4	4	18	33	87	12
London Caledonians	26	3	4	19	26	81	10

1945-46

Walthamstow Avenue	26	21	0	5	100	31	42
Oxford City	26	17	6	3	91	40	40
Romford	26	15	3	8	83	59	33
Dulwich Hamlet	26	14	2	10	63	59	30
Tufnell Park	26	12	4	10	70	55	28
Woking	26	10	7	9	56	54	27
Ilford	26	12	2	12	56	71	26
Leytonstone	26	11	3	12	61	75	25
Wycombe Wanderers	26	9	3	14	80	88	21
Wimbledon	26	7	6	13	52	72	20
Corinthian Casuals	26	8	4	14	58	83	20
Clapton	26	8	3	15	51	62	19
St Albans City	26	6	6	14	48	85	18
Kingstonian	26	6	3	17	48	86	15

1946-47

Leytonstone	26	19	2	5	92	36	40
Dulwich Hamlet	26	17	3	6	78	46	37
Romford	26	13	8	5	76	52	34
Walthamstow Avenue	26	13	4	9	64	37	30
Oxford City	26	12	6	8	70	51	30
Kingstonian	26	12	4	10	54	57	28
Wycombe Wanderers	26	9	8	9	62	62	26
Wimbledon	26	10	5	11	68	64	25
Ilford	26	7	7	12	66	78	21
Tufnell Park	26	8	5	13	45	69	21
Woking	26	7	7	12	34	62	21
Clapton	26	6	8	12	41	59	20
St Albans City	26	7	5	14	47	79	19
Corinthian Casuals	26	4	4	18	36	80	12

1947-48

Leytonstone	26	19	1	6	87	38	39
Kingstonian	26	16	6	4	74	39	38
Walthamstow Avenue	26	17	3	6	61	37	37
Dulwich Hamlet	26	17	2	7	71	39	36
Wimbledon	26	13	6	7	66	40	32
Romford	26	14	1	11	53	47	29
Oxford City	26	10	5	11	50	68	25
Woking	26	10	3	13	63	55	23
Ilford	26	7	8	11	51	59	22
St Albans City	26	9	2	15	43	56	20
Wycombe Wanderers	26	7	5	14	51	65	19
Tufnell Park	26	7	4	15	38	83	18
Clapton	26	5	4	17	35	69	14
Corinthian Casuals	26	5	2	19	33	81	12

1948-49

Dulwich Hamlet	26	15	6	5	60	31	36
Walthamstow Avenue	26	16	4	6	65	38	36
Wimbledon	26	15	4	7	64	41	34
Ilford	26	14	3	9	56	36	31
Oxford City	26	13	5	8	48	34	31
Leytonstone	26	12	6	8	49	41	30
Woking	26	14	1	11	64	59	29
Romford	26	11	3	12	47	54	25
Kingstonian	26	10	4	12	43	47	24
Corinthian Casuals	26	11	2	13	47	59	24
Wycombe Wanderers	26	11	2	13	49	61	24
St Albans City	26	6	6	14	40	60	16
Clapton	26	5	5	16	32	61	15
Tufnell Park	26	1	5	20	28	70	7

St Albans City had 2 points deducted

1949-50

Leytonstone	26	17	5	4	77	31	39
Wimbledon	26	18	2	6	72	51	38
Kingstonian	26	16	3	7	59	39	35
Walthamstow Avenue	26	14	6	6	73	42	34
Dulwich Hamlet	26	14	3	9	60	47	31
St Albans City	26	12	3	11	59	45	27
Woking	26	10	6	10	60	71	26
Wycombe Wanderers	26	9	7	10	51	52	25
Romford	26	10	4	12	45	49	24
Ilford	26	10	4	12	46	53	24
Clapton	26	8	6	12	51	59	22
Oxford City	26	6	6	14	35	54	18
Corinthian Casuals	26	4	5	17	41	69	13
Tufnell Park	26	3	2	21	24	91	8

1950-51

Leytonstone	26	20	3	3	72	26	43
Walthamstow Avenue	26	15	4	7	57	37	34
Romford	26	15	3	8	58	49	33
Wimbledon	26	13	5	8	58	39	31
Dulwich Hamlet	26	14	2	10	54	43	30
Woking	26	11	6	9	65	55	28
Ilford	26	12	4	10	44	45	28
Corinthian Casuals	26	13	0	13	62	60	26
St Albans City	26	11	4	11	32	36	26
Kingstonian	26	9	4	13	46	54	22
Wycombe Wanderers	26	8	3	15	46	64	19
Oxford City	26	7	4	15	47	65	18
Clapton	26	6	5	15	29	50	17
Tufnell Park Edmonton	26	4	1	21	24	73	9

1951-52

Leytonstone	26	13	9	4	63	36	35
Wimbledon	26	16	3	7	65	44	35
Walthamstow Avenue	26	15	4	7	71	43	34
Romford	26	14	4	8	64	42	32
Kingstonian	26	11	7	8	62	48	29
Wycombe Wanderers	26	12	5	9	64	59	29
Woking	26	11	5	10	60	71	27
Dulwich Hamlet	26	11	4	11	60	53	26
Corinthian Casuals	26	11	4	11	55	66	26
St Albans City	26	9	7	10	48	53	25
Ilford	26	8	5	13	32	47	21
Clapton	26	9	2	15	50	59	20
Oxford City	26	6	3	17	50	72	15
Tufnell Park Edmonton	26	2	6	18	25	73	10

1952-53

Walthamstow Avenue	28	19	6	3	53	25	44
Bromley	28	17	4	7	71	35	38
Leytonstone	28	14	6	8	60	38	34
Wimbledon	28	14	5	9	68	37	33
Kingstonian	28	13	6	9	62	50	32
Dulwich Hamlet	28	15	2	11	62	52	32
Romford	28	12	8	8	62	52	32
Wycombe Wanderers	28	14	2	12	54	62	30
St Albans City	28	11	6	11	43	57	28
Barking	28	9	7	12	42	51	25
Ilford	28	10	4	14	59	57	24
Woking	28	10	4	14	57	72	24
Corinthian Casuals	28	7	9	12	45	56	23
Oxford City	28	5	2	21	37	87	12
Clapton	28	2	5	21	27	71	9

1953-54

Bromley	28	18	3	7	76	45	39
Walthamstow Avenue	28	13	7	8	55	30	33
Wycombe Wanderers	28	15	3	10	65	44	33
Ilford	28	11	10	7	48	44	32
Corinthian Casuals	28	12	7	9	59	44	31
Woking	28	13	4	11	54	58	30
Leytonstone	28	12	5	11	58	48	29
St Albans City	28	11	6	11	54	55	28
Dulwich Hamlet	28	11	6	11	55	57	28
Romford	28	11	5	12	57	54	27
Clapton	28	11	5	12	42	56	27
Barking	28	11	2	15	59	84	24
Kingstonian	28	8	7	13	59	71	23
Wimbledon	28	7	8	13	43	59	22
Oxford City	28	4	6	18	49	84	14

1954-55

Walthamstow Avenue	28	21	1	6	80	38	43
St Albans City	28	18	3	7	61	41	39
Bromley	28	18	2	8	66	34	38
Wycombe Wanderers	28	16	3	9	68	43	35
Ilford	28	13	5	10	64	46	31
Barking	28	15	1	12	55	51	31
Woking	28	12	3	13	75	79	27
Kingstonian	28	10	7	11	47	57	27
Leytonstone	28	10	4	14	35	51	24
Oxford City	28	10	3	15	43	74	23
Clapton	28	9	4	15	41	50	22
Wimbledon	28	10	2	16	48	62	22
Corinthian Casuals	28	9	3	16	50	65	21
Dulwich Hamlet	28	7	5	16	48	60	19
Romford	28	4	10	14	43	73	18

1955-56

Wycombe Wanderers	28	19	5	4	82	36	43
Bromley	28	12	7	9	54	43	31
Leytonstone	28	12	7	9	50	44	31
Woking	28	14	3	11	62	60	31
Barking	28	12	7	9	41	45	31
Kingstonian	28	12	6	10	67	64	30
Walthamstow Avenue	28	13	3	12	61	45	29
Ilford	28	10	8	10	44	52	28
Oxford City	28	10	7	11	48	55	27
Clapton	28	9	8	11	45	48	26
Wimbledon	28	12	2	14	51	62	26
Corinthian Casuals	28	9	7	12	56	56	25
Dulwich Hamlet	28	9	6	13	55	67	24
Romford	28	9	6	13	42	55	24
St Albans City	28	2	10	16	36	62	14

1956-57

Wycombe Wanderers	30	18	6	6	86	53	42
Woking	30	20	1	9	104	47	41
Bromley	30	16	5	9	78	60	37
Oxford City	30	16	3	11	65	57	35
Ilford	30	12	8	10	59	65	32
Tooting & Mitcham United	30	10	11	9	53	48	31
Kingstonian	30	11	9	10	72	77	31
Walthamstow Avenue	30	11	8	11	48	46	30
Dulwich Hamlet	30	13	3	14	65	54	29
St Albans City	30	13	3	14	62	71	29
Leytonstone	30	11	6	13	50	50	28
Clapton	30	9	9	12	48	59	27
Wimbledon	30	10	5	15	47	66	25
Romford	30	10	5	15	53	81	25
Barking	30	7	6	17	48	72	20
Corinthian Casuals	30	7	4	19	46	78	18

1957-58

Tooting & Mitcham United	30	20	6	4	79	33	46
Wycombe Wanderers	30	19	4	7	78	42	42
Walthamstow Avenue	30	17	5	8	63	35	39
Bromley	30	13	9	8	66	51	35
Oxford City	30	13	6	11	59	48	32
Leytonstone	30	13	6	11	49	48	32
Wimbledon	30	15	2	13	64	66	32
Corinthian Casuals	30	12	8	10	62	68	32
Woking	30	12	7	11	70	58	31
Barking	30	10	6	14	49	61	26
St Albans City	30	11	3	16	56	76	25
Clapton	30	8	9	13	42	65	25
Kingstonian	30	7	8	15	45	66	22
Dulwich Hamlet	30	7	7	16	49	64	21
Ilford	30	8	4	18	46	70	20
Romford	30	6	8	16	45	71	20

1958-59

Wimbledon	30	22	3	5	91	38	47
Dulwich Hamlet	30	18	5	7	68	44	41
Wycombe Wanderers	30	18	4	8	93	50	40
Oxford City	30	17	4	9	87	58	38
Walthamstow Avenue	30	16	5	9	59	40	37
Tooting & Mitcham United	30	15	4	11	84	55	34
Barking	30	14	2	14	59	53	30
Woking	30	12	6	12	66	66	30
Bromley	30	11	7	12	56	55	29
Clapton	30	10	6	14	55	67	26
Ilford	30	10	6	14	46	67	26
Kingstonian	30	9	4	17	54	72	22
St Albans City	30	8	6	16	53	89	22
Leytonstone	30	7	6	17	40	87	20
Romford	30	7	5	18	54	76	19
Corinthian Casuals	30	7	5	18	44	92	19

1959-60

Tooting & Mitcham United	30	17	8	5	75	43	42
Wycombe Wanderers	30	19	3	8	84	46	41
Wimbledon	30	18	3	9	66	36	39
Kingstonian	30	18	3	9	76	51	39
Corinthian Casuals	30	18	1	11	69	61	37
Bromley	30	15	6	9	75	46	36
Dulwich Hamlet	30	14	6	10	65	47	34
Walthamstow Avenue	30	11	11	8	48	38	33
Oxford City	30	10	10	10	57	57	30
Leytonstone	30	10	8	12	43	46	28
Woking	30	10	6	14	54	61	26
St Albans City	30	10	6	14	50	65	26
Maidstone United	30	10	5	15	53	60	25
Barking	30	7	4	19	30	75	18
Ilford	30	5	6	19	34	86	16
Clapton	30	3	4	23	32	92	10

1960-61

Bromley	30	20	6	4	89	42	46
Walthamstow Avenue	30	20	5	5	87	38	45
Wimbledon	30	18	6	6	72	43	42
Dulwich Hamlet	30	17	4	9	71	59	35
Maidstone United	30	14	8	8	63	39	36
Leytonstone	30	15	6	9	46	34	36
Tooting & Mitcham United	30	14	3	13	69	51	31
Wycombe Wanderers	30	12	5	13	63	61	29
St Albans City	30	12	4	14	45	72	28
Oxford City	30	10	7	13	59	59	27
Corinthian Casuals	30	9	9	12	49	59	27
Kingstonian	30	10	6	14	55	61	26
Woking	30	10	6	14	58	71	26
Ilford	30	5	8	17	30	69	18
Barking	30	3	8	19	30	76	14
Clapton	30	3	5	22	25	77	11

1961-62

Wimbledon	30	19	6	5	68	24	44
Leytonstone	30	17	7	6	61	44	41
Walthamstow Avenue	30	14	8	8	51	31	36
Kingstonian	30	15	5	10	65	48	35
Tooting & Mitcham United	30	12	10	8	62	47	34
Oxford City	30	12	9	9	56	49	33
Wycombe Wanderers	30	12	7	11	57	51	31
Corinthian Casuals	30	12	7	11	45	51	31
St Albans City	30	10	9	11	55	55	29
Woking	30	9	9	12	51	60	27
Dulwich Hamlet	30	11	4	15	55	66	26
Barking	30	9	8	13	40	64	26
Ilford	30	7	10	13	50	59	24
Bromley	30	10	4	16	49	69	24
Clapton	30	6	8	16	45	67	20
Maidstone United	30	6	7	17	34	59	19

1962-63

Wimbledon	30	19	8	3	84	33	46
Kingstonian	30	18	8	4	79	37	44
Tooting & Mitcham United	30	17	8	5	65	37	42
Ilford	30	19	3	8	70	44	41
Walthamstow Avenue	30	14	7	9	51	44	35
Maidstone United	30	13	8	9	56	45	34
Bromley	30	12	10	8	57	51	34
Leytonstone	30	12	7	11	48	50	31
Wycombe Wanderers	30	10	10	10	56	61	30
St Albans City	30	11	5	14	54	49	27
Barking	30	8	10	12	39	50	26
Oxford City	30	8	9	13	55	64	25
Woking	30	8	6	16	42	66	22
Clapton	30	7	4	19	30	71	18
Dulwich Hamlet	30	4	5	21	30	71	13
Corinthian Casuals	30	4	4	22	28	71	12

1963-64

Wimbledon	38	27	6	5	87	44	60
Hendon	38	25	4	9	124	38	54
Kingstonian	38	24	4	10	100	62	52
Sutton United	38	23	5	10	99	64	51
Enfield	38	20	10	8	96	56	50
Oxford City	38	20	8	10	90	55	48
Tooting & Mitcham United	38	19	8	11	78	51	46
St Albans City	38	14	12	12	62	63	40
Ilford	38	16	8	14	75	79	40
Maidstone United	38	15	8	15	65	71	38
Walthamstow Avenue	38	15	6	17	70	66	36
Leytonstone	38	14	8	16	66	71	36
Wycombe Wanderers	38	13	6	19	74	80	32
Hitchin Town	38	14	4	20	67	100	32
Bromley	38	11	8	19	64	75	30
Barking	38	10	9	19	46	69	29
Woking	38	10	9	19	48	88	29
Corinthian Casuals	38	10	4	24	52	92	24
Dulwich Hamlet	38	6	12	20	47	97	24
Clapton	38	2	5	31	31	120	9

1964-65

Hendon	38	28	7	3	123	49	63
Enfield	38	29	5	4	98	35	63
Kingstonian	38	24	8	6	86	44	56
Leytonstone	38	24	5	9	115	62	53
Oxford City	38	20	7	11	76	51	47
St Albans City	38	18	9	11	63	43	45
Sutton United	38	17	11	10	74	57	45
Wealdstone	38	19	6	13	93	68	44
Bromley	38	14	11	13	71	80	39
Tooting & Mitcham United	38	15	7	16	71	66	37
Hitchin Town	38	13	9	16	61	66	35
Walthamstow Avenue	38	15	5	18	63	82	35
Wycombe Wanderers	38	13	7	18	70	85	33
Corinthian Casuals	38	13	7	18	56	77	33
Barking	38	10	8	20	58	80	28
Ilford	38	8	8	22	43	89	24
Maidstone United	38	8	6	24	49	86	22
Dulwich Hamlet	38	8	5	25	45	79	21
Clapton	38	8	3	27	43	91	19
Woking	38	7	4	27	45	113	18

Hendon beat Enfield in a play-off to decide the Championship

1965-66

Leytonstone	38	27	7	4	98	33	63
Hendon	38	27	5	6	111	55	59
Enfield	38	24	8	6	104	54	56
Wycombe Wanderers	38	25	6	7	100	65	56
Kingstonian	38	24	5	9	94	55	53
Wealdstone	38	20	6	12	90	64	46
Maidstone United	38	19	6	13	74	61	44
St Albans City	38	19	5	14	57	56	43
Sutton United	38	17	7	14	83	72	41
Tooting & Mitcham United	38	16	7	15	65	58	39
Corinthian Casuals	38	17	5	16	74	67	39
Woking	38	12	10	16	60	83	34
Walthamstow Avenue	38	12	9	17	81	75	33
Oxford City	38	10	9	19	49	72	29
Barking	38	10	7	21	51	72	27
Bromley	38	10	5	23	69	101	25
Ilford	38	7	10	21	50	84	24
Hitchin Town	38	6	8	24	57	118	20
Clapton	38	5	6	27	46	103	16
Dulwich Hamlet	38	5	5	28	30	95	15

1966-67

Sutton United	38	26	7	5	89	33	59
Walthamstow Avenue	38	22	12	4	89	47	56
Wycombe Wanderers	38	23	8	7	92	54	54
Enfield	38	25	2	11	87	33	52
Hendon	38	20	9	9	64	37	49
Tooting & Mitcham United	38	19	10	9	76	60	48
Leytonstone	38	19	9	10	67	38	47
St Albans City	38	16	12	10	59	45	44
Kingstonian	38	18	8	12	60	49	44
Oxford City	38	15	9	14	74	61	39
Woking	38	13	10	15	65	71	36
Wealdstone	38	13	8	17	72	73	34
Barking	38	11	12	15	56	61	34
Bromley	38	12	7	19	50	67	31
Clapton	38	10	8	20	49	92	28
Ilford	38	8	10	20	43	77	26
Corinthian Casuals	38	9	7	22	45	68	25
Maidstone United	38	6	10	22	43	90	22
Hitchin Town	38	8	6	24	39	89	22
Dulwich Hamlet	38	3	4	31	33	107	10

1967-68

Enfield	38	28	8	2	85	22	64
Sutton United	38	22	11	5	89	27	55
Hendon	38	23	6	9	90	36	52
Leytonstone	38	21	10	7	78	41	52
St Albans City	38	20	8	10	78	41	48
Walthamstow Avenue	38	19	9	10	81	64	47
Wealdstone	38	19	8	11	80	45	46
Tooting & Mitcham United	38	19	5	14	57	45	43
Barking	38	17	8	13	75	57	42
Oxford City	38	17	4	17	59	58	38
Kingstonian	38	14	10	14	56	61	38
Hitchin Town	38	14	9	15	61	73	37
Bromley	38	12	10	16	58	80	34
Wycombe Wanderers	38	13	5	20	73	85	31
Dulwich Hamlet	38	10	7	21	39	66	27
Clapton	38	10	7	21	51	88	27
Woking	38	8	8	22	50	90	24
Corinthian Casuals	38	7	10	21	40	80	24
Ilford	38	7	7	24	41	77	21
Maidstone United	38	3	4	31	26	131	10

1968-69

Enfield	38	27	7	4	103	28	61
Hitchin Town	38	23	10	5	67	41	56
Sutton United	38	22	9	7	83	29	53
Wycombe Wanderers	38	23	6	9	70	37	52
Wealdstone	38	20	11	7	73	48	51
Hendon	38	22	5	11	69	47	49
St Albans City	38	17	13	8	75	44	47
Barking	38	20	7	11	69	46	47
Oxford City	38	18	8	12	76	64	44
Tooting & Mitcham United	38	16	10	12	68	55	42
Leytonstone	38	18	4	16	71	53	40
Kingstonian	38	15	8	15	62	56	38
Walthamstow Avenue	38	10	10	18	47	71	30
Maidstone United	38	10	8	20	47	75	28
Clapton	38	10	7	21	52	76	27
Woking	38	8	7	23	45	77	23
Bromley	38	8	7	23	52	95	23
Dulwich Hamlet	38	6	9	23	31	77	21
Ilford	38	6	8	24	33	77	20
Corinthian Casuals	38	2	4	32	23	120	8

1969-70

Enfield	38	27	8	3	91	26	62
Wycombe Wanderers	38	25	11	2	85	24	61
Sutton United	38	24	9	5	75	35	57
Barking	38	21	9	8	93	47	51
Hendon	38	19	12	7	77	44	50
St Albans City	38	21	8	9	69	40	50
Hitchin Town	38	19	10	9	71	40	48
Tooting & Mitcham United	38	19	5	14	88	62	43
Leytonstone	38	17	7	14	57	41	41
Wealdstone	38	15	10	13	53	48	40
Oxford City	38	15	7	16	61	78	37
Kingstonian	38	13	9	16	55	57	35
Ilford	38	8	15	15	42	73	31
Dulwich Hamlet	38	8	12	18	46	66	28
Woking	38	10	7	21	46	69	27
Walthamstow Avenue	38	11	5	22	52	81	27
Clapton	38	9	7	22	45	87	25
Maidstone United	38	7	8	23	48	84	22
Corinthian Casuals	38	6	3	29	30	99	15
Bromley	38	3	4	31	28	111	10

1970-71

Wycombe Wanderers	38	28	6	4	93	32	62
Sutton United	38	29	3	6	76	35	61
St Albans City	38	23	10	5	87	26	56
Enfield	38	24	7	7	67	24	55
Ilford	38	21	7	10	74	51	49
Hendon	38	18	11	9	81	37	47
Barking	38	20	4	14	89	59	44
Leytonstone	38	17	10	11	68	50	44
Woking	38	18	6	14	57	50	42
Walthamstow Avenue	38	14	11	13	63	52	39
Oxford City	38	13	10	15	51	48	36
Hitchin Town	38	12	9	17	46	60	33
Wealdstone	38	12	8	18	45	64	32
Tooting & Mitcham United	38	11	9	18	44	66	31
Kingstonian	38	11	9	19	53	71	30
Bromley	38	10	6	22	34	77	26
Dulwich Hamlet	38	7	10	21	30	66	24
Maidstone United	38	7	6	25	42	84	20
Clapton	38	5	7	26	33	101	17
Corinthian Casuals	38	2	8	28	23	103	12

1971-72

Wycombe Wanderers	40	31	3	6	102	20	65
Enfield	40	26	8	6	90	41	60
Walton & Hersham	40	24	8	8	69	25	56
Hendon	40	23	10	7	79	35	56
Bishop's Stortford	40	24	5	11	61	37	53
Sutton United	40	21	10	9	77	43	52
St Albans City	40	23	4	13	74	47	50
Ilford	40	17	11	12	62	52	45
Barking	40	20	4	16	65	61	44
Hitchin Town	40	17	10	13	68	66	44
Bromley	40	16	10	14	67	64	42
Hayes	40	14	12	14	50	48	40
Oxford City	40	13	9	18	67	74	35
Woking	40	11	10	19	52	58	32
Kingstonian	40	10	12	18	49	59	32
Walthamstow Avenue	40	12	8	20	58	71	32
Leytonstone	40	11	8	21	48	68	30
Tooting & Mitcham United	40	6	9	25	38	93	21
Clapton	40	7	7	26	45	118	21
Dulwich Hamlet	40	4	12	24	35	81	20
Corinthian Casuals	40	3	4	33	21	116	10

1972-73

Hendon	42	34	6	2	88	18	74
Walton & Hersham	42	25	11	6	60	25	61
Leatherhead	42	23	10	9	76	32	56
Wycombe Wanderers	42	25	6	11	66	32	56
Walthamstow Avenue	42	20	12	10	66	48	52
Tooting & Mitcham United	42	20	11	11	73	39	51
Sutton United	42	21	9	12	69	48	51
Kingstonian	42	20	10	12	60	49	50
Enfield	42	20	8	14	90	54	48
Bishop's Stortford	42	18	12	12	58	51	48
Hayes	42	19	8	15	69	42	46
Dulwich Hamlet	42	18	9	15	59	52	45
Ilford	42	18	9	15	61	59	45
Leytonstone	42	17	11	14	55	54	45
Woking	42	18	8	16	61	56	44
Hitchin Town	42	15	9	18	52	64	39
Barking	42	8	7	27	45	88	23
St Albans City	42	5	12	25	34	76	22
Oxford City	42	6	7	29	30	101	19
Bromley	42	4	10	28	31	70	18
Clapton	42	3	11	28	31	100	17
Corinthian Casuals	42	3	8	31	30	106	14

1973-74

First Division

Wycombe Wanderers	42	27	9	6	96	34	90
Hendon	42	25	13	4	63	20	88
Bishop's Stortford	42	26	9	7	78	26	87
Dulwich Hamlet	42	22	11	9	71	38	77
Leatherhead	42	23	6	13	81	44	75
Walton & Hersham	42	20	12	10	68	50	72
Woking	42	22	6	14	63	55	72
Leytonstone	42	20	9	13	63	44	69
Ilford	42	20	8	14	60	44	68
Hayes	42	17	14	11	65	43	65
Oxford City	42	15	16	11	45	47	61
Sutton United	42	13	16	13	51	52	55
Hitchin Town	42	15	10	17	68	73	55
Barking	42	14	12	16	57	58	54
Kingstonian	42	12	15	15	47	46	51
Tooting & Mitcham United	42	14	9	19	57	62	51
Enfield	42	13	11	18	50	57	50
Walthamstow Avenue	42	11	13	18	46	62	46
Bromley	42	7	9	26	37	81	30
Clapton	42	8	3	31	36	128	27
St Albans City	42	4	7	31	30	92	19
Corinthian Casuals	42	3	4	35	31	107	13

Second Division

Dagenham	30	22	4	4	68	23	70
Slough Town	30	18	6	6	46	23	60
Hertford Town	30	17	5	8	46	29	56
Chesham Town	30	16	6	8	61	43	54
Aveley	30	16	5	9	50	28	53
Tilbury	30	14	5	11	47	36	47
Maidenhead United	30	12	11	7	36	30	47
Horsham	30	12	9	9	47	35	45
Harwich & Parkeston	30	11	9	10	46	41	42
Staines Town	30	10	8	12	34	41	38
Carshalton Athletic	30	8	8	14	34	51	32
Hampton	30	6	10	14	33	51	28
Harlow Town	30	6	9	15	33	48	27
Finchley	30	6	7	17	29	52	25
Southall	30	3	10	17	17	52	19
Wokingham Town	30	3	8	19	30	74	17

1974-75

First Division

Wycombe Wanderers	42	28	11	3	93	30	95
Enfield	42	29	8	5	78	26	95
Dagenham	42	28	5	9	95	44	89
Tooting & Mitcham United	42	25	9	8	78	46	84
Dulwich Hamlet	42	24	10	8	75	38	82
Leatherhead	42	23	10	9	83	42	79
Ilford	42	23	10	9	98	51	79
Oxford City	42	17	9	16	63	56	60
Slough Town	42	17	6	19	68	52	57
Sutton United	42	17	6	19	68	63	57
Bishop's Stortford	42	17	6	19	56	64	57
Hitchin Town	42	15	10	17	57	71	55
Hendon	42	15	7	20	59	74	52
Walthamstow Avenue	42	13	9	20	56	62	48
Woking	42	12	10	20	53	73	46
Hayes	42	10	14	18	52	66	44
Barking	42	12	8	22	59	67	44
Leytonstone	42	12	7	23	42	61	43
Kingstonian	42	13	4	25	48	73	43
Clapton	42	12	4	26	46	96	40
Walton & Hersham	42	9	4	29	37	108	31
Bromley	42	6	3	33	25	110	21

Second Division

Staines Town	34	23	2	9	65	23	71
Southall	34	20	3	11	55	41	63
Tilbury	34	19	5	10	64	36	60
Harwich & Parkeston	34	18	4	12	52	44	58
Chesham United	34	17	6	11	59	39	57
St Albans City	34	15	11	8	42	37	56
Harlow Town	34	16	6	12	53	47	54
Horsham	34	16	5	13	59	49	53
Maidenhead United	34	13	7	14	38	40	46
Hampton	34	12	7	15	44	42	43
Croydon	34	11	10	13	48	55	43
Hertford Town	34	10	7	17	35	52	37
Boreham Wood	34	7	15	12	41	49	36
Wokingham Town	34	10	6	18	32	43	36
Finchley	34	9	9	16	36	53	36
Carshalton Athletic	34	9	9	16	38	58	36
Aveley	34	9	7	18	34	63	34
Corinthian Casuals	34	8	9	17	35	59	33

Tilbury had 2 points deducted

1975-76

First Division

Enfield	42	26	9	7	83	38	87
Wycombe Wanderers	42	24	10	8	71	41	82
Dagenham	42	25	6	11	89	55	81
Ilford	42	22	10	10	58	39	76
Dulwich Hamlet	42	22	5	15	67	41	71
Hendon	42	20	11	11	60	41	71
Tooting & Mitcham United	42	19	11	12	73	49	68
Leatherhead	42	19	10	13	63	53	67
Staines Town	42	19	9	14	46	37	66
Slough Town	42	17	12	13	58	45	63
Sutton United	42	17	11	14	71	60	62
Bishop's Stortford	42	15	12	15	51	47	57
Walthamstow Avenue	42	14	11	17	47	60	53
Woking	42	14	9	19	58	62	51
Barking	42	15	6	21	57	70	51
Hitchin Town	42	13	11	18	45	57	50
Hayes	42	10	19	13	44	48	49
Kingstonian	42	13	8	21	53	87	47
Southall & Ealing Borough	42	11	9	22	56	69	42
Leytonstone	42	10	10	22	41	63	40
Oxford City	42	9	8	25	29	65	35
Clapton	42	3	3	36	19	112	12

Second Division

Tilbury	42	32	6	4	97	30	102
Croydon	42	28	14	0	81	27	98
Carshalton Athletic	42	28	6	8	75	37	90
Chesham United	42	21	12	9	91	51	75
Harwich & Parkeston	42	21	11	10	78	56	74
Hampton	42	21	9	12	72	52	72
St Albans City	42	18	12	12	59	48	66
Boreham Wood	42	17	12	13	68	50	63
Harrow Borough	42	15	12	15	71	74	57
Hornchurch	42	15	11	16	61	61	56
Horsham	42	14	13	15	60	55	55
Wembley	42	14	13	15	51	54	55
Wokingham Town	42	13	16	13	45	52	55
Walton & Hersham	42	14	12	16	61	56	54
Finchley	42	14	11	17	52	53	53
Bromley	42	11	11	20	64	86	44
Aveley	42	11	9	22	34	51	42
Harlow Town	42	11	9	22	50	73	42
Maidenhead United	42	6	17	19	32	65	35
Ware	42	7	12	23	50	95	33
Hertford Town	42	5	9	28	32	87	24
Corinthian Casuals	42	4	7	31	42	113	19

1976-77

First Division

Enfield	42	24	12	6	63	34	84
Wycombe Wanderers	42	25	8	9	71	34	83
Dagenham	42	23	10	9	80	39	79
Hendon	42	19	10	13	60	48	67
Tilbury	42	18	13	11	57	49	67
Tooting & Mitcham	42	18	10	14	85	72	64
Walthamstow Avenue	42	19	7	16	61	55	64
Slough Town	42	18	9	15	51	46	63
Hitchin Town	42	19	6	17	60	66	63
Leatherhead	42	18	7	17	61	47	61
Staines Town	42	16	13	13	52	48	61
Leytonstone	42	16	11	15	59	57	59
Barking	42	16	9	17	63	61	57
Southall & Ealing Borough	42	15	8	19	52	64	53
Croydon	42	13	10	19	38	52	49
Sutton United	42	14	7	21	40	55	49
Kingstonian	42	13	7	22	45	60	46
Hayes	42	12	10	20	49	69	46
Woking	42	11	12	19	47	61	45
Bishop's Stortford	42	11	11	20	51	71	44
Dulwich Hamlet	42	11	8	23	52	68	41
Ilford	42	10	8	24	32	73	38

Second Division

Boreham Wood	42	35	4	5	80	26	103
Carshalton Athletic	42	25	12	5	80	33	87
Harwich & Parkeston	42	23	8	11	93	61	77
Wembley	42	23	8	11	82	58	77
Harrow Borough	42	21	12	9	78	44	75
Horsham	42	23	5	14	67	56	74
Bromley	42	20	10	12	71	46	70
Oxford City	42	20	8	14	73	55	68
Hampton	42	20	8	14	62	45	68
Wokingham Town	42	16	14	12	60	44	62
Hornchurch	42	18	7	17	62	53	61
Chesham United	42	17	10	15	63	66	61
St Albans City	42	16	12	14	59	53	60
Walton & Hersham	42	17	9	16	57	56	60
Aveley	42	14	8	20	49	62	50
Corinthian Casuals	42	13	6	23	52	75	45
Harlow Town	42	11	8	23	39	77	41
Hertford Town	42	9	9	24	45	80	36
Maidenhead United	42	8	8	26	36	73	32
Clapton	42	7	9	28	43	87	30
Finchley	42	5	13	24	36	82	28
Ware	42	5	8	29	43	98	23

1977-78

Premier Division

Enfield	42	35	5	2	96	27	110
Dagenham	42	24	7	11	78	55	79
Wycombe Wanderers	42	22	9	11	66	41	75
Tooting & Mitcham United	42	22	8	12	64	49	74
Hitchin Town	42	20	9	13	69	53	69
Sutton United	42	18	12	12	66	57	66
Leatherhead	42	18	11	13	62	48	65
Croydon	42	18	10	14	61	52	64
Walthamstow Avenue	42	17	12	13	64	61	63
Barking	42	17	7	18	76	66	58
Carshalton Athletic	42	15	11	16	60	62	56
Hayes	42	15	11	16	46	53	56
Hendon	42	16	7	19	57	55	55
Woking	42	14	11	17	62	62	53
Boreham Wood	42	15	8	19	48	65	53
Slough Town	42	14	8	20	52	69	0
Staines Town	42	12	13	17	46	60	49
Tilbury	42	11	12	19	57	68	45
Kingstonian	42	8	13	21	43	65	37
Leytonstone	42	7	15	20	44	71	36
Southall & Ealing Borough	42	6	15	21	43	74	33
Bishop's Stortford	42	7	8	27	36	83	29

First Division

Dulwich Hamlet	42	28	9	5	91	25	93
Oxford City	42	26	5	11	85	44	83
Bromley	42	23	13	6	74	41	82
Walton & Hersham	42	22	11	9	69	41	77
Ilford	42	21	14	7	57	47	77
St Albans City	42	22	10	10	83	46	76
Wokingham Town	42	19	12	11	69	48	69
Harlow Town	42	19	8	15	63	49	65
Harrow Borough	42	17	10	15	59	54	61
Maidenhead United	42	16	13	13	55	54	61
Hertford Town	42	15	14	13	57	51	59
Chesham United	42	14	13	15	69	70	55
Hampton	42	13	13	16	49	53	52
Harwich & Parkeston	42	12	13	17	68	79	49
Wembley	42	15	3	24	56	82	48
Horsham	42	12	10	20	41	57	46
Finchley	42	11	13	18	41	68	46
Aveley	42	13	7	22	47	75	46
Ware	42	8	13	21	61	95	37
Clapton	42	10	6	26	46	78	36
Hornchurch	42	8	10	24	47	81	34
Corinthian Casuals	42	3	10	29	40	88	19

Second Division

Epsom & Ewell	32	21	5	6	65	34	68
Metropolitan Police	32	19	6	7	53	30	63
Farnborough Town	32	19	4	9	68	40	61
Molesey	32	17	8	7	47	27	59
Egham Town	32	15	9	8	52	34	54
Tring Town	32	14	11	7	62	32	53
Letchworth Garden City	32	14	11	7	67	48	53
Lewes	32	13	7	12	52	51	46
Rainham Town	32	13	6	13	42	50	45
Worthing	32	11	9	12	40	45	42
Eastbourne United	32	10	8	14	40	50	38
Cheshunt	32	9	6	17	43	60	33
Feltham	32	7	9	16	30	49	30
Camberley Town	32	6	11	15	32	49	29
Hemel Hempstead	32	6	9	17	33	50	27
Epping Town	32	7	6	19	37	64	27
Willesden	32	7	3	22	38	88	24

Second Division

Farnborough Town	34	26	3	5	77	34	81
Camberley Town	34	21	8	5	71	32	71
Molesey	34	19	11	4	55	33	68
Lewes	34	19	6	9	66	50	63
Feltham	34	16	7	11	47	36	55
Letchworth Garden City	34	14	10	10	56	48	52
Eastbourne United	34	16	4	14	47	45	52
Hemel Hempstead	34	13	11	10	46	37	50
Epping Town	34	14	7	13	49	44	49
Rainham Town	34	13	10	11	42	41	49
Cheshunt	34	11	8	15	43	49	41
Hungerford Town	34	11	8	15	48	58	41
Worthing	34	9	8	17	40	50	35
Hornchurch	34	9	8	17	39	62	35
Egham Town	34	7	12	15	48	54	33
Tring Town	34	6	8	20	33	56	26
Willesden	34	6	8	20	41	77	26
Corinthian Casuals	34	4	7	23	23	65	19

1978-79

Premier Division

Barking	42	28	9	5	92	50	93
Dagenham	42	25	6	11	83	63	81
Enfield	42	22	11	9	69	37	77
Dulwich Hamlet	42	21	13	8	69	39	76
Slough Town	42	20	12	10	61	44	72
Wycombe Wanderers	42	20	9	13	59	44	69
Woking	42	18	14	10	79	59	68
Croydon	42	19	9	14	61	51	66
Hendon	42	16	14	12	55	48	62
Leatherhead	42	17	9	16	57	45	60
Sutton United	42	17	9	16	62	51	60
Tooting & Mitcham United	42	15	14	13	52	52	59
Walthamstow Avenue	42	15	6	21	61	69	51
Tilbury	42	13	1	18	60	76	50
Boreham Wood	42	13	10	19	50	67	49
Hitchin Town	42	12	11	19	59	71	47
Carshalton Athletic	42	10	16	16	49	69	46
Hayes	42	9	18	15	45	58	45
Oxford City	42	12	7	23	50	80	43
Staines Town	42	6	16	20	40	64	34
Leytonstone	42	8	7	27	36	75	31
Kingstonian	42	3	15	24	35	72	24

1979-80

Premier Division

Enfield	42	25	9	8	74	32	84
Walthamstow Avenue	42	24	9	9	87	48	81
Dulwich Hamlet	42	21	16	5	66	37	79
Sutton United	42	20	13	9	67	40	73
Dagenham	42	20	13	9	82	56	73
Tooting & Mitcham United	42	21	6	15	62	59	69
Barking	42	19	10	13	72	51	67
Harrow Borough	42	17	15	10	64	51	66
Woking	42	17	13	12	78	59	64
Wycombe Wanderers	42	17	13	12	72	53	64
Harlow Town	42	14	12	16	55	61	54
Hitchin Town	42	13	15	14	55	69	54
Hendon	42	12	13	17	50	57	49
Slough Town	42	13	10	19	54	71	49
Boreham Wood	42	13	10	19	50	69	49
Staines Town	42	14	6	22	46	67	48
Hayes	42	12	9	21	48	68	45
Leatherhead	42	11	11	20	51	60	44
Carshalton Athletic	42	12	7	23	48	78	43
Croydon	42	10	10	22	51	59	40
Oxford City	42	10	9	23	49	87	39
Tilbury	42	7	11	24	41	90	30

Tilbury had 2 points deducted

First Division

Harlow Town	42	31	7	4	93	32	100
Harrow Borough	42	26	8	8	85	49	86
Maidenhead United	42	25	6	11	72	50	81
Bishop's Stortford	42	22	11	9	68	40	77
Horsham	42	23	7	12	63	47	76
Hertford Town	42	21	11	10	62	41	74
Harwich & Parkeston	42	22	5	15	90	57	71
Bromley	42	18	12	12	76	50	66
Hampton	42	17	11	14	59	47	62
Epsom & Ewell	42	18	7	17	69	41	61
Wembley	42	15	14	13	57	57	59
Aveley	42	17	6	19	57	67	57
Wokingham Town	42	17	8	17	64	68	56
Clapton	42	15	8	19	67	80	53
Metropolitan Police	42	12	13	17	58	55	49
Walton & Hersham	42	12	9	21	47	71	45
Ilford	42	13	5	24	48	80	44
Ware	42	11	10	21	46	69	43
Chesham United	42	11	9	22	46	66	42
Finchley	42	7	15	20	43	75	36
St Albans City	42	7	7	28	43	90	28
Southall & Ealing Borough	42	5	5	32	41	114	20

Wokingham Town had 3 points deducted

First Division

Leytonstone & Ilford	42	31	6	5	83	35	99
Bromley	42	24	10	8	93	44	82
Maidenhead United	42	24	8	10	81	46	80
Bishop's Stortford	42	24	8	10	74	47	80
Kingstonian	42	22	8	12	59	44	74
Chesham United	42	18	13	11	68	56	67
St Albans City	42	17	13	12	65	47	64
Farnborough Town	42	19	7	16	70	57	64
Epsom & Ewell	42	18	7	17	62	57	61
Camberley Town	42	16	10	16	43	38	58
Walton & Hersham	42	15	12	15	61	50	57
Wembley	42	16	8	18	46	52	56
Wokingham Town	42	14	11	17	45	49	53
Hertford Town	42	13	11	18	71	74	50
Aveley	42	12	13	17	45	55	49
Hampton	42	14	7	21	57	74	49
Finchley	42	13	9	20	44	59	48
Metropolitan Police	42	13	8	21	46	67	47
Ware	42	11	12	19	45	61	45
Clapton	42	14	3	25	48	77	45
Harwich & Parkeston	42	11	6	25	51	84	38
Horsham	42	6	4	32	29	113	22

Harwich & Parkeston had 1 point deducted

Second Division

Billericay Town	36	31	3	2	100	18	96
Lewes	36	24	7	5	82	33	79
Hungerford Town	36	21	8	7	78	36	71
Eastbourne United	36	21	6	9	77	45	69
Letchworth Garden City	36	21	6	9	63	32	69
Hornchurch	36	21	6	9	66	39	69
Molesey	36	15	9	12	67	60	54
Barton Rovers	36	15	7	14	49	49	52
Worthing	36	14	9	13	58	54	51
Cheshunt	36	13	7	16	47	52	46
Rainham Town	36	12	7	17	54	65	43
Egham Town	36	11	9	16	47	53	42
Southall & Ealing Borough	36	11	6	19	43	69	39
Feltham	36	8	11	17	23	49	35
Tring Town	36	7	13	16	38	55	34
Epping Town	36	10	4	22	44	69	34
Willesden	36	9	6	21	32	83	33
Hemel Hempstead	36	4	9	23	33	72	21
Corinthian Casuals	36	6	3	27	24	92	21

Second Division

Feltham	38	24	10	4	65	30	82
Hornchurch	38	25	6	7	74	35	81
Hungerford Town	38	23	10	5	84	29	79
Barton Rovers	38	19	11	8	61	25	68
Worthing	38	19	11	8	74	43	68
Cheshunt	38	19	11	8	57	33	68
Letchworth Garden City	38	18	7	13	49	40	61
Southall	38	14	11	13	48	52	53
Dorking Town	38	13	12	13	47	45	51
Horsham	38	16	3	19	47	47	51
Hemel Hempstead	38	14	7	17	47	54	49
Egham Town	38	13	9	16	45	62	48
Harwich & Parkeston	38	12	11	15	57	58	47
Rainham Town	38	11	13	14	44	45	46
Epping Town	38	12	7	19	37	50	43
Eastbourne United	38	11	10	17	59	75	43
Willesden	38	11	8	19	57	68	41
Tring Town	38	11	6	21	40	71	39
Molesey	38	4	9	25	31	83	21
Corinthian Casuals	38	1	8	29	17	95	11

1980-81

Premier Division

Slough Town	42	23	13	6	73	34	82
Enfield	42	23	11	8	81	43	80
Wycombe Wanderers	42	22	9	11	76	49	75
Leytonstone & Ilford	42	19	12	11	78	57	69
Sutton United	42	19	12	11	82	65	69
Hendon	42	18	10	14	66	58	64
Dagenham	42	17	11	14	79	66	62
Hayes	42	18	8	16	45	50	62
Harrow Borough	42	16	11	15	57	52	59
Bromley	42	16	9	17	63	69	57
Staines Town	42	15	9	18	60	61	54
Tooting & Mitcham United	42	15	8	19	49	53	53
Hitchin Town	42	14	10	18	64	62	52
Croydon	42	12	15	15	51	51	51
Dulwich Hamlet	42	13	12	17	62	67	51
Leatherhead	42	12	14	16	36	50	50
Carshalton Athletic	42	14	8	20	57	82	50
Barking	42	13	12	17	58	72	49
Harlow Town	42	11	15	16	53	66	48
Walthamstow Avenue	42	13	7	22	50	81	46
Boreham Wood	42	10	13	19	46	69	43
Woking	42	11	7	24	40	69	37

Barking had 1 point deducted
Woking had 3 points deducted

1981-82

Premier Division

Leytonstone & Ilford	42	26	5	11	91	52	83
Sutton United	42	22	9	11	72	49	75
Wycombe Wanderers	42	21	10	11	63	48	73
Staines Town	42	21	9	12	58	45	72
Walthamstow Avenue	42	21	7	14	81	62	70
Harrow Borough	42	18	13	11	77	55	67
Tooting & Mitcham United	42	19	10	13	58	47	67
Slough Town	42	17	13	12	64	54	64
Leatherhead	42	16	12	14	57	52	60
Hayes	42	16	10	16	58	52	58
Croydon	42	16	9	17	59	57	57
Barking	42	14	14	14	53	51	56
Hendon	42	13	13	16	56	65	52
Dulwich Hamlet	42	14	10	18	47	59	52
Bishop's Stortford	42	15	5	22	50	70	50
Carshalton Athletic	42	14	8	20	58	86	50
Billericay Town	42	11	16	15	41	50	49
Hitchin Town	42	12	11	19	56	77	47
Bromley	42	13	7	22	63	79	46
Woking	42	11	13	18	57	75	46
Harlow Town	42	10	11	21	50	73	41
Boreham Wood	42	8	13	21	47	58	37

First Division

Bishop's Stortford	42	30	6	6	84	28	96
Billericay Town	42	29	6	7	67	34	93
Epsom & Ewell	42	24	12	6	80	36	84
Farnborough Town	42	23	11	8	75	39	80
St Albans City	42	24	5	13	85	61	77
Kingstonian	42	20	9	13	63	52	66
Oxford City	42	18	9	15	71	48	63
Wokingham Town	42	16	15	11	70	56	63
Metropolitan Police	42	18	7	17	61	58	61
Chesham United	42	17	7	18	64	64	58
Lewes	42	17	7	18	72	83	58
Maidenhead United	42	16	7	19	58	62	55
Walton & Hersham	42	12	15	15	46	53	51
Hertford Town	42	13	11	18	46	65	50
Hampton	42	12	13	17	46	53	49
Aveley	42	13	9	20	54	55	48
Wembley	42	13	8	21	47	61	47
Clapton	42	12	8	22	53	86	44
Ware	42	9	13	20	50	69	40
Tilbury	42	10	8	24	42	84	35
Camberley Town	42	8	7	27	42	88	31
Finchley	42	6	11	25	36	77	29

Kingstonian and Tilbury both had 3 points deducted

First Division

Wokingham Town	40	29	5	6	86	30	92
Bognor Regis Town	40	23	10	7	65	34	79
Metropolitan Police	40	22	11	7	75	48	77
Oxford City	40	21	11	8	82	47	74
Feltham	40	20	8	12	65	49	68
Lewes	40	19	7	14	73	66	64
Hertford Town	40	16	10	14	62	54	58
Wembley	40	14	15	11	69	55	57
Farnborough Town	40	15	11	14	71	57	56
Epsom & Ewell	40	16	8	16	52	44	56
Kingstonian	40	16	7	17	57	56	55
Hampton	40	15	9	16	52	52	54
Hornchurch	40	13	15	12	42	50	54
Aveley	40	14	10	16	46	58	54
St Albans City	40	14	9	17	55	55	51
Maidenhead United	40	11	10	19	49	70	43
Tilbury	40	9	15	16	49	66	42
Walton & Hersham	40	10	11	19	43	65	41
Chesham United	40	9	9	22	41	71	36
Clapton	40	9	7	24	44	75	34
Ware	40	5	2	33	29	105	17

Second Division

Worthing	40	29	6	5	95	25	93
Cheshunt	40	25	7	8	79	33	82
Hungerford Town	40	22	10	8	89	42	74
Barton Rovers	40	22	8	10	65	32	74
Windsor & Eton	40	22	6	12	69	49	72
Corinthian Casuals	40	19	12	9	67	50	69
Harwich & Parkeston	40	19	12	9	64	47	69
Letchworth Garden City	40	15	11	14	67	55	56
Dorking Town	40	13	17	10	52	44	56
Hemel Hempstead	40	15	9	16	54	49	54
Basildon United	40	16	5	19	64	51	53
Finchley	40	14	9	17	57	68	51
Southall	40	12	14	14	36	42	50
Epping Town	40	12	11	17	48	62	47
Molesey	40	13	7	20	61	73	46
Egham Town	40	11	9	20	56	64	42
Rainham Town	40	11	9	20	53	83	42
Tring Town	40	9	13	18	49	78	40
Eastbourne United	40	9	12	19	51	73	39
Horsham	40	10	9	21	42	79	39
Camberley Town	40	3	2	35	21	140	11

Hungerford Town had 2 points deducted

Second Division

Clapton	42	30	4	8	96	46	94
Windsor & Eton	42	27	7	8	98	43	88
Barton Rovers	42	26	6	10	86	48	84
Leyton Wingate	42	25	8	9	111	41	83
Basildon United	42	23	13	6	92	42	82
Uxbridge	42	22	12	8	80	42	78
Hungerford Town	42	22	10	10	82	39	76
Corinthian Casuals	42	23	6	13	95	48	75
Egham Town	42	21	8	13	77	67	71
Tring Town	42	20	10	12	86	59	70
Letchworth Garden City	42	18	13	11	68	53	66
Southall	42	18	7	17	81	80	61
Molesey	42	17	9	16	73	56	60
Dorking Town	42	15	9	18	56	75	54
Hemel Hempstead	42	12	14	16	53	59	50
Rainham Town	42	14	4	24	57	94	46
Eastbourne United	42	10	6	26	54	104	36
Epping Town	42	6	8	28	29	89	26
Ware	42	6	6	30	34	97	24
Finchley	42	4	12	26	28	92	24
Horsham	42	5	7	30	32	106	22
Harwich & Parkeston	42	5	7	30	42	130	22

Letchworth Garden City had 1 point deducted

1982-83

Premier Division

Wycombe Wanderers	42	26	7	9	79	47	85
Leytonstone & Ilford	42	24	9	9	71	39	81
Harrow Borough	42	24	7	11	91	58	79
Hayes	42	23	9	10	63	41	78
Sutton United	42	20	8	14	96	71	68
Dulwich Hamlet	42	18	14	10	59	52	68
Slough Town	42	18	13	11	73	36	67
Bognor Regis Town	42	19	8	15	53	48	65
Tooting & Mitcham United	42	18	9	15	65	62	63
Billericay Town	42	17	10	15	54	51	61
Croydon	42	17	9	16	68	58	60
Hendon	42	18	6	18	68	61	60
Bishop's Stortford	42	17	9	16	61	58	60
Barking	42	14	14	14	47	55	56
Bromley	42	14	12	16	51	50	54
Carshalton Athletic	42	15	9	18	58	60	54
Wokingham Town	42	13	9	20	37	51	48
Walthamstow Avenue	42	12	11	19	48	64	47
Staines Town	42	12	11	19	62	79	47
Hitchin Town	42	11	9	22	49	77	42
Woking	42	6	6	30	30	79	24
Leatherhead	42	4	5	33	35	121	17

First Division

Worthing	40	25	6	9	76	39	81
Harlow Town	40	21	11	8	84	55	74
Farnborough Town	40	20	13	7	69	39	73
Hertford Town	40	20	11	9	70	61	71
Oxford City	40	19	13	8	70	49	70
Boreham Wood	40	21	6	13	62	42	69
Metropolitan Police	40	19	9	12	77	57	66
Walton & Hersham	40	17	6	17	65	59	57
Hampton	40	15	10	15	62	60	55
Wembley	40	14	10	16	62	61	52
Aveley	40	15	7	18	52	62	52
Kingstonian	40	13	12	15	53	53	51
Tilbury	40	12	10	18	41	47	46
Feltham	40	11	12	17	45	54	45
Chesham United	40	13	6	21	43	70	45
Epsom & Ewell	40	10	14	16	44	49	44
Lewes	40	12	8	20	47	71	44
Cheshunt	40	10	13	17	41	49	43
Hornchurch	40	11	8	21	45	74	41
Maidenhead United	40	10	10	20	57	87	40
St Albans City	40	10	9	21	52	79	37

St Albans City had 2 points deducted

1983-84

Premier Division

Harrow Borough	42	25	13	4	73	42	88
Worthing	42	20	11	11	89	72	71
Slough Town	42	20	9	13	73	56	69
Sutton United	42	18	12	12	67	45	66
Hayes	42	17	13	12	56	41	64
Hitchin Town	42	16	15	11	58	57	63
Wycombe Wanderers	42	16	14	12	63	52	62
Wokingham Town	42	18	10	14	78	55	61
Hendon	42	17	10	15	62	51	61
Dulwich Hamlet	42	16	11	15	61	64	59
Bishop's Stortford	42	15	13	14	56	57	58
Harlow Town	42	15	11	16	64	70	56
Bognor Regis Town	42	14	13	15	62	69	55
Staines Town	42	15	9	18	63	72	54
Billericay Town	42	15	8	19	53	73	53
Barking	42	13	13	16	60	64	52
Croydon	42	14	10	18	52	58	52
Walthamstow Avenue	42	13	10	19	53	67	49
Leytonstone & Ilford	42	13	9	20	54	67	48
Carshalton Athletic	42	11	10	21	59	72	43
Tooting & Mitcham United	42	10	13	19	50	63	43
Bromley	42	7	11	24	33	72	32

Wokingham Town had 3 points deducted

First Division

Windsor & Eton	42	26	7	9	89	44	85
Epsom & Ewell	42	23	9	10	73	51	78
Wembley	42	21	11	10	65	32	74
Maidenhead United	42	22	8	12	67	42	74
Boreham Wood	42	22	7	13	74	43	73
Farnborough Town	42	18	12	12	78	60	66
Hampton	42	18	12	12	65	49	66
Metropolitan Police	42	20	5	17	79	64	65
Chesham United	42	18	8	16	64	57	62
Tilbury	42	17	10	15	54	64	61
Leatherhead	42	15	10	17	67	56	55
Aveley	42	15	10	17	49	53	55
Woking	42	16	7	19	66	73	55
Hertford Town	42	15	9	18	56	73	54
Oxford City	42	14	9	19	57	56	51
Lewes	42	13	12	17	49	65	51
Walton & Hersham	42	13	10	19	52	70	49
Hornchurch	42	13	10	19	43	65	49
Kingstonian	42	13	9	20	47	67	48
Clapton	42	12	11	19	49	67	47
Cheshunt	42	12	8	22	45	64	44
Feltham	42	7	4	31	31	106	25

Second Division

Basildon United	42	30	7	5	88	27	97
St Albans City	42	29	9	5	100	46	96
Leyton Wingate	42	29	4	9	97	41	91
Tring Town	42	23	11	8	89	44	80
Corinthian Casuals	42	23	11	8	75	47	80
Hungerford Town	42	21	12	9	94	47	75
Uxbridge	42	18	15	9	61	36	69
Grays Athletic	42	20	9	13	72	57	69
Dorking	42	21	5	16	66	54	68
Southall	42	20	8	14	79	60	65
Egham Town	42	16	15	11	59	49	63
Epping Town	42	15	16	11	61	50	61
Molesey	42	13	14	15	59	68	53
Barton Rovers	42	15	8	19	54	64	53
Letchworth Garden City	42	15	7	20	48	66	52
Newbury Town	42	14	5	23	60	82	47
Hemel Hempstead	42	12	9	21	63	69	45
Rainham Town	42	7	5	30	38	114	26
Finchley	42	5	9	28	28	78	24
Eastbourne United	42	7	3	32	36	98	24
Ware	42	6	6	30	48	114	24
Horsham	42	7	4	31	40	104	23

Southall had 2 points deducted
Horsham had 3 points deducted

1984-85

Premier Division

Sutton United	42	23	15	4	115	55	84
Worthing	42	24	8	10	89	59	80
Wycombe Wanderers	42	24	6	12	68	46	78
Wokingham Town	42	20	13	9	74	54	73
Windsor & Eton	42	19	10	13	65	55	67
Bognor Regis Town	42	20	6	16	67	58	66
Dulwich Hamlet	42	16	17	9	82	57	65
Harrow Borough	42	18	8	16	70	56	62
Hayes	42	17	8	17	60	56	59
Tooting & Mitcham United	42	16	11	15	64	66	59
Walthamstow Avenue	42	15	11	16	64	65	56
Croydon	42	15	12	15	62	63	54
Epsom & Ewell	42	13	14	15	65	62	53
Slough Town	42	13	12	17	69	74	51
Carshalton Athletic	42	14	8	20	55	68	50
Bishop's Stortford	42	12	12	18	48	67	48
Hendon	42	9	19	14	62	65	46
Billericay Town	42	11	14	17	53	74	46
Barking	42	13	7	22	43	75	46
Hitchin Town	42	10	15	17	55	70	45
Leytonstone & Ilford	42	11	10	21	37	72	43
Harlow Town	42	5	12	25	45	95	27

Billercay Town had 1 point deducted
Croydon had 3 points deducted

First Division

Farnborough Town	42	26	8	8	101	45	86
Kingstonian	42	23	10	9	67	39	79
Leatherhead	42	23	10	9	109	61	76
Chesham United	42	22	8	12	78	46	74
Wembley	42	20	10	12	59	40	70
St Albans City	42	19	10	13	79	60	67
Tilbury	42	18	13	11	86	68	67
Bromley	42	18	9	15	71	64	63
Hampton	42	17	11	14	75	62	62
Staines Town	42	16	11	15	59	53	59
Maidenhead United	42	17	8	17	65	64	59
Walton & Hersham	42	16	8	18	60	69	55
Aveley	42	16	7	19	62	78	55
Oxford City	42	14	12	16	62	53	54
Lewes	42	15	9	18	70	72	54
Basildon United	42	15	8	19	55	61	53
Boreham Wood	42	15	7	20	72	83	52
Hornchurch	42	15	6	21	55	74	51
Woking	42	15	6	21	60	91	51
Metropolitan Police	42	10	12	20	65	92	42
Clapton	42	5	11	26	50	124	26
Hertford Town	42	5	10	27	36	97	25

Walton & Hersham had 1 point deducted
Leatherhead had 3 points deducted

Second Division North

Leyton Wingate	38	24	9	5	98	50	81
Finchley	38	24	8	6	66	31	79
Heybridge Swifts	38	22	9	7	71	33	75
Stevenage Borough	38	23	6	9	79	49	75
Saffron Walden Town	38	22	8	8	73	31	74
Tring Town	38	19	11	8	76	41	68
Chalfont St Peter	38	17	10	11	72	41	61
Flackwell Heath	38	16	11	11	54	40	59
Berkhamsted Town	38	15	12	11	50	42	57
Letchworth Garden City	38	17	6	15	66	69	57
Royston Town	38	13	9	16	47	77	48
Cheshunt	38	14	5	19	52	57	47
Marlow	38	13	6	19	64	81	45
Hemel Hempstead	38	11	7	20	49	65	40
Barton Rovers	38	9	8	21	40	62	35
Wolverton Town	38	9	8	21	38	77	35
Kingsbury Town	38	9	7	22	53	72	34
Harefield United	38	7	9	22	51	81	30
Haringey Borough	38	6	12	20	38	79	30
Ware	38	7	5	26	40	100	26

Finchley had 1 point deducted
The record of Epping Town was expunged

Second Division South

Grays Athletic	36	24	9	3	84	25	81
Uxbridge	36	22	10	4	81	20	76
Molesey	36	20	5	11	62	42	65
Hungerford Town	36	18	9	9	71	49	63
Whyteleafe	36	17	10	9	66	34	61
Egham Town	36	17	7	12	54	42	58
Southall	36	18	3	15	54	57	57
Bracknell Town	36	15	7	14	54	48	52
Banstead Athletic	36	14	8	14	63	70	50
Horsham	36	13	10	13	44	39	49
Ruislip Manor	36	13	10	13	48	49	49
Dorking	36	12	11	13	45	50	47
Rainham Town	36	12	8	16	58	61	44
Feltham	36	10	13	13	44	58	43
Camberley Town	36	10	12	14	44	54	42
Eastbourne United	36	10	9	17	66	72	39
Petersfield Town	36	9	5	22	41	80	32
Newbury Town	36	8	7	21	35	69	16
Chertsey Town	36	2	3	31	23	118	6

Chertsey Town had 3 points deducted
Newbury Town had 15 points deducted

1985-86

Premier Division

Sutton United	42	29	8	5	109	39	95
Yeovil Town	42	28	7	7	92	48	91
Farnborough Town	42	23	8	11	90	50	77
Croydon	42	23	7	12	70	50	76
Harrow Borough	42	21	8	13	76	66	71
Slough Town	42	18	8	16	66	68	62
Bishop's Stortford	42	17	10	15	55	61	61
Kingstonian	42	15	15	12	57	56	60
Dulwich Hamlet	42	17	9	16	64	79	60
Wokingham Town	42	16	10	16	67	64	58
Windsor & Eton	42	17	7	18	58	75	58
Tooting & Mitcham United	42	14	11	17	65	76	53
Walthamstow Avenue	42	12	14	16	69	70	50
Worthing	42	13	10	19	72	82	49
Bognor Regis Town	42	15	6	21	63	70	48
Hayes	42	10	17	15	36	42	47
Hitchin Town	42	11	14	17	53	69	47
Barking	42	11	13	18	45	55	46
Hendon	42	10	13	19	59	77	43
Carshalton Athletic	42	9	13	20	56	79	40
Billericay Town	42	9	12	21	59	78	39
Epsom & Ewell	42	8	12	22	63	90	36

Bognor Regis Town had 3 points deducted

First Division

St Albans City	42	23	11	8	92	61	80
Bromley	42	24	8	10	68	41	80
Wembley	42	22	12	8	59	30	78
Oxford City	42	22	11	9	75	51	77
Hampton	42	21	11	10	63	45	74
Leyton Wingate	42	21	10	11	77	56	73
Uxbridge	42	20	8	14	64	49	68
Staines Town	42	18	10	14	69	66	64
Boreham Wood	42	15	16	11	62	54	61
Walton & Hersham	42	16	10	16	68	71	58
Lewes	42	16	8	18	61	75	56
Leytonstone & Ilford	42	13	15	14	57	67	54
Finchley	42	12	17	13	61	59	53
Grays Athletic	42	13	11	18	69	75	50
Leatherhead	42	14	8	20	62	68	50
Tilbury	42	13	11	18	60	66	50
Maidenhead United	42	13	7	22	61	67	46
Basildon United	42	12	9	21	52	72	45
Hornchurch	42	11	11	20	44	59	44
Chesham United	42	12	6	24	51	87	42
Harlow Town	42	8	14	20	53	70	38
Aveley	42	8	6	28	59	98	30

Second Division North

Stevenage Borough	38	26	6	6	71	24	84
Kingsbury Town	38	25	8	5	84	35	83
Heybridge Swifts	38	20	8	10	65	46	68
Cheshunt	38	18	10	10	60	40	64
Hertford Town	38	17	7	14	60	50	58
Chalfont St Peter	38	15	11	12	53	50	56
Tring Town	38	14	13	11	58	46	55
Royston Town	38	13	13	12	59	57	52
Saffron Walden Town	38	13	12	13	61	65	51
Berkhamsted Town	38	14	8	16	45	52	50
Haringey Borough	38	14	7	17	49	51	49
Letchworth Garden City	38	13	8	17	46	52	47
Rainham Town	38	14	4	20	54	91	46
Hemel Hempstead	38	12	9	17	50	66	45
Ware	38	11	11	16	56	61	44
Vauxhall Motors	38	11	10	17	58	62	43
Barton Rovers	38	12	7	19	50	60	43
Harefield United	38	9	12	17	56	72	39
Clapton	38	10	7	21	51	90	37
Wolverton Town	38	8	11	19	42	58	35

Second Division South

Southwick	38	25	8	5	86	34	83
Bracknell Town	38	24	9	5	80	23	81
Woking	38	23	9	6	94	45	78
Newbury Town	38	22	7	9	86	53	73
Whyteleafe	38	21	10	7	61	41	73
Molesey	38	21	8	9	59	39	71
Metropolitan Police	38	20	6	12	72	48	66
Southall	38	19	7	12	76	58	64
Dorking	38	18	10	10	70	57	64
Feltham	38	16	7	15	65	60	55
Banstead Athletic	38	15	8	15	60	66	53
Petersfield United	38	12	9	17	61	71	45
Hungerford Town	38	11	6	21	57	78	39
Flackwell Heath	38	11	6	21	46	72	39
Eastbourne United	38	9	8	21	51	81	35
Camberley Town	38	9	7	22	53	64	34
Egham Town	38	7	8	23	41	83	29
Horsham	38	6	10	22	33	74	28
Ruislip Manor	38	5	12	21	44	87	27
Marlow	38	6	5	27	47	108	23

1986-87

Premier Division

Wycombe Wanderers	42	32	5	5	103	32	101
Yeovil Town	42	28	8	6	71	27	92
Slough Town	42	23	8	11	70	44	77
Hendon	42	22	7	13	67	53	73
Bognor Regis Town	42	20	10	12	85	61	70
Harrow Borough	42	20	10	12	68	44	70
Croydon	42	18	10	14	51	48	64
Barking	42	16	14	12	76	56	62
Farnborough Town	42	17	11	14	66	72	62
Bishop's Stortford	42	15	15	12	62	57	60
Bromley	42	16	11	15	63	72	59
Kingstonian	42	16	9	17	58	50	57
Windsor & Eton	42	13	15	14	47	52	54
St Albans City	42	14	9	19	61	70	51
Carshalton Athletic	42	13	9	20	55	68	48
Wokingham Town	42	14	6	22	47	61	48
Hayes	42	12	12	18	45	68	48
Dulwich Hamlet	42	12	10	20	62	71	46
Tooting & Mitcham United	42	12	9	21	51	53	45
Hitchin Town	42	13	5	24	56	69	44
Worthing	42	8	9	25	58	107	33
Walthamstow Avenue	42	4	6	32	36	113	18

First Division

Leytonstone & Ilford	42	30	5	7	78	29	95
Leyton Wingate	42	23	13	6	68	31	82
Bracknell Town	42	24	9	9	92	48	81
Southwick	42	23	7	12	80	66	76
Wembley	42	21	9	12	61	47	72
Grays Athletic	42	19	10	13	76	64	67
Kingsbury Town	42	20	7	15	69	67	67
Boreham Wood	42	20	6	16	59	52	66
Uxbridge	42	18	9	15	60	59	63
Leatherhead	42	17	11	14	45	48	62
Hampton	42	18	5	19	57	55	59
Basildon United	42	16	10	16	58	60	58
Billericay Town	42	14	12	16	57	52	54
Staines Town	42	13	13	16	40	51	52
Lewes	42	15	6	21	55	65	51
Stevenage Borough	42	12	11	19	61	67	47
Oxford City	42	11	10	21	64	72	43
Walton & Hersham	42	11	10	21	53	74	43
Tilbury	42	12	7	23	46	70	43
Epsom & Ewell	42	12	7	23	44	68	43
Maidenhead United	42	11	4	27	44	76	37
Finchley	42	6	11	25	44	90	29

Second Division North

Chesham United	42	28	6	8	81	48	90
Wolverton Town	42	23	14	5	74	32	83
Haringey Borough	42	22	13	7	86	40	79
Heybridge Swifts	42	21	11	10	81	54	74
Aveley	42	19	13	10	68	50	70
Letchworth Garden City	42	19	11	12	77	62	68
Barton Rovers	42	18	11	13	49	39	65
Tring Town	42	19	7	16	69	49	64
Collier Row	42	19	5	18	67	65	62
Ware	42	17	8	17	51	50	59
Saffron Walden Town	42	14	14	14	56	54	56
Wivenhoe Town	42	15	11	16	61	61	56
Vauxhall Motors	42	15	10	17	61	57	55
Hornchurch	42	13	16	13	60	60	55
Hertford Town	42	14	13	15	52	53	55
Berkhamsted Town	42	12	16	14	62	64	52
Harlow Town	42	13	11	18	45	55	50
Rainham Town	42	12	11	19	53	70	47
Clapton	42	10	11	21	45	63	41
Hemel Hempstead	42	9	12	21	48	77	39
Royston Town	42	4	12	26	37	109	24
Cheshunt	42	5	6	31	43	114	21

Second Division South

	P	W	D	L	F	A	Pts
Woking	40	27	7	6	110	32	88
Marlow	40	28	4	8	78	36	88
Dorking	40	24	12	4	78	30	84
Feltham	40	25	3	12	79	34	78
Ruislip Manor	40	22	10	8	85	47	76
Chertsey Town	40	18	11	11	56	44	65
Metropolitan Police	40	16	13	11	70	61	61
Chalfont St Peter	40	17	10	13	60	55	61
Hungerford Town	40	14	14	12	55	48	56
Harefield United	40	14	14	12	53	47	56
Eastbourne United	40	15	10	15	72	59	55
Whyteleafe	40	12	15	13	52	63	51
Horsham	40	14	8	18	54	61	50
Egham Town	40	14	6	20	45	77	48
Camberley Town	40	13	3	24	62	89	42
Flackwell Heath	40	9	11	20	34	63	38
Banstead Athletic	40	7	15	18	44	61	36
Petersfield United	40	9	8	23	45	84	34
Molesey	40	7	12	21	37	89	33
Newbury Town	40	6	14	20	51	83	32
Southall	40	6	6	28	28	85	24

Second Division North

	P	W	D	L	F	A	Pts
Wivenhoe Town	42	26	10	6	105	42	88
Collier Row	42	22	13	7	71	39	79
Tilbury	42	18	15	9	61	40	69
Berkhamsted Town	42	19	12	11	71	53	69
Harlow Town	42	17	16	9	67	36	67
Ware	42	17	15	10	63	58	66
Witham Town	42	17	14	11	69	47	65
Vauxhall Motors	42	16	17	9	56	42	65
Heybridge Swifts	42	17	13	12	56	50	64
Tring Town	42	18	6	18	69	67	60
Letchworth Garden City	42	18	5	19	59	64	59
Finchley	42	16	10	16	67	54	58
Clapton	42	14	15	13	50	62	57
Hornchurch	42	13	15	14	56	65	54
Barton Rovers	42	13	10	19	43	60	49
Rainham Town	42	12	12	18	63	66	48
Royston Town	42	13	8	21	49	70	47
Saffron Walden Town	42	13	7	22	34	67	46
Hemel Hempstead	42	11	12	19	38	71	45
Haringey Borough	42	11	8	23	54	78	41
Aveley	42	8	13	21	42	65	37
Hertford Town	42	8	4	30	45	92	28

Second Division South

	P	W	D	L	F	A	Pts
Chalfont St Peter	42	26	9	7	81	35	87
Metropolitan Police	42	23	17	2	80	32	86
Dorking	42	25	11	6	86	39	86
Feltham	42	21	12	9	74	41	75
Epsom & Ewell	42	21	11	10	71	49	74
Chertsey Town	42	22	7	13	63	47	73
Whyteleafe	42	20	11	11	84	55	71
Hungerford Town	42	21	7	14	66	54	70
Ruislip Manor	42	21	5	16	74	57	68
Yeading	42	19	10	13	83	56	67
Maidenhead United	42	18	12	12	69	54	66
Eastbourne United	42	18	10	14	67	57	64
Harefield Town	42	18	6	18	59	60	60
Egham Town	42	12	12	18	45	55	48
Horsham	42	12	10	20	45	66	46
Southall	42	13	7	22	45	72	46
Molesey	42	11	11	20	42	63	44
Newbury Town	42	8	13	21	40	81	37
Camberley Town	42	9	9	24	51	94	36
Flackwell Heath	42	6	8	28	42	96	26
Banstead Athletic	42	6	7	29	34	81	25
Petersfield United	42	6	7	29	45	102	25

1987-88

Premier Division

	P	W	D	L	F	A	Pts
Yeovil Town	42	24	9	9	66	34	81
Bromley	42	23	7	12	68	40	76
Slough Town	42	21	9	12	67	41	72
Leytonstone & Ilford	42	20	11	11	59	43	71
Wokingham Town	42	21	7	14	62	52	70
Hayes	42	20	9	13	62	48	69
Windsor & Eton	42	16	17	9	59	43	65
Farnborough Town	42	17	11	14	63	60	62
Carshalton Athletic	42	16	13	13	49	41	61
Hendon	42	16	12	14	62	58	60
Tooting & Mitcham United	42	15	14	13	57	59	59
Harrow Borough	42	15	11	16	53	58	56
Bishop's Stortford	42	15	10	17	55	58	55
Kingstonian	42	14	12	16	47	53	54
St Albans City	42	15	6	21	60	69	51
Bognor Regis Town	42	14	9	19	41	57	51
Leyton Wingate	42	14	8	20	58	64	50
Croydon	42	11	13	18	40	52	46
Barking	42	11	12	19	44	57	45
Dulwich Hamlet	42	10	11	21	46	64	41
Hitchin Town	42	10	8	24	46	79	38
Basingstoke Town	42	6	17	19	37	71	35

First Division

	P	W	D	L	F	A	Pts
Marlow	42	32	5	5	100	44	101
Grays Athletic	42	30	10	2	74	25	100
Woking	42	25	7	10	91	52	82
Boreham Wood	42	21	9	12	65	45	72
Staines Town	42	19	11	12	71	48	68
Wembley	42	18	11	13	54	46	65
Basildon United	42	18	9	15	65	58	63
Walton & Hersham	42	15	16	11	53	44	61
Hampton	42	17	10	15	59	54	61
Leatherhead	42	16	11	15	64	53	59
Southwick	42	13	12	17	59	63	51
Oxford City	42	13	12	17	70	77	51
Worthing	42	14	8	20	67	73	50
Kingsbury Town	42	11	17	14	62	69	50
Walthamstow Avenue	42	13	11	18	53	63	50
Lewes	42	12	13	17	83	77	49
Uxbridge	42	11	16	15	41	47	49
Chesham United	42	12	10	20	69	77	46
Bracknell Town	42	12	9	21	54	80	45
Billericay Town	42	11	11	20	58	88	44
Stevenage Borough	42	11	9	22	36	64	42
Wolverton Town	42	3	3	36	23	124	12

1988-89

Premier Division

	P	W	D	L	F	A	Pts
Leytonstone & Ilford	42	26	11	5	76	36	89
Farnborough Town	42	24	9	9	85	61	81
Slough Town	42	24	6	12	72	42	78
Carshalton Athletic	42	19	15	8	59	36	72
Grays Athletic	42	19	13	10	62	47	70
Kingstonian	42	19	11	12	54	37	68
Bishop's Stortford	42	20	6	16	70	56	66
Hayes	42	18	12	12	6	47	66
Bognor Regis Town	42	17	11	14	38	49	62
Barking	42	16	13	13	49	45	61
Wokingham Town	42	15	11	16	60	54	56
Hendon	42	13	17	12	51	68	56
Windsor & Eton	42	14	13	15	52	50	55
Bromley	42	13	15	14	61	48	54
Leyton Wingate	42	13	15	14	55	56	54
Dulwich Hamlet	42	12	12	18	58	57	48
St Albans City	42	12	9	21	51	59	45
Dagenham	42	11	12	19	53	68	45
Harrow Borough	42	9	13	20	53	75	40
Marlow	42	9	11	22	48	83	38
Tooting & Mitcham United	42	10	6	26	41	81	36
Croydon	42	4	9	29	27	81	21

First Division

Staines Town	40	26	9	5	79	29	87
Basingstoke Town	40	25	8	7	85	36	83
Woking	40	24	10	6	72	30	82
Hitchin Town	40	21	11	8	60	32	74
Wivenhoe Town	40	22	6	12	62	44	72
Lewes	40	21	8	11	72	54	71
Walton & Hersham	40	21	7	12	56	36	70
Kingsbury Town	40	20	7	13	65	41	67
Uxbridge	40	19	7	14	60	54	64
Wembley	40	18	6	16	45	58	60
Boreham Wood	40	16	9	15	57	52	57
Leatherhead	40	14	8	18	56	58	50
Metropolitan Police	40	13	9	18	52	68	48
Chesham United	40	12	9	19	54	67	45
Southwick	40	9	15	16	44	58	42
Chalfont St Peter	40	11	9	20	56	82	42
Hampton	40	7	14	19	37	62	35
Worthing	40	8	10	22	49	80	32
Collier Row	40	8	7	25	37	82	31
Bracknell Town	40	8	6	26	38	70	30
Basildon Town	40	6	7	27	34	77	25

Worthing had 2 points deducted.

Second Division North

Harlow Town	42	27	9	6	83	38	90
Purfleet	42	22	12	8	60	42	78
Tring Town	42	22	10	10	65	44	76
Stevenage Borough	42	20	13	9	84	55	73
Heybridge Swifts	42	21	9	12	64	43	72
Billericay Town	42	19	11	12	65	52	68
Clapton	42	18	11	13	65	56	65
Barton Rovers	42	18	11	13	58	50	65
Aveley	42	18	10	14	54	52	64
Hertford Town	42	16	13	13	62	49	59
Ware	42	17	8	17	60	65	59
Hemel Hempstead	42	16	10	16	55	58	58
Witham Town	42	16	7	19	69	67	55
Vauxhall Motors	42	15	9	18	53	57	54
Berkhamsted Town	42	14	10	18	57	70	52
Hornchurch	42	11	16	15	59	61	49
Tilbury	42	13	10	19	53	60	49
Royston Town	42	12	7	23	46	72	43
Rainham Town	42	9	15	18	49	62	42
Saffron Walden Town	42	8	16	18	54	72	40
Letchworth Garden City	42	4	18	20	34	71	30
Wolverton Town	42	5	7	30	42	95	13

Hertford Town 2 points deducted, Wolverton Town 9 points deducted.

Second Division South

Dorking	40	32	4	4	109	35	100
Whyteleafe	40	25	9	6	86	41	84
Finchley	40	21	9	10	70	45	72
Molesey	40	19	13	8	58	42	70
Harefield United	40	19	7	14	56	45	64
Hungerford Town	40	17	13	10	55	45	64
Ruislip Manor	40	16	9	15	56	43	57
Feltham	40	16	9	15	58	53	57
Epsom & Ewell	40	16	8	16	55	55	56
Egham Town	40	16	7	17	54	58	55
Eastbourne United	40	15	9	16	68	61	54
Chertsey Town	40	13	14	13	55	58	53
Flackwell Heath	40	13	11	16	51	49	50
Camberley Town	40	15	5	20	51	71	50
Yeading	40	13	9	18	47	63	46
Banstead Athletic	40	12	8	20	50	65	44
Maidenhead United	40	10	13	17	44	61	43
Southall	40	11	10	19	41	73	43
Newbury Town	40	11	8	21	47	65	41
Horsham	40	7	14	19	36	68	35
Petersfield United	40	5	7	28	36	87	22

Yeading had 2 points deducted.

1989-90

Premier Division

Slough Town	42	27	11	4	85	38	92
Wokingham Town	42	26	11	5	67	34	89
Aylesbury United	42	25	9	8	86	30	84
Kingstonian	42	24	9	9	87	51	81
Grays Athletic	42	19	13	10	59	44	70
Dagenham	42	17	15	10	54	43	66
Leyton Wingate	42	20	6	16	54	48	66
Basingstoke Town	42	18	9	15	65	55	63
Bishop's Stortford	42	19	6	17	60	59	63
Carshalton Athletic	42	19	5	18	63	59	59
Redbridge Forest	42	16	11	15	65	62	59
Hendon	42	15	10	17	54	63	55
Windsor & Eton	42	13	15	14	51	47	54
Hayes	42	14	11	17	61	59	53
St Albans City	42	13	10	19	49	59	49
Staines Town	42	14	6	22	53	69	48
Marlow	42	11	13	18	42	59	46
Harrow Borough	42	11	10	21	51	79	43
Bognor Regis Town	42	9	14	19	37	67	41
Barking	42	7	11	24	53	86	32
Bromley	42	7	11	24	32	69	32
Dulwich Hamlet	42	6	8	28	32	80	26

Carshalton Athletic had 3 points deducted.

First Division

Wivenhoe Town	42	31	7	4	94	36	100
Woking	42	30	8	4	102	29	98
Southwick	42	23	15	4	68	30	84
Hitchin Town	42	22	13	7	60	30	79
Walton & Hersham	42	20	10	12	68	50	70
Dorking	42	19	12	11	66	41	69
Boreham Wood	42	17	13	12	60	59	64
Harlow Town	42	16	13	13	60	53	61
Metropolitan Police	42	16	11	15	54	59	59
Chesham United	42	15	12	15	46	49	57
Chalfont St Peter	42	14	13	15	50	59	55
Tooting & Mitcham United	42	14	13	15	51	51	55
Worthing	42	15	8	19	56	63	53
Whyteleafe	42	11	16	15	50	65	49
Lewes	42	12	11	19	55	65	47
Wembley	42	11	10	21	57	68	43
Croydon	42	9	16	17	43	57	43
Uxbridge	42	11	10	21	52	75	43
Hampton	42	8	13	21	28	51	37
Leatherhead	42	7	10	25	34	77	31
Purfleet	42	7	8	27	33	78	29
Kingsbury Town	42	8	10	24	45	78	25

Kingsbury Town had 9 points deducted

Second Division North

Heybridge Swifts	42	26	9	7	79	29	87
Aveley	42	23	16	3	68	24	85
Hertford Town	42	24	11	7	92	51	83
Stevenage Borough	42	21	16	5	70	31	79
Barton Rovers	42	22	6	14	60	45	72
Tilbury	42	20	9	13	68	54	69
Basildon United	42	13	20	9	50	44	59
Collier Row	42	15	13	14	43	45	58
Royston Town	42	15	11	16	63	72	56
Saffron Walden Town	42	15	11	16	60	73	56
Vauxhall Motors	42	14	13	15	55	54	55
Clapton	42	13	16	13	50	46	54
Ware	42	14	11	17	53	59	53
Hemel Hempstead	42	12	15	15	58	70	51
Billericay Town	42	13	11	18	49	58	50
Hornchurch	42	12	12	18	49	64	48
Berkhamsted Town	42	9	16	17	44	68	43
Finchley	42	11	10	21	50	75	43
Tring Town	42	10	9	23	48	70	39
Witham Town	42	8	14	20	44	56	38
Rainham Town	42	9	11	22	48	75	38
Letchworth Garden City	42	7	12	23	30	68	33

Clapton had 1 point deducted

Second Division South

Yeading	40	29	4	7	86	37	91
Molesey	40	24	11	5	76	30	83
Abingdon Town	40	22	9	9	64	39	75
Ruislip Manor	40	20	12	8	60	32	72
Maidenhead United	40	20	12	8	66	39	72
Southall	40	22	5	13	56	33	71
Newbury Town	40	21	7	12	50	36	70
Flackwell Heath	40	16	11	13	69	65	59
Hungerford Town	40	14	16	10	54	51	58
Egham Town	40	12	14	14	39	38	50
Banstead Athletic	40	14	8	18	46	47	50
Harefield United	40	13	9	18	44	46	48
Chertsey Town	40	13	9	18	53	58	48
Epsom & Ewell	40	13	9	18	49	54	48
Malden Vale	40	13	7	20	36	67	46
Eastbourne United	40	11	10	19	47	65	43
Camberley Town	40	11	9	20	44	66	42
Feltham	40	11	7	22	47	80	40
Bracknell Town	40	10	9	21	40	57	39
Petersfield United	40	10	8	22	48	93	38
Horsham	40	4	8	28	29	70	20

Second Division North

Stevenage Borough	42	34	5	3	122	29	107
Vauxhall Motors	42	24	10	8	82	50	82
Billericay Town	42	22	8	12	70	41	74
Ware	42	22	8	12	78	51	74
Berkhamsted Town	42	19	11	12	60	51	68
Witham Town	42	19	10	13	70	59	67
Purfleet	42	17	14	11	68	57	65
Rainham Town	42	19	7	16	57	46	64
Hemel Hempstead	42	16	14	12	62	56	62
Barton Rovers	42	17	10	15	61	58	61
Saffron Walden Town	42	16	13	13	72	77	61
Collier Row	42	16	11	15	63	63	59
Kingsbury Town	42	17	8	17	64	72	59
Edgware Town	42	17	7	18	73	65	58
Hertford Town	42	16	10	16	69	70	58
Royston Town	42	14	15	13	78	62	57
Tilbury	42	14	6	22	70	79	48
Basildon United	42	11	10	21	61	90	43
Hornchurch	42	10	9	23	53	87	39
Clapton	42	9	10	23	54	93	34
Finchley	42	6	7	29	50	112	24
Tring Town	42	1	9	32	30	99	12

Finchley had 1 point deducted
Clapton had 3 points deducted

1990-91

Premier Division

Redbridge Forest	42	29	6	7	74	43	93
Enfield	42	26	11	5	83	30	89
Aylesbury United	42	24	11	7	90	47	83
Woking	42	24	10	8	84	39	82
Kingstonian	42	21	12	9	86	57	75
Grays Athletic	42	20	8	14	66	53	68
Marlow	42	18	13	11	72	49	67
Hayes	42	20	5	17	60	57	65
Carshalton Athletic	42	19	7	16	80	67	64
Wivenhoe Town	42	16	11	15	69	66	59
Wokingham Town	42	15	13	14	58	54	58
Windsor & Eton	42	15	10	17	48	63	55
Bishop's Stortford	42	14	12	16	54	49	54
Dagenham	42	13	11	18	62	68	50
Hendon	42	12	10	20	48	62	46
St Albans City	42	11	12	19	60	74	45
Bognor Regis Town	42	12	8	22	44	71	44
Basingstoke Town	42	12	7	23	57	95	43
Staines Town	42	10	10	22	46	79	39
Harrow Borough	42	10	8	24	57	84	38
Barking	42	8	10	24	41	85	34
Leyton Wingate	42	7	7	28	44	91	28

Staines Town had 1 point deducted

Second Division South

Abingdon Town	42	29	7	6	95	28	94
Maidenhead United	42	28	8	6	85	33	92
Egham Town	42	27	6	9	100	46	87
Malden Vale	42	26	5	11	72	44	83
Ruislip Manor	42	25	5	12	93	44	80
Southall	42	23	10	9	84	43	79
Harefield United	42	23	10	9	81	56	79
Newbury Town	42	23	8	11	71	45	77
Hungerford Town	42	16	13	13	84	69	61
Leatherhead	42	17	9	16	82	55	60
Banstead Athletic	42	15	13	14	58	62	58
Hampton	42	14	15	13	62	43	57
Epsom & Ewell	42	15	12	15	49	50	57
Chertsey Town	42	15	9	18	76	72	54
Horsham	42	14	7	21	58	67	49
Flackwell Heath	42	11	11	20	56	78	44
Bracknell Town	42	11	7	24	60	97	40
Feltham	42	10	8	24	45	80	38
Cove	42	10	7	25	51	94	37
Eastbourne United	42	10	7	25	53	109	37
Petersfield United	42	6	3	33	35	119	21
Camberley Town	42	1	6	35	27	143	9

First Division

Chesham United	42	27	8	7	102	37	89
Bromley	42	22	14	6	62	37	80
Yeading	42	23	8	11	75	45	77
Aveley	42	21	9	12	76	43	72
Hitchin Town	42	21	9	12	78	50	72
Tooting & Mitcham United	42	20	12	10	71	48	72
Walton & Hersham	42	21	8	13	73	48	71
Molesey	42	22	5	15	65	46	71
Whyteleafe	42	21	6	15	62	53	69
Dorking	42	20	5	17	78	67	65
Chalfont St Peter	42	19	5	18	56	63	62
Dulwich Hamlet	42	16	11	15	67	54	59
Harlow Town	42	17	8	17	73	64	59
Boreham Wood	42	15	8	19	46	53	53
Wembley	42	13	12	17	62	59	51
Uxbridge	42	15	5	22	45	61	50
Croydon	42	15	5	22	44	85	50
Heybridge Swifts	42	13	10	19	46	59	49
Southwick	42	13	8	21	49	75	47
Lewes	42	10	8	24	49	82	38
Metropolitan Police	42	9	6	27	55	76	33
Worthing	42	2	4	36	28	157	10

1991-92

Premier Division

Woking	42	30	7	5	96	25	97
Enfield	42	24	7	11	59	45	79
Sutton United	42	19	13	10	88	51	70
Chesham United	42	20	10	12	67	48	70
Wokingham Town	42	19	10	13	73	58	67
Marlow	42	20	7	15	56	50	67
Ayelsbury United	42	16	17	9	69	46	65
Carshalton Athletic	42	18	8	16	64	67	62
Dagenham	42	15	16	11	70	59	61
Kingstonian	42	17	8	17	71	65	59
Windsor & Eton	42	15	11	16	56	56	56
Bromley	42	14	12	16	51	57	54
St Albans City	42	14	11	17	66	70	53
Basingstoke Town	42	14	11	17	56	65	53
Grays Athletic	42	14	11	17	53	68	53
Wivenhoe Town	42	16	4	22	56	81	52
Hendon	42	13	9	20	59	73	48
Harrow Borough	42	11	13	18	58	78	46
Hayes	42	10	14	18	52	63	44
Staines Town	42	11	10	21	43	73	43
Bognor Regis Town	42	9	11	22	51	89	38
Bishop's Stortford	42	7	12	23	41	68	33

First Division

Stevenage Borough	40	30	6	4	95	37	96
Yeading	40	24	10	6	83	34	82
Dulwich Hamlet	40	22	9	9	71	40	75
Boreham Wood	40	22	7	11	65	40	73
Wembley	40	21	6	13	54	43	69
Abingdon Town	40	19	8	13	60	47	65
Tooting & Mitcham United	40	16	13	11	57	45	61
Hitchin Town	40	17	10	13	55	45	61
Walton & Hersham	40	15	13	12	62	50	58
Molesey	40	16	9	15	55	61	57
Dorking	40	16	7	17	68	65	55
Barking	40	14	11	15	51	54	53
Chalfont St Peter	40	15	6	19	62	70	51
Leyton Wingate	40	13	11	16	53	56	50
Uxbridge	40	13	8	19	47	62	47
Maidenhead United	40	13	7	20	52	61	46
Harlow Town	40	11	9	20	50	70	42
Croydon	40	11	6	23	44	68	39
Heybridge Swifts	40	8	9	23	33	71	33
Whyteleafe	40	7	10	23	42	78	31
Aveley	40	8	3	29	33	95	27

Second Division

Purfleet	42	27	8	7	97	48	89
Lewes	42	23	14	5	74	36	83
Billericay Town	42	24	8	10	75	44	80
Leatherhead	42	23	6	13	68	40	75
Ruislip Manor	42	20	9	13	74	51	69
Egham Town	42	19	12	11	81	62	69
Metropolitan Police	42	20	9	13	76	58	69
Saffron Walden Town	42	19	11	12	86	67	68
Hemel Hempstead	42	18	10	14	63	50	64
Hungerford Town	42	18	7	17	53	58	61
Barton Rovers	42	17	8	17	61	64	59
Worthing	42	17	8	17	67	72	59
Witham Town	42	16	11	15	56	61	59
Banstead Athletic	42	16	10	16	69	58	58
Malden Vale	42	15	12	15	63	48	57
Rainham Town	42	14	13	15	53	48	55
Ware	42	14	9	19	58	62	51
Berkhamsted Town	42	13	11	18	56	57	50
Harefield United	42	11	7	24	47	66	40
Southall	42	8	7	27	39	93	31
Southwick	42	6	2	34	29	115	20
Newbury Town	42	4	8	30	30	117	20

Third Division

Edgware Town	40	30	3	7	106	44	93
Chertsey Town	40	29	4	7	115	44	91
Tilbury	40	26	9	5	84	40	87
Hampton	40	26	5	9	93	35	83
Horsham	40	23	8	9	92	51	77
Cove	40	21	9	10	74	49	72
Flackwell Heath	40	19	12	9	78	50	69
Thame United	40	19	7	14	73	46	64
Epsom & Ewell	40	17	11	12	55	50	62
Collier Row	40	17	9	14	67	59	60
Royston Town	40	17	7	16	59	58	58
Kingsbury Town	40	12	10	18	54	61	46
Hertford Town	40	12	10	18	55	73	46
Petersfield United	40	12	9	19	45	67	45
Camberley Town	40	11	8	21	52	69	41
Feltham & Hounslow	40	11	2	22	53	78	40
Bracknell Town	40	10	7	23	48	90	37
Hornchurch	40	8	7	25	40	87	31
Tring Town	40	9	4	27	35	94	31
Clapton	40	9	3	28	47	92	30
Eastbourne United	40	5	5	30	34	121	20

1992-93

Premier Division

Chesham United	42	30	8	4	104	34	98
St Albans City	42	28	9	5	103	50	93
Enfield	42	25	6	11	94	48	81
Carshalton Athletic	42	22	10	10	96	56	76
Sutton United	42	18	14	10	74	57	68
Grays Athletic	42	18	11	13	61	64	65
Stevenage Borough	42	18	8	16	62	60	62
Harrow Borough	42	16	14	12	59	60	62
Hayes	42	16	13	13	64	59	61
Aylesbury United	42	18	6	18	70	77	60
Hendon	42	12	18	12	52	54	54
Basingstoke Town	42	12	17	13	49	45	53
Kingstonian	42	14	10	18	59	58	52
Dulwich Hamlet	42	12	14	16	52	66	50
Marlow	42	12	11	19	72	73	47
Wokingham Town	42	11	13	18	62	81	46
Bromley	42	11	13	18	51	72	46
Wivenhoe Town	42	13	7	22	41	75	46
Yeading	42	11	12	19	58	66	45
Staines Town	42	10	13	19	59	77	43
Windsor & Eton	42	8	7	27	40	90	31
Bognor Regis Town	42	5	10	27	46	106	25

First Division

Hitchin Town	40	25	7	8	67	29	82
Molesey	40	23	11	6	81	38	80
Dorking	40	23	9	8	73	40	78
Purfleet	40	19	12	9	67	42	69
Bishop's Stortford	40	19	10	11	63	42	67
Abingdon Town	40	17	13	10	65	47	64
Tooting & Mitcham United	40	17	12	11	68	46	63
Billericay Town	40	18	6	16	67	61	60
Wembley	40	14	15	11	44	34	57
Walton & Hersham	40	14	12	14	58	54	54
Boreham Wood	40	12	14	14	44	43	50
Maidenhead United	40	10	18	12	45	50	48
Leyton	40	11	14	15	56	61	47
Whyteleafe	40	12	10	18	63	71	46
Uxbridge	40	11	13	16	50	59	46
Heybridge Swifts	40	11	9	20	47	65	42
Croydon	40	11	9	20	54	82	42
Chalfont St Peter	40	7	17	16	48	70	38
Barking	40	10	8	22	42	80	38
Lewes	40	9	10	21	34	80	37
Aveley	40	9	7	24	45	87	34

Second Division

Worthing	42	28	7	7	105	50	91
Ruislip Manor	42	25	12	5	78	33	87
Berkhamsted Town	42	24	8	10	77	55	80
Hemel Hempstead	42	22	12	8	84	52	78
Metropolitan Police	42	22	6	14	84	51	72
Malden Vale	42	20	9	13	78	54	69
Chertsey Town	42	20	7	15	84	60	67
Saffron Walden Town	42	19	10	13	63	49	67
Newbury Town	42	14	18	10	53	51	60
Hampton	42	16	11	15	59	59	59
Edgware Town	42	16	10	16	84	75	58
Egham Town	42	16	9	17	60	71	57
Banstead Athletic	42	14	13	15	67	52	55
Leatherhead	42	14	11	17	66	61	53
Ware	42	12	11	19	68	76	47
Witham Town	42	10	16	16	54	65	46
Tilbury	42	12	8	22	55	101	44
Barton Rovers	42	9	14	19	40	66	41
Hungerford Town	42	11	8	23	37	93	41
Rainham Town	42	9	10	23	56	80	37
Harefield United	42	10	7	25	37	72	37
Southall	42	7	7	28	43	106	28

Third Division

Aldershot Town	38	28	8	2	90	35	92
Thame United	38	21	11	6	84	38	74
Collier Row	38	21	11	6	68	30	74
Leighton Town	38	21	10	7	89	47	73
Cove	38	21	8	9	69	42	71
Northwood	38	19	11	8	84	68	68
Royston Town	38	17	8	13	59	42	59
East Thurrock United	38	17	7	14	69	58	58
Kingsbury Town	38	15	9	14	62	59	54
Hertford Town	38	14	10	14	61	64	52
Flackwell Heath	38	15	6	17	82	76	51
Tring Town	38	12	11	15	59	63	47
Hornchurch	38	11	13	14	53	52	46
Horsham	38	12	7	19	63	72	43
Epsom & Ewell	38	10	11	17	52	67	41
Bracknell Town	38	7	13	18	52	94	34
Clapton	38	8	7	23	46	74	31
Camberley Town	38	8	7	23	37	72	31
Petersfield United	38	6	12	20	36	90	30
Feltham & Hounslow	38	5	4	29	47	119	19

Second Division

Newbury Town	42	32	7	3	115	36	103
Chertsey Town	42	33	3	6	121	48	102
Aldershot Town	42	30	7	5	78	27	97
Barton Rovers	42	25	8	9	68	37	83
Witham Town	42	21	10	11	68	51	73
Malden Vale	42	20	10	12	70	49	70
Thame United	42	19	12	11	87	51	69
Metropolitan Police	42	20	9	13	75	54	69
Banstead Athletic	42	19	9	14	56	53	66
Aveley	42	19	5	18	60	66	62
Edgware Town	42	16	10	16	88	75	58
Saffron Walden Town	42	17	7	18	61	62	58
Hemel Hempstead	42	14	11	17	47	43	53
Egham Town	42	14	8	20	48	65	50
Ware	42	14	7	21	48	76	49
Hungerford Town	42	13	7	22	56	66	46
Tilbury	42	13	3	26	59	81	42
Hampton	42	12	5	25	42	70	41
Leatherhead	42	10	6	26	46	92	36
Lewes	42	8	11	24	38	85	34
Collier Row	42	7	8	27	37	88	29
Rainham Town	42	4	2	36	24	116	14

1993-94

Premier Division

Stevenage Borough	42	31	4	7	88	39	97
Enfield	42	28	8	6	80	28	92
Marlow	42	25	7	10	90	67	82
Chesham United	42	24	8	10	73	45	80
Sutton United	42	23	10	9	77	31	79
Carshalton Athletic	42	22	7	13	81	53	73
St Albans City	42	21	10	11	81	54	73
Hitchin Town	42	21	7	14	81	56	70
Harrow Borough	42	18	11	13	54	56	65
Kingstonian	42	18	9	15	101	64	63
Hendon	42	18	9	15	61	51	63
Aylesbury United	42	17	7	18	64	67	58
Hayes	42	15	8	19	63	72	53
Grays Athletic	42	15	5	22	56	69	50
Bromley	42	14	7	21	56	69	49
Dulwich Hamlet	42	13	8	21	52	74	47
Yeading	42	11	13	18	58	66	46
Molesey	42	11	11	20	44	62	44
Wokingham Town	42	11	6	25	38	67	39
Dorking	42	9	4	29	58	104	31
Basingstoke Town	42	5	12	25	38	86	27
Wivenhoe Town	42	5	3	34	38	152	18

First Division

Bishop's Stortford	42	24	13	5	83	31	85
Purfleet	42	22	12	8	70	44	78
Walton & Hersham	42	22	11	9	81	53	77
Tooting & Mitcham United	42	21	12	9	66	37	75
Heybridge Swifts	42	20	11	11	72	45	71
Billericay Town	42	20	11	11	70	51	71
Abingdon Town	42	20	10	12	61	50	70
Worthing	42	19	11	12	79	46	68
Leyton	42	20	8	14	88	66	68
Boreham Wood	42	17	15	10	69	50	66
Staines Town	42	18	9	15	85	56	63
Bognor Regis Town	42	15	14	13	57	48	59
Wembley	42	16	10	16	66	52	58
Barking	42	15	11	16	63	69	56
Uxbridge	42	15	8	19	57	58	53
Whyteleafe	42	15	6	21	71	90	51
Maidenhead United	42	12	13	17	52	48	49
Berkhamsted Town	42	12	9	21	65	77	45
Ruislip Manor	42	10	8	24	42	79	38
Chalfont St Peter	42	7	10	25	40	79	31
Windsor & Eton	42	8	7	27	47	94	31
Croydon	42	3	3	36	37	198	12

Third Division

Bracknell Town	40	25	8	7	78	29	83
Cheshunt	40	23	12	5	62	34	81
Oxford City	40	24	6	10	94	55	78
Harlow Town	40	22	11	7	61	36	77
Southall	40	17	12	11	66	53	63
Camberley Town	40	18	7	15	56	50	61
Hertford Town	40	18	6	16	67	65	60
Royston Town	40	15	11	14	44	41	56
Northwood	40	15	11	14	78	77	56
Epsom & Ewell	40	15	9	16	63	62	54
Harefield United	40	12	15	13	45	55	51
Cove	40	15	6	19	59	74	51
Kingsbury Town	40	12	14	14	57	54	50
Feltham & Hounslow	40	14	7	19	60	63	49
Leighton Town	40	12	11	17	51	64	47
East Thurrock Town	40	10	15	15	65	64	45
Clapton	40	12	9	19	51	65	45
Hornchurch	40	12	8	20	42	60	44
Tring Town	40	10	11	19	48	64	41
Flackwell Heath	40	9	11	20	44	83	38
Horsham	40	6	8	26	43	86	26

1994-95

Premier Division

Enfield	42	26	9	5	106	43	93
Slough Town	42	22	13	7	82	56	79
Hayes	42	20	14	8	66	47	74
Aylesbury United	42	21	6	15	86	59	69
Hitchin Town	42	18	12	12	68	59	66
Bromley	42	18	11	13	76	67	65
St Albans City	42	17	13	12	96	81	64
Molesey	42	18	8	16	65	61	62
Yeading	42	14	15	13	60	59	57
Harrow Borough	42	17	6	19	64	67	57
Dulwich Hamlet	42	16	9	17	70	82	57
Carshalton Athletic	42	16	9	17	69	84	57
Kingstonian	42	16	8	18	62	57	56
Walton & Hersham	42	14	11	17	75	73	53
Sutton United	42	13	12	17	74	69	51
Purfleet	42	13	12	17	76	90	51
Hendon	42	12	14	16	57	65	50
Grays Athletic	42	11	16	15	57	61	49
Bishop's Stortford	42	12	11	19	53	76	47
Chesham United	42	12	9	21	60	87	45
Marlow	42	10	9	23	52	84	39
Wokingham Town	42	6	9	27	39	86	27

First Division

Boreham Wood	42	31	5	6	90	38	98
Worthing	42	21	13	8	93	49	76
Chertsey Town	42	21	11	10	109	57	74
Aldershot Town	42	23	5	14	80	53	74
Billericay Town	42	20	9	13	68	52	69
Staines Town	42	17	12	13	83	65	63
Basingstoke Town	42	17	10	15	81	71	61
Tooting & Mitcham United	42	15	14	13	58	48	59
Wembley	42	16	11	15	70	61	59
Abingdon Town	42	16	11	15	67	69	59
Whyteleafe	42	17	7	18	70	78	58
Maidenhead United	42	15	12	15	73	76	57
Uxbridge	42	15	11	16	54	62	56
Leyton	42	15	10	17	67	66	55
Barking	42	16	7	19	74	77	55
Heybridge Swifts	42	16	6	20	73	78	54
Ruislip Manor	42	14	11	17	70	75	53
Bognor Regis Town	42	13	14	15	57	63	53
Berkhamsted Town	42	14	10	18	54	70	52
Newbury Town	42	12	15	15	58	71	51
Wivenhoe Town	42	8	7	27	47	94	31
Dorking	42	3	3	36	40	163	12

Second Division

Thame United	42	30	3	9	97	49	93
Barton Rovers	42	25	7	10	93	51	82
Oxford City	42	24	8	10	86	47	80
Bracknell Town	42	23	9	10	86	47	78
Metropolitan Police	42	19	12	11	81	65	69
Hampton	42	20	9	13	79	74	69
Croydon	42	20	5	17	85	65	65
Banstead Athletic	42	18	10	14	73	59	64
Saffron Walden Town	42	17	13	12	64	59	64
Chalfont St Peter	42	17	12	13	67	54	63
Witham Town	42	18	9	15	75	64	63
Leatherhead	42	16	12	14	71	75	60
Edgware Town	42	16	10	16	70	66	58
Tilbury	42	15	9	18	62	82	54
Cheshunt	42	13	13	16	66	81	52
Ware	42	14	7	21	61	81	49
Egham Town	42	11	14	17	60	65	47
Hemel Hempstead	42	10	11	21	45	76	41
Hungerford Town	42	11	7	24	55	81	40
Windsor & Eton	42	10	8	24	58	84	38
Aveley	42	9	5	28	48	95	32
Malden Vale	42	5	9	28	46	108	24

Third Division

Collier Row	40	30	5	5	86	23	95
Canvey Island	40	28	4	8	88	42	88
Bedford Town	40	22	11	7	90	50	77
Northwood	40	22	8	10	80	47	74
Horsham	40	22	6	12	84	61	72
Southall	40	21	8	11	87	59	71
Leighton Town	40	20	8	12	66	43	68
Camberley Town	40	19	8	13	59	39	65
Kingsbury Town	40	18	11	1	72	54	65
Hornchurch	40	17	8	15	64	63	59
Clapton	40	14	11	15	69	61	53
Tring Town	40	13	12	15	68	69	51
East Thurrock United	40	14	8	18	60	79	50
Epsom & Ewell	40	13	10	17	58	62	49
Harlow Town	40	13	8	19	53	83	47
Harefield United	40	12	8	20	51	79	44
Hertford Town	40	11	10	19	56	78	43
Feltham & Hounslow	40	13	4	23	64	87	43
Flackwell Heath	40	8	4	28	50	99	28
Lewes	40	6	5	29	34	104	23
Cove	40	3	5	32	37	94	14

1995-96

Premier Division

Hayes	42	24	14	4	76	32	86
Enfield	42	26	8	8	78	35	86
Boreham Wood	42	24	1	7	69	29	83
Yeovil Town	42	23	11	8	83	51	80
Dulwich Hamlet	42	23	11	8	85	59	80
Carshalton Athletic	42	22	8	12	68	49	74
St Albans City	42	20	12	10	70	41	72
Kingstonian	42	20	11	11	62	38	71
Harrow Borough	42	19	10	13	70	56	67
Sutton United	42	17	14	11	71	56	65
Aylesbury United	42	17	12	13	71	58	63
Bishop's Stortford	42	16	9	17	61	62	57
Yeading	42	11	14	17	48	60	47
Hendon	42	12	10	20	52	65	46
Chertsey Town	42	13	6	23	45	71	45
Purfleet	42	12	8	22	48	67	44
Grays Athletic	42	11	11	20	43	63	44
Hitchin Town	42	10	10	22	41	74	40
Bromley	42	10	7	25	52	91	37
Molesey	42	9	9	24	46	81	36
Walton & Hersham	42	9	7	26	42	79	34
Worthing	42	4	7	31	42	106	19

First Division

Oxford City	42	28	7	7	98	60	91
Heybridge Swifts	42	27	7	8	97	43	88
Staines Town	42	23	11	8	82	59	80
Leyton Pennant	42	22	7	13	77	57	73
Aldershot Town	42	21	9	12	81	46	72
Billericay Town	42	19	9	14	58	58	66
Bognor Regis Town	42	18	11	13	71	53	65
Marlow	42	19	5	18	72	75	62
Basingstoke Town	42	16	13	13	70	60	61
Uxbridge	42	16	12	14	46	49	60
Wokingham Town	42	16	10	16	62	65	58
Chesham United	42	15	12	15	51	44	57
Thame United	42	14	13	15	64	73	55
Maidenhead United	42	12	14	16	50	63	50
Whyteleafe	42	12	13	17	71	81	49
Abingdon Town	42	13	9	20	63	80	48
Barton Rovers	42	12	10	20	69	87	46
Berkhamsted Town	42	11	11	20	52	68	44
Tooting & Mitcham United	42	11	10	21	45	64	43
Ruislip Manor	42	11	9	22	55	77	42
Wembley	42	11	8	23	49	66	41
Barking	42	4	12	26	35	90	24

Second Division

Canvey Island	40	25	12	3	91	36	87
Croydon	40	25	6	9	78	42	81
Hampton	40	23	10	7	74	44	79
Banstead Athletic	40	21	11	8	72	36	74
Collier Row	40	21	11	8	73	41	74
Wivenhoe Town	40	21	8	11	82	57	71
Metropolitan Police	40	18	10	12	57	45	64
Bedford Town	40	18	10	12	69	59	64
Bracknell Town	40	18	8	14	69	50	62
Edgware Town	40	16	9	15	72	67	57
Tilbury	40	12	11	17	52	62	47
Ware	40	13	8	19	55	80	47
Chalfont St Peter	40	11	13	16	58	68	46
Leatherhead	40	12	10	18	71	77	46
Saffron Walden Town	40	11	12	17	56	58	45
Cheshunt	40	10	12	18	56	90	42
Hemel Hempstead	40	10	10	20	46	62	40
Egham Town	40	12	3	25	42	74	39
Witham Town	40	8	10	22	35	68	34
Hungerford Town	40	9	7	24	44	79	34
Dorking	40	8	5	27	44	104	29

Third Division

Horsham	40	29	5	6	95	40	92
Leighton Town	40	28	5	7	95	34	89
Windsor & Eton	40	27	6	7	117	46	87
Wealdstone	40	23	8	9	104	39	77
Harlow Town	40	22	10	8	85	62	76
Northwood	40	20	9	11	76	56	69
Epsom & Ewell	40	18	14	8	95	57	68
Kingsbury Town	40	15	16	9	61	48	61
East Thurrock United	40	17	8	15	61	50	59
Aveley	40	16	10	14	62	53	58
Wingate & Finchley	40	16	7	17	74	70	55
Lewes	40	14	7	19	56	72	49
Flackwell Heath	40	14	5	21	60	84	47
Hornchurch	40	11	8	21	55	77	41
Harefield United	40	11	7	22	49	89	40
Tring Town	40	10	8	22	40	78	38
Camberley Town	40	9	9	22	45	81	36
Hertford Town	40	10	5	25	72	103	35
Cove	40	8	10	22	37	89	34
Clapton	40	9	6	25	48	89	33
Southall	40	9	5	26	34	104	32

1996-97

Premier Division

Yeovil Town	42	31	8	3	83	34	101
Enfield	42	28	11	3	91	29	98
Sutton United	42	18	13	11	87	70	67
Dagenham & Redbridge	42	18	11	13	57	43	65
Yeading	42	17	14	11	58	47	65
St Albans City	42	18	11	13	65	55	65
Aylesbury United	42	18	11	13	64	54	65
Purfleet	42	17	11	14	67	63	62
Heybridge Swifts	42	16	14	12	62	62	62
Boreham Wood	42	15	13	14	56	52	58
Kingstonian	42	16	8	18	79	79	56
Dulwich Hamlet	42	14	13	15	57	57	55
Carshalton Athletic	42	14	11	17	51	56	53
Hitchin Town	42	15	7	20	67	73	52
Oxford City	42	14	10	18	67	83	52
Hendon	42	13	12	17	53	59	51
Harrow Borough	42	12	14	16	58	62	50
Bromley	42	13	9	20	67	72	48
Bishop's Stortford	42	10	13	19	43	64	43
Staines Town	42	10	8	24	46	71	38
Grays Athletic	42	8	9	25	43	78	33
Chertsey Town	42	8	7	27	40	98	31

First Division

Chesham United	42	27	6	9	80	46	87
Basingstoke Town	42	22	13	7	81	38	79
Walton & Hersham	42	21	13	8	67	41	76
Hampton	42	21	12	9	62	39	75
Billericay Town	42	21	12	9	69	49	75
Bognor Regis Town	42	21	9	12	63	44	72
Aldershot Town	42	19	14	9	67	45	71
Uxbridge	42	15	17	10	65	48	62
Whyteleafe	42	18	7	17	71	68	61
Molesey	42	17	9	16	50	53	60
Abingdon Town	42	15	11	16	44	42	56
Leyton Pennant	42	14	12	16	71	72	54
Maidenhead United	42	15	10	17	57	57	52
Wokingham Town	42	14	10	18	41	45	52
Thame United	42	13	10	19	57	69	49
Worthing	42	11	11	20	58	77	44
Barton Rovers	42	11	11	20	61	58	44
Croydon	42	11	10	21	40	57	43
Berkhamsted Town	42	11	9	22	47	66	42
Canvey Island	42	9	14	19	52	71	41
Marlow	42	11	6	25	41	84	39
Tooting & Mitcham United	42	8	8	26	40	85	32

Maidenhead United had 3 points deducted

Second Division

Collier Row & Romford	42	28	12	2	93	33	96
Leatherhead	42	30	5	7	116	45	95
Wembley	42	23	11	8	92	45	80
Barking	42	22	13	7	69	40	79
Horsham	42	22	11	9	78	48	77
Edgware Town	42	20	14	8	74	50	74
Bedford Town	42	21	8	13	77	43	71
Banstead Athletic	42	21	5	16	75	52	68
Windsor & Eton	42	17	13	12	65	62	64
Leighton Town	42	17	12	13	64	52	63
Bracknell Town	42	17	9	16	78	71	60
Wivenhoe Town	42	17	9	16	69	62	60
Chalfont St Peter	42	14	13	15	53	61	55
Hungerford Town	42	14	13	15	68	77	55
Metropolitan Police	42	14	7	21	72	75	49
Tilbury	42	14	7	21	68	77	49
Witham Town	42	11	10	21	39	67	43
Egham Town	42	10	9	23	47	86	39
Cheshunt	42	9	3	30	37	101	30
Ware	42	7	8	27	44	80	29
Dorking	42	7	6	29	40	100	27
Hemel Hempstead	42	5	6	31	34	125	21

Third Division

Wealdstone	32	24	3	5	72	24	75
Braintree Town	32	23	5	4	99	29	74
Northwood	32	18	10	4	60	31	64
Harlow Town	32	19	4	9	60	41	61
Aveley	32	17	6	9	64	39	57
East Thurrock United	32	16	6	10	58	51	54
Camberley Town	32	15	6	11	55	44	51
Wingate & Finchley	32	11	7	14	52	63	40
Hornchurch	32	11	6	15	35	51	39
Clapton	32	11	6	15	31	49	39
Lewes	32	10	8	14	45	53	38
Kingsbury Town	32	11	4	17	41	54	37
Hertford Town	32	10	6	16	55	65	36
Epsom & Ewell	32	8	5	19	62	78	29
Flackwell Heath	32	8	5	19	36	71	29
Tring Town	32	7	3	22	33	74	24
Southall	32	6	4	22	28	69	22

1997-98

Premier Division

Kingstonian	42	25	12	5	84	35	87
Boreham Wood	42	23	11	8	81	42	80
Sutton United	42	22	12	8	83	56	78
Dagenham & Redbridge	42	21	10	11	73	50	73
Hendon	42	21	10	11	69	50	73
Heybridge Swifts	42	18	11	13	74	62	65
Enfield	42	18	8	16	66	58	62
Basingstoke Town	42	17	11	14	56	60	62
Walton & Hersham	42	18	6	18	50	70	60
Purfleet	42	15	13	14	57	58	58
St Albans City	42	17	7	18	54	59	58
Harrow Borough	42	15	10	17	60	67	55
Gravesend & Northfleet	42	15	8	19	65	67	53
Chesham United	42	14	10	18	71	70	52
Bromley	42	13	13	16	53	53	52
Dulwich Hamlet	42	13	11	18	56	67	50
Carshalton Athletic	42	13	9	20	54	77	48
Aylesbury United	42	13	8	21	55	70	47
Bishop's Stortford	42	14	5	23	53	69	47
Yeading	42	12	11	19	49	65	47
Hitchin Town	42	8	15	19	45	62	39
Oxford City	42	7	9	26	35	76	30

First Division

Aldershot Town	42	28	8	6	89	36	92
Billericay Town	42	25	6	11	78	44	81
Hampton	42	22	15	5	75	47	81
Maidenhead United	42	25	5	12	76	37	80
Uxbridge	42	23	6	13	66	59	75
Grays Athletic	42	21	10	11	79	49	73
Romford	42	21	8	13	92	59	71
Bognor Regis Town	42	20	9	13	77	45	69
Leatherhead	42	18	11	13	70	51	65
Leyton Pennant	42	17	11	14	66	58	62
Chertsey Town	42	16	13	13	83	70	61
Worthing	42	17	6	19	64	71	57
Berkhamsted Town	42	15	8	19	59	69	53
Staines Town	42	13	10	19	54	74	49
Croydon	42	13	10	19	47	64	49
Barton Rovers	42	11	13	18	53	72	46
Wembley	42	10	15	17	38	61	45
Molesey	42	10	11	21	47	65	41
Whyteleafe	42	10	10	22	48	83	40
Wokingham Town	42	7	10	25	41	74	31
Abingdon Town	42	9	4	29	47	101	31
Thame United	42	7	9	25	33	96	30

Second Division

Canvey Island	42	30	8	4	116	41	98
Braintree Town	42	29	11	2	117	45	98
Wealdstone	42	24	11	7	81	46	83
Bedford Town	42	22	12	8	55	25	78
Metropolitan Police	42	21	8	13	80	65	71
Wivenhoe Town	42	18	12	12	84	66	66
Edgware Town	42	18	10	14	81	65	64
Chalfont St Peter	42	17	13	12	63	60	64
Northwood	42	17	11	14	65	69	62
Windsor & Eton	42	17	7	18	75	72	58
Tooting & Mitcham United	42	16	9	17	58	56	57
Barking	42	15	12	15	62	75	57
Banstead Athletic	42	15	9	18	60	63	54
Marlow	42	16	5	21	64	78	53
Horsham	42	13	9	20	67	75	48
Bracknell Town	42	13	8	21	68	93	47
Leighton Town	42	13	6	23	45	78	45
Hungerford Town	42	11	11	20	66	77	44
Witham Town	42	9	13	20	55	68	40
Tilbury	42	9	12	21	57	88	39
Egham Town	42	9	5	28	47	101	32
Cheshunt	42	4	10	28	31	90	32

Third Division

Hemel Hempstead	38	27	6	5	86	28	87
Hertford Town	38	26	5	7	77	31	83
Harlow Town	38	24	11	3	81	43	83
Camberley Town	38	24	7	7	93	43	79
Ford United	38	23	9	6	90	34	78
East Thurrock United	38	23	7	8	70	40	76
Epsom & Ewell	38	17	6	15	69	57	57
Ware	38	17	6	15	69	57	57
Aveley	38	16	7	15	65	57	55
Corinthian Casuals	38	16	6	16	59	57	54
Hornchurch	38	12	9	17	55	68	45
Clapton	38	13	6	19	46	61	45
Flackwell Heath	38	12	9	17	50	76	45
Croydon Athletic	38	12	7	19	58	63	43
Tring Town	38	12	7	19	51	69	43
Southall	38	10	6	22	41	85	46
Dorking	38	9	6	23	49	94	33
Wingate & Finchley	38	7	8	23	46	80	29
Lewes	38	7	5	26	34	88	26
Kingsbury Town	38	5	3	30	35	93	18

1998-99

Premier Division

Sutton United	42	27	7	8	89	39	88
Aylesbury United	42	23	8	11	67	38	77
Dagenham & Redbridge	42	20	13	9	71	44	73
Purfleet	42	22	7	13	71	54	73
Enfield	42	21	9	12	73	49	72
St Albans City	42	17	17	8	71	52	68
Aldershot Town	42	16	14	12	83	48	62
Basingstoke Town	42	17	10	15	63	53	61
Harrow Borough	42	17	9	16	72	66	60
Gravesend & Northfleet	42	18	6	18	54	53	60
Slough Town	42	16	11	15	60	53	59
Billericay Town	42	15	13	14	54	56	58
Hendon	42	16	9	17	70	71	57
Boreham Wood	42	14	15	13	59	63	57
Chesham United	42	15	9	18	58	79	54
Dulwich Hamlet	42	14	8	20	53	63	50
Heybridge Swifts	42	13	9	20	51	85	48
Walton & Hersham	42	12	7	23	50	77	43
Hampton	42	10	12	20	41	71	42
Carshalton Athletic	42	10	10	22	47	82	40
Bishops Stortford	42	9	10	23	49	90	37
Bromley	42	8	11	23	50	72	35

First Division

Canvey Island	42	28	6	8	76	41	90
Hitchin Town	42	25	10	7	75	38	85
Wealdstone	42	26	6	10	75	48	84
Braintree Town	42	20	10	12	75	48	70
Bognor Regis Town	42	20	8	14	63	44	68
Grays Athletic	42	19	11	12	56	42	68
Oxford City	42	16	14	12	58	51	62
Croydon	42	16	13	13	53	53	61
Chertsey Town	42	14	16	12	57	57	58
Romford	42	14	15	13	58	63	57
Maidenhead United	42	13	15	14	50	46	54
Worthing	42	13	13	16	47	61	52
Leyton Pennant	42	13	12	17	62	70	51
Uxbridge	42	13	11	18	54	51	50
Barton Rovers	42	11	15	16	43	49	48
Yeading	42	12	10	20	51	55	46
Leatherhead	42	12	9	21	48	59	45
Whyteleafe	42	13	6	23	51	72	45
Staines Town	42	10	15	17	33	57	45
Molesey	42	8	20	14	35	52	44
Wembley	42	10	10	22	36	71	40
Berkhamsted Town	42	10	7	25	53	81	37

Second Division

Bedford Town	42	29	7	6	89	31	94
Harlow Town	42	27	8	7	100	47	89
Thame United	42	26	8	8	89	50	86
Hemel Hempstead	42	21	12	9	90	50	75
Windsor & Eton	42	22	6	14	87	55	72
Banstead Athletic	42	21	8	13	83	62	71
Northwood	42	20	7	15	67	68	67
Tooting & Mitcham United	42	19	9	14	63	62	66
Chalfont St Peter	42	16	12	14	70	71	60
Metropolitan Police	42	17	8	17	61	58	59
Leighton Town	42	16	10	16	60	64	58
Horsham	42	17	6	19	74	67	57
Marlow	42	16	9	17	72	68	57
Edgware Town	42	14	10	18	65	68	52
Witham Town	42	12	15	15	64	64	51
Hungerford Town	42	13	12	17	59	61	51
Wivenhoe Town	42	14	8	20	71	83	50
Wokingham Town	42	14	4	24	44	79	46
Barking	42	10	11	21	50	75	41
Hertford Town	42	11	2	29	44	96	35
Bracknell Town	42	7	10	25	48	92	31
Abingdon Town	42	6	6	30	48	124	24

Third Division

Ford United	38	27	5	6	110	42	86
Wingate & Finchley	38	25	5	8	79	38	80
Cheshunt	38	23	10	5	70	41	79
Lewes	38	25	3	10	86	45	78
Epsom & Ewell	38	19	5	14	61	51	62
Ware	38	19	4	15	79	60	61
Tilbury	38	17	8	13	74	52	59
Croydon Athletic	38	16	10	12	82	59	58
East Thurrock United	38	15	13	10	74	56	58
Egham Town	38	16	8	14	65	58	56
Corinthian Casuals	38	16	7	15	70	71	55
Southall	38	14	9	15	68	66	51
Camberley Town	38	14	8	16	66	77	50
Aveley	38	12	7	19	50	67	43
Flackwell Heath	38	11	9	18	59	70	42
Hornchurch	38	10	9	19	48	73	39
Clapton	38	11	6	21	48	89	39
Dorking	38	8	7	23	52	98	31
Kingsbury Town	38	6	3	29	40	98	21
Tring Town	38	5	6	27	38	108	21

1999-2000

Premier Division

Dagenham & Redbridge	42	32	5	5	97	35	101
Aldershot Town	42	24	5	13	71	51	77
Chesham United	42	20	10	12	64	50	70
Purfleet	42	18	15	9	70	48	69
Canvey Island	42	21	6	15	70	53	69
St Albans City	42	19	10	13	75	55	67
Billericay Town	42	18	12	12	62	62	66
Hendon	42	18	8	16	61	64	62
Slough Town	42	17	9	16	61	59	60
Dulwich Hamlet	42	17	5	20	62	68	56
Gravesend & Northfleet	42	15	10	17	66	67	55
Farnborough Town	42	14	11	17	52	55	53
Hampton & Richmond Borough	42	13	13	16	49	57	52
Enfield	42	13	11	18	64	68	50
Heybridge Swifts	42	13	11	18	57	65	50
Hitchin Town	42	13	11	18	59	72	50
Carshalton Athletic	42	12	12	18	55	65	48
Basingstoke Town	42	13	9	20	56	71	48
Harrow Borough	42	14	6	22	54	70	48
Aylesbury United	42	13	9	20	64	81	48
Boreham Wood	42	11	10	21	44	71	43
Walton & Hersham	42	11	8	23	44	70	41

First Division

Croydon	42	25	9	8	85	47	84
Grays Athletic	42	21	12	9	80	44	75
Maidenhead United	42	20	15	7	72	45	75
Thame United	42	20	13	9	61	38	73
Worthing	42	19	12	11	80	60	69
Staines Town	42	19	12	11	63	52	69
Whyteleafe	42	20	9	13	60	49	69
Bedford Town	42	17	12	13	59	52	63
Bromley	42	17	9	16	63	65	60
Uxbridge	42	15	13	14	60	44	58
Bishop's Stortford	42	16	10	16	57	62	58
Barton Rovers	42	16	8	18	64	83	56
Oxford City	42	17	4	21	57	55	55
Braintree Town	42	15	10	17	65	74	55
Yeading	42	12	18	12	53	54	54
Wealdstone	42	13	12	17	51	58	51
Bognor Regis Town	42	12	13	17	47	53	49
Harlow Town	42	11	13	18	62	76	46
Romford	42	12	9	21	51	70	45
Leatherhead	42	9	13	20	47	70	40
Chertsey Town	42	9	5	28	50	84	32
Leyton Pennant	42	7	9	26	34	85	30

Second Division

Hemel Hempstead	42	31	8	3	98	27	101
Northwood	42	29	9	4	109	40	96
Ford United	42	28	8	6	108	41	92
Berkhamsted Town	42	22	8	12	75	52	74
Windsor & Eton	42	20	13	9	73	53	73
Wivenhoe Town	42	20	9	13	61	47	69
Barking	42	18	13	11	70	51	67
Marlow	42	20	4	18	86	66	64
Metropolitan Police	42	18	7	17	75	71	61
Banstead Athletic	42	16	11	15	55	56	59
Tooting & Mitcham United	42	16	7	19	72	74	55
Wokingham Town	42	15	9	18	58	80	54
Wembley	42	14	11	17	47	53	53
Edgware Town	42	13	11	18	72	71	50
Hungerford Town	42	13	10	19	61	78	49
Cheshunt	42	12	12	18	53	65	48
Horsham	42	13	8	21	66	81	47
Leighton Town	42	13	8	21	65	84	47
Molesey	42	10	12	20	54	69	42
Wingate & Finchley	42	11	7	24	54	97	40
Witham Town	42	7	9	26	39	110	30
Chalfont St Peter	42	2	8	32	39	124	14

Third Division

East Thurrock United	40	26	7	7	89	42	85
Great Wakering Rovers	40	25	7	8	81	41	82
Tilbury	40	21	12	7	67	39	75
Hornchurch	40	19	12	9	72	57	69
Croydon Athletic	40	19	11	10	85	52	68
Epsom & Ewell	40	18	12	10	67	46	66
Lewes	40	18	10	12	73	51	64
Bracknell Town	40	15	16	9	81	64	61
Aveley	40	17	10	13	73	64	61
Corinthian Casuals	40	16	10	14	59	51	58
Flackwell Heath	40	17	6	17	74	76	57
Ware	40	16	8	16	74	62	56
Egham Town	40	14	13	13	48	43	55
Hertford Town	40	15	10	15	63	60	55
Abingdon Town	40	10	12	18	48	64	42
Kingsbury Town	40	11	8	21	55	86	41
Camberley Town	40	11	7	22	44	79	40
Tring Town	40	10	9	21	37	64	39
Dorking	40	9	10	21	53	69	37
Clapton	40	9	7	24	50	93	34
Southall	40	3	5	32	33	123	14

2000-2001

Premier Division

Farnborough Town	42	31	6	5	86	27	99
Canvey Island	42	27	8	7	79	41	89
Basingstoke Town	42	22	13	7	73	40	79
Aldershot Town	41	21	11	9	73	39	74
Chesham United	42	22	6	14	78	52	72
Gravesend & Northfleet	42	22	5	15	62	45	71
Heybridge Swifts	42	18	13	11	74	60	67
Billericay Town	41	18	13	10	62	54	67
Hampton & Richmond Borough	42	18	12	12	73	60	66
Hitchin Town	42	18	5	19	72	69	59
Purfleet	42	14	13	15	55	55	55
Hendon	42	16	6	18	62	62	54
Sutton United	41	14	11	16	74	70	53
St Albans City	42	15	5	22	50	69	50
Grays Athletic	42	14	8	20	49	68	50
Maidenhead United	42	15	2	25	47	63	47
Croydon	42	12	10	20	55	77	46
Enfield	42	12	9	21	48	74	45
Harrow Borough	41	10	11	20	61	90	41
Slough Town	42	10	9	23	40	72	39
Carshalton Athletic	42	10	6	26	40	85	36
Dulwich Hamlet	42	4	10	28	33	84	22

First Division

Boreham Wood	42	26	7	9	82	49	85
Bedford Town	42	22	16	4	81	40	82
Braintree Town	42	25	6	11	112	60	81
Bishop's Stortford	42	24	6	12	103	76	78
Thame United	42	22	8	12	86	54	74
Ford United	42	19	12	11	70	58	69
Uxbridge	42	21	5	16	73	55	68
Northwood	42	20	8	14	89	81	68
Whyteleafe	42	20	6	16	62	69	66
Oxford City	42	16	13	13	64	49	61
Harlow Town	42	15	16	11	70	66	61
Worthing	42	16	9	17	69	69	57
Staines Town	42	16	8	18	60	66	56
Aylesbury United	42	17	4	21	65	55	55
Yeading	42	15	9	18	72	74	54
Bognor Regis Town	42	13	11	18	71	71	50
Walton & Hersham	42	14	8	20	59	80	50
Bromley	42	14	6	22	63	86	48
Wealdstone	42	12	9	21	54	73	45
Leatherhead	42	12	4	26	37	87	40
Romford	42	9	4	29	53	113	31
Barton Rovers	42	2	9	31	30	94	15

Second Division

Tooting & Mitcham United	42	26	11	5	92	35	89
Windsor	42	24	10	8	70	40	82
Barking	42	23	13	6	82	54	82
Berkhamsted Town	42	24	8	10	99	49	80
Wivenhoe Town	42	23	11	8	78	52	80
Hemel Hempstead	42	22	10	10	74	44	76
Horsham	42	19	9	14	84	61	66
Chertsey Town	42	18	9	15	59	59	63
Great Wakering Rovers	42	16	13	13	69	59	61
Tilbury	42	18	6	18	61	67	60
Banstead Athletic	42	17	8	17	69	58	59
East Thurrock United	42	16	11	15	72	64	59
Metropolitan Police	42	18	4	20	64	77	58
Marlow	42	15	11	16	62	61	56
Molesey	42	14	9	19	53	61	51
Wembley	42	12	10	20	39	63	46
Hungerford Town	42	11	9	22	40	73	42
Leyton Pennant	42	10	11	21	47	74	41
Cheshunt	42	11	6	25	48	77	39
Edgware Town	42	9	9	24	41	77	36
Leighton Town	42	8	10	24	44	87	34
Wokingham Town	42	3	12	27	39	94	20

Wokingham Town had 1 point deducted

Third Division

Arlesey Town	42	34	6	2	138	37	108
Lewes	41	25	11	5	104	34	86
Ashford Town	42	26	7	9	102	49	85
Flackwell Heath	42	24	10	8	93	51	82
Corinthian Casuals	42	24	10	8	83	50	82
Aveley	42	24	3	15	85	61	75
Epsom & Ewell	42	23	4	15	76	52	73
Witham Town	42	21	9	12	76	57	72
Bracknell Town	41	19	10	12	90	70	67
Croydon Athletic	41	15	12	14	78	63	57
Ware	42	17	6	19	75	76	57
Tring Town	42	16	9	17	60	71	57
Egham Town	42	15	11	16	60	60	56
Hornchurch	42	14	13	15	73	60	55
Wingate & Finchley	42	15	7	20	75	75	52
Kingsbury Town	42	11	8	23	74	100	41
Abingdon Town	42	12	7	23	53	102	40
Dorking	42	10	9	23	59	99	39
Hertford Town	41	9	8	24	57	97	35
Camberley Town	42	8	8	26	53	107	32
Clapton	42	5	9	28	48	121	24
Chalfont St Peter	42	4	1	37	30	150	13

Abingdon Town had 3 points deducted

2001-2002

Premier Division

Gravesend & Northfleet	42	31	6	5	90	33	99
Canvey Island	42	30	5	7	107	41	95
Aldershot Town	42	22	7	13	76	51	73
Braintree Town	42	23	4	15	66	61	73
Purfleet	42	19	15	8	67	44	72
Grays Athletic	42	20	10	12	65	55	70
Chesham United	42	19	10	13	69	53	67
Hendon Town	42	19	5	18	66	54	62
Billericay Town	42	16	13	13	59	60	61
St Albans City	42	16	9	17	71	60	57
Hitchin Town	42	15	10	17	73	81	55
Sutton Albion	42	13	15	14	62	62	54
Heybridge Swifts	42	15	9	18	68	85	54
Kingstonian	42	13	13	16	50	56	52
Boreham Wood	42	15	6	21	49	62	51
Maidenhead United	42	15	5	22	51	63	50
Bedford Town	42	12	12	18	64	69	48
Basingstoke Town	42	11	15	16	50	68	48
Enfield	42	11	9	22	48	77	42
Hampton & Richmond Borough	42	9	13	20	51	71	40
Harrow Borough	42	8	10	24	50	89	34
Croydon	42	7	5	30	36	93	26

First Division

Ford United	42	27	7	8	92	56	88
Bishop's Stortford	42	26	9	7	104	51	87
Aylesbury United	42	23	10	9	96	64	79
Bognor Regis Town	42	20	13	9	74	55	73
Northwood	42	19	11	12	92	64	68
Carshalton Athletic	42	17	16	9	64	53	67
Harlow Town	42	19	9	14	77	65	66
Slough Town	42	17	11	14	68	51	62
Uxbridge	42	18	6	18	68	65	60
Oxford City	42	17	9	16	59	66	60
Thame United	42	15	14	13	75	61	59
Tooting & Mitcham United	42	16	11	15	70	70	59
Walton & Hersham	42	16	10	16	75	70	58
Yeading	42	16	10	16	84	90	58
Worthing	42	15	8	19	69	65	53
Staines Town	42	12	11	19	45	60	47
Dulwich Hamlet	42	11	13	18	64	76	46
Wealdstone	42	11	12	19	60	82	45
Bromley	42	10	11	21	44	74	41
Whyteleafe	42	10	11	21	46	86	41
Barking & East Ham United	42	8	7	27	61	123	31
Windsor & Eton	42	7	5	30	53	93	26

Second Division

Lewes	42	29	9	4	108	31	96
Horsham	42	27	9	6	104	44	90
Berkhamstead Town	42	23	10	9	82	51	79
Arlesey Town	42	23	6	13	89	55	75
Banstead Athletic	42	22	8	12	83	54	74
Leyton Pennant	42	22	8	12	84	60	74
Great Wakering Rovers	42	21	8	13	64	37	71
East Thurrock United	42	21	8	13	67	59	71
Marlow	42	18	13	11	73	63	67
Hemel Hempstead Town	42	18	10	14	82	66	64
Leatherhead	42	17	6	19	72	62	57
Ashford Town	42	15	11	16	58	71	56
Metropolitan Police	42	16	7	19	84	84	55
Barton Rovers	42	15	9	18	54	60	54
Hungerford Town	42	14	9	19	56	75	51
Tilbury	42	15	6	21	55	74	51
Chertsey Town	42	10	14	18	79	112	44
Wembley	42	9	10	23	51	82	37
Molesey	42	10	6	26	40	93	36
Cheshunt	42	7	13	22	51	84	34
Wivenhoe Town	42	8	9	25	55	111	33
Romford	42	4	7	31	42	105	19

Third Division

Croydon Athletic	42	30	5	7	138	41	95
Hornchurch	42	25	11	6	96	46	86
Aveley	42	26	6	10	109	55	84
Bracknell Town	42	25	8	9	96	54	83
Epsom & Ewell	42	20	15	7	79	51	75
Egham Town	42	21	11	10	72	59	74
Wingate & Finchley	42	20	9	13	80	60	69
Dorking	42	18	14	10	77	66	68
Tring Town	42	19	11	12	64	62	68
Corinthian-Casuals	42	18	13	11	69	44	67
Hertford Town	42	20	7	15	88	74	67
Witham Town	42	15	10	17	66	72	55
Ware	42	14	10	18	74	76	52
Chalfont St Peter	42	15	4	23	69	92	49
Wokingham Town	42	14	6	22	79	105	48
Abingdon Town	42	13	7	22	61	75	46
Leighton Town	42	8	12	22	56	95	36
Kingsbury Town	42	8	11	23	58	91	35
Edgware Town	42	9	7	26	65	101	34
Flackwell Heath	42	9	8	25	53	99	32
Clapton	42	9	4	29	45	118	31
Camberley Town	42	7	9	26	37	95	30

2002-2003

Premier Division

Aldershot Town	46	33	6	7	81	36	105
Canvey Island	46	28	8	10	112	56	92
Hendon	46	22	13	11	70	56	79
St. Albans City	46	23	8	15	73	65	77
Basingstoke Town	46	23	7	16	80	60	76
Sutton United	46	22	9	15	77	62	75
Hayes	46	20	13	13	67	54	73
Purfleet	46	19	15	12	68	48	72
Bedford Town	46	21	9	16	66	58	72
Maidenhead United	46	16	17	13	75	63	65
Kingstonian	46	16	17	13	71	64	65
Billericay Town	46	17	11	18	46	44	62
Bishop's Stortford	46	16	11	19	74	72	59
Hitchin Town	46	15	13	18	69	67	58
Ford United	46	15	12	19	78	84	57
Braintree Town	46	14	12	20	59	71	54
Aylesbury United	46	13	15	18	62	75	54
Harrow Borough	46	15	9	22	54	75	54
Grays Athletic	46	14	11	21	53	59	53
Heybridge Swifts	46	13	14	19	52	80	53
Chesham United	46	14	10	22	56	81	52
Boreham Wood	46	11	15	20	50	58	48
Enfield	46	9	11	26	47	101	38
Hampton & Richmond Borough	46	3	14	29	35	86	23

Division One (North)

Northwood	46	28	7	11	109	56	91
Hornchurch	46	25	15	6	85	48	90
Hemel Hempstead Town	46	26	7	13	70	55	85
Slough Town	46	22	14	10	86	59	80
Uxbridge	46	23	10	13	62	41	79
Aveley	46	21	14	11	66	48	77
Berkhamsted Town	46	21	13	12	92	68	76
Thame United	46	20	12	14	84	51	72
Wealdstone	46	21	9	16	85	69	72
Harlow Town	46	20	12	14	66	53	72
Marlow	46	19	10	17	74	63	67
Barking & East Ham United	46	19	9	18	73	76	66
Yeading	46	18	11	17	77	69	65
Great Wakering Rovers	46	17	14	15	64	70	65
Oxford City	46	17	13	16	55	51	64
Arlesey Town	46	17	12	17	69	71	63
East Thurrock United	46	17	10	19	75	79	61
Wingate & Finchley	46	15	11	20	70	74	56
Barton Rovers	46	15	7	24	53	65	52
Tilbury	46	14	7	25	55	96	49
Wivenhoe Town	46	9	11	26	56	94	38
Leyton Pennant	46	9	7	30	38	81	34
Wembley	46	7	11	28	57	111	32
Hertford Town	46	6	6	34	46	119	24

Division One (South)

Carshalton Athletic	46	28	8	10	73	44	92
Bognor Regis Town	46	26	10	10	92	34	88
Lewes	46	24	16	6	106	50	88
Dulwich Hamlet	46	23	12	11	73	49	81
Whyteleafe	46	21	13	12	74	51	76
Bromley	46	21	13	12	70	53	76
Walton & Hersham	46	20	13	13	87	63	73
Horsham	46	21	9	16	80	58	72
Epsom & Ewell	46	19	12	15	67	66	69
Egham Town	46	19	10	17	62	71	67
Tooting & Mitcham United	46	18	9	19	83	78	63
Worthing	46	17	12	17	78	75	63
Windsor & Eton	46	18	9	19	66	65	63
Leatherhead	46	16	13	17	71	66	61
Staines Town	46	14	16	16	57	63	58
Banstead Athletic	46	14	15	17	58	59	57
Ashford Town (Middlesex)	46	14	11	21	47	70	53
Croydon	46	15	8	23	56	87	53
Croydon Athletic	46	13	13	20	52	66	52
Bracknell Town	46	12	16	18	57	74	52
Corinthian Casuals	46	12	14	20	50	68	50
Molesey	46	13	9	24	52	79	48
Metropolitan Police	46	12	10	24	50	76	46
Chertsey Town	46	3	7	36	43	139	16

Division Two

Cheshunt	30	25	3	2	91	29	78
Leyton	30	21	5	4	77	22	68
Flackwell Heath	30	17	3	10	52	44	54
Abingdon Town	30	14	11	5	65	42	53
Hungerford Town	30	12	12	6	49	36	48
Leighton Town	30	14	3	13	61	43	45
Witham Town	30	12	8	10	40	47	44
Ware	30	12	5	13	47	53	41
Clapton	30	12	5	13	40	47	41
Tring Town	30	11	5	14	49	58	38
Kingsbury Town	30	9	11	10	38	48	38
Edgware Town	30	10	3	17	49	65	33
Wokingham Town	30	7	7	16	34	81	28
Dorking	30	6	6	18	49	63	24
Chalfont St. Peter	30	6	5	19	34	63	23
Camberley Town	30	4	4	22	23	61	16

2003-2004

Premier Division

Canvey Island	46	32	8	6	106	42	104
Sutton United	46	25	10	11	94	56	85
Thurrock	46	24	11	11	87	45	83
Hendon	46	25	8	13	68	47	83
* Hornchurch	46	24	11	11	63	35	82
Grays Athletic	46	22	15	9	82	39	81
Carshalton Athletic	46	24	9	13	66	55	81
Hayes	46	21	11	14	56	46	74
Kettering Town	46	20	11	15	63	63	71
Bognor Regis Town	46	20	10	16	69	67	70
Bishop's Stortford	46	20	9	17	78	61	69
Maidenhead United	46	18	9	19	60	68	63
Ford United	46	16	14	16	69	63	62
Basingstoke Town	46	17	9	20	58	64	60
Bedford Town	46	14	13	19	62	63	55
Heybridge Swifts	46	14	11	21	57	78	53
Harrow Borough	46	12	14	20	47	63	50
Kingstonian	46	12	13	21	40	56	49
St. Albans City	46	12	12	22	55	83	48
Hitchin Town	46	13	8	25	55	89	47
Northwood	46	12	9	25	65	95	45
Billericay Town	46	11	11	24	51	66	44
Braintree Town	46	11	6	29	41	88	39
Aylesbury United	46	5	14	27	41	101	29

* Hornchurch had 1 point deducted

Division One (North)

Yeading	46	32	7	7	112	54	103
Leyton	46	29	9	8	90	53	96
Cheshunt	46	27	10	9	119	54	91
Chesham United	46	24	9	13	104	60	81
Dunstable Town	46	23	9	14	86	61	78
Hemel Hempstead Town	46	22	12	12	75	72	78
Wealdstone	46	23	7	16	81	51	76
Arlesey Town	46	23	7	16	95	70	76
Boreham Wood	46	20	13	13	82	59	73
Harlow Town	46	20	10	16	75	51	70
Wingate & Finchley	46	19	13	14	68	63	70
East Thurrock United	46	19	11	16	62	54	68
Uxbridge	46	15	14	17	59	57	59
Aveley	46	15	14	17	67	71	59
Thame United	46	16	9	21	72	83	57
* Waltham Forest	46	15	13	18	62	60	55
Wivenhoe Town	46	15	10	21	79	104	55
Barton Rovers	46	16	6	24	52	80	54
Oxford City	46	14	11	21	55	65	53
Berkhamstead Town	46	12	10	24	66	88	46
Great Wakering Rovers	46	10	13	23	47	97	43
Tilbury	46	10	9	27	56	100	39
Barking & East Ham United	46	8	7	31	37	100	31
Enfield	46	5	7	34	44	138	22

* Waltham Forest had 3 points deducted.

2004-2005

Premier Division

Yeading	42	25	11	6	74	48	86
Billericay Town	42	23	11	8	78	40	80
Eastleigh	42	22	13	7	84	49	79
Braintree Town	42	19	17	6	67	33	74
Leyton	42	21	8	13	71	57	71
Hampton & Richmond	42	21	8	13	64	53	71
Heybridge Swifts	42	18	9	15	76	65	63
Chelmsford City	42	17	11	14	63	58	62
Staines Town	42	17	9	16	59	53	60
Worthing	42	16	11	15	50	45	59
Hendon	42	17	7	18	48	60	58
Salisbury City	42	16	9	17	60	64	57
Slough Town	42	15	10	17	61	66	55
Folkestone Invicta	42	14	10	18	51	53	52
Windsor & Eton	42	12	14	16	48	62	50
Harrow Borough	42	13	10	19	41	54	49
Northwood	42	14	7	21	49	66	49
Wealdstone	42	13	8	21	60	73	47
Cheshunt	42	12	11	19	58	71	47
Tonbridge Angels	42	11	10	21	47	73	43
Dover Athletic	42	10	9	23	50	66	39
Kingstonian	42	7	5	30	43	93	26

Division One (South)

Lewes	46	29	7	10	113	61	94
Worthing	46	26	14	6	87	46	92
Windsor & Eton	46	26	13	7	75	39	91
Slough Town	46	28	6	12	103	63	90
Hampton & Richmond Borough	46	26	11	9	82	45	89
Staines Town	46	26	9	11	85	52	87
Dulwich Hamlet	46	23	15	8	77	57	84
Bromley	46	22	10	14	80	58	76
Walton & Hersham	46	20	14	12	76	55	74
Croydon Athletic	46	20	10	16	70	54	70
Tooting & Mitcham United	46	20	9	17	82	68	69
Ashford Town (Middlesex)	46	18	13	15	69	62	67
Leatherhead	46	19	9	18	83	88	66
Bracknell Town	46	19	6	21	81	87	63
Horsham	46	16	11	19	71	69	59
Marlow	46	16	11	19	50	64	59
Whyteleafe	46	17	4	25	66	93	55
Banstead Athletic	46	15	8	23	56	73	53
Molesey	46	12	12	22	45	84	48
Metropolitan Police	46	9	14	23	58	84	41
Croydon	46	10	10	26	57	88	40
Egham Town	46	8	8	30	55	92	32
Corinthian Casuals	46	6	6	34	48	110	24
Epsom & Ewell	46	5	8	33	40	117	23

Division One

AFC Wimbledon	42	29	10	3	91	33	97
Walton & Hersham	42	28	4	10	69	34	88
Horsham	42	24	6	12	90	61	78
Bromley	42	22	9	11	69	44	75
Metropolitan Police	42	22	8	12	72	51	74
Cray Wanderers	42	19	16	7	95	54	73
Leatherhead	42	20	13	9	73	55	73
Tooting & Mitcham United	42	18	15	9	92	60	69
Whyteleafe	42	20	6	16	60	59	66
Burgess Hill Town	42	19	6	17	73	62	63
Hastings United	42	15	11	16	55	57	56
Croydon Athletic	42	13	16	13	66	65	55
Corinthian-Casuals	42	15	9	18	56	64	54
Bashley	42	13	13	16	68	74	52
Dulwich Hamlet	42	10	14	18	61	64	44
Molesey	42	12	8	22	46	70	44
Banstead Athletic	42	10	10	22	50	64	40
Newport IOW	42	10	10	22	50	88	40
Fleet Town	42	11	5	26	47	86	38
Ashford Town	42	8	12	22	47	85	36
Dorking	42	8	11	23	43	89	35
Croydon	42	5	10	27	37	91	25

Division Two

Leighton Town	42	28	7	7	111	36	91
Dorking	42	27	8	7	87	47	89
Hertford Town	42	24	9	9	74	35	81
Chertsey Town	42	22	9	11	75	53	75
Flackwell Heath	42	22	5	15	71	53	71
Witham Town	42	20	10	12	75	54	70
Kingsbury Town	42	14	11	17	60	64	53
Ware	42	14	10	18	67	60	52
Abingdon Town	42	15	6	21	83	81	51
Camberley Town	42	15	6	21	51	71	51
Wembley	42	13	9	20	46	67	48
Wokingham Town	42	12	7	23	55	94	43
Edgware Town	42	12	6	24	62	88	42
Chalfont St. Peter	42	12	6	24	57	89	42
Clapton	42	8	5	29	47	129	29

Division Two

Ilford	30	22	3	5	62	23	69
Enfield	30	21	3	6	64	33	66
Brook House	30	20	4	6	65	25	64
Hertford Town	30	17	7	6	65	40	58
Witham Town	30	16	3	11	67	53	51
Chertsey Town	30	15	6	9	55	48	51
Abingdon Town	30	13	9	8	65	42	48
Edgware Town	30	12	3	15	40	41	39
Flackwell Heath	30	11	5	14	50	55	38
Ware	30	9	10	11	41	55	37
Chalfont St Peter	30	9	7	14	41	52	34
Camberley Town	30	9	5	16	36	44	32
Wembley	30	8	5	17	41	55	29
Epsom & Ewell	30	8	4	18	41	64	28
Kingsbury Town	30	5	4	21	35	76	19
Clapton	30	3	6	21	20	82	15

2005-2006

Premier Division

Braintree Town	42	28	10	4	74	32	94
Heybridge Swifts	42	28	3	11	70	46	87
Fisher Athletic	42	26	7	9	84	46	85
AFC Wimbledon	42	22	11	9	67	36	77
Hampton & Richmond	42	24	3	15	73	54	75
Staines Town	42	20	10	12	74	56	70
Billericay Town	42	19	12	11	69	45	69
Worthing	42	19	10	13	71	60	67
Walton & Hersham	42	19	7	16	55	50	64
Chelmsford City	42	18	10	14	57	62	64
Bromley	42	16	14	12	57	49	62
East Thurrock United	42	18	5	19	60	60	59
Folkestone Invicta	42	16	10	16	47	51	58
Margate	42	11	17	14	49	55	50
Leyton	42	13	9	20	58	61	48
Harrow Borough	42	13	9	20	56	73	48
Slough Town	42	13	8	21	63	75	47
Wealdstone	42	13	5	24	68	82	44
Hendon	42	9	12	21	44	64	39
Maldon Town	42	8	11	23	41	73	35
Windsor & Eton	42	8	8	26	37	75	32
Redbridge	42	3	5	34	28	97	14

Division One

Ramsgate	44	24	14	6	84	38	86
Horsham	44	25	11	8	94	55	86
Tonbridge Angels	44	24	8	12	71	48	80
Metropolitan Police	44	24	7	13	72	46	79
Dover Athletic	44	21	14	9	69	46	77
Tooting & Mitcham United	44	22	9	13	93	62	75
Kingstonian	44	20	14	10	82	56	74
Croydon Athletic	44	20	13	11	56	41	73
Bashley	44	20	10	14	63	61	70
Leatherhead	44	18	14	12	64	50	68
Cray Wanderers	44	20	8	16	80	74	68
Hastings United	44	19	10	15	65	58	67
Dulwich Hamlet	44	19	8	17	55	43	65
Fleet Town	44	13	19	12	50	56	58
Walton Casuals	44	16	10	18	68	75	58
Lymington & New Milton	44	12	11	21	61	80	47
Molesey	44	12	10	22	56	79	46
Whyteleafe	44	10	14	20	50	66	44
Burgess Hill Town	44	10	10	24	57	83	40
Banstead Athletic	44	8	13	23	43	71	37
Ashford Town	44	8	11	25	41	81	35
Newport IOW	44	6	11	27	38	97	29
Corinthian Casuals	44	6	9	29	39	85	27

Division Two

Ware	30	19	4	7	77	36	61
Witham Town	30	17	7	6	61	30	58
Brook House	30	17	7	6	63	33	58
Flackwell Heath	30	15	7	8	54	49	52
Egham Town	30	15	5	10	39	36	50
Chertsey Town	30	14	7	9	47	37	49
Edgware Town	30	13	5	12	46	41	44
Chalfont St Peter	30	13	2	15	50	53	41
Dorking	30	11	8	11	48	51	41
Croydon	30	11	7	12	43	43	40
Wembley	30	11	6	13	44	43	39
Kingsbury Town	30	9	10	11	32	37	37
Hertford Town	30	7	10	13	35	54	31
Camberley Town	30	5	8	17	31	57	23
Epsom & Ewell	30	5	6	19	32	64	21
Clapton	30	4	9	17	33	71	16

Clapton had 5 points deducted.

2006-2007

Premier Division

Hampton & Richmond	42	24	10	8	77	53	82
Bromley	42	23	11	8	83	43	80
Chelmsford City	42	23	8	11	96	51	77
Billericay Town	42	22	11	9	71	42	77
AFC Wimbledon	42	21	15	6	76	37	75
Margate	42	20	11	11	79	48	71
Boreham Wood	42	19	12	11	71	49	69
Horsham	42	18	14	10	70	57	68
Ramsgate	42	20	5	17	63	63	65
Heybridge Swifts	42	17	13	12	57	40	64
Tonbridge Angels	42	20	4	18	74	72	64
Staines Town	42	15	12	15	64	64	57
Carshalton Athletic	42	14	12	16	54	59	54
Hendon	42	16	6	20	53	64	54
Leyton	42	13	10	19	55	77	49
East Thurrock United	42	14	6	22	56	70	48
Ashford Town (Middlesex)	42	11	13	18	59	71	46
Folkestone Invicta	42	12	10	20	45	66	46
Harrow Borough	42	13	6	23	61	71	45
Worthing	42	8	11	23	57	82	35
Walton & Hersham	42	9	6	27	38	83	33
Slough Town	42	4	6	32	26	123	18

AFC Wimbledon had 3 points deducted.

Division One North

AFC Hornchurch	42	32	7	3	96	27	103
Harlow Town	42	24	10	8	71	31	82
Enfield Town	42	24	7	11	74	39	79
Maldon Town	42	20	11	11	50	42	71
AFC Sudbury	42	19	13	10	67	41	70
Canvey Island	42	19	10	13	65	47	67
Ware	42	19	10	13	70	56	67
Waltham Forest	42	17	14	11	60	56	65
Wingate & Finchley	42	16	11	15	58	49	59
Waltham Abbey	42	15	13	14	65	51	58
Wivenhoe Town	42	16	9	17	50	52	57
Great Wakering Rovers	42	16	9	17	57	64	57
Enfield	42	16	6	20	65	63	54
Potters Bar Town	42	14	9	19	60	62	51
Aveley	42	14	9	19	47	57	51
Redbridge	42	15	5	22	42	48	50
Bury Town	42	13	11	18	57	69	50
Arlesey Town	42	13	11	18	44	63	50
Tilbury	42	11	10	21	43	72	43
Witham Town	42	10	7	25	52	90	37
Ilford	42	9	5	28	36	97	32
Flackwell Heath	42	7	9	26	37	90	30

Division One South

Maidstone United	42	23	11	8	79	47	80
Tooting & Mitcham	42	22	13	7	70	41	79
Dover Athletic	42	22	11	9	77	41	77
Hastings United	42	22	10	10	79	56	76
Fleet Town	42	21	12	9	65	52	75
Metropolitan Police	42	18	15	9	65	48	69
Dartford	42	19	11	12	86	65	68
Dulwich Hamlet	42	18	13	11	83	56	67
Horsham YMCA	42	17	7	18	59	69	58
Sittingbourne	42	14	15	13	68	63	57
Leatherhead	42	15	10	17	58	63	55
Cray Wanderers	42	14	12	16	67	69	54
Kingstonian	42	13	13	16	60	63	52
Burgess Hill Town	42	13	12	17	58	81	51
Molesey	42	12	13	17	52	63	49
Chatham Town	42	12	11	19	52	62	47
Walton Casuals	42	11	13	18	57	71	46
Ashford Town	42	10	14	18	52	65	44
Croydon Athletic	42	12	8	22	44	77	44
Whyteleafe	42	9	15	18	52	65	42
Corinthian-Casuals	42	8	10	24	53	88	34
Godalming Town	42	8	9	25	45	76	33

NORTHERN PREMIER LEAGUE

1968-69

Macclesfield Town	38	27	6	5	82	38	60
Wigan Athletic	38	18	12	8	59	41	48
Morecambe	38	16	14	8	64	37	46
Gainsborough Trinity	38	19	8	11	64	43	46
South Shields	38	19	8	11	78	56	46
Bangor City	38	18	9	11	102	64	45
Hyde United	38	16	10	12	71	65	42
Goole Town	38	15	10	13	80	78	40
Altrincham	38	14	10	14	69	52	38
Fleetwood	38	16	6	16	58	58	38
Gateshead	38	14	9	15	42	48	37
South Liverpool	38	12	13	13	56	66	37
Northwich Victoria	38	16	5	17	59	82	37
Boston United	38	14	8	16	59	65	36
Runcorn	38	12	11	15	59	63	35
Netherfield	38	12	4	22	51	69	28
Scarborough	38	9	10	19	49	68	28
Ashington	38	10	8	20	48	74	28
Chorley	38	8	9	21	46	75	25
Worksop Town	38	6	8	24	34	88	20

1969-70

Macclesfield Town	38	22	8	8	72	41	52
Wigan Athletic	38	20	12	6	56	32	52
Boston United	38	21	8	9	65	33	50
Scarborough	38	20	10	8	74	39	50
South Shields	38	19	7	12	66	43	45
Gainsborough Trinity	38	16	11	11	64	49	43
Stafford Rangers	38	16	7	15	59	52	39
Bangor City	38	15	9	14	68	63	39
Northwich Victoria	38	15	8	15	60	66	38
Netherfield	38	14	9	15	56	54	37
Hyde United	38	15	7	16	59	59	37
Altincham	38	14	8	16	62	65	36
Fleetwood	38	13	10	15	53	60	36
Runcorn	38	11	13	14	57	72	35
Morecambe	38	10	13	15	41	51	33
South Liverpool	38	11	11	16	44	55	33
Great Harwood	38	10	9	19	63	92	29
Matlock Town	38	8	12	18	52	67	28
Goole Town	38	10	6	22	50	71	26
Gateshead	38	5	12	21	37	94	22

1970-71

Wigan Athletic	42	27	13	2	91	32	67
Stafford Rangers	42	27	7	8	87	51	61
Scarborough	42	23	12	7	83	40	58
Boston United	42	22	12	8	69	31	56
Macclesfield Town	42	23	10	9	84	45	56
Northwich Victoria	42	22	5	15	71	55	49
Bangor City	42	19	10	13	72	61	48
Altrincham	42	19	10	13	80	76	48
South Liverpool	42	15	15	12	67	57	45
Chorley	42	14	14	14	58	61	42
Gainsborough Trinity	42	15	11	16	65	63	41
Morecambe	42	14	11	17	67	79	39
South Shields	42	12	14	16	67	66	38
Bradford Park Avenue	42	15	8	19	54	73	38
Lancaster City	42	12	12	18	53	76	36
Netherfield	42	13	9	20	59	57	35
Matlock Town	42	10	13	19	58	80	33
Fleetwood	42	10	11	21	56	90	31
Great Harwood	42	8	13	21	66	98	29
Runcorn	42	10	5	27	58	84	25
Kirkby Town	42	6	13	23	57	93	25
Goole Town	42	10	4	28	44	98	24

1971-72

Stafford Rangers	46	30	11	5	91	32	71
Boston United	46	28	13	5	87	37	69
Wigan Athletic	46	27	10	9	70	43	64
Scarborough	46	21	15	10	75	46	57
Northwich Victoria	46	20	14	12	65	59	54
Macclesfield Town	46	18	15	13	61	50	51
Gainsborough Trinity	46	21	9	16	93	79	51
South Shields	46	18	14	14	75	57	50
Bangor City	46	20	8	18	93	74	48
Altrincham	46	18	11	17	72	58	47
Skelmersdale United	46	19	9	18	61	58	47
Matlock Town	46	20	7	19	67	75	47
Chorley	46	17	12	17	66	59	46
Lancaster City	46	15	14	17	84	84	44
Great Harwood	46	15	14	17	60	74	44
Ellesmere Port Town	46	17	9	20	67	71	43
Morecambe	46	15	10	21	51	64	40
Bradford Park Avenue	46	13	13	20	54	71	39
Netherfield	46	16	5	25	51	73	37
Fleetwood	46	11	15	20	43	67	37
South Liverpool	46	12	12	22	61	73	36
Runcorn	46	8	14	24	48	80	30
Goole Town	46	9	10	27	51	97	28
Kirkby Town	46	6	12	28	38	104	24

1972-73

Boston United	46	27	16	3	88	34	70
Scarborough	46	26	9	11	72	39	61
Wigan Athletic	46	23	14	9	69	38	60
Altrincham	46	22	16	8	75	55	60
Bradford Park Avenue	46	19	17	10	63	50	55
Stafford Rangers	46	20	11	15	63	46	51
Gainsborough Trinity	46	18	13	15	70	50	49
Northwich Victoria	46	17	15	14	74	62	49
Netherfield	46	20	9	17	68	65	49
Macclesfield Town	46	16	16	14	58	47	48
Ellesmere Port Town	46	18	11	17	52	56	47
Skelmersdale United	46	15	16	15	58	59	46
Bangor City	46	16	13	17	70	60	45
Mossley	46	17	11	18	70	73	45
Morecambe	46	17	11	18	62	70	45
Great Harwood	46	14	15	17	63	74	43
South Liverpool	46	12	19	15	47	57	43
Runcorn	46	15	12	19	75	78	42
Goole Town	46	13	13	20	64	73	39
South Shields	46	17	4	25	64	81	38
Matlock Town	46	11	11	24	42	80	33
Lancaster City	46	10	11	25	53	78	31
Barrow	46	12	6	28	52	101	30
Fleetwood	46	5	15	26	31	77	25

1973-74

Boston United	46	27	11	8	69	32	65
Wigan Athletic	46	28	8	10	96	39	64
Altrincham	46	26	11	9	77	34	63
Stafford Rangers	46	27	9	10	101	45	63
Scarborough	46	22	14	10	62	43	58
South Shields	46	25	6	15	87	48	56
Runcorn	46	21	14	11	72	47	56
Macclesfield Town	46	18	15	13	48	47	51
Bangor City	46	19	11	16	65	56	49
Gainsborough Trinity	46	18	11	17	77	64	47
South Liverpool	46	16	15	15	55	47	47
Skelmersdale United	46	16	13	17	50	59	45
Goole Town	46	14	15	17	60	69	43
Fleetwood	46	14	15	17	48	68	43
Mossley	46	15	11	20	53	65	41
Northwich Victoria	46	14	13	19	68	75	41
Morecambe	46	13	13	20	62	84	39
Buxton	46	14	10	22	45	71	38
Matlock Town	46	11	14	21	50	79	36
Great Harwood	46	10	14	22	52	74	34
Bradford Park Avenue	46	9	15	22	42	84	33
Barrow	46	13	7	26	46	94	33
Lancaster City	46	10	12	24	52	67	32
Netherfield	46	11	5	30	42	88	27

1974-75

Team	P	W	D	L	F	A	Pts
Wigan Athletic	46	33	6	7	94	38	72
Runcorn	46	30	8	8	102	42	68
Altrincham	46	26	12	8	87	43	64
Stafford Rangers	46	25	13	8	81	39	63
Scarborough	46	24	12	10	73	45	60
Mossley	46	23	11	12	78	52	57
Gateshead United	46	22	12	12	74	48	56
Goole Town	46	19	12	15	75	71	50
Northwich Victoria	46	18	12	16	83	71	48
Great Harwood	46	17	14	15	69	66	48
Matlock Town	46	19	8	19	87	79	46
Boston United	46	16	14	16	64	63	46
Morecambe	46	14	15	17	71	87	43
Worksop Town	46	14	14	18	69	66	42
South Liverpool	46	14	14	18	59	71	42
Buxton	46	11	17	18	50	77	39
Macclesfield Town	46	11	14	21	46	62	36
Lancaster City	46	13	10	23	53	76	36
Bangor City	46	13	9	24	56	67	35
Gainsborough Trinity	46	10	15	21	46	79	35
Skelmersdale United	46	13	7	26	63	93	33
Barrow	46	9	15	22	45	72	33
Netherfield	46	12	8	26	42	91	32
Fleetwood	46	5	10	31	26	97	20

1975-76

Team	P	W	D	L	F	A	Pts
Runcorn	46	29	10	7	95	42	68
Stafford Rangers	46	26	15	5	81	41	67
Scarborough	46	26	10	10	84	43	62
Matlock Town	46	26	9	11	96	63	61
Boston United	46	27	6	13	95	58	60
Wigan Athletic	46	21	15	10	81	42	57
Altrincham	46	20	14	12	77	57	54
Bangor City	46	21	12	13	80	70	54
Mossley	46	21	11	14	70	58	53
Goole Town	46	20	13	13	58	49	53
Northwich Victoria	46	17	17	12	79	59	51
Lancaster City	46	18	9	19	61	70	45
Worksop Town	46	17	10	19	63	56	44
Gainsborough Trinity	46	13	17	16	58	69	43
Macclesfield Town	46	15	12	19	50	64	42
Gateshead United	46	17	7	22	64	63	41
Buxton	46	11	13	22	37	62	35
Skelmersdale United	46	12	10	24	45	74	34
Netherfield	46	11	11	24	55	76	33
Morecambe	46	11	11	24	47	67	33
Great Harwood	46	13	7	26	58	86	33
South Liverpool	46	12	9	25	45	78	33
Barrow	46	12	9	25	47	84	33
Fleetwood	46	3	9	34	36	131	15

1976-77

Team	P	W	D	L	F	A	Pts
Boston United	44	27	11	6	82	35	65
Northwich Victoria	44	27	11	6	85	43	65
Matlock Town	44	26	11	7	108	57	63
Bangor City	44	22	11	11	87	52	55
Scarborough	44	21	12	11	77	66	54
Goole Town	44	23	6	15	64	50	52
Lancaster City	44	21	9	14	71	58	51
Gateshead United	44	18	12	14	80	64	48
Mossley	44	17	14	13	74	59	48
Altrincham	44	19	9	16	60	53	47
Stafford Rangers	44	16	14	14	60	55	46
Runcorn	44	15	14	15	57	49	44
Worksop Town	44	16	12	16	50	58	44
Wigan Athletic	44	14	15	15	62	54	43
Morecambe	44	13	11	20	59	75	37
Gainsborough Trinity	44	13	10	21	58	74	36
Great Harwood	44	11	14	19	63	84	36
Buxton	44	11	13	20	48	63	35
Macclesfield Town	44	8	15	21	41	68	31
Frickley Athletic	44	11	8	25	53	93	30
Barrow	44	11	6	27	56	87	28
South Liverpool	44	10	8	26	51	104	28
Netherfield	44	9	8	27	47	92	26

1977-78

Team	P	W	D	L	F	A	Pts
Boston United	46	31	9	6	85	35	71
Wigan Athletic	46	25	15	6	83	45	65
Bangor City	46	26	10	10	92	50	62
Scarborough	46	26	10	10	80	39	62
Altrincham	46	22	15	9	84	49	59
Northwich Victoria	46	22	14	10	83	55	50
Stafford Rangers	46	22	13	11	71	41	57
Runcorn	46	19	18	9	70	44	56
Mossley	46	22	11	13	85	73	55
Matlock Town	46	21	12	13	79	60	54
Lancaster City	46	15	14	17	66	82	44
Frickley Athletic	46	15	12	19	77	81	42
Barrow	46	14	12	20	50	61	40
Goole Town	46	15	9	22	60	68	39
Great Harwood	46	13	13	20	66	83	39
Gainsborough Trinity	46	14	10	22	61	74	38
Gateshead	46	16	5	25	65	74	37
Netherfield	46	11	13	22	50	80	35
Workington	46	13	8	25	48	80	34
Worksop Town	46	12	10	24	45	84	34
Morecambe	46	11	11	24	67	92	33
Macclesfield Town	46	12	9	25	60	92	33
Buxton	46	13	6	27	60	95	32
South Liverpool	46	9	7	30	53	111	25

1978-79

Team	P	W	D	L	F	A	Pts
Mossley	44	32	5	7	117	48	69
Altrincham	44	25	11	8	93	39	61
Matlock Town	44	24	8	12	100	59	56
Scarborough	44	19	14	11	61	44	52
Southport	44	19	14	11	62	49	52
Boston United	44	17	18	9	40	33	52
Runcorn	44	21	9	14	79	54	51
Stafford Rangers	44	18	14	12	67	41	50
Goole Town	44	17	15	12	56	61	49
Northwich Victoria	44	18	11	15	64	52	47
Lancaster City	44	17	12	15	62	54	46
Bangor City	44	15	14	15	65	66	44
Worksop Town	44	13	14	17	55	67	40
Workington	44	16	7	21	62	74	39
Netherfield	44	13	11	20	39	69	37
Barrow	44	14	9	21	47	78	37
Gainsborough Trinity	44	12	12	20	52	67	36
Morecambe	44	11	13	20	55	65	35
Frickley Athletic	44	13	9	22	58	70	35
South Liverpool	44	12	10	22	48	85	34
Gateshead	44	11	11	22	42	63	33
Buxton	44	11	9	24	50	84	31
Macclesfield Town	44	8	10	26	40	92	26

1979-80

Team	P	W	D	L	F	A	Pts
Mossley	42	28	9	5	96	41	65
Witton Albion	42	28	8	6	89	30	64
Frickley Athletic	42	24	13	5	93	48	61
Burton Albion	42	25	6	11	83	42	56
Matlock Town	42	18	17	7	87	53	53
Buxton	42	21	9	12	61	48	51
Worksop Town	42	20	10	12	65	52	50
Macclesfield Town	42	18	11	13	67	53	47
Grantham	42	18	8	16	71	65	44
Marine	42	16	10	16	65	57	42
Goole Town	42	14	13	15	61	63	41
Lancaster City	42	13	13	16	74	77	39
Oswestry Town	42	12	14	16	44	60	38
Gainsborough Trinity	42	14	8	20	64	75	36
Runcorn	42	11	11	20	46	63	33
Gateshead	42	11	11	20	50	77	33
Morecambe	42	10	12	20	40	59	32
Netherfield	42	7	15	20	37	66	29
Southport	42	8	13	21	30	75	29
South Liverpool	42	7	14	21	51	84	28
Workington	42	8	12	22	50	85	28
Tamworth	42	8	9	25	26	77	25

1980-81

Runcorn	42	32	7	3	99	22	71
Mossley	42	24	7	11	95	55	55
Marine	42	22	10	10	60	41	54
Buxton	42	21	7	14	64	50	49
Gainsborough Trinity	42	17	13	12	50	57	47
Burton Albion	42	19	8	15	63	54	46
Witton Albion	42	19	8	15	70	62	46
Goole Town	42	14	16	12	56	50	44
South Liverpool	42	19	6	17	59	64	44
Workington	42	15	13	14	57	48	43
Gateshead	42	12	18	12	65	61	42
Worksop Town	42	15	11	16	66	61	41
Macclesfield Town	42	13	13	16	52	69	39
Grantham	42	14	9	19	57	74	37
Matlock Town	42	12	12	18	57	80	36
Lancaster City	42	13	9	20	48	70	35
Netherfield	42	11	12	19	73	81	34
Oswestry Town	42	13	8	21	54	67	34
King's Lynn	42	8	18	16	46	65	34
Southport	42	11	11	26	42	68	33
Morecambe	42	11	8	23	42	74	30
Tamworth	42	9	12	21	38	76	30

1981-82

Bangor City	42	27	8	7	108	60	62
Mossley	42	24	11	7	76	43	59
Witton Albion	42	22	10	10	75	44	54
Gateshead	42	19	14	9	65	49	52
King's Lynn	42	19	12	11	61	36	50
Grantham	42	18	13	11	65	53	49
Burton Albion	42	19	9	14	71	62	47
Southport	42	16	14	12	63	55	46
Marine	42	17	12	13	64	57	46
Macclesfield Town	42	17	9	16	67	58	43
Workington	42	18	7	17	62	60	43
Worksop Town	42	15	13	14	52	60	43
South Liverpool	42	13	13	16	55	57	39
Goole Town	42	13	13	16	56	60	39
Oswestry Town	42	14	11	17	55	59	39
Buxton	42	14	11	17	48	56	39
Lancaster City	42	13	12	17	47	50	38
Gainsborough Trinity	42	10	13	19	60	69	33
Tamworth	42	10	9	23	31	56	29
Morecambe	42	9	11	22	43	86	29
Matlock Town	42	7	12	23	38	72	26
Netherfield	42	5	9	28	31	91	19

1982-83

Gateshead	42	32	4	6	114	43	100
Mossley	42	25	9	8	77	42	84
Burton Albion	42	24	9	9	81	53	81
Chorley	42	23	11	8	77	49	80
Macclesfield Town	42	24	8	10	71	49	80
Marine	42	17	17	8	81	57	68
Workington	42	19	10	13	71	55	67
Hyde United	42	18	12	12	91	63	66
King's Lynn	42	17	13	12	62	44	64
Matlock Town	42	18	10	14	70	65	64
Witton Albion	42	17	12	13	82	52	63
Buxton	42	17	9	16	60	62	60
Morecambe	42	16	11	15	75	66	59
Grantham	42	15	13	14	49	50	58
Southport	42	11	14	17	58	65	47
Goole Town	42	13	7	22	52	66	46
Gainsborough Trinity	42	11	9	22	60	71	42
Oswestry Town	42	10	8	24	56	99	38
South Liverpool	42	7	15	20	57	91	36
Tamworth	42	7	8	27	44	97	29
Worksop Town	42	5	10	27	50	98	25
Netherfield	42	2	9	31	28	129	15

1983-84

Barrow	42	29	10	3	92	38	97
Matlock Town	42	23	8	11	72	48	77
South Liverpool	42	22	11	9	55	44	77
Grantham	42	20	8	14	64	51	68
Burton Albion	42	17	13	12	61	47	64
Macclesfield Town	42	18	10	14	65	55	64
Rhyl	42	19	6	17	64	55	63
Horwich	42	18	9	15	64	59	63
Gainsborough Trinity	42	17	11	14	82	66	62
Stafford Rangers	42	15	17	10	65	52	62
Hyde United	42	17	8	17	61	63	59
Marine	42	16	10	16	63	68	58
Witton Albion	42	14	14	14	64	57	56
Chorley	42	14	11	17	68	65	53
Workington	42	14	9	19	53	57	51
Southport	42	14	8	20	57	74	50
Worksop Town	42	13	8	21	57	74	47
Goole Town	42	12	10	20	59	80	46
Morecambe	42	11	12	19	59	75	45
Oswestry Town	42	11	8	23	66	97	41
Buxton	42	11	6	25	52	91	39
Mossley	42	9	9	24	47	74	33

Mossley had 3 points deducted

1984-85

Stafford Rangers	42	26	8	8	81	40	86
Macclesfield Town	42	23	13	6	67	39	82
Witton Albion	42	22	8	12	57	39	74
Hyde United	42	21	8	13	68	52	71
Marine	42	18	15	9	59	34	69
Burton Albion	42	18	15	9	70	49	69
Worksop Town	42	19	10	13	68	56	67
Workington	42	18	9	15	59	53	53
Horwich	42	16	14	12	67	50	62
Bangor City	42	17	9	16	70	61	60
Gainsborough Trinity	42	14	14	14	72	73	56
Southport	42	15	9	18	65	66	54
Matlock Town	42	14	9	19	56	66	51
Oswestry Town	42	14	9	19	59	75	51
Mossley	42	14	9	19	45	65	51
Goole Town	42	13	11	18	60	65	50
Rhyl	42	11	14	17	52	63	47
Morecambe	42	11	14	17	51	67	47
Chorley	42	12	10	20	47	63	46
South Liverpool	42	9	15	18	43	71	42
Grantham	42	8	13	21	41	69	36
Buxton	42	8	6	28	38	79	30

Grantham had 1 point deducted

1985-86

Gateshead	42	24	10	8	85	51	82
Marine	42	23	11	8	63	35	80
Morecambe	42	17	17	8	59	39	68
Gainsborough Trinity	42	18	14	10	66	52	68
Burton Albion	42	18	12	12	64	47	66
Southport	42	17	11	14	70	66	62
Worksop Town	42	17	10	15	51	48	61
Workington	42	14	18	10	54	46	59
Macclesfield Town	42	17	8	17	67	65	59
Hyde United	42	14	15	13	63	62	57
Witton Albion	42	15	13	14	56	59	57
Mossley	42	13	16	13	56	60	55
Bangor City	42	13	15	14	51	51	54
Rhyl	42	14	10	18	65	71	52
South Liverpool	42	11	17	14	43	44	50
Horwich	42	15	6	21	53	63	50
Caernarfon Town	42	11	17	14	51	63	50
Oswestry Town	42	12	13	17	51	60	49
Buxton	42	11	12	19	55	76	45
Chorley	42	9	15	18	56	64	42
Matlock Town	42	9	15	18	59	75	42
Goole Town	42	7	11	24	37	78	31

Workington, Witton Albion, Horwich and Goole Town all had 1 point deducted.

1986-87

Macclesfield Town	42	26	10	6	80	47	88
Bangor City	42	25	12	5	74	35	87
Caernarfon Town	42	20	16	6	67	40	76
Marine	42	21	10	11	70	43	73
South Liverpool	42	21	10	11	58	40	73
Morecambe	42	20	12	10	68	49	72
Matlock Town	42	20	10	12	81	67	70
Southport	42	19	11	12	67	49	68
Chorley	42	16	12	14	58	59	60
Mossley	42	15	12	15	57	52	57
Hyde United	42	15	10	17	81	70	55
Burton Albion	42	16	6	20	56	68	54
Buxton	42	13	14	15	71	68	53
Witton Albion	42	15	8	19	68	79	53
Barrow	42	15	7	20	42	57	52
Goole Town	42	13	12	17	58	62	51
Oswestry Town	42	14	8	20	55	83	50
Rhyl	42	10	15	17	56	74	45
Worksop Town	42	9	13	20	56	74	40
Gainsborough Trinity	42	9	10	23	53	77	37
Workington	42	5	14	23	38	70	28
Horwich RMI	42	3	12	27	36	85	20

Workington and Horwich RMI both had 1 point deducted.

1987-88

Premier Division

Chorley	42	26	10	6	78	35	88
Hyde United	42	25	10	7	91	52	85
Caernarfon Town	42	22	10	10	56	34	76
Morecambe	42	19	15	8	61	41	72
Barrow	42	21	8	13	70	41	71
Worksop Town	42	20	11	11	74	55	71
Bangor City	42	20	10	12	71	55	70
Rhyl	42	18	13	11	70	42	67
Marine	42	19	10	13	67	45	67
Frickley Athletic	42	18	11	13	61	55	65
Witton Albion	42	16	12	14	61	47	60
Goole Town	42	17	9	16	71	61	60
Horwich	42	17	9	16	46	42	60
Southport	42	15	12	15	43	48	57
South Liverpool	42	10	19	13	56	64	49
Buxton	42	11	14	17	72	76	47
Mossley	42	11	11	20	54	75	44
Gateshead	42	11	7	24	52	71	40
Matlock Town	42	10	8	24	58	89	38
Gainsborough Trinity	42	8	10	24	38	81	34
Oswestry Town	42	6	10	26	44	101	28
Workington	42	6	3	33	28	113	21

First Division

Fleetwood Town	36	22	7	7	85	45	73
Stalybridge Celtic	36	22	6	8	72	42	72
Leek Town	36	20	10	6	63	38	70
Accrington Stanley	36	21	6	9	71	39	69
Farsley Celtic	36	18	9	9	64	48	60
Droylsden	36	16	10	10	63	48	58
Eastwood Hanley	36	14	12	10	50	37	54
Winsford United	36	15	6	15	59	47	51
Congleton Town	36	12	16	8	43	39	51
Harrogate Town	36	13	9	14	51	50	48
Alfreton Town	36	13	8	15	53	54	47
Radcliffe Borough	36	11	13	12	66	62	46
Irlam Town	36	12	10	14	39	45	46
Penrith	36	11	11	14	46	51	44
Sutton Town	36	11	5	20	51	96	38
Lancaster City	36	10	6	20	45	72	36
Eastwood Town	36	8	10	18	45	65	34
Curzon Ashton	36	8	4	24	43	73	28
Netherfield	36	4	4	28	35	93	16

Congleton Town had 1 point deducted
Farsley Celtic had 3 points deducted

1988-89

Premier Division

Barrow	42	26	9	7	89	35	87
Hyde United	42	24	8	10	77	44	80
Witton Albion	42	22	13	7	67	39	79
Bangor City	42	22	10	10	77	48	76
Marine	42	23	7	12	69	48	76
Goole Town	42	22	7	13	75	60	73
Fleetwood Town	42	19	16	7	53	44	73
Rhyl	42	18	10	14	75	65	64
Frickley Athletic	42	17	10	15	64	53	61
Mossley	42	17	9	16	56	58	60
South Liverpool	42	15	13	14	65	57	58
Caernarfon Town	42	15	10	17	49	53	55
Matlock Town	42	16	5	21	65	73	53
Southport	42	13	12	17	66	52	51
Buxton	42	12	14	16	61	63	50
Morecambe	42	13	9	20	55	60	47
Gainsborough Trinity	42	12	11	19	56	73	47
Shepshed Charterhouse	42	14	8	20	19	80	44
Stalybridge Celtic	42	9	13	20	16	81	40
Horwich	42	7	14	21	12	70	35
Gateshead	42	7	13	22	36	70	34
Worksop Town	42	6	5	31	42	103	23

Morecambe had 1 point deducted
Shepshed Charterhouse had 6 points deducted

First Division

Colne Dynamo	42	30	11	1	102	21	98
Bishop Auckland	42	28	5	9	78	28	89
Leek Town	42	25	11	6	74	41	85
Droylsden	42	25	9	8	84	48	84
Whitley Bay	42	23	6	13	77	49	75
Accrington Stanley	42	21	10	11	81	60	73
Lancaster City	42	21	8	13	76	54	71
Harrogate Town	42	19	7	16	68	61	64
Newtown	42	15	12	15	65	59	57
Congleton Town	42	15	11	16	62	66	56
Workington	42	17	3	22	59	74	54
Eastwood Town	42	14	10	13	55	61	52
Curzon Ashton	42	13	11	18	74	72	50
Farsley Celtic	42	12	13	17	52	73	49
Irlam Town	42	11	14	17	53	63	47
Penrith	42	14	5	23	61	91	47
Radcliffe Borough	42	12	10	20	62	86	46
Eastwood Hanley	42	11	12	10	46	67	45
Winsford United	42	13	6	23	58	93	35
Alfreton Town	42	8	11	23	44	92	35
Netherfield	42	8	9	25	57	90	32
Sutton Town	42	7	6	29	70	109	23

Leek Town and Netherfield both had 1 point deducted
Colne Dynamo had 3 points deducted
Sutton Town had 4 points deducted

1989-90

Premier Division

Colne Dynamoes	42	32	6	4	86	40	102
Gateshead	42	22	10	10	78	58	76
Witton Albion	42	22	7	13	67	39	73
Hyde United	42	21	8	13	73	50	71
South Liverpool	42	20	9	13	89	79	69
Matlock Town	42	18	12	12	61	42	66
Southport	42	17	14	11	54	48	65
Fleetwood Town	42	17	12	13	73	66	63
Marine	42	16	14	12	59	55	62
Bangor City	42	15	15	12	64	58	60
Bishop Auckland	42	17	8	17	72	64	59
Frickley Athletic	42	16	8	18	56	61	56
Horwich	42	15	13	14	66	69	55
Morecambe	42	15	9	18	58	70	54
Gainsborough Trinity	42	16	8	18	59	55	53
Buxton	42	15	8	19	59	72	53
Stalybridge Celtic	42	12	9	21	48	61	45
Mossley	42	11	10	21	61	82	43
Goole Town	42	12	5	25	54	77	41
Shepshed	42	11	7	24	55	82	40
Caernarfon Town	42	10	8	24	56	86	38
Rhyl	42	7	10	25	43	77	30

Rhyl had 1 point deducted
Horwich and Gainsborough Trinity both had 3 points deducted

First Division

Leek Town	42	26	8	8	70	31	86
Droylsden	42	27	6	9	81	46	80
Accrington Stanley	42	22	10	10	80	53	76
Whitley Bay	42	21	11	10	93	59	74
Emley	42	20	9	13	70	42	69
Congleton Town	42	20	12	10	65	53	69
Winsford United	42	18	10	14	65	53	64
Curzon Ashton	42	17	11	14	66	60	62
Harrogate Town	42	17	9	16	68	62	60
Lancaster City	42	15	14	13	73	54	59
Eastwood Town	42	16	11	15	61	64	59
Farsley Celtic	42	17	6	19	71	75	57
Rossendale United	42	15	9	18	73	69	54
Newtown	42	14	12	16	49	62	54
Irlam Town	42	14	11	17	61	66	53
Workington	42	14	8	20	56	64	50
Radcliffe Borough	42	14	7	21	47	63	49
Alfreton Town	42	13	8	21	59	85	47
Worksop Town	42	13	5	24	56	95	44
Netherfield	42	11	6	25	56	89	39
Eastwood Hanley	42	10	6	26	45	76	36
Penrith	42	9	9	24	44	88	36

Congleton Town 3 points deducted. Droylsden 7 points deducted.

1990-91

Premier Division

Witton Albion	40	28	9	3	81	31	93
Stalybridge Celtic	40	22	11	7	44	26	77
Morecambe	40	19	16	5	72	44	73
Fleetwood Town	40	20	9	11	69	44	69
Southport	40	18	14	8	66	48	68
Marine	40	18	11	11	56	39	65
Bishop Auckland	40	17	10	13	62	56	61
Buxton	40	17	11	12	66	61	59
Leek Town	40	15	11	14	48	44	56
Frickley Athletic	40	16	6	18	64	62	54
Hyde United	40	14	11	15	73	63	53
Goole Town	40	14	10	16	68	74	52
Droylsden	40	12	11	17	67	70	47
Chorley	40	12	10	18	55	55	46
Mossley	40	13	10	17	55	68	45
Horwich	40	13	6	21	62	81	45
Matlock Town	40	12	7	21	52	70	43
Bangor City	40	9	12	19	52	70	39
South Liverpool	40	10	9	21	58	92	39
Gainsborough Trinity	40	9	11	20	57	84	38
Shepshed Charterhouse	40	6	7	27	38	83	25

First Division

Whitley Bay	42	25	10	7	95	38	85
Emley	42	24	12	6	78	37	84
Worksop Town	42	25	7	10	85	56	82
Accrington Stanley	42	21	13	8	83	57	76
Rhyl	42	21	7	14	62	63	70
Eastwood Town	42	17	11	14	70	60	62
Warrington Town	42	17	10	15	68	52	61
Lancaster City	42	19	8	15	58	56	61
Bridlington Town	42	15	15	12	72	52	60
Curzon Ashton	42	14	14	14	49	57	56
Congleton Town	42	14	12	16	57	71	54
Netherfield	42	14	11	17	67	66	53
Newtown	42	13	12	17	68	75	51
Caernarfon Town	42	13	10	19	51	64	49
Rossendale United	42	12	13	17	66	67	48
Radcliffe Borough	42	12	12	18	50	69	48
Irlam Town	42	12	11	19	55	76	47
Winsford United	42	11	13	18	51	66	46
Harrogate Town	42	11	13	18	55	73	46
Workington	42	11	11	20	54	67	41
Farsley Celtic	42	11	9	22	49	78	39
Alfreton Town	42	7	12	23	41	84	33

1991-92

Premier Division

Stalybridge Celtic	42	26	14	2	84	33	92
Marine	42	23	9	10	64	32	78
Morecambe	42	21	13	8	70	44	76
Leek Town	42	21	10	11	62	49	73
Buxton	42	21	9	12	65	47	72
Emley	42	18	11	13	69	47	65
Southport	42	16	17	9	57	48	65
Accrington Stanley	42	17	12	13	78	62	63
Hyde United	42	17	9	16	69	67	60
Fleetwood United	42	17	8	17	67	64	59
Bishop Auckland	42	16	9	17	48	58	57
Goole Town	42	15	9	18	60	72	54
Horwich	42	13	14	15	44	52	53
Frickley Athletic	42	12	16	14	61	57	52
Droylsden	42	12	14	16	62	72	50
Mossley	42	15	4	23	51	73	49
Whitley Bay	42	13	9	20	53	79	48
Gainsborough Trinity	42	11	13	18	48	63	46
Matlock Town	42	12	9	21	59	87	45
Bangor City	42	11	10	21	46	57	43
Chorley	42	11	9	22	61	82	42
Shepshed Albion	42	6	8	28	46	79	26

First Division

Colwyn Bay	42	30	4	8	99	49	94
Winsford United	42	29	6	7	96	41	93
Worksop Town	42	25	5	12	101	54	80
Guiseley	42	22	12	8	93	56	78
Caernarfon Town	42	23	9	10	78	47	78
Bridlington Town	42	22	9	11	86	46	75
Warrington Town	42	20	8	14	79	64	68
Knowsley United	42	18	10	14	69	52	64
Netherfield	42	18	7	17	54	61	61
Harrogate Town	42	14	16	12	73	69	58
Curzon Ashton	42	15	9	18	71	83	54
Farsley Celtic	42	15	9	18	79	101	53
Radcliffe Borough	42	15	9	18	67	72	51
Newtown	42	15	6	21	60	95	51
Eastwood Town	42	13	11	18	59	70	50
Lancaster City	42	10	19	13	55	62	49
Congleton Town	42	14	5	23	59	81	47
Rhyl	42	11	10	21	59	69	43
Rossendale United	42	9	11	22	61	90	38
Alfreton Town	42	12	2	28	63	98	38
Irlam Town	42	9	7	26	45	95	33
Workington	42	7	8	27	45	99	28

Farsley Celtic 1 point deducted. Radcliffe Borough 3 points deducted.

1992-93

Premier Division

Southport	42	29	9	4	103	31	96
Winsford United	42	27	9	6	91	43	90
Morecambe	42	25	11	6	93	51	86
Marine	42	26	8	8	83	47	86
Leek Town	42	21	11	10	86	51	74
Accrington Stanley	42	20	13	9	79	45	73
Frickley Athletic	42	21	6	15	62	52	69
Barrow	42	18	11	13	71	55	65
Hyde United	42	17	13	12	87	71	64
Bishop Auckland	42	17	11	14	63	52	62
Gainsborough Trinity	42	17	8	17	63	66	59
Colwyn Bay	42	16	6	20	80	79	54
Horwich	42	14	10	18	72	79	52
Buxton	42	13	10	19	60	75	49
Matlock Town	42	13	11	18	56	79	47
Emley	42	13	6	23	62	91	45
Whitley Bay	42	11	8	23	57	96	41
Chorley	42	10	10	22	52	93	40
Fleetwood Town	42	10	7	25	50	77	37
Droylsden	42	10	7	25	47	84	37
Mossley	42	7	8	27	53	95	29
Goole Town	42	6	9	27	47	105	27

Matlock Town had 3 points deducted

First Division

Bridlington Town	40	25	11	4	84	35	86
Knowsley United	40	23	7	10	86	48	76
Ashton United	40	22	8	10	81	54	74
Guiseley	40	20	10	10	90	64	70
Warrington Town	40	19	10	11	85	57	67
Gretna	40	17	12	11	64	47	63
Curzon Ashton	40	16	15	9	69	63	63
Great Harwood Town	40	17	9	14	66	57	60
Alfreton Town	40	15	9	16	80	80	54
Harrogate Town	40	14	12	14	77	81	54
Worksop Town	40	15	9	16	66	70	54
Radcliffe Borough	40	13	14	13	66	69	53
Workington	40	13	13	14	51	61	52
Eastwood Town	40	3	11	16	49	52	50
Netherfield	40	11	14	15	68	63	47
Caernarfon Town	40	13	8	19	66	74	47
Farsley Celtic	40	12	8	20	64	77	44
Lancaster City	40	10	12	18	49	76	42
Shepshed Albion	40	9	12	19	46	66	39
Congleton Town	40	10	7	23	58	95	37
Rossendale United	40	5	5	30	50	126	20

1993-94

Premier Division

Marine	42	27	9	6	106	62	90
Leek Town	42	27	8	7	79	50	89
Boston United	42	23	9	10	90	43	78
Bishop Auckland	42	23	9	10	73	58	78
Frickley Athletic	42	21	12	9	90	51	75
Colwyn Bay	42	18	14	10	74	51	68
Morecambe	42	20	7	15	90	56	67
Barrow	42	18	10	14	59	51	64
Hyde United	42	17	10	15	80	71	61
Chorley	42	17	10	15	70	67	61
Whitley Bay	42	17	9	16	61	72	60
Gainsborough Trinity	42	15	11	16	64	66	56
Emley	42	12	16	14	63	71	52
Matlock Town	42	13	12	17	71	76	51
Buxton	42	13	10	19	67	73	49
Accrington Stanley	42	14	7	21	63	85	49
Droylsden	42	11	14	17	57	82	47
Knowsley United	42	11	11	20	52	66	44
Winsford United	42	9	11	22	50	74	38
Horwich RMI	42	8	12	22	50	75	35
Bridlington Town	42	7	10	25	41	91	28
Fleetwood Town	42	7	7	28	55	114	28

Horwich RMI 1 point deducted. Bridlington Town 3 points deducted

First Division

Guiseley	40	29	6	5	87	37	93
Spennymoor United	40	25	6	9	95	50	81
Ashton United	40	24	7	9	85	41	79
Lancaster City	40	20	10	10	74	46	70
Netherfield	40	20	6	14	68	60	66
Alfreton Town	40	18	10	12	83	70	64
Warrington Town	40	17	11	12	52	48	62
Goole Town	40	16	11	13	72	58	59
Great Harwood Town	40	15	14	11	56	60	59
Gretna	40	16	7	17	64	65	55
Workington	40	14	10	16	70	74	52
Worksop Town	40	14	9	17	79	87	51
Bamber Bridge	40	13	11	16	62	59	50
Curzon Ashton	40	13	8	19	62	71	47
Congleton Town	40	12	9	19	53	68	45
Radcliffe Borough	40	10	14	16	62	75	44
Mossley	40	10	12	18	44	68	39
Caernarfon Town	40	9	11	20	54	88	38
Farsley Celtic	40	6	16	18	42	77	34
Harrogate Town	40	8	9	23	40	86	33
Eastwood Town	40	7	11	22	47	63	32

Mossley had 3 points deducted

1994-95

Premier Division

Marine	42	29	11	2	83	27	98
Morecambe	42	28	10	4	99	34	94
Guiseley	42	28	9	5	96	50	93
Hyde United	42	22	10	10	89	59	76
Boston United	42	20	11	11	80	43	71
Spennymoor United	42	20	11	11	66	52	71
Buxton	42	18	9	15	65	62	63
Gainsborough Trinity	42	16	13	13	69	61	61
Bishop Auckland	42	16	12	14	68	55	57
Witton Albion	42	14	14	14	54	56	56
Barrow	42	17	5	20	68	71	56
Colwyn Bay	42	16	8	18	71	80	56
Emley	42	14	13	15	62	68	55
Matlock Town	42	15	5	22	62	72	50
Accrington Stanley	42	12	13	17	55	77	49
Knowsley United	42	11	14	17	64	83	47
Winsford United	42	10	11	21	56	75	41
Chorley	42	11	7	24	64	87	40
Frickley Athletic	42	10	10	22	53	79	40
Droylsden	42	10	8	24	56	93	38
Whitley Bay	42	8	8	26	46	97	32
Horwich RMI	42	9	4	29	49	94	31

Bishop Auckland had 3 points deducted

First Division

Blyth Spartans	42	26	9	7	95	55	87
Bamber Bridge	42	25	10	7	101	51	85
Warrington Town	42	25	9	8	74	40	84
Alfreton Town	42	25	7	10	94	49	82
Lancaster City	42	23	10	9	81	44	79
Worksop Town	42	19	14	9	95	68	71
Radcliffe Borough	42	18	10	14	76	70	64
Ashton United	42	18	8	16	80	70	62
Netherfield	42	17	7	118	54	56	58
Eastwood Town	42	14	13	15	67	61	55
Gretna	42	14	13	15	64	66	55
Atherton Laburnum Rovers	42	14	8	20	60	67	50
Harrogate Town	42	14	8	20	57	78	50
Caernarfon Town	42	13	10	19	59	62	49
Curzon Ashton	42	10	16	16	64	80	46
Great Harwood Town	42	11	13	18	66	87	46
Congleton Town	42	11	13	18	52	75	46
Fleetwood	42	12	11	19	51	74	44
Farsley Celtic	42	12	7	23	66	100	43
Workington	42	12	6	24	61	91	42
Goole Town	42	11	7	24	46	81	40
Mossley	42	11	5	26	52	90	37

Mossley had 1 point deducted. Fleetwood had 3 points deducted

1995-96

Premier Division

Bamber Bridge	42	20	16	6	81	49	76
Boston United	42	23	6	13	86	59	75
Hyde United	42	21	11	10	86	51	74
Barrow	42	20	13	9	69	42	73
Gainsborough Trinity	42	20	13	9	60	41	73
Blyth Spartans	42	17	13	12	75	61	64
Accrington Stanley	42	17	14	11	62	54	62
Emley	42	17	10	15	57	53	61
Spennymoor United	42	14	18	10	67	61	60
Guiseley	42	15	14	13	62	57	59
Bishop Auckland	42	16	11	15	60	55	59
Marine	42	15	14	13	59	54	59
Witton Albion	42	17	8	17	60	62	59
Chorley	42	14	9	19	67	74	48
Knowsley United	42	14	6	22	61	89	48
Winsford United	42	10	16	16	56	79	46
Leek Town	42	10	15	17	52	55	45
Colwyn Bay	42	8	21	13	43	57	45
Frickley Athletic	42	11	14	17	63	87	44
Buxton	42	9	11	22	43	72	38
Droylsden	42	10	8	24	58	100	38
Matlock Town	42	8	11	23	71	86	35

Accrington Stanley, Chorley & Frickley Town all had 3 points deducted

First Division

Lancaster City	40	24	11	5	79	38	83
Alfreton Town	40	23	9	8	79	47	78
Lincoln United	40	22	7	11	80	56	73
Curzon Ashton	40	20	7	13	73	53	67
Farsley Celtic	40	19	9	12	66	61	66
Radcliffe Borough	40	17	13	10	70	48	64
Eastwood Town	40	18	9	13	60	47	63
Whitley Bay	40	18	8	14	72	62	62
Ashton United	40	19	7	14	73	65	60
Atherton Laburnum Rovers	40	15	12	13	60	61	57
Worksop Town	40	16	8	16	84	90	56
Gretna	40	13	13	14	75	65	52
Warrington Town	40	13	10	17	75	72	49
Leigh	40	14	7	19	53	59	49
Netherfield	40	13	10	17	64	73	49
Workington	40	11	12	17	50	62	45
Bradford Park Avenue	40	9	14	17	57	72	41
Congleton Town	40	11	11	18	36	59	41
Great Harwood Town	40	9	7	24	44	78	33
Fleetwood	40	7	10	23	41	81	31
Harrogate Town	40	7	10	23	54	96	31

Great Harwood Town had 1 point deducted, Congleton Town had 3 points deducted and Ashton United had 4 points deducted

1996-97

Premier Division

Leek Town	44	28	9	7	71	35	93
Bishop Auckland	44	23	14	7	88	43	83
Hyde United	44	22	16	6	93	46	82
Emley	44	23	12	9	89	54	81
Barrow	44	23	11	10	71	45	80
Boston United	44	22	13	9	74	47	79
Blyth Spartans	44	22	11	11	74	49	77
Marine	44	20	15	9	53	37	75
Guiseley	44	20	11	13	63	54	71
Gainsborough Trinity	44	18	12	14	65	46	66
Accrington Stanley	44	18	12	14	77	70	66
Runcorn	44	15	15	14	63	62	60
Chorley	44	16	9	19	69	66	57
Winsford United	44	13	14	17	50	56	53
Knowsley United	44	12	14	18	58	79	49
Colwyn Bay	44	11	13	20	60	76	46
Lancaster City	44	12	9	23	48	75	45
Frickley Athletic	44	12	8	24	62	91	44
Spennymoor United	44	10	10	24	52	68	40
Bamber Bridge	44	11	7	26	59	99	40
Alfreton Town	44	8	13	23	45	83	37
Witton Albion	44	5	14	25	41	91	39
Buxton	44	5	12	27	33	86	27

Knowsley United had 1 point deducted

First Division

Radcliffe Borough	42	26	7	9	77	33	85
Leigh	42	24	11	7	65	33	83
Lincoln United	42	25	8	9	78	47	83
Farsley Celtic	42	23	8	11	75	48	77
Worksop Town	42	20	12	10	68	38	69
Stocksbridge Park Steels	42	19	11	12	66	54	68
Bradford Park Avenue	42	20	8	14	58	50	68
Ashton United	42	17	14	11	73	52	65
Great Harwood Town	42	16	12	14	56	46	60
Droylsden	42	15	14	13	69	67	59
Matlock Town	42	16	10	16	61	69	58
Whitley Bay	42	14	12	16	47	54	54
Flixton	42	15	7	20	57	72	52
Netherfield	42	12	14	16	54	56	50
Eastwood Town	42	12	14	16	42	50	50
Gretna	42	10	18	14	55	68	48
Harrogate Town	42	13	8	21	55	76	47
Congleton Town	42	12	9	21	47	64	45
Workington	42	10	12	20	45	63	42
Curzon Ashton	42	8	10	24	48	79	34
Warrington Town	42	5	18	19	42	79	33
Atherton Laburnum Rovers	42	7	9	26	45	85	30

Worksop Town had 3 points deducted

1997-98

Premier Division

Barrow	42	25	8	9	61	29	83
Boston United	42	22	12	8	55	40	78
Leigh RMI	42	21	13	8	63	41	76
Runcorn	42	22	9	11	80	50	75
Gainsborough Trinity	42	22	9	11	60	39	75
Emley	42	22	8	12	81	61	74
Winsford United	42	19	12	11	54	43	69
Altrincham	42	18	11	13	76	44	65
Guiseley	42	16	16	10	61	53	64
Bishop Auckland	42	17	12	13	78	60	63
Marine	42	15	11	16	56	59	56
Hyde United	42	13	16	13	60	55	55
Colwyn Bay	42	15	9	18	53	57	54
Spennymoor United	42	14	11	17	58	72	52
Chorley	42	14	7	21	51	70	49
Frickley Athletic	42	12	12	18	45	62	48
Lancaster City	42	13	8	21	55	74	47
Blyth Spartans	42	12	13	17	52	63	39
Bamber Bridge	42	9	12	21	51	74	39
Accrington Stanley	42	8	14	20	49	68	38
Radcliffe Borough	42	6	12	24	39	70	30
Alfreton Town	42	3	13	26	32	86	22

Spennymoor United had 1 point deducted
Blyth Spartans had 10 points deducted

First Division

Whitby Town	42	30	8	4	99	48	98
Worksop Town	42	28	7	7	93	44	91
Ashton United	42	26	9	7	93	43	87
Droylsden	42	24	8	10	70	49	80
Lincoln United	42	20	11	11	76	62	71
Farsley Celtic	42	20	10	12	72	66	70
Witton Albion	42	19	9	14	77	55	66
Eastwood Town	42	18	12	12	68	51	66
Bradford Park Avenue	42	18	11	13	62	46	65
Belper Town	42	18	7	17	68	66	61
Stocksbridge Park Steels	42	17	9	16	68	63	60
Trafford	42	16	6	20	59	61	54
Whitley Bay	42	14	12	16	60	63	54
Matlock Town	42	14	11	17	68	65	53
Gretna	42	13	9	20	58	64	48
Netherfield	42	12	11	19	55	75	47
Flixton	42	10	12	20	45	73	42
Congleton Town	42	11	8	23	65	101	41
Harrogate Town	42	8	14	20	57	80	38
Great Harwood Town	42	8	12	22	42	88	36
Workington	42	8	7	27	38	84	31
Buxton	42	7	3	32	41	87	24

1998-99

Premier Division

Team	P	W	D	L	F	A	Pts
Altrincham	42	23	11	8	67	33	80
Worksop Town	42	22	10	10	66	48	76
Guiseley	42	21	9	12	64	47	72
Bamber Bridge	42	18	15	9	63	48	69
Gateshead	42	18	11	13	69	58	65
Gainsborough Trinity	42	19	8	15	65	59	65
Whitby Town	42	17	13	12	77	62	64
Leigh	42	16	15	11	63	54	63
Hyde United	42	16	11	15	61	48	59
Stalybridge Celtic	42	16	11	15	71	63	59
Winsford United	42	14	15	13	56	52	57
Runcorn	42	12	19	11	46	49	55
Emley	42	12	17	13	47	49	53
Blyth Spartans	42	14	9	19	56	64	51
Colwyn Bay	42	12	13	17	60	71	49
Frickley Athletic	42	11	15	16	55	71	48
Marine	42	10	17	15	61	69	47
Spennymoor United	42	12	11	19	52	71	47
Lancaster City	42	11	13	18	50	62	46
Bishop Auckland	42	10	15	17	49	67	45
Chorley	42	8	15	19	45	68	39
Accrington Stanley	42	9	9	24	47	77	36

First Division

Team	P	W	D	L	F	A	Pts
Droylsden	42	26	8	8	97	55	86
Hucknall Town	42	26	11	5	80	38	86
Ashton United	42	22	12	8	79	46	78
Lincoln United	42	20	12	10	94	65	72
Eastwood Town	42	20	8	14	65	69	68
Radcliffe Borough	42	19	8	15	78	62	65
Burscough	42	19	8	15	67	61	65
Witton Albion	42	18	9	15	70	63	63
Bradford Park Avenue	42	17	11	14	64	55	62
Stocksbridge Park Steels	42	16	13	13	64	60	61
Harrogate Town	42	17	7	18	75	77	58
Gretna	42	16	10	16	73	80	58
Belper Town	42	15	11	16	58	57	56
Trafford	42	14	11	17	50	58	53
Netherfield Kendal	42	13	10	19	51	64	49
Flixton	42	12	12	18	50	64	48
Matlock Town	42	14	6	22	53	72	48
Farsley Celtic	42	11	13	18	56	73	46
Whitley Bay	42	10	9	23	53	77	39
Congleton Town	42	8	15	19	65	91	39
Great Harwood Town	42	10	8	24	51	73	38
Alfreton Town	42	9	8	25	53	86	35

Hucknall Town had 3 points deducted

1999-2000

Premier Division

Team	P	W	D	L	F	A	Pts
Leigh	44	28	8	8	91	45	92
Hyde United	44	24	13	7	77	44	85
Gateshead	44	23	13	8	79	41	82
Marine	44	21	16	7	78	46	79
Emley	44	20	12	12	54	41	72
Lancaster City	44	20	11	13	65	55	71
Stalybridge Celtic	44	18	12	14	64	54	66
Bishop Auckland	44	18	11	15	63	61	65
Runcorn	44	18	10	16	64	55	64
Worksop Town	44	19	6	19	78	65	63
Gainsborough Trinity	44	16	15	13	59	49	63
Whitby Town	44	15	13	16	66	66	58
Barrow	44	14	15	15	65	59	57
Blyth Spartans	44	15	9	20	62	67	54
Droylsden	44	14	12	18	53	60	54
Frickley Athletic	44	15	9	20	64	85	54
Bamber Bridge	44	14	11	19	70	67	53
Hucknall Town	44	14	11	19	55	61	53
Leek Town	44	14	10	20	58	79	52
Colwyn Bay	44	12	12	20	46	85	48
Spennymoor United	44	10	13	21	41	71	42
Guiseley	44	8	17	19	52	72	41
Winsford United	44	3	7	34	40	116	16

Spennymoor United had 1 point deducted

First Division

Team	P	W	D	L	F	A	Pts
Accrington Stanley	42	25	9	8	96	43	84
Burscough	42	22	18	2	81	35	84
Witton Albion	42	23	15	4	88	46	84
Bradford Park Avenue	42	23	9	10	77	48	78
Radcliffe Borough	42	22	12	8	71	48	78
Farsley Celtic	42	19	11	12	66	52	68
Matlock Town	42	17	16	9	72	55	67
Ossett Town	42	17	8	17	77	55	59
Stocksbridge Park Steels	42	16	8	18	55	70	56
Eastwood Town	42	15	11	16	64	65	55
Harrogate Town	42	14	12	16	65	67	54
Congleton Town	42	14	12	16	63	73	54
Chorley	42	13	15	14	53	64	54
Ashton United	42	12	16	14	65	67	52
Workington	42	13	13	16	49	55	52
Lincoln United	42	13	12	17	52	80	51
Belper Town	42	13	11	18	59	72	50
Trafford	42	11	12	19	55	63	45
Gretna	42	11	7	24	48	78	40
Netherfield Kendal	42	8	9	25	46	82	33
Flixton	42	7	9	26	47	85	30
Whitley Bay	42	7	9	26	41	87	30

Eastwood Town had 1 point deducted

2000-2001

Premier Division

Team	P	W	D	L	F	A	Pts
Stalybridge Celtic	44	31	9	4	96	32	102
Emley	44	31	8	5	86	42	101
Bishop Auckland	44	26	7	11	89	53	85
Lancaster City	44	24	9	11	84	60	81
Worksop Town	44	20	13	11	102	60	73
Barrow	44	21	9	14	83	53	72
Altrincham	44	20	10	14	80	59	70
Gainsborough Trinity	44	17	14	13	59	56	65
Accrington Stanley	44	18	10	16	72	65	64
Hucknall Town	44	17	12	15	57	63	63
Gateshead	44	16	12	16	67	61	60
Bamber Bridge	44	17	8	19	63	65	59
Runcorn	44	15	10	19	56	71	55
Blyth Spartans	44	15	9	20	61	64	54
Burscough	44	14	10	20	59	68	52
Hyde United	44	13	12	19	72	79	51
Whitby Town	44	13	11	20	60	76	50
Marine	44	12	13	19	62	78	49
Colwyn Bay	44	12	10	22	68	102	46
Frickley Athletic	44	10	15	19	50	79	45
Droylsden	44	13	6	25	50	80	45
Leek Town	44	12	8	24	45	70	44
Spennymoor United	44	4	5	35	32	108	17

First Division

Team	P	W	D	L	F	A	Pts
Bradford Park Avenue	42	28	5	9	83	40	89
Vauxhall Motors	42	23	10	9	95	50	79
Ashton United	42	23	9	10	91	49	78
Stocksbridge Park Steels	42	19	13	10	80	60	70
Trafford	42	20	9	13	70	62	68
Belper Town	42	18	11	13	71	62	65
Witton Albion	42	15	16	11	51	50	61
Ossett Town	42	16	12	14	66	58	60
Radcliffe Borough	42	17	8	17	72	71	59
Chorley	42	15	14	13	71	70	59
Harrogate Town	42	15	10	17	60	70	55
Matlock Town	42	14	10	18	70	74	52
North Ferriby United	42	14	10	18	64	73	52
Workington	42	13	12	17	53	60	51
Lincoln United	42	13	12	17	60	75	51
Gretna	42	12	12	18	72	82	48
Guiseley	42	11	15	16	37	50	48
Kendal Town	42	12	12	18	60	69	47
Farsley Celtic	42	12	11	19	53	71	47
Eastwood Town	42	12	8	21	40	63	47
Winsford United	42	13	11	18	61	70	44
Congleton Town	42	6	28	8	43	94	30

Trafford and Kendal Town both had 1 point deducted
Winsford United had 6 points deducted

2001-2002

Premier Division

Burton Albion	44	31	11	2	106	30	104
Vauxhall Motors	44	27	8	9	86	55	89
Lancaster City	44	23	9	12	80	57	78
Worksop Town	44	23	9	12	74	51	78
Emley	44	22	9	13	69	55	75
Accrington Stanley	44	21	9	14	89	64	72
Runcorn FC Halton	44	21	8	15	76	53	71
Barrow	44	19	10	15	75	59	67
Altrincham	44	19	9	16	66	58	66
Bradford Park Avenue	44	18	5	21	77	76	59
Droylsden	44	17	8	19	65	78	59
Blyth Spartans	44	14	16	14	59	62	58
Frickley Athletic	44	16	11	17	63	69	58
Gateshead	44	14	14	16	58	71	56
Whitby Town	44	15	8	21	61	76	53
Hucknall Town	44	14	9	21	50	68	51
Marine	44	11	17	16	62	71	50
Burscough	44	15	5	24	69	86	50
Gainsborough Trinity	44	13	10	21	61	76	49
Colwyn Bay	44	12	11	21	49	82	47
Bishop Auckland	44	12	8	24	46	68	44
Hyde United	44	10	10	24	61	87	40
Bamber Bridge	44	7	10	27	38	88	30

First Division

Harrogate Town	42	25	11	6	80	35	86
Ossett Town	42	21	13	8	73	44	76
Ashton United	42	21	12	9	90	63	75
Spennymoor United	42	22	6	14	75	73	72
Radcliffe Borough	42	20	8	14	73	51	68
Leek Town	42	20	8	14	67	51	68
Gretna	42	19	7	16	66	66	63
Eastwood Town	42	17	11	14	61	59	62
Rossendale United	42	17	10	15	69	58	61
Witton Albion	42	17	10	15	72	68	61
Guiseley	42	18	7	17	60	67	61
North Ferriby United	42	14	16	12	71	60	58
Chorley	42	16	9	17	59	57	57
Matlock Town	42	15	9	18	49	48	54
Trafford	42	14	9	19	64	80	51
Workington	42	12	12	18	51	57	48
Farsley Celtic	42	12	11	19	64	78	47
Belper Town	42	12	11	19	49	66	47
Lincoln United	42	11	14	17	62	80	47
Stocksbridge Park Steels	42	12	9	21	55	76	45
Kendal Town	42	9	9	24	52	76	36
Ossett Albion	42	8	8	26	43	92	32

2002-2003

Premier Division

Accrington Stanley	44	30	10	4	97	44	100
Barrow	44	24	12	8	84	52	84
Vauxhall Motors	44	22	10	12	81	46	76
Stalybridge Celtic	44	21	13	10	77	51	76
Worksop Town	44	21	9	14	82	67	72
Harrogate Town	44	21	8	15	75	63	71
Bradford Park Avenue	44	20	10	14	73	70	70
Hucknall Town	44	17	15	12	72	62	66
Droylsden	44	18	10	16	62	52	64
Whitby Town	44	17	12	15	80	69	63
Marine	44	17	10	17	63	60	61
Wakefield & Emley	44	14	18	12	46	49	60
Runcorn FC Halton	44	15	15	14	69	74	60
Altrincham	44	17	9	18	58	63	60
Gainsborough Trinity	44	16	11	17	67	66	59
Ashton United	44	15	13	16	71	79	58
Lancaster City	44	16	9	19	71	75	57
Burscough	44	14	9	21	44	51	51
Blyth Spartans	44	14	9	21	67	87	51
Frickley Athletic	44	13	8	23	45	78	47
Gateshead	44	10	11	23	60	81	41
Colwyn Bay	44	5	9	30	52	99	24
Hyde United	44	5	8	31	40	98	23

Division One

Alfreton Town	42	26	9	7	106	59	87
Spennymoor United	42	27	6	9	81	42	87
Radcliffe Borough	42	25	10	7	90	46	85
North Ferriby United	42	23	9	10	78	45	78
Chorley	42	21	10	11	80	51	73
Belper Town	42	20	13	9	53	42	73
Witton Albion	42	19	15	8	67	50	72
Matlock Town	42	20	10	12	67	48	70
Leek Town	42	20	9	13	63	46	69
Workington	42	19	10	13	73	60	67
Farsley Celtic	42	17	11	14	66	67	62
Kendal Town	42	18	7	17	68	58	61
Bamber Bridge	42	15	9	18	55	59	54
Guiseley	42	14	11	17	68	63	53
Bishop Auckland	42	13	10	19	58	83	49
Lincoln United	42	12	9	21	67	77	45
Stocksbridge PS	42	11	9	22	54	81	42
Rossendale United	42	12	5	25	58	88	41
Kidsgrove Athletic	42	9	11	22	49	71	38
Ossett Town	42	8	9	25	39	80	33
Eastwood Town	42	5	8	29	33	92	23
Trafford	42	5	6	31	34	99	21

2003-2004

Premier Division

Hucknall Town	44	29	8	7	83	38	95
Droylsden	44	26	8	10	96	64	86
Barrow	44	22	14	8	82	52	80
Alfreton Town	44	23	9	12	73	43	78
Harrogate Town	44	24	5	15	79	63	77
Southport	44	20	10	14	71	52	70
Worksop Town	44	19	13	12	69	50	70
Lancaster City	44	20	9	15	62	49	69
Vauxhall Motors	44	19	10	15	78	75	67
Gainsborough Trinity	44	17	13	14	70	52	64
Stalybridge Celtic	44	18	10	16	72	66	64
Altrincham	44	16	15	13	66	51	63
Runcorn FC Halton	44	16	13	15	67	63	61
Ashton United	44	17	8	19	59	79	59
Whitby Town	44	14	11	19	55	70	53
Marine	44	13	12	19	62	74	51
Bradford Park Avenue	44	12	14	18	48	62	50
Spennymoor United	44	14	6	24	55	93	48
Burscough	44	10	15	19	47	67	45
Radcliffe Borough	44	12	6	26	74	99	42
Blyth Spartans	44	10	10	24	54	74	40
Frickley Athletic	44	11	7	26	51	83	40
Wakefield & Emley	44	8	6	30	45	99	30

Division One

Hyde United	42	24	8	10	79	49	80
Matlock Town	42	23	7	12	78	51	76
Farsley Celtic	42	20	14	8	78	56	74
Lincoln United	42	20	11	11	73	53	71
Witton Albion	42	17	12	13	61	56	63
Gateshead	42	21	4	17	65	68	63
Workington	42	17	11	14	70	58	62
Leek Town	42	16	13	13	56	47	61
Guiseley	42	16	12	14	66	54	60
Bamber Bridge	42	16	12	14	64	53	60
Bridlington Town	42	16	10	16	70	68	58
Prescot Cables	42	16	10	16	63	65	58
Bishop Auckland	42	14	13	15	61	64	55
Ossett Town	42	15	10	17	62	73	52
Rossendale United	42	13	12	17	53	62	51
Colwyn Bay	42	14	9	19	56	82	51
North Ferriby United	42	13	11	18	64	70	50
Chorley	42	13	10	19	54	70	49
Stocksbridge Park Steels	42	12	12	18	57	69	48
Belper Town	42	9	15	18	44	58	42
Kendal Town	42	11	7	24	53	79	40
Kidsgrove Athletic	42	10	9	23	45	67	39

2004-2005
Premier Division

Hyde United	42	25	13	4	80	43	88
Workington	42	26	7	9	73	30	85
Farsley Celtic	42	25	8	9	81	41	83
Whitby Town	42	23	11	8	65	49	80
Prescot Cables	42	21	8	13	63	54	71
Burscough	42	21	7	14	93	74	70
Leek Town	42	16	15	11	63	52	63
Witton Albion	42	15	17	10	56	44	62
Radcliffe Borough	42	16	14	12	60	60	62
Guiseley	42	16	13	13	70	64	61
Matlock Town	42	14	13	15	59	67	55
Blyth Spartans	42	13	13	16	53	55	52
Wakefield & Emley	42	14	10	18	60	67	52
Lincoln United	42	15	4	23	53	66	49
Marine	42	10	18	14	53	60	48
Ossett Town	42	11	13	18	53	62	46
Gateshead	42	11	12	19	61	84	45
Frickley Athletic	42	10	14	18	44	57	44
Bishop Auckland	42	11	7	24	51	74	40
Bridlington Town	42	7	14	21	43	66	35
Bamber Bridge	42	9	7	26	48	92	34
Spennymoor United	42	9	10	23	44	65	25

Spennymoor United had 12 points deducted.

Division One

North Ferriby United	42	25	8	9	83	49	83
Ilkeston Town	42	24	9	9	64	40	81
AFC Telford United	42	23	11	8	78	44	80
Willenhall Town	42	22	12	8	71	46	78
Kendal Town	42	21	8	13	89	69	71
Eastwood Town	42	20	9	13	73	54	69
Mossley	42	20	6	16	81	56	66
Brigg Town	42	15	19	8	59	46	64
Gresley Rovers	42	17	12	13	57	53	63
Kidsgrove Athletic	42	15	15	12	60	55	60
Woodley Sports	42	16	11	15	68	74	59
Ossett Albion	42	15	13	14	83	74	58
Colwyn Bay	42	14	13	15	54	62	55
Stocksbridge Park Steels	42	15	9	18	58	58	51
Shepshed Dynamo	42	13	11	18	53	75	50
Chorley	42	13	9	20	62	69	48
Belper Town	42	13	8	21	57	66	47
Spalding United	42	13	8	21	57	69	47
Clitheroe	42	12	10	20	47	57	46
Warrington Town	42	11	13	18	45	59	46
Rossendale United	42	10	10	22	64	87	40
Rocester	42	0	6	36	31	132	6

Stocksbridge Park Steels had 3 points deducted.

2005-2006
Premier Division

Blyth Spartans	42	26	11	5	79	32	89
Frickley Athletic	42	26	8	8	72	36	86
Marine	42	23	12	7	61	25	81
Farsley Celtic	42	23	10	9	84	34	79
North Ferriby United	42	21	10	11	77	54	73
Whitby Town	42	18	10	14	60	59	64
Burscough	42	19	6	17	64	64	63
Witton Albion	42	17	9	16	68	55	60
Matlock Town	42	16	11	15	60	55	59
AFC Telford United	42	14	17	11	54	52	59
Ossett Town	42	17	7	18	57	61	58
Leek Town	42	14	14	14	50	53	56
Prescot Cables	42	15	8	19	49	60	53
Guiseley	42	14	9	19	45	58	51
Ashton United	42	13	10	19	62	63	49
Ilkeston Town	42	12	13	17	48	51	49
Gateshead	42	12	10	20	52	77	46
Radcliffe Borough	42	12	8	22	54	62	44
Lincoln United	42	14	10	18	44	64	44
Wakefield Emley	42	11	9	22	38	69	42
Bradford Park Avenue	42	10	9	23	64	86	39
Runcorn FC Halton	42	6	11	25	36	108	29

Division One

Mossley	42	23	9	10	83	55	78
Fleetwood Town	42	22	10	10	72	48	76
Kendal Town	42	22	10	10	81	58	76
Woodley Sports	42	22	8	12	85	53	74
Gresley Rovers	42	20	10	12	79	64	70
Stocksbridge PS	42	17	16	9	66	43	67
Eastwood Town	42	16	14	12	66	58	62
Brigg Town	42	16	14	12	70	64	62
Belper Town	42	17	8	17	53	56	59
Shepshed Dynamo	42	15	13	14	57	56	58
Bridlington Town	42	16	10	16	61	68	58
Colwyn Bay	42	15	11	16	56	53	56
Bamber Bridge	42	13	15	14	65	59	54
Ossett Albion	42	15	9	18	54	64	54
Rossendale United	42	12	17	13	58	61	53
Clitheroe	42	15	8	19	54	73	53
Kidsgrove Athletic	42	14	9	19	66	69	51
Chorley	42	14	8	20	58	59	50
Warrington Town	42	11	15	16	62	74	48
Spalding United	42	10	15	17	49	70	45
Goole	42	11	11	20	55	85	43
Bishop Auckland	42	3	6	33	39	99	15

Goole had 1 point deducted.

2006-2007
Premier Division

Burscough	42	23	12	7	80	37	80
Witton Albion	42	24	8	10	90	48	80
AFC Telford United	42	21	15	6	72	40	78
Marine	42	22	8	12	70	53	74
Matlock Town	42	21	9	12	70	43	72
Guiseley	42	19	12	11	71	49	69
Hednesford Town	42	18	14	10	49	41	68
Fleetwood Town	42	19	10	13	71	60	67
Gateshead	42	17	14	11	75	57	65
Ossett Town	42	18	10	14	61	52	64
Whitby Town	42	18	6	18	63	78	60
Ilkeston Town	42	16	11	15	66	62	59
North Ferriby United	42	15	9	18	54	61	54
Prescot Cables	42	13	14	15	52	56	53
Lincoln United	42	12	15	15	40	58	51
Frickley Athletic	42	13	10	19	50	69	49
Leek Town	42	13	9	20	49	61	48
Ashton United	42	13	9	20	52	72	48
Kendal Town	42	12	11	19	59	79	47
Mossley	42	10	5	27	48	79	35
Radcliffe Borough	42	7	11	24	39	71	32
Grantham Town	42	3	8	31	39	94	17

Burscough had one point deducted.

Division One

Buxton	46	30	11	5	94	37	101
Cammell Laird	46	28	10	8	105	56	94
Eastwood Town	46	26	9	11	89	43	87
Bradford Park Avenue	46	24	10	12	77	47	82
Colwyn Bay	46	22	11	13	74	65	77
Stocksbridge Park Steels	46	22	10	14	82	49	76
Goole	46	21	9	16	80	84	72
Kidsgrove Athletic	46	21	7	18	91	80	70
Rossendale United	46	21	7	18	64	59	70
Woodley Sports	46	19	11	16	89	71	68
Ossett Albion	46	19	11	16	71	66	68
Harrogate Railway	46	21	5	20	72	78	68
Bamber Bridge	46	18	8	20	78	75	62
Alsager Town	46	18	7	21	72	75	61
Skelmersdale United	46	17	10	19	72	77	61
Clitheroe	46	18	6	22	78	75	60
Brigg Town	46	16	10	20	57	72	58
Gresley Rovers	46	16	7	23	59	75	55
Belper Town	46	17	4	25	58	86	55
Shepshed Dynamo	46	15	7	24	62	96	52
Wakefield	46	13	10	23	48	71	49
Warrington Town	46	13	8	25	64	84	47
Chorley	46	10	6	30	52	99	36
Bridlington Town	46	3	14	29	33	101	23

MIDLAND COMBINATION

Formation

The Midland Combination was formed as the Worcestershire Combination after a meeting held at the Seven Stars Hotel, Oldswinford near Stourbridge on 28th April 1927. This meeting was organised by Mr S. Bloye and Mr E.J. Rivers who worked at Stewarts & Lloyds' Coombs Wood works. They felt there was a need for a league for amateur clubs, particularly in the north of the county.

The 10 founder members were: Bewdley, Blackheath Town, Cookley St. Peters, Halesowen Labour, Highley Colliers, Kidderminster Harriers Reserves, Oldbury Town, Old Carolians, Stewarts & Lloyds and Stourbridge Reserves.

The Worcestershire Combination changed its name to the Midland Combination in 1968, a year after the neighbouring Warwickshire Combination closed down.

Some of the published tables contained errors. Additional research has found corrections for many of these, totals that still do not balance are shown below the relevant columns in italics.

Abbreviations used:

WMRL = West Midlands Regional League.

BYOB = Birmingham Youths & Old Boys F.A.

WWMA = Warwickshire & West Midland Alliance.

& DL = & District League.

WORCESTERSHIRE COMBINATION

1927-28

Blackheath Town	18	12	2	4	74	29	26
Kidderminster Harriers Reserves	18	12	2	4	61	25	26
Stourbridge Reserves	18	12	2	4	88	42	26
Halesowen Labour	18	11	1	6	61	45	23
Oldbury Town	18	7	4	7	55	54	18
Stewart & Lloyds	18	7	2	9	65	58	16
Highley Colliers	18	6	1	11	50	64	13
Bewdley	18	6	0	12	41	80	12
Old Carolians	18	4	2	12	52	85	10
Cookley St. Peters	18	3	4	11	29	94	10

Highley Colliers left and were replaced by Halesowen St. John.

1928-29

Blackheath Town	16	12	2	2	66	32	26
Halesowen Labour	16	10	2	4	57	35	22
Stourbridge Reserves	16	9	3	4	62	43	21
Stewart & Lloyds	16	8	1	7	48	41	17
Oldbury Town	17	6	3	8	43	39	15
Bewdley	17	4	6	7	56	58	14
Cookley St. Peters	13	5	2	6	32	43	12
Halesowen St. John	18	5	2	11	48	76	12
Kidderminster Harriers Reserves	8	3	2	3	27	21	8
Old Carolians	17	3	1	13	44	104	7
					483	*492*	

Not all fixtures were completed.
Blackheath Town, Stourbridge Reserves, Oldbury Town, Cookley St. Peters, Halesowen St. John, Kidderminster Harriers Reserves and Old Carolians all left. Dudley Town and Netherton Liberals joined from the Cradley Heath & DL and Hanbury Conservatives also joined.

1929-30

First Series

Halesowen Labour	10	7	1	2	48	23	15
Netherton Liberals	10	6	1	3	29	19	13
Bewdley	10	6	0	4	25	21	12
Dudley Town	10	3	1	6	28	35	7
Stewart & Lloyds	10	3	1	6	20	40	7
Hanbury Conservatives	10	2	2	6	22	34	6

Second Series

Dudley Town	10	8	1	1	27	7	17
Bewdley	10	6	0	4	38	26	12
Stewart & Lloyds	10	6	0	4	31	23	12
Halesowen Labour	10	5	0	5	27	32	10
Hanbury Conservatives	10	3	0	7	19	36	6
Netherton Liberals	10	1	1	8	10	28	3

Hanbury Conservatives left. Stourport Swifts joined from the Kidderminster League and Brintons, Bromley, Bromsgrove Rovers Reserves, Burton Delingpole, Lye & Wollescote, Round Oak, Stoke Works and Wordsley Olympic also joined.

1930-31

Halesowen Labour	25	19	2	4	135	51	40
Dudley Town	25	18	2	5	92	43	38
Lye & Wollescote	26	16	5	5	89	69	37
Burton Delingpole	25	17	2	6	104	53	36
Round Oak	24	11	4	9	71	44	26
Bromley	25	12	2	11	72	56	26
Wordsley Olympic	25	11	1	13	81	76	23
Bewdley	26	10	3	13	68	87	23
Stewart & Lloyds	25	9	3	13	64	86	21
Stoke Works	25	7	5	13	58	76	19
Brintons	26	8	3	15	60	97	19
Stourport Swifts	25	7	4	14	48	93	18
Netherton Liberals	26	5	2	19	32	90	12
Bromsgrove Rovers Reserves	16	3	0	13	23	76	6

Bromsgrove Rovers Reserves did not complete their fixtures and left at the end of the season.
Lye & Wollescote were reformed as Lye Town. Stewart & Lloyds left. Brierley Hill Alliance Reserves, Coombs Wood, B.T.H. and Stourbridge Reserves joined.

1931-32

Dudley Town	30	22	4	4	115	55	48
Brierley Hill Alliance Reserves	30	21	3	6	109	57	45
Brintons	30	22	2	6	104	54	46
Coombs Wood	30	16	6	8	108	65	38
Round Oak	30	17	3	10	98	83	37
Lye Town	30	14	8	8	100	64	36
Bromley	30	16	3	11	77	64	35
Burton Delingpole	30	15	2	13	104	96	32
Halesowen Labour	30	12	7	11	93	101	31
B.T.H.	30	14	2	14	73	88	30
Stourbridge Reserves	30	10	6	14	79	91	26
Wordsley Olympic	30	10	3	17	67	104	23
Stourport Swifts	30	9	4	17	80	93	22
Netherton Liberals	30	8	3	19	66	99	19
Stoke Works	30	4	1	25	62	120	9
Bewdley	30	1	1	28	36	137	3

Dudley Town moved to the Birmingham Combination and Stourport Swifts moved to the Kidderminster League.
Stoke Works, Halesowen Labour, Brintons and Burton Delingpole left. Woodside Wanderers, Coombs Wood Works, Darby End Institute and Tarmac joined.

1932-33

Tarmac	26	19	2	5	100	31	40
Lye Town	26	19	1	6	125	58	39
Bromley	26	15	4	7	77	45	34
Woodside Wanderers	26	16	1	9	104	50	33
Brierley Hill Alliance Reserves	26	15	2	9	76	56	32
Round Oak	26	14	3	9	73	69	31
Stourbridge Reserves	26	14	2	10	69	62	30
Darby End Institute	26	12	4	10	73	77	28
Wordsley Olympic	26	10	1	15	69	88	21
Netherton Liberals	26	9	2	15	55	73	20
Coombs Wood Works	26	9	2	15	53	91	20
Bewdley	26	7	2	17	54	99	16
B.T.H.	26	6	2	18	48	98	14
Coombs Wood	26	3	0	23	29	108	6

Coombs Wood left.
Horseley Sports, Greets Green Wesley and Catshill Village joined.

1933-34

Woodside Wanderers	30	26	1	3	157	38	53
Tarmac	30	22	4	4	132	44	48
Brierley Hill Alliance Reserves	30	20	3	7	88	64	43
Lye Town	30	17	4	9	100	63	38
Horseley Sports	30	16	5	9	97	59	37
Darby End Institute	30	16	4	10	90	62	36
Coombs Wood Works	30	15	3	12	61	83	33
Greets Green Wesley	30	15	2	13	64	75	32
Netherton Liberals	30	11	7	12	64	67	29
Stourbridge Reserves	30	11	6	13	71	77	28
Catshill Village	30	10	3	17	68	94	23
Bromley	30	8	5	17	62	90	21
Wordsley Olympic	30	6	6	18	52	115	18
Bewdley	30	7	1	22	46	100	15
Round Oak	30	4	5	21	64	118	13
B.T.H.	30	4	5	21	44	111	13

Coombs Wood Works, Horseley Sports and Darby End Institute left.
Dudley Town Reserves joined.

1934-35

Catshill Village	26	19	3	4	117	45	41
Lye Town	26	18	3	5	82	46	39
Dudley Town Reserves	26	16	3	7	81	41	35
Tarmac	26	16	3	7	70	40	35
Netherton Liberals	26	13	4	9	70	42	30
Greets Green Wesley	26	12	4	10	60	54	28
Woodside Wanderers	26	12	4	10	58	49	28
Stourbridge Reserves	26	11	4	11	61	78	26
Bromley	26	9	4	13	50	68	22
Bewdley	26	8	4	14	57	70	20
Wordsley Olympic	26	8	2	16	50	90	18
Brierley Hill Alliance Reserves	26	6	4	16	42	74	16
B.T.H.	26	6	4	16	57	98	16
Round Oak	26	3	4	19	51	111	10

Round Oak and Woodside Wanderers left. Whiteheath joined.

1935-36

Lye Town	24	21	0	3	119	40	42
Catshill Village	24	18	4	2	90	33	40
Netherton Liberals	24	12	7	5	70	47	31
Tarmac	24	13	2	9	66	35	28
Greets Green Wesley	24	9	7	8	44	48	25
Brierley Hill Alliance Reserves	24	11	2	11	71	57	24
Bewdley	24	11	2	11	60	87	24
Whiteheath	24	9	3	12	57	77	21
Dudley Town Reserves	24	8	4	12	71	75	20
Stourbridge Reserves	24	5	5	14	50	79	15
Wordsley Olympic	24	5	5	14	49	86	15
Bromley	24	6	3	15	51	96	15
B.T.H.	24	5	2	17	46	84	12

Greets Green Wesley left.
Goodyears and Halesowen Town Reserves joined.

1936-37

Catshill Village	26	23	2	1	110	25	48
Goodyears	25	17	4	4	72	32	38
Lye Town	26	18	2	6	97	46	38
Netherton Liberals	24	17	3	4	78	31	37
Tarmac	25	13	5	7	68	41	31
Dudley Town Reserves	26	11	5	10	46	50	27
Bewdley	25	10	2	13	50	64	22
Halesowen Town Reserves	26	9	4	13	54	71	22
Stourbridge Reserves	26	10	1	15	61	65	21
Wordsley Olympic	24	7	4	13	62	72	18
Whiteheath	25	6	3	16	45	72	15
Bromley	20	3	4	13	32	71	10
Brierley Hill Alliance Reserves	25	4	1	20	39	97	9
B.T.H.	21	3	2	16	20	97	8

Not all fixtures were completed.
Tarmac, Dudley Town Reserves, Halesowen Town Reserves, Wordsley Olympic, Whiteheath, Bromley and B.T.H. left. Stourport Swifts joined from the Kidderminster League and Jack Moulds Athletic, Wrockwardine Wood and Worcester City Reserves also joined.

1937-38

Catshill Village	20	16	1	3	70	32	33
Lye Town	20	14	2	4	76	31	30
Jack Moulds Athletic	20	9	7	4	38	29	25
Netherton Liberals	20	10	4	6	42	36	24
Goodyears	20	10	3	7	54	44	23
Wrockwardine Wood	20	9	4	7	50	38	22
Stourport Swifts	20	7	2	11	49	53	16
Stourbridge Reserves	20	6	3	11	38	50	15
Worcester City Reserves	20	5	4	11	47	69	14
Brierley Hill Alliance Reserves	20	4	5	11	40	66	13
Bewdley	20	2	1	17	26	82	5

Bewdley, Brierley Hill Alliance Reserves and Worcester City Reserves left. Bridgnorth Town, Woodsetton, Weoley Castle and Stourbridge Glazed Brickworks joined.

1938-39

Catshill Village	20	17	2	1	84	25	36
Wrockwardine Wood	21	15	2	4	62	33	32
Lye Town	21	14	3	4	75	42	31
Bridgnorth Town	22	11	1	10	60	57	23
Goodyears	21	8	4	9	51	61	20
Netherton Liberals	22	8	4	10	38	53	20
Woodsetton	21	8	3	10	51	38	19
Jack Moulds Athletic	16	7	2	7	31	30	16
Weoley Castle	22	7	2	13	40	61	16
Stourport Swifts	22	5	5	12	43	51	15
Stourbridge Glazed Brickworks	21	6	3	12	42	66	15
Stourbridge Reserves	21	3	1	17	24	84	7

Not all fixtures were completed.

1939-48

The Worcestershire Combination closed down upon the outbreak of war in 1939 and was not restarted until 1948. Of the pre-war members, only Jack Moulds Athletic, Stourport Swifts and Stourbridge Reserves rejoined. They were joined by 13 new members: Bournville Athletic, British Legion (Austin), Bromsgrove Rovers Reserves, Dudley Town Reserves, Halesowen Town Reserves, Handsworth Wood, High Duty Alloys, Kingswinford Wanderers, Lye Town Reserves, Moor Green Reserves, Round Oak, Smethwick Highfield and Wordsley.

1948-49

Jack Moulds Athletic	30	23	5	2	106	35	51
Smethwick Highfield	30	19	4	7	91	56	42
Halesowen Town Reserves	30	18	3	9	99	55	39
Stourport Swifts	30	14	7	9	72	64	35
Lye Town Reserves	30	14	7	9	73	73	35
Moor Green Reserves	30	14	6	10	72	57	34
British Legion (Austin)	30	14	6	10	78	70	34
Stourbridge Reserves	30	13	5	12	87	67	31
Round Oak	30	12	5	13	74	74	29
Kingswinford Wanderers	30	12	5	13	70	85	29
Bromsgrove Rovers Reserves	30	13	2	15	73	61	28
Dudley Town Reserves	30	11	4	15	68	78	26
Bournville Athletic	30	10	6	14	59	76	26
Handsworth Wood	30	5	6	19	47	88	16
High Duty Alloys	30	4	5	21	57	94	13
Wordsley	30	4	4	22	39	132	12

High Duty Alloys moved to the Redditch & DL and Dudley Town Reserves also left. Brierley Hill Alliance Reserves joined from the Walsall Senior League, Boldmere St. Michaels Reserves joined from the BYOB and Herman Smith and Cradley Heath Reserves also joined.

1949-50

Bournville Athletic	34	25	3	6	95	34	53
Jack Moulds Athletic	34	22	5	7	112	49	49
Smethwick Highfield	34	22	5	7	115	59	49
Bromsgrove Rovers Reserves	34	22	5	7	99	58	49
Brierley Hill Alliance Reserves	34	16	9	9	97	66	41
Stourport Swifts	34	17	7	10	74	60	41
Halesowen Town Reserves	34	14	6	14	74	72	34
Stourbridge Reserves	34	16	2	16	71	76	34
Herman Smith	34	11	8	15	57	85	30
Kingswinford Wanderers	34	12	5	17	71	83	29
Lye Town Reserves	34	12	5	17	68	85	29
Cradley Heath Reserves	34	12	5	17	56	72	29
Boldmere St. Michaels Reserves	34	11	6	17	63	60	28
Handsworth Wood	34	12	4	18	69	88	28
Moor Green Reserves	34	9	10	15	54	84	28
British Legion (Austin)	34	12	2	20	82	104	26
Round Oak	34	9	4	21	76	105	22
Wordsley	34	3	7	24	49	142	13

Stourport Swifts moved to the Kidderminster League and Round Oak, Wordsley and Cradley Heath Reserves also left. Paget Rangers joined from the Central Amateur League and Richard Thomas & Baldwins and Wolverhampton Wanderers "B" also joined.

1950-51

Jack Moulds Athletic	32	24	3	5	96	30	51
Smethwick Highfield	32	21	6	5	133	58	48
Halesowen Town Reserves	32	21	3	8	86	43	45
Bournville Athletic	32	17	8	7	87	57	42
Wolverhampton Wanderers "B"	32	17	5	10	116	54	39
Brierley Hill Alliance Reserves	32	18	2	12	109	82	38
Paget Rangers	32	17	4	11	72	60	38
Richard Thomas & Baldwins	32	14	5	13	55	71	33
Moor Green Reserves	32	14	4	14	71	60	32
Boldmere St. Michaels Reserves	32	13	5	14	53	66	31
Bromsgrove Rovers Reserves	32	9	8	15	76	82	26
Lye Town Reserves	32	11	3	18	68	91	25
Kingswinford Wanderers	32	10	5	17	55	92	25
Handsworth Wood	32	8	6	18	44	88	22
Stourbridge Reserves	32	10	0	22	51	87	20
British Legion (Austin)	32	9	2	21	49	117	20
Herman Smith	32	3	3	26	29	112	9

Herman Smith left. Evesham United joined from the Worcester & DL, Lower Gornal Athletic joined from the Wolverhampton Amateur League and Walsall Wood joined from the Walsall Senior League.

1951-52

Walsall Wood	36	31	2	3	129	37	64
Smethwick Highfield	36	30	2	4	140	48	62
Evesham United	36	23	6	7	108	65	52
Wolverhampton Wanderers "B"	36	19	7	10	113	71	45
Paget Rangers	36	18	5	13	88	68	41
Halesowen Town Reserves	36	19	3	14	74	64	41
Brierley Hill Alliance Reserves	36	18	4	14	99	103	40
Jack Moulds Athletic	36	16	6	14	86	66	38
Lower Gornal Athletic	36	14	7	15	102	89	35
Moor Green Reserves	36	13	9	14	82	78	35
Bromsgrove Rovers Reserves	36	15	3	18	94	99	33
Stourbridge Reserves	36	13	7	16	72	84	33
Richard Thomas & Baldwins	36	13	6	17	63	81	32
Bournville Athletic	36	12	4	20	68	82	28
Lye Town Reserves	36	9	8	19	67	87	26
Kingswinford Wanderers	36	12	1	23	61	101	25
British Legion (Austin)	36	8	7	21	59	119	23
Boldmere St. Michaels Reserves	36	9	3	24	48	80	21
Handsworth Wood	36	3	4	29	54	185	10

Smethwick Highfield changed their name to Smethwick Town. Handsworth Wood left and joined the Birmingham AFA.

1952-53

Evesham United	34	28	3	3	147	41	59
Smethwick Town	34	26	3	5	130	44	55
Walsall Wood	34	23	6	5	97	38	52
Wolverhampton Wanderers "B"	34	22	2	10	109	61	46
Paget Rangers	34	19	3	12	73	69	41
Jack Moulds Athletic	34	18	4	12	96	80	40
Bournville Athletic	34	17	4	13	108	76	38
Stourbridge Reserves	34	14	9	11	66	66	37
Boldmere St. Michaels Reserves	34	15	7	12	70	80	37
Moor Green Reserves	34	15	5	14	82	69	35
Lower Gornal Athletic	34	15	3	16	106	102	33
Bromsgrove Rovers Reserves	34	10	7	17	69	113	27
Halesowen Town Reserves	34	11	4	19	63	86	26
Richard Thomas & Baldwins	34	9	4	21	42	77	22
Brierley Hill Alliance Reserves	34	9	3	22	45	92	21
Kingswinford Wanderers	34	6	6	22	63	117	18
Lye Town Reserves	34	6	3	25	55	109	15
British Legion (Austin)	34	4	2	28	45	146	10

Kingswinford Wanderers were replaced by Kingswinford & Wallheath and British Legion (Austin) left. Quarry Bank Celtic joined from the WWMA.

1953-54

Brierley Hill Alliance Reserves	34	26	3	5	100	52	55
Walsall Wood	34	25	2	7	102	53	52
Evesham United	34	24	4	6	84	45	52
Wolverhampton Wanderers "B"	34	19	4	11	83	50	42
Smethwick Town	34	19	3	12	92	61	41
Paget Rangers	34	17	7	10	75	60	41
Jack Moulds Athletic	34	18	4	12	81	59	40
Lower Gornal Athletic	34	16	6	12	76	74	38
Bournville Athletic	34	15	5	14	101	73	35
Halesowen Town Reserves	34	14	6	14	77	73	34
Stourbridge Reserves	34	15	3	16	81	69	33
Lye Town Reserves	34	13	5	16	88	75	31
Quarry Bank Celtic	34	10	7	17	61	85	27
Bromsgrove Rovers Reserves	34	9	4	21	66	114	22
Moor Green Reserves	34	7	7	20	38	71	21
Boldmere St. Michaels Reserves	34	7	3	24	48	113	17
Richard Thomas & Baldwins	34	7	2	25	47	113	16
Kingswinford & Wallheath	34	4	7	23	48	108	15

Kingswinford & Wallheath left. Stratford Town joined from the WWMA.

1954-55

Evesham United	34	26	4	4	120	40	56
Walsall Wood	34	24	3	7	99	52	51
Jack Moulds Athletic	34	18	8	8	76	55	44
Stratford Town	34	19	5	10	120	61	43
Bromsgrove Rovers Reserves	34	19	4	11	89	60	42
Bournville Athletic	34	18	5	11	91	79	41
Stourbridge Reserves	34	17	2	15	70	71	36
Quarry Bank Celtic	34	14	7	13	83	82	35
Smethwick Town	34	14	5	15	80	79	33
Halesowen Town Reserves	34	13	7	14	71	78	33
Paget Rangers	34	13	7	14	62	72	33
Wolverhampton Wanderers "B"	34	11	10	13	82	74	32
Brierley Hill Alliance Reserves	34	14	3	17	69	75	31
Moor Green Reserves	34	11	4	19	59	86	26
Lye Town Reserves	34	9	4	21	51	117	22
Boldmere St. Michaels Reserves	34	8	5	21	56	89	21
Richard Thomas & Baldwins	34	7	5	22	57	109	19
Lower Gornal Athletic	34	4	6	24	55	111	14

Evesham United moved to the Birmingham League.
Malvern Town joined from the Worcester & DL.

1957-58

Wolverhampton Wanderers "B"	34	26	3	5	125	36	55
Walsall Wood	34	25	4	5	122	49	54
Jack Moulds Athletic	34	19	5	10	89	54	43
Malvern Town	34	17	8	9	80	63	42
Lower Gornal Athletic	34	19	2	13	101	63	40
Bromsgrove Rovers Reserves	34	18	4	12	75	59	40
Allens Cross	34	17	4	13	68	58	38
Smethwick Town	34	15	4	15	77	75	34
Paget Rangers	34	13	7	14	73	65	33
Bournville Athletic	34	15	3	16	80	88	33
Lye Town Reserves	34	14	5	15	72	80	33
Quarry Bank Celtic	34	14	4	16	64	77	32
Brierley Hill Alliance Reserves	34	13	4	17	82	69	30
Halesowen Town Reserves	34	12	6	16	70	86	30
Boldmere St. Michaels Reserves	34	10	5	19	63	98	25
Moor Green Reserves	34	9	5	20	59	88	23
Stourbridge Reserves	34	9	4	21	49	97	22
Worcester City "A"	34	1	3	30	32	176	5

Worcester City "A" left.
Shelfield Athletic joined from the Staffordshire County League.

1955-56

Malvern Town	34	20	9	5	96	41	49
Stratford Town	34	21	6	7	95	42	48
Halesowen Town Reserves	34	20	8	6	97	55	48
Jack Moulds Athletic	34	20	4	10	84	52	44
Wolverhampton Wanderers "B"	34	17	9	8	92	60	43
Lower Gornal Athletic	34	16	8	10	74	54	40
Bromsgrove Rovers Reserves	34	17	4	13	82	69	38
Smethwick Town	34	15	7	12	71	64	37
Walsall Wood	34	12	11	11	77	73	35
Quarry Bank Celtic	34	15	4	15	95	89	34
Lye Town Reserves	34	13	7	14	75	90	33
Moor Green Reserves	34	11	9	14	55	62	31
Paget Rangers	34	13	5	16	58	68	31
Bournville Athletic	34	11	5	18	69	81	27
Brierley Hill Alliance Reserves	34	9	8	17	74	93	26
Stourbridge Reserves	34	7	9	18	54	82	23
Boldmere St. Michaels Reserves	34	7	5	22	46	90	19
Richard Thomas & Baldwins	34	1	4	29	31	160	6

Richard Thomas & Baldwins moved to the Wolverhampton Works
League. Allens Cross joined from the WWMA.

1958-59

Shelfield Athletic	34	25	4	5	115	43	54
Walsall Wood	34	24	5	5	108	40	53
Wolverhampton Wanderers "B"	34	24	4	6	110	44	52
Halesowen Town Reserves	34	21	3	10	93	70	45
Lower Gornal Athletic	34	19	4	11	88	73	42
Paget Rangers	34	15	6	13	75	64	36
Quarry Bank Celtic	34	17	0	17	73	70	34
Malvern Town	34	15	4	15	80	84	34
Brierley Hill Alliance Reserves	34	13	8	13	54	61	34
Stourbridge Reserves	34	13	7	14	87	85	33
Bromsgrove Rovers Reserves	34	12	9	13	70	82	33
Moor Green Reserves	34	12	6	16	55	70	30
Allens Cross	34	12	4	18	73	78	28
Bournville Athletic	34	10	5	19	73	109	25
Jack Moulds Athletic	34	8	7	19	56	81	23
Boldmere St. Michaels Reserves	34	9	4	21	60	107	22
Smethwick Town	34	7	6	21	39	84	20
Lye Town Reserves	34	4	6	24	43	107	14

1956-57

Stratford Town	34	25	5	4	98	35	55
Wolverhampton Wanderers "B"	34	23	3	8	110	57	49
Malvern Town	34	21	6	7	102	58	48
Allens Cross	34	20	5	9	89	54	45
Jack Moulds Athletic	34	19	5	10	92	54	43
Walsall Wood	34	19	3	12	94	61	41
Bournville Athletic	34	17	7	10	87	64	41
Smethwick Town	34	14	5	15	76	80	33
Lower Gornal Athletic	34	12	8	14	86	86	32
Bromsgrove Rovers Reserves	34	12	7	15	68	72	31
Paget Rangers	34	15	1	18	63	75	31
Moor Green Reserves	34	12	6	16	53	66	30
Stourbridge Reserves	34	10	6	18	64	83	26
Quarry Bank Celtic	34	12	2	20	72	96	26
Halesowen Town Reserves	34	12	1	21	79	120	25
Lye Town Reserves	34	11	2	21	72	93	24
Brierley Hill Alliance Reserves	34	10	3	21	54	100	23
Boldmere St. Michaels Reserves	34	3	3	28	48	143	9
					1407	1397	

Stratford Town moved to the Birmingham League.
Worcester City "A" joined from the Warwickshire Combination.

1959-60

Paget Rangers	34	25	7	2	100	31	57
Shelfield Athletic	34	25	1	8	99	43	51
Wolverhampton Wanderers "B"	34	21	5	8	104	47	47
Malvern Town	34	18	7	9	124	71	43
Lower Gornal Athletic	34	20	3	11	93	57	43
Allens Cross	34	17	6	11	73	51	40
Walsall Wood	34	14	11	9	62	47	39
Halesowen Town Reserves	34	16	5	13	77	65	37
Bromsgrove Rovers Reserves	34	17	3	14	86	83	37
Quarry Bank Celtic	34	12	6	16	72	89	30
Smethwick Town	34	12	6	16	63	87	30
Brierley Hill Alliance Reserves	34	12	6	16	63	94	30
Bournville Athletic	34	10	5	19	80	106	25
Moor Green Reserves	34	7	11	16	48	80	25
Boldmere St. Michaels Reserves	34	10	4	20	55	104	24
Jack Moulds Athletic	34	10	3	21	68	86	23
Stourbridge Reserves	34	6	6	22	47	99	18
Lye Town Reserves	34	4	5	25	45	119	13

Lye Town Reserves left.
Blakenall joined from the Staffordshire County League.

1960-61

Paget Rangers	34	26	4	4	136	45	56
Walsall Wood	34	24	4	6	110	48	52
Blakenall	34	23	4	7	110	50	50
Allens Cross	34	23	4	7	101	51	50
Smethwick Town	34	19	6	9	70	65	44
Malvern Town	34	19	5	10	104	62	43
Bromsgrove Rovers Reserves	34	20	3	11	96	82	43
Wolverhampton Wanderers "B"	34	19	4	11	101	68	42
Stourbridge Reserves	34	13	6	15	69	63	32
Halesowen Town Reserves	34	13	5	16	86	78	31
Lower Gornal Athletic	34	10	10	14	72	81	30
Quarry Bank Celtic	34	9	7	18	76	88	25
Jack Moulds Athletic	34	11	2	21	62	83	24
Bournville Athletic	34	9	3	22	65	118	21
Brierley Hill Alliance Reserves	34	7	6	21	84	110	20
Boldmere St. Michaels Reserves	34	9	2	23	50	127	20
Moor Green Reserves	34	6	6	22	54	118	18
Shelfield Athletic	34	3	5	26	41	150	11

Shelfield Athletic left.
Alvechurch joined from the West Midland Alliance, Premier Division.

A new Second Division was formed by the following clubs:
Castle Rovers and Yardley Wood Social (both ex-West Midland Alliance), British Legion (Austin) (ex-Kings Norton League), Olton (ex-BYOB), Crabbs Cross and Lye Town Reserves, plus 11 Division One Reserve sides:
Allens Cross, Bournville Athletic and Paget Rangers (all ex-BYOB), Alvechurch (ex-West Midland Alliance Division One), Jack Moulds Athletic and Smethwick Town (both ex-West Midland Alliance), Blakenall and Walsall Wood (both ex-Staffordshire County League), Malvern Town (ex-Worcester League), Lower Gornal Athletic and Quarry Bank Celtic.

1961-62

Division One

Allens Cross	34	22	7	5	92	33	51
Jack Moulds Athletic	34	22	7	5	90	37	51
Walsall Wood	34	23	5	6	99	42	51
Malvern Town	34	18	8	8	113	48	44
Blakenall	34	16	8	10	87	53	40
Paget Rangers	34	16	7	11	88	69	39
Alvechurch	34	15	8	11	81	62	38
Bromsgrove Rovers Reserves	34	15	5	14	63	71	35
Halesowen Town Reserves	34	12	8	14	80	75	32
Wolverhampton Wanderers "B"	34	13	5	16	60	78	31
Quarry Bank Celtic	34	12	6	16	75	76	30
Smethwick Town	34	13	4	17	64	67	30
Lower Gornal Athletic	34	12	6	16	62	98	30
Brierley Hill Alliance Reserves	34	13	2	19	59	90	28
Stourbridge Reserves	34	12	3	19	54	76	27
Moor Green Reserves	34	7	7	20	49	103	21
Bournville Athletic	34	6	8	20	46	83	20
Boldmere St. Michaels Reserves	34	3	8	23	30	111	14

Division Two

Allens Cross Reserves	32	24	4	4	101	44	52
Yardley Wood Social	32	22	4	6	85	35	48
Castle Rovers	32	22	2	8	83	50	46
Paget Rangers Reserves	32	20	5	7	87	48	45
Lye Town Reserves	32	17	5	10	83	52	39
Walsall Wood Reserves	32	17	4	11	77	55	38
Blakenall Reserves	32	15	4	13	66	74	34
Malvern Town Reserves	32	14	5	13	74	70	33
Alvechurch Reserves	32	13	5	14	71	56	31
British Legion (Austin)	32	14	2	16	90	85	30
Olton	32	14	2	16	66	69	30
Jack Moulds Athletic Reserves	32	13	2	17	60	64	28
Smethwick Town Reserves	32	9	5	18	69	92	23
Bournville Athletic Reserves	32	10	2	20	59	99	22
Lower Gornal Athletic Reserves	32	7	6	19	51	104	20
Crabbs Cross	32	5	5	22	44	104	15
Quarry Bank Celtic Reserves	32	2	6	24	55	120	10

Quarry Bank Celtic Reserves left. Hall Green Amateurs joined from the West Midland Alliance and Shirley Town also joined.

1962-63

Division One

Alvechurch	34	27	3	4	117	46	57
Wolverhampton Wanderers "B"	34	23	4	7	127	37	50
Paget Rangers	34	21	3	10	77	59	45
Blakenall	34	18	7	9	84	56	43
Malvern Town	34	20	3	11	97	65	43
Allens Cross	34	18	4	12	75	46	40
Jack Moulds Athletic	34	18	4	12	75	64	40
Walsall Wood	34	15	6	13	64	76	36
Halesowen Town Reserves	34	14	7	13	75	65	35
Stourbridge Reserves	34	15	4	15	73	77	34
Lower Gornal Athletic	34	12	8	14	58	96	32
Smethwick Town	34	13	2	19	67	75	28
Brierley Hill Alliance Reserves	34	11	6	17	59	71	28
Bromsgrove Rovers Reserves	34	10	7	17	59	77	27
Quarry Bank Celtic	34	10	6	18	46	72	26
Bournville Athletic	34	8	1	25	45	99	17
Boldmere St. Michaels Reserves	*34*	*7*	*2*	*25*	*48*	*119*	*16*
Moor Green Reserves	34	6	3	25	46	92	15

Smethwick Town changed their name to Smethwick Highfield.
Lower Gornal Athletic moved to the WMRL and Boldmere St. Michaels joined from the WMRL.

Division Two

Hall Green Amateurs	**34**	**28**	**2**	**4**	**93**	**28**	**58**
Yardley Wood Social	34	25	3	6	122	34	53
Allens Cross Reserves	34	24	4	6	91	37	52
Shirley Town	34	20	7	7	76	43	47
Castle Rovers	34	20	6	8	83	44	46
Paget Rangers Reserves	34	16	8	10	95	59	40
Blakenall Reserves	34	18	4	12	74	55	40
Alvechurch Reserves	34	18	4	12	87	85	40
Lye Town Reserves	34	18	2	14	93	67	38
Malvern Town Reserves	34	13	5	16	97	98	31
Jack Moulds Athletic Reserves	34	14	3	17	64	74	31
Walsall Wood Reserves	34	12	5	17	72	77	29
Olton	34	11	5	18	66	88	27
Smethwick Town Reserves	34	8	7	19	46	85	23
British Legion (Austin)	34	6	5	23	45	133	17
Lower Gornal Athletic Reserves	34	6	4	24	54	94	16
Bournville Athletic Reserves	34	6	2	26	63	125	14
Crabbs Cross	34	4	2	28	45	140	10

Crabbs Cross left.
Coleshill Hall Hospital joined from the BYOB as Coleshill Hall.

1963-64

Division One

Hall Green Amateurs	34	28	4	2	85	28	60
Alvechurch	34	23	5	6	102	40	51
Walsall Wood	34	19	5	10	67	49	43
Halesowen Town Reserves	34	19	5	10	75	60	43
Wolverhampton Wanderers "B"	34	15	10	9	69	46	40
Quarry Bank Celtic	34	16	8	10	72	65	40
Moor Green Reserves	34	14	5	15	60	67	33
Boldmere St. Michaels	34	11	10	13	46	55	32
Allens Cross	34	12	7	15	56	63	31
Smethwick Highfield	34	12	7	15	64	76	31
Blakenall	34	10	10	14	61	63	30
Stourbridge Reserves	34	12	6	16	65	74	30
Paget Rangers	34	11	8	15	59	73	30
Jack Moulds Athletic	34	12	5	17	66	82	29
Brierley Hill Alliance Reserves	34	10	8	16	59	69	28
Malvern Town	34	11	5	18	69	81	27
Bromsgrove Rovers Reserves	34	9	4	21	48	68	22
Bournville Athletic	*34*	*4*	*4*	*26*	*47*	*111*	*12*

Kidderminster Harriers Reserves joined from the Warwickshire Combination.

Division Two

Castle Rovers	33	27	3	3	115	27	57
Coleshill Hall	34	26	2	6	143	61	54
Lower Gornal Athletic Reserves	33	25	2	6	99	34	52
Lye Town Reserves	34	20	6	8	102	55	46
Paget Rangers Reserves	33	21	2	10	87	39	44
Boldmere St. Michaels Reserves	33	17	6	10	76	61	40
Walsall Wood Reserves	33	16	5	12	66	63	37
Allens Cross Reserves	34	16	3	15	80	85	35
Shirley Town	27	11	3	13	57	57	25
Blakenall Reserves	34	13	4	17	75	95	30
Yardley Wood Social	34	10	8	16	66	68	28
Olton	34	10	4	20	53	86	24
Jack Moulds Athletic Reserves	34	9	6	19	46	90	24
Alvechurch Reserves	34	10	3	21	67	117	23
Smethwick Highfield Reserves	33	7	8	18	34	69	22
Malvern Town Reserves	34	10	1	23	61	97	21
British Legion (Austin)	34	9	3	22	73	134	21
Bournville Athletic Reserves	33	5	5	23	47	109	15

Shirley Town resigned in mid-season. Their position was decided on points average. British Legion (Austin) moved to the Kings Norton League and Yardley Wood Social moved to the WWMA. Bournville Athletic Reserves also left. Highgate United joined from the WWMA and Alkamatic joined from the Redditch League. Hall Green Amateurs Reserves also joined.

1964-65

Division One

Alvechurch	34	26	2	6	112	43	54
Hall Green Amateurs	34	24	4	6	73	32	52
Boldmere St. Michaels	34	18	7	9	75	53	43
Blakenall	34	19	4	11	75	57	42
Kidderminster Harriers Reserves	34	18	4	12	71	63	40
Allens Cross	34	15	8	11	74	65	38
Halesowen Town Reserves	34	16	4	14	63	56	36
Walsall Wood	34	16	4	14	59	64	36
Stourbridge Reserves	34	15	5	14	67	64	35
Bromsgrove Rovers Reserves	34	14	5	15	72	72	33
Jack Moulds Athletic	34	14	5	15	57	70	33
Wolverhampton Wanderers "B"	34	11	9	14	72	71	31
Paget Rangers	34	12	7	15	53	61	31
Malvern Town	34	11	6	17	62	77	28
Brierley Hill Alliance Reserves	34	11	3	20	56	74	25
Smethwick Highfield	34	8	7	19	49	81	23
Quarry Bank Celtic	*34*	*7*	*5*	*22*	*54*	*86*	*19*
Moor Green Reserves	*34*	*4*	*5*	*25*	*31*	*86*	*13*

Stourbridge Reserves and Kidderminster Harriers Reserves moved to the WMRL and Hall Green Amateurs also left.
Evesham United joined from the Warwickshire Combination and Moor Green and Sutton Coldfield Town joined from the WMRL.

Division Two

Hall Green Amateurs Reserves	34	24	5	5	89	44	53
Lower Gornal Athletic Reserves	34	22	7	5	100	39	51
Coleshill Hall	34	22	7	5	101	52	51
Highgate United	**34**	**20**	**5**	**9**	**94**	**58**	**45**
Alvechurch Reserves	34	20	5	9	98	62	45
Lye Town Reserves	34	20	3	11	87	53	43
Paget Rangers Reserves	34	18	4	12	104	80	40
Bournville Athletic	34	14	5	15	83	72	33
Castle Rovers	**34**	**14**	**4**	**16**	**58**	**77**	**32**
Walsall Wood Reserves	34	9	10	15	69	96	28
Malvern Town Reserves	34	10	7	17	78	87	27
Allens Cross Reserves	34	12	3	19	69	86	27
Alkamatic	34	10	6	18	74	109	26
Olton	34	11	3	20	74	99	25
Boldmere St. Michaels Reserves	34	10	4	20	76	105	24
Blakenall Reserves	34	9	4	21	62	110	22
Jack Moulds Athletic Reserves	34	9	3	22	54	96	21
Smethwick Highfield Reserves	34	8	3	23	57	102	19

Olton changed their name to Olton F.C. (Holdings) Ltd.
Lower Gornal Athletic Reserves moved to the WMRL and Blakenall Reserves, Walsall Wood Reserves and Hall Green Amateurs Reserves also left. Alcester Town and Castle Rovers Reserves joined from the Warwickshire Combination, Highgate United Reserves joined from the Birmingham AFA and Sutton Coldfield Town Reserves also joined.

1965-66

Division One

Evesham United	34	27	4	3	142	45	58
Alvechurch	34	23	5	6	101	27	51
Moor Green	34	23	4	7	87	42	50
Blakenall	34	16	10	8	80	53	42
Castle Rovers	34	17	8	9	56	43	42
Paget Rangers	34	13	9	12	51	47	35
Jack Moulds Athletic	34	14	5	15	59	65	33
Smethwick Highfield	34	14	5	15	59	74	33
Walsall Wood	34	9	12	13	58	71	30
Malvern Town	34	12	6	16	76	95	30
Boldmere St. Michaels	34	12	5	17	68	76	29
Bromsgrove Rovers Reserves	34	10	7	17	57	59	27
Halesowen Town Reserves	34	12	3	19	55	76	27
Sutton Coldfield Town	34	11	5	18	59	100	27
Brierley Hill Alliance Reserves	34	9	8	17	49	95	26
Highgate United	34	10	5	19	47	64	25
Allens Cross	34	11	3	20	53	95	25
Wolverhampton Wanderers "B"	34	8	6	20	49	79	22

Allens Cross and Castle Rovers merged to form Cross Castle United. Oldbury United joined from the WWMA.

Division Two

Alvechurch Reserves	34	27	2	5	111	32	56
Coleshill Hall	34	26	1	7	116	53	53
Alkamatic	34	25	2	7	101	54	52
Moor Green Reserves	34	19	4	11	85	62	42
Alcester Town	34	17	6	11	77	58	40
Quarry Bank Celtic	34	14	10	10	85	75	38
Jack Moulds Athletic Reserves	34	15	3	16	59	70	33
Bournville Athletic	34	13	6	15	64	68	32
Boldmere St. Michaels Reserves	34	13	6	15	68	95	32
Paget Rangers Reserves	34	13	4	17	67	62	30
Malvern Town Reserves	34	12	6	16	72	83	30
Castle Rovers Reserves	34	9	9	16	57	74	27
Allens Cross Reserves	34	9	9	16	54	83	27
Sutton Coldfield Town Reserves	34	10	6	18	70	75	26
Lye Town Reserves	34	9	8	17	63	82	26
Olton F.C. (Holdings) Ltd.	34	8	10	16	53	74	26
Smethwick Highfield Reserves	34	10	5	19	58	97	25
Highgate United Reserves	34	6	5	23	38	101	17

Coleshill Hall disbanded and Olton F.C. (Holdings) Ltd. also left. Knowle joined from the WWMA and Evesham United Reserves also joined.

1966-67

Division One

Alvechurch	34	26	5	3	94	20	57
Evesham United	34	25	5	4	115	39	55
Boldmere St. Michaels	34	23	4	7	75	44	50
Highgate United	34	21	7	6	79	37	49
Moor Green	34	18	6	10	87	54	42
Malvern Town	34	15	7	12	57	44	37
Jack Moulds Athletic	34	14	8	12	55	57	36
Paget Rangers	34	12	11	11	69	65	35
Walsall Wood	34	14	7	13	65	74	35
Oldbury United	34	12	10	12	80	67	34
Cross Castle United	34	14	4	16	42	46	32
Sutton Coldfield Town	34	12	6	16	63	61	30
Bromsgrove Rovers Reserves	34	7	10	17	51	92	24
Halesowen Town Reserves	34	9	4	21	53	89	22
Brierley Hill Alliance Reserves	34	9	4	21	50	90	22
Smethwick Highfield	34	8	4	22	51	90	20
Blakenall	34	8	3	23	62	103	19
Wolverhampton Wanderers "B"	34	3	7	24	33	109	13

Division Two

Highgate United Reserves	32	22	3	7	84	48	47
Alkamatic	32	17	9	6	65	41	43
Lye Town Reserves	32	16	7	9	79	57	39
Alcester Town	32	15	8	9	69	61	38
Knowle	32	16	5	11	74	61	37
Boldmere St. Michaels Reserves	32	15	6	11	80	69	36
Bournville Athletic	32	15	5	12	75	60	35
Alvechurch Reserves	32	13	8	11	73	57	34
Moor Green Reserves	32	14	6	12	63	59	34
Jack Moulds Athletic Reserves	32	14	5	13	95	78	33
Malvern Town Reserves	32	15	2	15	71	72	32
Paget Rangers Reserves	32	12	7	13	70	71	31
Cross Castle United Reserves	32	12	7	13	46	51	31
Quarry Bank Celtic	32	11	6	15	78	79	28
Sutton Coldfield Town Reserves	32	11	3	18	59	69	25
Smethwick Highfield Reserves	32	6	3	23	49	89	15
Evesham United Reserves	32	2	2	28	39	147	6

Alkamatic and Evesham United Reserves left.
Coleshill Town joined from the BYOB Mercian League, Whitmore Old Boys joined from the Wolverhampton Amateur League and Oldbury United Reserves also joined.

1967-68

Division One

Evesham United	34	27	2	5	90	43	56
Alvechurch	34	26	1	7	98	30	53
Moor Green	34	19	9	6	76	44	47
Malvern Town	34	18	9	7	63	40	45
Highgate United	34	19	6	9	82	40	44
Oldbury United	34	16	9	9	63	41	41
Paget Rangers	34	14	10	10	60	47	38
Jack Moulds Athletic	34	15	7	12	59	45	37
Boldmere St. Michaels	34	16	3	15	52	45	35
Bromsgrove Rovers Reserves	34	11	9	14	56	67	31
Cross Castle United	34	9	11	14	54	65	29
Blakenall	34	11	7	16	55	74	29
Walsall Wood	34	10	8	16	51	70	28
Sutton Coldfield Town	34	8	11	15	51	64	27
Brierley Hill Alliance Reserves	34	10	4	20	53	89	24
Smethwick Highfield	34	8	5	21	47	77	21
Halesowen Town Reserves	34	8	5	21	32	72	21
Wolverhampton Wanderers "B"	*34*	*2*	*2*	*30*	*25*	*114*	*6*

Jack Moulds Athletic changed their name to Solihull Amateurs.
Halesowen Town Reserves and Brierley Hill Alliance Reserves moved to the WMRL and Bromsgrove Rovers Reserves also left.
Lydbrook Athletic and Warwickshire Constabulary joined from the Warwickshire Combination and Bridgnorth Town joined from the Kidderminster League.

Division Two

Whitmore Old Boys	**34**	**25**	**3**	**6**	**92**	**38**	**53**
Coleshill Town	34	18	11	5	84	51	47
Bournville Athletic	34	19	7	8	71	48	45
Boldmere St. Michaels Reserves	34	18	8	8	67	43	44
Sutton Coldfield Town Reserves	34	18	4	12	71	65	40
Smethwick Highfield Reserves	34	17	4	13	72	68	38
Paget Rangers Reserves	34	14	8	12	63	55	36
Alcester Town	34	14	7	13	54	47	35
Moor Green Reserves	34	13	9	12	66	68	35
Quarry Bank Celtic	34	15	4	15	66	77	34
Lye Town Reserves	34	12	7	15	52	73	31
Highgate United Reserves	34	11	8	15	68	71	30
Malvern Town Reserves	34	10	8	16	56	74	28
Cross Castle United Reserves	34	9	7	18	57	82	25
Alvechurch Reserves	34	9	6	19	51	60	24
Jack Moulds Athletic Reserves	34	8	8	18	53	68	24
Knowle	34	7	8	19	46	76	22
Oldbury United Reserves	34	7	7	20	51	76	21

Lye Town Reserves moved to the WMRL.
Blakenall Reserves joined from the Bloxwich Combination.

MIDLAND COMBINATION

1968-69

Division One

Evesham United	34	23	8	3	107	39	54
Alvechurch	34	24	3	7	81	31	51
Oldbury United	34	21	8	5	67	29	50
Paget Rangers	34	23	3	8	69	34	49
Malvern Town	34	21	5	8	101	45	47
Sutton Coldfield Town	34	21	3	10	75	48	45
Moor Green	34	16	7	11	76	61	39
Highgate United	34	16	7	11	79	64	39
Boldmere St. Michaels	34	13	11	10	59	49	37
Solihull Amateurs	34	14	6	14	53	53	34
Cross Castle United	34	11	7	16	57	61	29
Whitmore Old Boys	34	10	8	16	48	69	28
Lydbrook Athletic	34	10	6	18	48	73	26
Blakenall	34	9	6	19	46	90	24
Bridgnorth Town	34	9	5	20	56	85	23
Smethwick Highfield	34	7	5	22	46	79	19
Walsall Wood	34	6	2	26	38	90	14
Warwickshire Constabulary	34	0	4	30	49	155	4

Warwickshire Constabulary changed name to Birmingham City Police.
Cross Castle United changed their name to Northfield Amateurs.

Division Two

Highgate United Reserves	34	25	6	3	94	42	56
Knowle	34	22	7	5	88	42	51
Moor Green Reserves	34	20	7	7	85	44	47
Malvern Town Reserves	34	20	6	8	85	57	46
Coleshill Town	34	20	5	9	97	60	45
Alcester Town	34	17	5	12	82	68	39
Bournville Athletic	34	15	5	12	66	66	39
Paget Rangers Reserves	34	14	7	13	64	58	35
Oldbury United Reserves	34	14	6	14	59	58	34
Alvechurch Reserves	34	13	6	15	76	66	32
Cross Castle United Reserves	34	13	5	16	65	68	31
Solihull Amateurs Reserves	34	11	8	15	59	66	30
Sutton Coldfield Town Reserves	34	10	8	16	52	66	28
Quarry Bank Celtic	34	8	9	17	59	87	25
Wolverhampton Wanderers "B"	34	10	4	20	57	82	24
Smethwick Highfield Reserves	34	8	5	21	50	82	21
Blakenall Reserves	34	5	5	24	45	115	15
Boldmere St. Michaels Reserves	34	5	4	25	36	92	14

Blakenall Reserves left.
Solihull Borough joined from the BYOB Mercian League.

1969-70

Division One

Paget Rangers	34	23	7	4	97	31	53
Sutton Coldfield Town	34	21	6	7	75	31	48
Alvechurch	34	18	11	5	72	35	47
Evesham United	34	18	9	7	75	43	45
Malvern Town	34	18	6	10	75	53	42
Bridgnorth Town	34	17	4	13	78	66	38
Moor Green	34	11	14	9	57	48	36
Oldbury United	34	12	11	11	70	48	35
Solihull Amateurs	34	12	10	12	57	56	34
Blakenall	34	13	8	13	46	58	34
Birmingham City Police	34	13	7	14	51	55	33
Highgate United	34	12	6	16	58	72	30
Smethwick Highfield	34	9	8	17	52	66	26
Northfield Amateurs	34	9	8	17	47	72	26
Whitmore Old Boys	34	10	6	18	43	79	26
Boldmere St. Michaels	34	7	9	18	43	72	23
Walsall Wood	34	7	9	18	33	76	23
Lydbrook Athletic	34	5	3	26	33	101	13

Northfield Amateurs changed their name to Northfield.
Solihull Amateurs moved to the WMRL and Lydbrook Athletic moved to the Gloucestershire County League.
Stratford Town joined from the WMRL.

Division Two

Coleshill Town	34	27	4	3	99	30	58
Bournville Athletic	34	19	8	7	86	59	46
Moor Green Reserves	34	17	10	7	74	44	44
Alcester Town	34	17	8	9	56	41	42
Knowle	**34**	**17**	**4**	**13**	**77**	**61**	**38**
Solihull Borough	34	14	9	11	66	56	37
Highgate United Reserves	34	12	13	9	63	58	37
Wolverhampton Wanderers "B"	34	16	4	14	63	54	36
Malvern Town Reserves	34	14	6	14	78	80	34
Smethwick Highfield Reserves	34	10	12	12	55	71	32
Paget Rangers Reserves	34	10	11	13	39	41	31
Alvechurch Reserves	34	12	7	15	66	74	31
Sutton Coldfield Town Reserves	34	13	2	19	52	62	28
Northfield Amateurs Reserves	34	12	3	19	60	68	27
Oldbury United Reserves	34	9	7	18	62	80	25
Boldmere St. Michaels Reserves	34	11	3	20	55	94	25
Quarry Bank Celtic	34	7	7	20	52	84	21
Solihull Amateurs Reserves	34	5	10	19	36	82	20

Solihull Amateurs Reserves and Wolverhampton Wanderers "B" left.
Mile Oak Rovers joined from the BYOB Mercian League and Solihull
Town and Astwood Bank Rovers joined from the Worcester & DL.

1970-71

Division One

Paget Rangers	34	25	5	4	81	32	55
Sutton Coldfield Town	34	22	8	4	75	32	52
Evesham United	34	19	8	7	78	45	46
Moor Green	34	17	9	8	63	33	43
Alvechurch	34	17	7	10	67	47	41
Boldmere St. Michaels	34	16	9	9	62	52	41
Malvern Town	34	15	8	11	60	59	38
Blakenall	34	16	5	13	65	56	37
Oldbury United	34	14	8	12	64	40	36
Highgate United	34	13	8	13	58	52	34
Bridgnorth Town	34	12	5	17	70	83	29
Smethwick Highfield	34	10	8	16	45	70	28
Walsall Wood	34	10	7	17	49	71	27
Knowle	34	8	10	16	57	70	26
Birmingham City Police	34	9	5	20	39	76	23
Northfield	34	8	6	20	41	68	22
Stratford Town	34	6	6	22	27	70	18
Whitmore Old Boys	**34**	**5**	**6**	**23**	**45**	**90**	**16**

Division Two

Solihull Town	34	22	8	4	80	33	52
Solihull Borough	**34**	**22**	**8**	**4**	**77**	**35**	**52**
Highgate United Reserves	34	21	5	8	89	56	47
Oldbury United Reserves	34	18	9	7	62	36	45
Astwood Bank Rovers	34	19	4	11	58	48	42
Moor Green Reserves	34	12	16	6	65	32	40
Coleshill Town	34	17	5	12	67	47	39
Mile Oak Rovers	34	14	8	12	64	67	36
Bournville Athletic	34	10	11	13	50	61	31
Sutton Coldfield Town Reserves	34	11	8	15	59	61	30
Alvechurch Reserves	34	13	4	17	61	70	30
Paget Rangers Reserves	34	11	7	16	49	51	29
Northfield Reserves	34	11	7	16	40	59	29
Malvern Town Reserves	34	9	9	16	47	60	27
Alcester Town	34	10	5	19	37	75	25
Quarry Bank Celtic	34	10	3	21	59	88	23
Boldmere St. Michaels Reserves	34	6	7	21	30	71	19
Smethwick Highfield Reserves	34	4	8	22	33	77	16

Smethwick Highfield Reserves, Paget Rangers Reserves and Alvechurch
Reserves left.
Albion Haden United joined from the West Midland Metropolitan
League and Bridgnorth Town Reserves and Westphalians also joined.

1971-72

Division One

Alvechurch	34	27	1	6	111	27	55
Oldbury United	34	23	6	5	68	35	52
Sutton Coldfield Town	34	17	11	6	65	44	45
Highgate United	34	18	8	8	63	31	44
Evesham United	34	18	7	9	62	44	43
Moor Green	34	13	12	9	55	44	38
Malvern Town	34	13	10	11	50	44	36
Bridgnorth Town	34	13	7	14	48	50	33
Walsall Wood	34	14	4	16	48	54	32
Knowle	34	12	7	15	50	54	31
Solihull Borough	34	11	9	14	52	59	31
Blakenall	34	10	7	17	46	62	27
Boldmere St. Michaels	34	9	9	16	38	54	27
Birmingham City Police	34	10	7	17	42	73	27
Paget Rangers	34	8	10	16	35	52	26
Stratford Town	34	7	11	16	41	66	25
Northfield	34	10	4	20	46	70	24
Smethwick Highfield	**34**	**4**	**8**	**22**	**30**	**87**	**16**

Racing F.C. (Warwick) joined from the West Midlands Regional League.

Division Two

Highgate United Reserves	34	21	10	3	83	31	52
Alcester Town	34	19	12	3	77	43	50
Moor Green Reserves	34	21	6	7	79	46	48
Coleshill Town	34	18	10	6	67	30	46
Albion Haden United	34	21	4	9	93	50	46
Bridgnorth Town Reserves	34	17	6	11	80	64	40
Astwood Bank Rovers	34	17	4	13	62	43	38
Solihull Town	34	13	8	13	45	52	34
Whitmore Old Boys	34	12	7	15	55	62	31
Oldbury United Reserves	34	14	2	18	40	50	30
Mile Oak Rovers	34	10	8	16	51	56	28
Northfield Reserves	34	12	4	18	52	71	28
Boldmere St. Michaels Reserves	34	9	10	15	47	65	28
Bournville Athletic	34	11	6	17	45	71	28
Sutton Coldfield Town Reserves	34	9	9	16	49	56	27
Malvern Town Reserves	34	8	6	20	42	72	22
Westphalians	34	6	9	19	37	78	21
Quarry Bank Celtic	34	5	5	24	28	92	15

Westphalians and Quarry Bank Celtic left.
Chelmsley Town joined from the BYOB Mercian League.

1972-73

Division One

Highgate United	34	28	5	1	85	21	61
Alvechurch	34	27	4	3	104	23	58
Sutton Coldfield Town	34	23	5	6	75	31	51
Evesham United	34	20	8	6	70	35	48
Malvern Town	34	17	8	9	64	53	42
Oldbury United	34	16	8	10	50	39	40
Racing Club (Warwick)	34	14	8	12	50	45	36
Paget Rangers	34	14	7	13	45	52	35
Moor Green	34	12	10	12	45	43	34
Birmingham City Police	34	10	10	14	46	61	30
Bridgnorth Town	34	10	8	16	44	66	28
Stratford Town	34	9	9	16	35	38	27
Walsall Wood	34	9	6	19	36	71	24
Solihull Borough	34	7	9	18	42	57	23
Northfield	34	6	10	18	33	60	22
Boldmere St. Michaels	34	6	8	20	41	71	20
Knowle	34	8	4	22	36	70	20
Blakenall	34	4	5	25	17	82	13

Alvechurch moved to the West Midlands Regional League.

Division Two

Albion Haden United	34	21	9	4	80	40	51
Whitmore Old Boys	34	20	10	4	68	32	50
Solihull Town	34	20	8	6	72	26	48
Astwood Bank Rovers	34	19	5	10	57	33	43
Alcester Town	34	14	12	8	50	37	40
Sutton Coldfield Town Reserves	34	16	5	13	56	46	37
Oldbury United Reserves	34	11	14	9	45	39	36
Smethwick Highfield	34	13	8	13	47	57	34
Northfield Reserves	34	14	6	14	44	55	34
Chelmsley Town	34	12	9	13	57	54	33
Coleshill Town	34	12	9	13	47	52	33
Boldmere St. Michaels Reserves	34	12	4	18	52	71	28
Highgate United Reserves	34	9	8	17	44	58	26
Bournville Athletic	34	8	10	16	46	65	26
Moor Green Reserves	34	10	5	19	59	80	25
Mile Oak Rovers	34	8	9	17	46	63	25
Malvern Town Reserves	34	7	11	16	37	57	25
Bridgnorth Town Reserves	34	6	6	22	28	70	18

Solihull Town and Highgate United Reserves left.
Rowley Regis joined from the Staffordshire County League,
Wolverhampton Wanderers "A" joined from the WMRL and Racing Club
(Warwick) Reserves and Coventry Amateurs Reserves also joined.

1973-74

Division One

Highgate United	32	27	3	2	95	16	57
Malvern Town	32	19	7	6	69	34	45
Solihull Borough	32	17	8	7	58	31	42
Sutton Coldfield Town	32	14	10	8	52	35	38
Blakenall	32	12	14	6	47	32	38
Northfield	32	14	8	10	52	49	36
Bridgnorth Town	32	13	9	10	43	35	35
Evesham United	32	13	9	10	54	46	35
Moor Green	32	13	9	10	51	48	35
Racing Club (Warwick)	32	11	10	11	41	39	32
Paget Rangers	32	13	5	14	48	49	31
Oldbury United	32	11	5	16	40	46	27
Birmingham City Police	32	9	5	18	45	53	23
Stratford Town	32	7	7	18	38	66	21
Boldmere St. Michaels	32	7	5	20	31	72	19
Knowle	32	5	5	22	26	85	15
Walsall Wood	32	4	7	21	23	77	15

Birmingham City Police changed their name to West Midlands Police
and Northfield changed their name to Northfield Town.
Cinderford Town joined from the Gloucestershire County League.

Division Two

Astwood Bank Rovers	38	26	6	6	88	31	58
Moor Green Reserves	38	27	4	7	84	39	58
Wolverhampton Wanderers "B"	38	20	7	11	88	50	47
Albion Haden United	38	17	13	8	71	49	47
Coleshill Town	38	18	7	13	85	60	43
Chelmsley Town	38	15	11	12	75	65	41
Whitmore Old Boys	38	16	8	14	78	62	40
Bridgnorth Town Reserves	38	11	16	11	54	59	38
Smethwick Highfield	38	12	14	12	54	62	38
Malvern Town Reserves	38	15	7	16	67	69	37
Northfield Reserves	38	13	11	14	55	67	37
Oldbury United Reserves	38	14	8	16	68	61	36
Sutton Coldfield Town Reserves	38	14	8	16	61	70	36
Mile Oak Rovers	38	12	9	17	69	66	33
Racing Club (Warwick) Reserves	38	12	9	17	65	68	33
Bournville Athletic	38	15	3	20	75	107	33
Rowley Regis	38	12	5	21	56	81	29
Coventry Amateurs Reserves	38	10	8	20	49	66	28
Alcester Town	38	11	6	21	45	74	28
Boldmere St. Michaels Reserves	38	7	6	25	46	127	20

Coventry Amateurs changed their name to Coventry Sporting.
Racing Club (Warwick) Reserves and Bridgnorth Town Reserves left.
Walsall Sportsco joined from the Birmingham Works League and Hurley
Daw Mill Welfare joined from the BYOB Mercian League.

1974-75

Division One

Highgate United	34	22	10	2	71	20	54
Moor Green	34	22	6	6	67	38	50
Solihull Borough	34	17	10	7	49	40	44
Blakenall	34	16	11	7	53	32	43
Sutton Coldfield Town	34	16	8	10	59	40	40
Cinderford Town	34	15	8	11	64	44	38
West Midlands Police	34	15	8	11	42	39	38
Malvern Town	34	15	7	12	55	39	37
Northfield Town	34	13	11	10	55	45	37
Bridgnorth Town	34	12	10	12	43	50	34
Evesham United	34	13	7	14	54	47	33
Paget Rangers	34	11	10	13	45	44	32
Oldbury United	34	12	8	14	45	46	32
Stratford Town	34	10	7	17	45	64	27
Racing Club (Warwick)	34	7	8	19	26	59	22
Knowle	34	7	6	21	42	62	20
Boldmere St. Michaels	34	6	6	22	30	72	18
Walsall Wood	***34***	***3***	***7***	***24***	***23***	***87***	***13***

Stratford Town moved to the Hellenic League.
Cadbury Heath joined from the Gloucestershire County League.

Division Two

Whitmore Old Boys	38	27	7	4	94	32	61
Coleshill Town	**38**	**26**	**5**	**7**	**80**	**36**	**57**
Alcester Town	38	20	11	7	78	41	51
Smethwick Highfield	38	21	8	9	86	49	50
Walsall Sportsco	38	19	9	10	69	35	47
Albion Haden United	38	18	9	11	72	50	45
Astwood Bank Rovers	38	17	10	11	71	60	44
Wolverhampton Wanderers "A"	38	16	9	13	74	56	41
Malvern Town Reserves	38	14	12	12	66	50	40
Mile Oak Rovers	38	16	7	15	65	65	39
Hurley Daw Mill Welfare	38	17	3	18	77	88	37
Moor Green Reserves	38	10	14	14	45	52	34
Chelmsley Town	38	15	4	19	57	71	34
Rowley Regis	38	10	11	17	41	77	31
Northfield Town Reserves	38	12	6	20	60	72	30
Sutton Coldfield Town Reserves	38	12	5	21	60	78	29
Coventry Sporting Reserves	38	11	7	20	51	68	29
Oldbury United Reserves	38	10	7	21	42	79	27
Bournville Athletic	38	7	6	25	45	106	20
Boldmere St. Michaels Reserves	38	4	6	28	36	104	14

Albion Haden United changed their name to Cradley Town.
Northfield Town Reserves left.
Studley Sporting joined from the BYOB Mercian League.

1975-76

Division One

Northfield Town	34	23	5	6	63	30	51
Moor Green	34	20	10	4	72	39	50
Malvern Town	34	20	9	5	66	30	49
Paget Rangers	34	19	7	8	50	39	45
Racing Club (Warwick)	34	17	8	9	42	29	42
Sutton Coldfield Town	34	16	9	9	57	33	41
West Midlands Police	34	14	10	10	46	40	38
Blakenall	34	12	13	9	54	33	37
Bridgnorth Town	34	9	18	7	48	45	36
Evesham United	34	12	11	11	51	40	35
Solihull Borough	34	9	15	10	41	43	33
Cadbury Heath	34	11	8	15	47	47	30
Highgate United	34	11	8	15	46	53	30
Cinderford Town	34	8	8	18	40	60	24
Oldbury United	34	6	10	18	35	57	22
Boldmere St. Michaels	34	5	12	17	23	49	22
Coleshill Town	34	2	11	21	26	72	15
Knowle	34	2	8	24	21	89	12

Division Two

Whitmore Old Boys	38	27	4	7	79	35	58
Cradley Town	38	25	7	6	112	42	57
Alcester Town	38	24	8	6	90	41	56
Hurley Daw Mill Welfare	38	24	7	7	79	35	55
Astwood Bank Rovers	38	21	11	6	101	53	53
Walsall Sportsco	38	18	11	9	59	41	47
Studley Sporting	38	20	6	12	81	54	46
Walsall Wood	38	18	9	11	61	46	45
Moor Green Reserves	38	16	6	16	70	66	38
Chelmsley Town	38	13	10	15	53	65	36
Smethwick Highfield	38	12	11	15	61	60	35
Malvern Town Reserves	38	12	10	16	55	66	34
Mile Oak Rovers	38	9	12	17	45	70	30
Oldbury United Reserves	38	11	7	20	53	71	29
Coventry Sporting Reserves	38	8	11	19	44	67	27
Boldmere St. Michaels Reserves	38	12	3	23	42	81	27
Wolverhampton Wanderers "A"	38	10	7	21	44	87	27
Rowley Regis	38	6	9	23	44	94	21
Bournville Athletic	38	5	10	23	46	94	20
Sutton Coldfield Town Reserves	38	7	5	26	33	84	19

Astwood Bank Rovers changed their name to Astwood Bank.
Whitmore Old Boys merged with Oxley of the WMRL where they played as Wolverhampton United. Coventry Sporting Reserves moved to the WMRL and Oldbury United Reserves also left.
Polesworth joined from the BYOB Mercian League, Rockwood Albion joined from the West Midland Metropolitan League and West Midlands Police Reserves also joined.

1976-77

Division One

Blakenall	34	19	10	5	52	24	48
Bridgnorth Town	34	22	4	8	77	36	48
West Midlands Police	34	19	8	7	47	26	46
Cinderford Town	34	16	9	9	59	46	41
Malvern Town	34	16	8	10	44	35	40
Evesham United	34	17	5	12	52	41	39
Sutton Coldfield Town	34	15	8	11	46	35	38
Highgate United	34	13	9	12	44	36	35
Paget Rangers	34	14	7	13	45	45	35
Knowle	34	11	10	13	50	52	32
Moor Green	34	13	4	17	46	54	30
Coleshill Town	34	12	6	16	39	54	30
Oldbury United	34	12	5	17	41	49	29
Boldmere St. Michaels	34	12	5	17	38	49	29
Racing Club (Warwick)	34	8	12	14	33	46	28
Solihull Borough	34	11	4	19	42	65	26
Northfield Town	34	9	7	18	40	58	25
Cadbury Heath	34	2	9	23	18	62	13

Cadbury Heath moved to the Avon Premier Combination.
Stratford Town joined from the Hellenic League.

Division Two

Astwood Bank	38	27	3	8	93	44	57
Walsall Sportsco	**38**	**22**	**9**	**7**	**68**	**33**	**53**
Polesworth	38	23	5	10	68	41	51
Moor Green Reserves	38	18	13	7	87	49	49
Cradley Town	38	22	4	12	82	53	48
Hurley Daw Mill Welfare	38	16	13	9	54	41	45
Mile Oak Rovers	**38**	**18**	**8**	**12**	**58**	**48**	**44**
Rowley Regis	38	18	6	14	62	41	42
Sutton Coldfield Town Reserves	38	14	11	13	47	51	39
Studley Sporting	38	14	11	13	58	70	39
Alcester Town	38	14	10	14	70	63	38
Walsall Wood	38	15	7	16	64	58	37
Wolverhampton Wanderers "A"	38	11	10	17	51	56	32
Malvern Town Reserves	38	10	11	17	49	80	31
Chelmsley Town	38	11	8	19	41	56	30
West Midlands Police Reserves	38	6	15	17	42	56	27
Rockwood Albion	38	10	7	21	53	86	27
Smethwick Highfield	38	7	11	20	49	89	25
Bournville Athletic	38	7	9	22	56	100	23
Boldmere St. Michaels Reserves	38	6	11	21	36	73	23

Polesworth changed their name to Polesworth North Warwick.
Wolverhampton Wanderers "A" left. Stafford F.C. joined from the Staffordshire County League, Kings Heath joined from the BYOB Mercian League and Tamworth Reserves also joined.

1977-78

Division One

Sutton Coldfield Town	38	20	12	6	77	34	52
Paget Rangers	38	21	9	8	74	36	51
Blakenall	38	19	13	6	57	24	51
Walsall Sportsco	38	20	10	8	62	32	50
Cinderford Town	38	18	10	10	73	39	46
Bridgnorth Town	38	16	14	8	60	28	46
Moor Green	38	16	14	8	66	41	46
Malvern Town	38	16	13	9	59	41	45
Racing Club (Warwick)	38	16	10	12	51	44	42
Evesham United	38	15	12	11	49	46	42
Solihull Borough	38	10	17	11	45	48	37
Highgate United	38	14	7	17	56	62	35
Mile Oak Rovers	38	9	17	12	35	47	35
Northfield Town	38	11	12	15	55	60	34
Boldmere St. Michaels	38	11	10	17	35	48	32
Oldbury United	38	10	12	16	51	65	32
Coleshill Town	38	8	10	20	38	79	26
West Midlands Police	38	4	17	17	32	61	25
Knowle	38	7	6	25	38	80	20
Stratford Town	*38*	*4*	*5*	*29*	*29*	*127*	*13*

Division Two

Hurley Daw Mill Welfare	38	27	8	3	69	19	62
Cradley Town	38	24	9	5	76	35	57
Walsall Wood	**38**	**19**	**13**	**6**	**72**	**49**	**51**
Sutton Coldfield Town Reserves	38	20	9	9	85	50	49
Rowley Regis	38	19	9	10	58	39	47
Astwood Bank	38	18	8	12	61	43	44
Studley Sporting	38	16	10	12	70	53	42
Stafford F.C.	38	15	11	12	62	60	41
Tamworth Reserves	38	15	9	14	53	61	39
Rockwood Albion	38	13	12	13	55	48	38
Boldmere St. Michaels Reserves	38	15	8	15	52	47	38
Moor Green Reserves	38	16	6	16	71	70	38
Kings Heath	38	13	7	18	45	53	33
Chelmsley Town	38	10	13	15	39	49	33
Smethwick Highfield	38	10	11	17	46	52	31
West Midlands Police Reserves	38	13	5	20	52	75	31
Bournville Athletic	38	10	9	19	58	76	29
Polesworth North Warwick	38	10	8	20	45	61	28
Alcester Town	38	6	5	27	32	91	17
Malvern Town Reserves	38	3	6	29	30	100	12

Malvern Town Reserves left and Witton Social joined.

1978-79

Division One

Sutton Coldfield Town	38	26	9	3	104	30	61
Oldbury United	38	20	11	7	49	29	51
Bridgnorth Town	38	19	11	8	54	31	49
Boldmere St. Michaels	38	20	9	9	44	35	49
Walsall Sportsco	38	18	11	9	58	41	47
Blakenall	38	17	10	11	57	38	44
Solihull Borough	38	18	8	12	59	46	44
Paget Rangers	38	16	10	12	50	41	42
Knowle	38	17	7	14	51	44	41
Mile Oak Rovers	38	15	10	13	42	37	40
Moor Green	38	16	7	15	70	55	39
Highgate United	38	13	7	18	46	54	33
Malvern Town	38	9	15	14	39	51	33
West Midlands Police	38	11	11	16	32	46	33
Racing Club (Warwick)	38	11	10	17	41	46	32
Walsall Wood	38	10	11	17	43	65	31
Cinderford Town	38	10	10	18	36	64	30
Northfield Town	38	12	5	21	41	62	29
Evesham United	38	7	5	26	29	80	19
Coleshill Town	38	1	11	26	22	72	13

Malvern Town, Blakenall & Sutton Coldfield Town moved to the WMRL.
Chipping Norton Town joined from the Hellenic League.

Division Two

Stafford F.C.	38	27	6	5	82	29	60
Studley Sporting	38	25	6	7	105	46	56
Stratford Town	38	21	12	5	69	32	54
Cradley Town	38	21	7	10	73	44	49
Rowley Regis	38	19	10	9	76	39	48
Astwood Bank	38	18	11	9	74	52	47
Hurley Daw Mill Welfare	38	18	10	10	70	40	46
Chelmsley Town	38	17	8	13	61	44	42
Kings Heath	38	14	12	12	51	49	40
Moor Green Reserves	38	16	6	16	63	56	38
Witton Social	38	12	12	14	40	44	36
Polesworth North Warwick	38	12	10	16	51	59	34
Alcester Town	38	12	10	16	48	67	34
Sutton Coldfield Town Reserves	38	13	7	18	69	83	33
Smethwick Highfield	38	11	9	18	56	80	31
Rockwood Albion	38	8	14	16	55	71	30
Boldmere St. Michaels Reserves	38	8	7	23	46	79	23
West Midlands Police Reserves	38	7	8	23	47	90	22
Tamworth Reserves	38	9	4	25	46	97	22
Bournville Athletic	38	4	7	27	32	113	15

Witton Social changed their name to GEC Witton Social.
Boldmere St. Michaels Reserves and West Midlands Police Reserves left.
Ludlow Colts, Bedworth United Reserves, Mile Oak Rovers Reserves and Highgate United Reserves joined.

A new Third Division was formed with 18 founder members:
Bartley Green, Bilston United, Darlaston Old Boys, Hay Green, Kingsbury United, Littleton, Sheldon Promovere, Solihull Social, Stone Town, Wythall, Yardley Wood United and the Reserves of:
Boldmere St. Michaels, Bridgnorth Town, Bromsgrove Brookfield, Cradley Town, GEC Witton Social, Studley Sporting and Walsall Wood.

1979-80

Division One

Bridgnorth Town	38	26	7	5	78	20	59
Moor Green	38	24	8	6	83	39	56
Oldbury United	38	21	8	9	71	41	50
Walsall Sportsco	38	18	13	7	55	36	49
Highgate United	38	18	8	12	65	56	44
Chipping Norton Town	38	16	11	11	56	41	43
Mile Oak Rovers	38	13	16	9	46	42	42
Boldmere St. Michaels	38	14	13	11	51	34	41
Evesham United	38	16	9	13	58	42	41
West Midlands Police	38	16	8	14	52	56	40
Cinderford Town	38	12	15	11	41	41	39
Solihull Borough	38	13	10	15	53	63	36
Knowle	38	11	11	16	36	43	33
Coleshill Town	38	12	9	17	42	54	33
Racing Club (Warwick)	38	8	15	15	31	54	31
Walsall Wood	38	7	15	16	36	57	29
Paget Rangers	38	9	9	20	41	64	27
Cradley Town	38	9	8	21	34	57	26
Studley Sporting	38	6	9	23	40	97	21
Northfield Town	38	5	10	23	31	63	20

Division Two

Hurley Daw Mill Welfare	38	26	7	5	77	32	59
Smethwick Highfield	38	26	5	7	100	39	57
GEC Witton Social	38	23	7	8	64	34	53
Bedworth United Reserves	38	20	12	6	76	45	52
Mile Oak Rovers Reserves	38	20	11	7	70	42	51
Chelmsley Town	38	20	7	11	61	44	47
Stratford Town	38	19	7	12	71	48	45
Stafford F.C.	38	19	7	12	59	46	45
Moor Green Reserves	38	15	13	10	78	56	43
Rockwood Albion	38	15	6	17	55	63	36
Kings Heath	38	11	13	14	47	49	35
Polesworth North Warwick	38	12	10	16	49	49	34
Alcester Town	38	12	10	16	38	51	34
Sutton Coldfield Town Reserves	38	12	8	18	58	59	32
Astwood Bank	38	11	9	18	29	54	31
Tamworth Reserves	38	10	6	22	37	76	26
Ludlow Colts	38	7	10	21	42	79	24
Bournville Athletic	38	5	10	23	37	82	20
Rowley Regis	38	5	9	24	37	77	19
Highgate United Reserves	38	5	7	26	41	101	17

Tamworth Reserves moved to the WMRL and Rowley Regis also left.
Banbury United Reserves joined.

Division Three

Sheldon Promovere	34	30	3	1	140	30	63
Wythall	34	21	5	8	83	40	47
Yardley Wood United	34	21	4	9	66	44	46
Stone Town	34	19	4	11	83	58	42
Kingsbury United	34	17	7	10	56	41	41
Bartley Green	34	15	8	11	55	54	38
Bromsgrove Brookfield	34	15	6	13	57	52	36
Darlaston Old Boys	34	11	12	11	50	60	34
Bridgnorth Town Reserves	34	14	5	15	49	57	33
Littleton	34	13	4	17	44	50	30
Hay Green	34	10	9	15	50	72	29
Studley Sporting Reserves	34	8	11	15	44	55	27
Solihull Social	34	11	5	18	46	68	27
Walsall Wood Reserves	34	10	6	18	49	58	26
Boldmere St. Michaels Reserves	34	8	10	16	45	64	26
GEC Witton Social Reserves	34	8	9	17	52	81	25
Cradley Town Reserves	34	9	6	19	41	73	24
Bilston United	34	6	6	22	43	90	18
					1053	*1047*	

Bilston United, Stone Town, Studley Sporting Reserves and Solihull Social left.
Bolehall Swifts joined from the Staffordshire County League, Southam United joined from the Coventry & North Warwickshire League and Polesworth North Warwick Reserves also joined.

1980-81

Division One

Moor Green	38	28	7	3	109	30	63
Bridgnorth Town	38	22	7	9	76	38	51
Mile Oak Rovers	38	21	8	9	63	43	50
Cinderford Town	38	22	5	11	68	30	49
Boldmere St. Michaels	38	18	11	9	50	39	47
Oldbury United	38	18	10	10	65	47	46
Chipping Norton Town	38	16	11	11	58	45	43
Racing Club (Warwick)	38	16	10	12	66	46	42
Knowle	38	16	10	12	50	42	42
Hurley Daw Mill Welfare	38	14	11	13	54	56	39
Highgate United	38	16	6	16	79	61	38
West Midlands Police	38	11	15	12	62	58	37
Paget Rangers	38	13	11	14	42	41	37
Solihull Borough	38	13	10	15	58	69	36
Evesham United	38	10	10	18	57	81	30
Walsall Sportsco	38	8	12	18	49	69	28
Walsall Wood	38	10	8	20	42	71	28
Smethwick Highfield	38	8	10	20	37	74	26
Cradley Town	38	5	4	29	33	100	14
Coleshill Town	38	5	4	29	27	104	14

Division Two

Sheldon Promovere	38	27	11	0	123	41	65
Bedworth United Reserves	38	22	7	9	73	37	51
Kings Heath	38	21	8	9	79	52	50
Stratford Town	38	21	8	9	59	47	50
Moor Green Reserves	38	17	9	12	78	56	43
Astwood Bank	38	17	9	12	63	43	43
GEC Witton Social	38	17	8	13	74	58	42
Northfield Town	38	16	9	13	78	58	41
Studley Sporting	38	17	7	14	66	61	41
Sutton Coldfield Town Reserves	38	17	6	15	67	60	40
Yardley Wood United	38	16	6	16	74	63	38
Banbury United Reserves	38	13	9	16	46	59	35
Chelmsley Town	38	11	12	15	52	75	34
Mile Oak Rovers Reserves	38	13	7	18	48	72	33
Alcester Town	38	12	8	18	60	69	32
Bournville Athletic	38	9	10	19	51	78	28
Polesworth North Warwick	38	11	5	22	55	90	27
Stafford F.C.	38	9	8	21	42	74	26
Ludlow Colts	38	8	5	25	34	78	21
Rockwood Albion	38	7	6	25	34	77	20

Stafford F.C. changed their name to Stafford Town.
Sheldon Promovere left.
Alvechurch Reserves joined from the WMRL and Knowle Reserves also joined.

Division Three

Southam United	30	26	3	1	103	28	55
Walsall Wood Reserves	30	19	5	6	68	34	43
Kingsbury United	30	15	6	9	59	37	36
Boldmere St. Michaels Reserves	30	14	6	10	47	47	34
Littleton	30	14	6	10	40	40	34
Bromsgrove Brookfield	30	14	5	11	50	35	33
Bolehall Swifts	30	12	8	10	50	46	32
Bartley Green	30	12	6	12	48	43	30
Hay Green	30	12	5	13	51	47	29
Wythall	30	11	6	13	61	62	28
Darlaston Old Boys	30	8	8	14	48	63	24
Bridgnorth Town Reserves	30	7	8	15	33	50	22
Polesworth North Warwick Res.	30	9	4	17	34	70	22
GEC Witton Social Reserves	30	9	2	19	33	62	20
Cradley Town Reserves	30	8	4	18	32	70	20
Highgate United Reserves	30	6	6	18	43	66	18

Darlaston Old Boys and Bartley Green left.
Ashted Rovers, Enville Athletic and the Reserves of Paget Rangers, Coleshill Town, Smethwick Highfield, Stratford Town and Solihull Borough all joined.

Goal difference replaced goal average from the next season onwards.

1981-82

Division One

Chipping Norton Town	42	27	9	6	106	43	63
Highgate United	42	27	6	9	85	46	60
Mile Oak Rovers	42	24	10	8	78	49	58
Cinderford Town	42	19	16	7	71	40	54
Oldbury United	42	22	8	12	67	44	52
Bridgnorth Town	42	20	12	10	65	47	52
Moor Green	42	22	7	13	84	59	51
Knowle	42	16	16	10	64	50	48
Walsall Sportsco	42	18	10	14	68	54	46
Racing Club (Warwick)	42	16	13	13	68	64	45
West Midlands Police	42	14	14	14	70	70	42
Boldmere St. Michaels	42	14	14	14	59	60	42
Coleshill Town	42	16	8	18	57	68	40
Stratford Town	42	12	12	18	37	49	36
Smethwick Highfield	42	13	10	19	49	64	36
Northfield Town	42	15	6	21	56	76	36
Solihull Borough	42	11	13	18	46	68	35
Cradley Town	42	12	10	20	60	80	34
Paget Rangers	42	10	14	18	43	63	34
Walsall Wood	42	9	8	25	40	82	26
Evesham United	42	6	9	27	40	83	21
Hurley Daw Mill Welfare	42	3	7	32	42	96	13

Walsall Sportsco and Walsall Wood merged to form Walsall Borough. Oldbury United moved to the Southern League.

Division Two

Bedworth United Reserves	38	29	3	6	93	37	61
Southam United	38	24	11	3	82	40	59
Studley Sporting	38	24	9	5	87	50	57
Kings Heath	38	23	7	8	86	45	53
GEC Witton Social	38	21	7	10	65	40	49
Knowle Reserves	38	19	8	11	66	56	46
Mile Oak Rovers Reserves	38	19	4	15	85	73	42
Alvechurch Reserves	38	13	12	13	65	64	38
Moor Green Reserves	38	16	4	18	66	66	36
Sutton Coldfield Town Reserves	38	11	13	14	56	68	35
Chelmsley Town	38	11	12	15	52	55	34
Yardley Wood United	38	14	6	18	63	77	34
Astwood Bank	38	10	13	15	53	52	33
Kingsbury United	38	12	9	17	64	71	33
Alcester Town	38	11	9	18	51	67	31
Bournville Athletic	38	12	7	19	51	70	31
Polesworth North Warwick	38	9	7	22	51	75	25
Stafford Town	38	9	7	22	49	92	25
Walsall Wood Reserves	38	8	6	24	42	82	22
Banbury United Reserves	38	4	8	26	40	87	16

GEC Witton Social changed their name to Witton Social.
Stafford Town moved to the Staffordshire County League and Yardley Wood United, Knowle Reserves and Banbury United Reserves also left. Redditch United Reserves joined.

Division Three

Paget Rangers Reserves	38	25	7	6	93	60	57
Boldmere St. Michaels Reserves	38	26	2	10	99	46	54
Hay Green	38	21	9	8	93	52	51
Wythall	38	23	5	10	94	62	51
Littleton	38	17	12	9	54	37	46
Rockwood Albion	38	15	12	11	63	57	42
Ludlow Colts	38	16	9	13	50	52	41
Coleshill Town Reserves	38	13	13	12	60	57	39
Bridgnorth Town Reserves	38	14	10	14	62	54	38
Smethwick Highfield Reserves	38	14	8	16	46	51	36
Enville Athletic	38	14	8	16	46	51	36
GEC Witton Social Reserves	38	14	7	17	51	53	35
Stratford Town Reserves	38	11	12	15	58	68	34
Bromsgrove Brookfield	38	12	10	16	47	66	34
Highgate United Reserves	38	12	9	17	47	57	33
Bolehall Swifts	38	13	5	20	62	69	31
Cradley Town Reserves	38	11	7	20	61	72	29
Ashted Rovers	38	9	10	19	55	84	28
Solihull Borough Reserves	38	11	6	21	52	81	28
Polesworth North Warwick Res.	38	5	7	26	28	92	17

Littleton, Ashted Rovers, Solihull Borough Reserves and Polesworth North Warwick Reserves all left. Earlswood Town joined from the BYOB Mercian League and Whitmore Old Boys and the Reserves of Oldbury United, Racing Club (Warwick) and Hurley Daw Mill Welfare also joined.

1982-83

Division One

Bridgnorth Town	38	29	6	3	102	30	64
Moor Green	38	27	6	5	106	44	60
Boldmere St. Michaels	38	25	7	6	60	36	57
Highgate United	38	20	12	6	74	38	52
Cinderford Town	38	21	7	10	76	51	49
Paget Rangers	38	17	9	12	63	40	43
Stratford Town	38	15	11	12	59	62	41
Mile Oak Rovers	38	15	10	13	58	50	40
Hurley Daw Mill Welfare	38	13	10	15	60	62	36
Evesham United	38	13	10	15	52	58	36
Cradley Town	38	14	7	17	62	74	35
West Midlands Police	38	10	13	15	66	73	33
Racing Club (Warwick)	38	12	9	17	52	65	33
Coleshill Town	38	13	7	18	45	58	33
Walsall Borough	38	10	9	19	34	67	29
Smethwick Highfield	38	8	12	18	38	58	28
Northfield Town	38	10	6	22	53	81	26
Chipping Norton Town	38	7	11	20	32	59	25
Solihull Borough	38	6	8	24	43	83	20
Knowle	38	6	8	24	43	89	20

Knowle changed their name to Knowle North Star and Hurley Daw Mill Welfare changed their name to Hurley Daw Mill.
Bridgnorth Town and Moor Green moved to the Southern League and Cradley Town moved to the WMRL.

Division Two

Studley Sporting	36	25	5	6	88	37	55
Kings Heath	36	22	9	5	76	38	53
Southam United	36	19	7	10	71	51	45
Astwood Bank	36	18	8	10	69	48	44
Paget Rangers Reserves	36	17	7	12	76	61	41
Sutton Coldfield Town Reserves	36	17	7	12	62	51	41
Moor Green Reserves	36	15	8	13	80	61	38
Polesworth North Warwick	36	16	5	15	56	57	37
Bournville Athletic	36	12	12	12	56	53	36
Bedworth United Reserves	36	13	10	13	63	72	36
Alvechurch Reserves	36	13	7	16	54	60	33
Boldmere St. Michaels Reserves	36	13	6	17	51	57	32
Mile Oak Rovers Reserves	36	11	10	15	45	73	32
Kingsbury United	36	13	5	18	58	66	31
Witton Social	*36*	*12*	*7*	*17*	*53*	*68*	*31*
Alcester Town	36	10	9	17	51	59	29
Chelmsley Town	36	9	8	19	46	73	26
Redditch United Reserves	*36*	*8*	*6*	*22*	*47*	*81*	*22*
Walsall Borough Reserves	36	8	6	22	42	79	22
						1144	*1145*

Banbury United Reserves withdrew when their record was

	17	5	2	10	20	39	12

Astwood Bank, Walsall Borough Reserves and Bedworth United Reserves left. Bloxwich AFC joined from the Staffordshire County League and New World also joined.

Division Three

Bridgnorth Town Reserves	36	26	4	6	88	36	56
Oldbury United Reserves	36	25	3	8	92	46	53
Bromsgrove Brookfield	36	23	5	8	75	44	51
Earlswood Town	36	20	9	7	92	50	49
Wythall	36	17	10	9	75	41	44
Highgate United Reserves	36	18	8	10	63	41	44
Whitmore Old Boys	36	18	6	12	69	55	42
Enville Athletic	36	18	5	13	60	42	41
Bolehall Swifts	36	13	10	13	67	63	36
Ludlow Colts	36	14	6	16	45	53	34
Racing Club (Warwick) Reserves	36	14	6	16	58	69	34
Witton Social Reserves	36	13	5	18	50	58	31
Coleshill Town Reserves	36	14	1	21	50	71	29
Hay Green	36	11	6	19	64	89	28
Rockwood Albion	36	9	8	19	35	64	26
Smethwick Highfield Reserves	36	9	7	20	30	46	25
Hurley Daw Mill Welfare Reserves	36	9	6	21	39	81	24
Cradley Town Reserves	36	8	3	25	51	100	19
Stratford Town Reserves	36	6	6	24	30	84	18

Hay Green and the Reserves of Hurley Daw Mill Welfare, Cradley Town and Witton Social left.
Kingswinford Town, Princes End United, Sedgley Rovers, Henley Forest of Arden, Colinthians '83, Kings Norton Old Boys and Northfield Town Reserves joined.

The Divisions were renamed Premier, One and Two from next season.

1983-84

Premier Division

Studley Sporting	38	22	8	8	83	49	52
Coleshill Town	38	22	7	9	77	43	51
West Midlands Police	38	20	10	8	82	52	50
Highgate United	38	17	14	7	70	41	48
Racing Club (Warwick)	38	21	4	13	79	66	46
Paget Rangers	38	15	15	8	55	35	45
Hurley Daw Mill	38	16	11	11	68	55	43
Evesham United	38	16	10	12	55	49	42
Stratford Town	38	16	6	16	58	71	38
Boldmere St. Michaels	38	14	9	15	46	37	37
Northfield Town	38	14	9	15	63	56	37
Mile Oak Rovers	38	15	7	16	58	53	37
Solihull Borough	38	15	7	16	54	57	37
Chipping Norton Town	38	13	10	15	49	51	36
Kings Heath	38	11	14	13	50	59	36
Cinderford Town	38	12	9	17	51	63	33
Walsall Borough	38	13	6	19	54	58	32
Smethwick Highfield	38	7	13	18	45	66	27
Southam United	38	7	8	23	35	76	22
Knowle North Star	38	3	5	30	34	129	11

Cinderford Town moved to the Gloucestershire County League and Chipping Norton Town moved to the Oxfordshire Senior League.

Division One

New World	34	25	6	3	94	25	56
Polesworth North Warwick	34	21	7	6	70	27	49
Bromsgrove Brookfield	34	17	6	11	51	42	40
Bridgnorth Town Reserves	34	15	9	10	60	42	39
Kingsbury United	34	17	4	13	59	55	38
Moor Green Reserves	34	16	6	12	50	51	38
Bloxwich AFC	34	14	8	12	54	58	36
Sutton Coldfield Town Reserves	34	14	7	13	81	59	35
Oldbury United Reserves	34	12	9	13	55	48	33
Chelmsley Town	34	13	7	14	54	63	33
Alcester Town	34	14	3	17	52	62	31
Alvechurch Reserves	34	9	12	13	42	52	30
Bournville Athletic	34	9	11	14	49	55	29
Wythall	34	12	5	17	44	61	29
Boldmere St. Michaels Reserves	34	10	7	17	29	51	27
Mile Oak Rovers Reserves	34	8	9	17	39	64	25
Paget Rangers Reserves	34	8	8	18	31	59	24
Highgate United Reserves	34	7	6	21	47	87	20

Alvechurch Reserves left and Cheltenham Town Reserves joined.

Division Two

Kingswinford Town	36	23	7	6	89	38	53
Princes End United	36	23	5	8	91	43	51
Sedgley Rovers	36	22	7	7	82	47	51
Enville Athletic	36	21	6	9	63	29	48
Henley Forest of Arden	36	19	9	8	74	39	47
Whitmore Old Boys	36	20	7	9	73	46	47
Northfield Town Reserves	36	18	6	12	82	54	42
Smethwick Highfield Reserves	36	16	9	11	45	36	41
Coleshill Town Reserves	36	17	6	13	62	56	40
Colinthians '83	36	16	7	13	70	57	39
Racing Club (Warwick) Reserves	36	16	5	15	62	59	37
Bolehall Swifts	36	15	3	18	57	69	33
Kings Norton Old Boys	36	11	10	15	52	55	32
Redditch United Reserves	36	12	6	18	55	76	30
Earlswood Town	36	9	6	21	49	62	24
Ludlow Colts	36	6	9	21	42	98	21
Rockwood Albion	36	7	6	23	30	94	20
Witton Social	36	4	8	24	37	79	16
Stratford Town Reserves	36	3	6	27	31	109	12

Witton Social changed their name to Witton.
Ludlow Colts and Redditch United Reserves left.
Wilmcote joined from the Stratford Alliance and Priors Sports, Triplex, West Heath United and the Reserves of Bedworth United, Bournville Athletic, Kings Heath and Solihull Borough all joined.

1984-85

Premier Division

Mile Oak Rovers	38	27	6	5	91	28	60
Solihull Borough	38	22	10	6	68	36	54
Paget Rangers	38	21	10	7	60	35	52
Boldmere St. Michaels	38	21	8	9	67	40	50
New World	38	21	6	11	71	41	48
Highgate United	38	20	8	10	73	47	48
Polesworth North Warwick	38	20	8	10	58	34	48
West Midlands Police	38	17	9	12	80	56	43
Stratford Town	38	15	13	10	53	40	43
Racing Club (Warwick)	38	13	12	13	69	67	38
Walsall Borough	38	13	10	15	47	44	36
Smethwick Highfield	38	10	13	15	50	58	33
Evesham United	38	13	7	18	57	81	33
Hurley Daw Mill	38	11	9	18	43	56	31
Studley Sporting	38	8	14	16	50	69	30
Northfield Town	38	11	7	20	63	76	29
Coleshill Town	38	10	8	20	44	60	28
Kings Heath	38	7	11	20	31	61	25
Southam United	38	6	5	27	45	102	17
Knowle North Star	38	4	6	28	40	129	14

Mile Oak Rovers moved to the Southern League.

Division One

Cheltenham Town Reserves	40	24	10	6	106	40	58
Sutton Coldfield Town Reserves	40	23	8	9	99	50	54
Paget Rangers Reserves	40	19	14	7	63	35	52
Bridgnorth Town Reserves	40	21	9	10	86	59	51
Princes End United	40	19	9	12	98	59	47
Sedgley Rovers	40	19	9	12	77	57	47
Bromsgrove Brookfield	40	18	11	11	78	67	47
Chelmsley Town	40	20	6	14	78	60	46
Kingsbury United	40	18	9	13	84	67	45
Enville Athletic	40	14	12	14	62	54	40
Bloxwich AFC	40	15	10	15	58	64	40
Moor Green Reserves	40	17	6	17	67	74	40
Mile Oak Rovers Reserves	40	14	9	17	57	80	37
Boldmere St. Michaels Reserves	40	12	11	17	61	58	35
Henley Forest of Arden	40	16	3	21	62	68	35
Alcester Town	40	12	10	18	56	73	34
Highgate United Reserves	40	12	9	19	65	67	33
Wythall	40	11	10	19	55	76	32
Oldbury United Reserves	40	9	8	23	47	121	26
Kingswinford Town	40	7	10	23	50	90	24
Bournville Athletic	40	5	7	28	39	129	17

Bournville Athletic changed their name to Bournville.
Bromsgrove Brookfield, Kingswinford Town and Oldbury United Reserves left.

Division Two

Bolehall Swifts	38	27	7	4	80	32	61
West Heath United	38	26	6	6	105	43	58
Racing Club (Warwick) Res.	38	21	6	11	80	52	48
Smethwick Highfield Reserves	38	21	5	12	63	41	47
Rockwood Albion	38	17	11	10	77	54	45
Northfield Town Reserves	38	18	9	11	72	56	45
Colinthians '83	38	19	6	13	84	63	44
Bedworth United Reserves	38	18	8	12	75	58	44
Stratford Town Reserves	38	17	9	12	68	54	43
Kings Norton Old Boys	38	15	10	13	58	57	40
Triplex	38	16	8	14	50	51	40
Kings Heath Reserves	38	13	11	14	47	46	37
Wilmcote	38	15	6	17	64	70	36
Coleshill Town Reserves	38	12	8	18	53	58	32
Solihull Borough Reserves	38	11	9	18	51	68	31
Whitmore Old Boys	38	11	6	21	72	84	28
Earlswood Town	38	9	8	21	58	93	26
Witton	38	7	9	22	35	68	23
Bournville Athletic Reserves	38	8	7	23	51	106	23
Priors Sports	38	1	7	30	30	119	9

Colinthians '83 and Bournville Athletic Reserves left.
Dudley Sports joined from the Birmingham Works League, Fairfield Villa joined from the Kidderminster League and Alvechurch Reserves, Bromsgrove Rovers Reserves, Enville Athletic Reserves, Little Bloxwich Strollers, Shelfield United and Wellesbourne also joined.

1985-86   Premier Division

Boldmere St. Michaels	38	25	10	3	72	24	60
Paget Rangers	38	24	9	5	94	31	57
West Midlands Police	38	23	8	7	65	41	54
Northfield Town	38	18	12	8	74	50	48
Bloxwich AFC	38	18	11	9	77	50	47
Stratford Town	38	17	12	9	53	32	46
Solihull Borough	38	18	7	13	62	45	43
Walsall Borough	38	15	13	10	52	37	43
Polesworth North Warwick	38	16	10	12	52	46	42
Racing Club (Warwick)	38	13	15	10	52	50	41
Coleshill Town	38	14	13	11	54	54	41
Highgate United	38	16	8	14	56	55	40
Evesham United	38	12	9	17	62	80	33
Hurley Daw Mill	38	12	8	18	44	59	32
New World	38	9	7	22	46	73	25
Knowle North Star	38	8	9	21	35	63	25
Southam United	38	6	12	20	52	90	24
Studley Sporting	38	7	8	23	43	75	22
Smethwick Highfield	38	5	11	22	31	75	21
Kings Heath	38	5	6	27	24	70	16

Walsall Borough changed their name to Walsall Wood and Smethwick Highfield changed their name to Ashtree Highfield.
Hurley Daw Mill and New World left.

Division One

Moor Green Reserves	40	28	6	6	90	45	62
Boldmere St. Michaels Reserves	40	24	9	7	95	42	57
Paget Rangers Reserves	40	25	7	8	76	30	57
Princes End United	40	23	10	7	68	36	56
Bolehall Swifts	40	19	16	5	71	36	54
Cheltenham Town Reserves	40	21	7	12	83	52	49
West Heath United	40	20	5	15	80	56	45
Sutton Coldfield Town Reserves	40	17	8	15	72	61	42
Alcester Town	40	15	11	14	48	48	41
Mile Oak Rovers Reserves	40	16	8	16	49	44	40
Highgate United Reserves	40	15	9	16	76	75	39
Chelmsley Town	40	14	11	15	58	72	39
Racing Club (Warwick) Reserves	40	12	11	17	54	69	35
Kingsbury United	40	10	12	18	46	62	32
Wythall	40	11	10	19	42	64	32
Bridgnorth Town Reserves	40	12	8	20	59	82	32
Sedgley Rovers	40	13	5	22	56	81	31
Enville Athletic	40	11	7	22	58	67	29
Northfield Town Reserves	40	8	10	22	38	84	26
Smethwick Highfield Reserves	40	7	7	26	24	80	21
Henley Forest of Arden	40	7	7	26	36	93	21

Henley Forest of Arden, Sedgley Rovers and the Reserves of Northfield Town, Smethwick Highfield, Bridgnorth Town, Racing Club (Warwick), Moor Green, Boldmere St. Michaels, Paget Rangers, Cheltenham Town, Sutton Coldfield Town and Mile Oak Rovers all left and a new, separate Reserve Section was formed.
Shirley Town and Shifnal Wanderers United joined.

Division Two

Stratford Town Reserves	42	28	7	7	73	32	63
Kings Norton Old Boys	42	26	8	8	99	43	60
Bromsgrove Rovers Reserves	42	23	12	7	103	59	58
Wilmcote	42	23	9	10	82	54	55
Little Bloxwich Strollers	42	23	8	11	88	61	54
Triplex	42	22	10	10	88	62	54
Rockwood Albion	42	19	11	12	68	55	49
Shelfield United	42	18	9	15	78	58	45
Dudley Sports	42	15	12	15	81	72	42
Earlswood Town	42	16	9	17	68	67	41
Solihull Borough Reserves	42	16	8	18	64	57	40
Wellesbourne	42	15	9	18	68	85	39
Witton	42	15	9	18	66	86	39
Coleshill Town Reserves	42	16	6	20	67	70	38
Whitmore Old Boys	42	15	8	19	82	98	38
Fairfield Villa	42	13	10	19	67	72	36
Alvechurch Reserves	42	12	12	18	69	77	36
Kings Heath Reserves	42	14	7	21	76	91	35
Bedworth United Reserves	42	11	10	21	66	91	32
Enville Athletic Reserves	42	8	8	26	45	91	24
Bournville	42	6	12	24	54	101	24
Priors Sports	42	8	6	28	56	126	22

Kings Norton Old Boys changed their name to Kings Norton ex-Servicemen's Club and Little Bloxwich Strollers changed their name to Bloxwich Strollers.
Rockwood Albion, Priors Sports and the Reserves of Stratford Town, Bromsgrove Rovers, Alvechurch and Bedworth United left. Handrahan Timbers joined from the Staffordshire County League (South), West Midland Fire Service joined from the Birmingham AFA and Bromsgrove Athletic, College Celtic, C.P. Dunchurch and the Reserves of Knowle North Star, Southam United and Dudley Sports also joined.

1986-87

Premier Division

Stratford Town	38	23	13	2	81	29	59
Paget Rangers	38	24	9	5	98	30	57
Racing Club (Warwick)	38	24	8	6	93	29	56
Boldmere St. Michaels	38	22	11	5	73	32	55
West Midlands Police	38	14	16	8	65	51	44
Northfield Town	38	15	10	13	57	46	40
Solihull Borough	38	13	13	12	58	69	39
Walsall Wood	38	16	6	16	54	52	38
Highgate United	38	15	7	16	50	49	37
Ashtree Highfield	38	15	6	17	47	59	36
Polesworth North Warwick	38	13	10	15	51	64	36
Princes End United	38	14	8	16	51	69	36
Evesham United	38	10	11	17	62	75	31
Knowle North Star	38	11	8	19	51	66	30
Kings Heath	38	9	12	17	36	52	30
Bloxwich AFC	38	12	5	21	56	73	29
Southam United	38	9	11	18	42	75	29
Coleshill Town	38	11	5	22	49	81	27
Studley Sporting	38	9	8	21	43	78	26
Bolehall Swifts	38	7	11	20	46	84	25

Knowle North Star changed their name to Knowle.
Paget Rangers moved to the Southern League. Studley Sporting left.
Leamington joined from the Southern League.

Division One

Wilmcote	32	19	6	7	73	41	44
Kings Norton ex-Servicemen's C.	32	22	3	7	78	39	47
Wythall	32	16	9	7	67	43	41
Kingsbury United	32	16	8	8	49	34	40
West Heath United	32	15	9	8	61	48	39
Chelmsley Town	32	13	11	8	59	36	37
Triplex	32	16	5	11	65	50	37
Shelfield United	32	12	10	10	38	39	34
Highgate United Reserves	32	11	8	13	53	53	30
Shirley Town	32	12	6	14	47	55	30
Bloxwich Strollers	32	12	5	15	39	53	29
Enville Athletic	32	10	9	13	31	48	29
Dudley Sports	32	9	9	14	38	42	27
Coleshill Town Reserves	32	9	7	16	54	68	25
Alcester Town	32	8	8	16	55	60	24
Solihull Borough Reserves	32	4	8	20	31	81	16
Shifnal Wanderers United	32	5	5	22	39	87	15

Kingsbury United, Shifnal Wanderers United and Highgate United Reserves left.

Division Two

Bromsgrove Athletic	30	17	9	4	71	28	43
College Celtic	30	17	9	4	64	30	43
West Midland Fire Service	30	17	6	7	64	44	40
Fairfield Villa	30	16	5	9	69	43	37
Whitmore Old Boys	30	15	4	11	72	56	34
Kings Heath Reserves	30	13	7	10	63	51	33
Witton	30	10	12	8	43	37	32
Handrahan Timbers	30	11	10	9	61	52	32
Bournville	30	10	11	9	42	43	31
Knowle North Star Reserves	30	10	9	11	50	61	29
Earlswood Town	30	11	5	14	47	43	27
Enville Athletic Reserves	30	8	7	15	34	69	23
C.P. Dunchurch	30	7	8	15	48	71	22
Southam United Reserves	30	7	6	17	41	62	20
Wellesbourne	30	6	7	17	51	96	19
Dudley Sports Reserves	30	5	5	20	40	74	15

Bournville, Whitmore Old Boys and Southam United Reserves left. Streetly Celtic joined from the BYOB Mercian League and Weston United also joined. Studley BKL joined from Sunday football.

Division Two

West Midland Fire Service	30	22	3	5	70	25	47
Streetly Celtic	30	20	6	4	62	29	46
Weston United	30	18	5	7	71	36	41
Wellesbourne	30	17	4	9	64	36	38
Southam United	30	15	8	7	52	31	38
Studley BKL	30	15	5	10	60	39	35
College Celtic	30	14	7	9	42	42	35
Witton	30	12	6	12	45	48	30
Kings Heath Reserves	30	10	8	12	44	49	28
Earlswood Town	30	11	3	16	36	46	25
Fairfield Villa	30	7	10	13	40	57	24
Enville Athletic Reserves	30	7	9	14	25	49	23
Dudley Sports Reserves	30	10	3	17	30	55	23
Knowle North Star Reserves	30	9	3	18	40	54	21
Handrahan Timbers	30	7	2	21	25	54	16
C.P. Dunchurch	30	2	6	22	23	79	10

C.P. Dunchurch, College Celtic, Witton, Enville Athletic Reserves and Knowle North Star Reserves left.
Upton Town joined from the Kidderminster League and Chelmsley Town Reserves and Shirley Town Reserves also joined.

1987-88

Premier Division

Racing Club (Warwick)	36	22	12	2	74	23	56
Boldmere St. Michaels	36	22	6	8	69	30	50
Ashtree Highfield	36	20	10	6	70	44	50
Stratford Town	36	20	8	8	65	40	48
Evesham United	36	20	6	10	81	47	46
West Midlands Police	36	20	3	13	77	57	43
Coleshill Town	36	16	10	10	61	41	42
Princes End United	36	16	9	11	55	55	41
Northfield Town	36	14	12	10	48	40	40
Kings Heath	36	12	12	12	45	50	36
Solihull Borough	36	14	6	16	62	65	34
Bolehall Swifts	36	11	8	17	40	53	30
Walsall Wood	36	10	9	17	51	61	29
Knowle	36	10	8	18	40	60	28
Leamington	36	8	11	17	37	59	27
Polesworth North Warwick	36	8	8	20	53	85	24
Highgate United	36	9	6	21	44	80	24
Wilmcote	*36*	*5*	*8*	*23*	*28*	*65*	*18*
Bloxwich AFC	*36*	*7*	*4*	*25*	*45*	*90*	*18*

Ashtree Highfield moved to the Southern League and Leamington ceased to run.
Hinckley FC joined from the Central Midlands League.

Division One

Chelmsley Town	26	16	7	3	72	31	39
Shirley Town	26	16	6	4	51	30	38
Bloxwich Strollers	26	12	8	6	51	38	32
Kings Norton ex-Servicemen's C.	26	11	9	6	47	38	31
West Heath United	26	12	7	7	45	38	31
Bromsgrove Athletic	26	12	5	9	44	32	29
Dudley Sports	26	9	8	9	48	42	26
Alcester Town	26	9	7	10	33	34	25
Wythall	26	8	6	12	39	38	22
Shelfield United	26	9	4	13	32	43	22
Triplex	26	7	6	13	33	45	20
Solihull Borough Reserves	26	6	6	14	27	66	18
Coleshill Town Reserves	*26*	*5*	*6*	*15*	*34*	*55*	*16*
Enville Athletic	*26*	*3*	*9*	*14*	*28*	*54*	*15*

1988-89

Premier Division

Boldmere St. Michaels	34	23	9	2	76	22	55
Racing Club (Warwick)	34	22	8	4	77	31	52
Evesham United	34	21	7	6	82	30	49
Princes End United	34	17	9	8	58	37	43
West Midlands Police	34	18	6	10	66	41	42
Northfield Town	34	15	10	9	55	43	40
Stratford Town	34	14	10	10	60	44	38
Walsall Wood	34	13	10	11	49	52	36
Hinckley FC	34	12	11	11	49	55	35
Highgate United	34	9	15	10	60	61	33
Bolehall Swifts	34	12	8	14	44	55	32
Kings Heath	34	9	11	14	42	52	29
Chelmsley Town	34	10	7	17	37	65	27
Knowle	34	8	10	16	34	58	26
Polesworth North Warwick	34	4	14	16	37	62	22
Coleshill Town	34	8	6	20	46	73	22
Solihull Borough	34	7	6	21	41	72	20
Shirley Town	*34*	*4*	*3*	*27*	*20*	*80*	*11*

Racing Club (Warwick) moved to the Southern League.
Stapenhill joined from the Leicestershire Senior League and Mile Oak Rovers joined from the Southern League.

Division One

Bloxwich AFC	26	18	4	4	78	28	40
Streetly Celtic	26	16	7	3	53	29	39
West Heath United	26	16	4	6	72	24	36
Dudley Sports	26	14	8	4	82	39	36
Bloxwich Strollers	26	13	9	4	51	29	35
Wythall	26	13	7	6	49	36	33
Kings Norton ex-Servicemen's C.	26	10	8	8	58	49	28
Wilmcote	26	7	9	10	45	39	23
Triplex	26	8	7	11	36	58	23
Bromsgrove Athletic	26	4	8	14	25	41	16
West Midland Fire Service	26	5	6	15	38	71	16
Alcester Town	*26*	*5*	*5*	*16*	*29*	*77*	*15*
Shelfield United	26	4	5	17	22	58	13
Solihull Borough Reserves	26	4	3	19	37	97	11

Bloxwich AFC changed their name to Bloxwich Town.
Shelfield United and Solihull Borough Reserves left.
Stapenhill Reserves joined.

Division Two

	P	W	D	L	F	A	Pts
Upton Town	26	16	7	3	72	25	39
Wellesbourne	26	18	2	6	73	30	38
Studley BKL	26	15	4	7	73	47	34
Southam United	26	12	7	7	55	45	31
Weston United	26	11	6	9	54	55	28
Enville Athletic	26	12	4	10	38	39	28
Handrahan Timbers	26	12	3	11	54	37	27
Kings Heath Reserves	26	10	6	10	50	43	26
Coleshill Town Reserves	26	9	8	9	37	46	26
Fairfield Villa	26	8	8	10	41	41	24
Earlswood Town	26	6	8	12	34	48	20
Dudley Sports Reserves	26	5	8	13	44	64	18
Chelmsley Town Reserves	26	4	8	14	26	55	16
Shirley Town Reserves	26	3	3	20	24	100	9

Becketts Sporting and Hams Hall joined from the BYOB Mercian League Archdale '73', Emerald Social, Greenway Sports, Kenilworth Rangers, Pershore Town '88 (a newly reformed club) and also Thimblemill R.E.C. joined.

Three points were awarded for a win from the next season onwards.

Division Two

	P	W	D	L	F	A	Pts
Pershore Town '88	32	21	7	4	63	27	70
Alcester Town	32	16	11	5	66	35	59
Becketts Sporting	32	17	7	8	63	36	58
Earlswood Town	32	17	6	9	60	42	57
Hams Hall	32	16	8	8	72	37	56
Weston United	32	16	5	11	69	58	53
Kenilworth Rangers	32	13	10	9	65	59	49
Emerald Social	32	12	9	11	51	49	45
Archdale '73	'32	12	8	12	70	65	44
Thimblemill R.E.C.	32	11	9	12	54	57	42
Enville Athletic	32	9	9	14	48	55	36
Chelmsley Town Reserves	32	8	11	13	37	50	35
Fairfield Villa	32	9	7	16	35	54	34
Greenway Sports	32	9	6	17	45	65	33
Coleshill Town Reserves	32	8	7	17	45	64	31
Dudley Sports Reserves	32	7	6	19	33	69	27
Shirley Town Reserves	32	6	4	22	30	84	22

Greenway Sports and Shirley Town Reserves left.
Chelmsley Town Reserves disbanded and reformed as a separate club, continuing in the league as Marston Green.
Badsey Rangers joined from the Worcester & DL and Monica Star, Sherwood Celtic and Mile Oak Rovers Reserves also joined.

1989-90

Premier Division

	P	W	D	L	F	A	Pts
Boldmere St. Michaels	38	24	9	5	72	24	81
Northfield Town	38	22	8	8	79	32	74
Evesham United	38	22	7	9	79	44	73
Stapenhill	38	21	7	10	77	35	70
Stratford Town	38	18	9	11	77	50	63
West Midlands Police	38	18	8	12	80	66	62
Bloxwich Town	38	17	9	12	65	62	60
Bolehall Swifts	38	16	6	16	70	58	54
Princes End United	38	14	11	13	68	55	53
Solihull Borough	38	16	3	19	53	52	51
Highgate United	38	12	13	13	46	50	49
Hinckley FC	38	13	9	16	39	69	48
Chelmsley Town	38	13	6	19	46	66	45
Polesworth North Warwick	38	11	10	17	51	72	43
Kings Heath	38	10	12	16	55	74	42
Coleshill Town	38	11	8	19	38	54	41
Walsall Wood	38	9	12	17	50	73	39
Knowle	38	10	9	19	50	81	39
Mile Oak Rovers	38	8	14	16	47	74	38
Streetly Celtic	*38*	*7*	*6*	*25*	*38*	*89*	*27*

Sandwell Borough joined from the Southern League.

Division One

	P	W	D	L	F	A	Pts
Stapenhill Reserves	32	21	3	8	60	44	66
Kings Norton ex-Servicemen's	32	17	10	5	75	39	61
Studley BKL	32	18	6	8	57	42	60
Dudley Sports	32	16	7	9	67	38	55
West Heath United	32	13	12	7	50	36	51
Wythall	32	14	8	10	55	51	50
Southam United	32	14	5	13	56	44	47
Handrahan Timbers	32	13	7	12	52	41	46
Wellesbourne	32	13	7	12	63	56	46
Triplex	32	13	7	12	51	50	46
Upton Town	32	13	6	13	55	49	45
Bloxwich Strollers	32	12	9	11	60	58	45
West Midland Fire Service	32	9	8	15	49	55	35
Kings Heath Reserves	32	8	8	16	49	78	32
Wilmcote	32	9	5	18	39	73	32
Bromsgrove Athletic	32	6	5	21	35	67	23
Shirley Town	*32*	*5*	*3*	*24*	*29*	*81*	*18*

Bloxwich Strollers moved to the WMRL. Bromsgrove Athletic also left.

1990-91

Premier Division

	P	W	D	L	F	A	Pts
West Midlands Police	40	22	14	4	84	41	80
Solihull Borough	40	24	6	10	74	35	78
Evesham United	40	21	11	8	83	46	74
Sandwell Borough	40	20	14	6	63	31	74
Stratford Town	40	19	12	9	81	43	69
Northfield Town	40	18	13	9	63	37	67
Stapenhill	40	18	12	10	60	50	66
Coleshill Town	40	18	11	11	57	42	65
Highgate United	40	18	11	11	48	35	65
Hinckley FC	40	18	9	13	56	47	63
Walsall Wood	40	17	8	15	53	48	59
Boldmere St. Michaels	40	14	11	15	51	56	53
Kings Heath	40	12	14	14	65	62	50
Knowle	40	14	7	19	47	66	49
Bloxwich Town	40	11	11	18	64	73	44
Bolehall Swifts	40	12	5	23	41	79	41
Mile Oak Rovers	40	9	10	21	40	73	37
Chelmsley Town	40	9	9	22	43	77	36
Princes End United	40	10	6	24	34	71	36
Polesworth North Warwick	*40*	*5*	*12*	*23*	*39*	*86*	*27*
Kings Norton ex-Servicemen's	*40*	*4*	*8*	*28*	*32*	*80*	*20*

Solihull Borough moved to the Southern League and Princes End United disbanded.
Armitage '90 joined from the Staffordshire Senior League and Barlestone St. Giles joined from the Leicestershire Senior League.

Division One

	P	W	D	L	F	A	Pts
Alcester Town	28	20	4	4	85	28	64
Wilmcote	28	19	3	6	47	20	60
Pershore Town '88	28	17	6	5	63	20	57
Studley BKL	28	16	8	4	56	27	56
Stapenhill Reserves	28	12	7	9	58	57	43
Wellesbourne	28	11	7	10	57	52	40
Dudley Sports	28	11	5	12	42	45	38
Handrahan Timbers	28	10	7	11	43	52	37
Triplex	28	9	8	11	33	41	35
Southam United	28	9	7	12	39	48	34
Kings Heath Reserves	28	7	7	14	41	54	28
West Midland Fire Service	28	8	4	16	37	63	28
West Heath United	28	6	5	17	39	65	23
Upton Town	28	5	7	16	31	57	22
Wythall	*28*	*5*	*5*	*18*	*28*	*70*	*20*

Streetly Celtic resigned during the season. Their record was expunged.
Wigston Fields joined from the Leicestershire Senior League and Ledbury Town '84 and Solihull Borough Reserves also joined.

Division Two

Badsey Rangers	**34**	**25**	**6**	**3**	**78**	**29**	**81**
Becketts Sporting	**34**	**21**	**5**	**8**	**82**	**43**	**68**
Monica Star	34	18	8	8	64	39	62
Coleshill Town Reserves	34	18	7	9	73	45	61
Marston Green	34	18	6	10	55	34	60
Archdale '73'	34	15	10	9	63	53	55
Thimblemill R.E.C.	34	16	5	13	67	62	53
Kenilworth Rangers	34	16	3	15	58	43	51
Emerald Social	34	14	8	12	61	57	50
Earlswood Town	34	13	9	12	52	58	48
Enville Athletic	34	11	8	15	57	66	41
Weston United	34	12	5	17	46	69	41
Hams Hall	34	10	10	14	61	60	40
Sherwood Celtic	34	11	7	16	47	57	40
Shirley Town	34	9	7	18	48	60	34
Dudley Sports Reserves	34	8	5	21	38	77	29
Mile Oak Rovers Reserves	34	6	7	21	39	75	25
Fairfield Villa	34	4	6	24	38	100	18

Weston United moved to the Shropshire County League and Mile Oak Rovers Reserves also left.

Swift Personalised Products joined from the Birmingham Works League as Swift PP, and the Reserves of Pershore Town '88, Wellesbourne, Wigston Fields and Barlestone St. Giles also joined.

1991-92

Premier Division

Evesham United	40	28	7	5	76	31	91
Armitage '90	40	27	7	6	84	28	88
West Midlands Police	40	24	8	8	86	44	80
Highgate United	40	22	11	7	71	34	77
Sandwell Borough	40	21	8	11	81	45	71
Pershore Town '88	40	19	11	10	76	41	68
Walsall Wood	40	18	13	9	66	42	67
Stapenhill	40	18	9	13	83	67	63
Boldmere St. Michaels	40	17	9	14	69	52	60
Bolehall Swifts	40	15	14	11	59	47	59
Northfield Town	40	14	15	11	48	54	57
Coleshill Town	40	12	15	13	46	48	51
Alcester Town	40	11	9	20	53	74	42
Stratford Town	40	11	8	21	47	64	41
Chelmsley Town	40	12	5	23	61	111	41
Knowle	40	10	9	21	59	77	39
Barlestone St. Giles	40	10	9	21	39	78	39
Kings Heath	*40*	*10*	*8*	*22*	*45*	*68*	*38*
Hinckley FC	40	10	8	22	49	79	38
Bloxwich Town	40	9	8	23	48	83	35
Mile Oak Rovers	40	3	7	30	35	114	16

Hinckley FC continued as Barwell after merging with Barwell Athletic of the Leicestershire Senior League. Evesham United moved to the Southern League and Walsall Wood moved to the Staffordshire Senior League. Meir KA joined from the Staffordshire Senior League.

Division One

Studley BKL	**36**	**22**	**10**	**4**	**68**	**35**	**76**
Badsey Rangers	36	22	7	7	78	37	73
Wellesbourne	36	21	8	7	76	41	71
West Heath United	36	21	7	8	77	37	70
Dudley Sports	36	18	8	10	57	46	62
Becketts Sporting	36	15	12	9	67	44	57
Southam United	36	13	12	11	52	50	51
Solihull Borough Reserves	36	14	7	15	65	66	49
Kings Norton ex-Servicemen's Cl.	36	13	9	14	55	56	48
Handrahan Timbers	36	11	14	11	45	38	47
Wigston Fields	36	12	10	14	47	45	46
Polesworth North Warwick	36	13	6	17	54	65	45
Triplex	36	11	10	15	50	59	43
Upton Town	36	12	6	18	49	51	42
Wilmcote	36	11	4	21	53	64	37
West Midland Fire Service	36	8	12	16	44	61	36
Ledbury Town '84	36	10	5	21	41	91	35
Stapenhill Reserves	36	7	8	21	60	106	29
Kings Heath Reserves	36	5	11	20	34	80	26

Kings Heath Reserves and Stapenhill Reserves left.

Division Two

Marston Green	**38**	**24**	**13**	**1**	**87**	**34**	**85**
Hams Hall	**38**	**24**	**7**	**7**	**96**	**42**	**79**
Kenilworth Rangers	**38**	**23**	**8**	**7**	**82**	**59**	**77**
Sherwood Celtic	**38**	**22**	**8**	**8**	**93**	**42**	**74**
Thimblemill R.E.C.	38	20	9	9	107	62	69
Monica Star	38	17	9	12	71	51	60
Pershore Town '88 Reserves	38	18	6	14	71	57	60
Enville Athletic	38	16	7	15	60	56	55
Emerald Social	38	14	10	14	76	83	52
Shirley Town	38	13	11	14	64	56	50
Wellesbourne Reserves	38	14	8	16	67	67	50
Swift PP	38	14	8	16	56	66	50
Coleshill Town Reserves	38	13	9	16	60	65	48
Earlswood Town	38	12	11	15	49	65	47
Wythall	38	10	11	17	60	75	41
Archdale '73'	38	11	6	21	68	88	39
Wigston Fields Reserves	38	8	12	18	49	93	36
Barlestone St. Giles Reserves	38	8	6	24	50	91	30
Fairfield Villa	38	9	3	26	37	85	30
Dudley Sports Reserves	38	7	4	27	46	112	25

Kenilworth Rangers changed their name to Kenilworth Town. Wythall and Emerald Social left. Ansells joined from the Birmingham Works League, Colletts Green joined from Sunday football, Holly Lane joined as a new club and Burntwood Town and the Reserves of Meir KA, Kenilworth Town and Studley BKL Reserves also joined.

1992-93   Premier Division

Armitage '90	38	26	6	6	91	32	84
Stapenhill	38	25	4	9	105	45	79
Stratford Town	38	21	13	4	70	33	76
Sandwell Borough	38	21	9	8	89	47	72
Pershore Town '88	38	21	8	9	74	38	71
West Midlands Police	38	20	10	8	77	39	70
Coleshill Town	38	21	6	11	63	44	69
Boldmere St. Michaels	38	17	12	9	74	48	63
Bolehall Swifts	38	15	10	13	66	56	55
Knowle	38	15	10	13	70	71	55
Barwell	38	14	12	12	63	70	54
Northfield Town	38	13	12	13	58	59	51
Meir KA	38	9	12	17	47	60	39
Mile Oak Rovers	38	9	9	20	37	72	36
Studley BKL	38	7	14	17	39	71	35
Chelmsley Town	38	7	13	18	51	75	34
Highgate United	38	8	10	20	48	80	34
Bloxwich Town	38	5	11	22	28	74	26
Barlestone St. Giles	*38*	*5*	*5*	*28*	*40*	*104*	*20*
Alcester Town	38	3	10	25	30	102	19

Armitage '90 moved to the Southern League and Alcester Town disbanded. Shifnal Town joined from the Shropshire County League and Shepshed Albion joined from the Northern Premier League.

Division One

Wellesbourne	**40**	**27**	**8**	**5**	**89**	**41**	**89**
Kings Heath	**40**	**24**	**7**	**9**	**100**	**44**	**79**
Kenilworth Town	40	23	7	10	86	49	76
West Heath United	40	23	4	13	92	64	73
Handrahan Timbers	40	19	10	11	66	52	67
Kings Norton ex-Servicemen's Cl.	40	20	6	14	71	54	66
Southam United	40	17	13	10	66	45	64
Becketts Sporting	40	17	13	10	69	61	64
Sherwood Celtic	40	19	6	15	76	63	63
West Midland Fire Service	40	18	7	15	71	58	61
Badsey Rangers	39	16	8	15	64	63	56
Hams Hall	40	15	11	14	68	68	56
Solihull Borough Reserves	40	15	10	15	65	64	55
Marston Green	40	14	8	18	69	75	50
Wilmcote	40	12	10	18	67	85	46
Polesworth North Warwick	40	12	8	20	68	95	44
Triplex	40	11	10	19	41	57	43
Dudley Sports	40	11	3	26	55	84	36
Wigston Fields	39	9	8	22	57	80	35
Upton Town	40	9	8	23	45	84	35
Ledbury Town '84	*40*	*5*	*1*	*34*	*31*	*130*	*16*

Badsey Rangers vs Wigston Fields was not played.

West Heath United changed their name to Olton Royale after being taken over by the Sunday League side of that name.

Wigston Fields moved to the Leicestershire Senior League, Marston Green moved into Sunday football and Triplex disbanded.

Division Two

Ansells	40	32	4	4	137	41	100
Shirley Town	40	29	5	6	142	57	92
Colletts Green	40	27	5	8	122	52	86
Monica Star	40	26	5	9	104	41	83
Coleshill Town Reserves	40	24	3	13	92	57	75
Fairfield Villa	40	22	8	10	96	60	74
Enville Athletic	40	20	9	11	88	67	69
Meir KA Reserves	40	20	9	11	75	57	69
Archdale '73'	40	15	12	13	87	78	57
Holly Lane	40	16	9	15	90	82	57
Swift PP	40	17	5	18	78	67	56
Pershore Town '88 Reserves	40	15	10	15	76	59	55
Thimblemill R.E.C.	40	16	7	17	86	78	55
Burntwood Town	40	15	6	19	65	75	51
Kenilworth Town Reserves	40	13	10	17	65	89	49
Studley BKL Reserves	40	12	8	20	67	86	44
Earlswood Town	40	10	5	25	65	110	35
Wigston Fields Reserves	40	7	6	27	49	119	27
Barlestone St. Giles Reserves	40	6	4	30	42	164	22
Wellesbourne Reserves	40	6	2	32	42	133	20
Dudley Sports Reserves	40	3	6	31	45	141	15

Ansells were promoted to the Premier Division.
Wigston Fields Reserves and Pershore Town '88 Reserves left.
Massey Ferguson, Jaguar-Daimler, Sphinx, GPT (Coventry) and Alvis SGL joined from the Coventry Alliance, Rugby Town joined from the Coventry & North Warwickshire League and Sutton Coldfield Town Reserves also joined.

A new Third Division was formed by:
Albright & Wilson, Blackheath Electrodrives, Mitchells & Butlers and Park Rangers who all joined from the WMRL, Alveston from the Stratford Alliance, Bilston Community College from the Staffordshire County League (South), Continental Star from the Birmingham Works League, the Reserves of West Midlands Police, Stapenhill, Ansells, Wilmcote and Enville Athletic plus the Reserves of Barlestone St. Giles, Wellesbourne, Dudley Sports and Kenilworth Town who were relegated from Division Two.

1993-94

Premier Division

Pershore Town '88	42	25	13	4	84	35	88
West Midlands Police	42	25	10	7	95	49	85
Shifnal Town	42	25	8	9	112	35	83
Shepshed Albion	42	23	10	9	87	47	79
Boldmere St. Michaels	42	22	7	13	74	54	73
Northfield Town	42	20	9	13	83	65	69
Studley BKL	42	19	11	12	91	76	68
Wellesbourne	42	18	11	13	78	60	65
Stratford Town	42	19	8	15	73	56	65
Meir KA	42	17	11	14	101	78	62
Stapenhill	42	17	11	14	77	55	62
Barwell	42	18	8	16	69	61	62
Sandwell Borough	42	15	14	13	82	71	59
Bolehall Swifts	42	17	7	18	61	77	58
Knowle	42	12	13	17	63	67	49
Bloxwich Town	42	14	6	22	65	108	48
Coleshill Town	42	10	15	17	53	72	45
Kings Heath	42	11	9	22	65	99	42
Highgate United	42	12	6	24	58	98	42
Chelmsley Town	42	8	9	25	59	94	33
Ansells	42	5	11	26	43	109	26
Mile Oak Rovers	42	2	9	31	32	135	15

The following left to become founder members of the Midland Alliance: Pershore Town '88, West Midlands Police, Shifnal Town, Shepshed Albion (as Shepshed Dynamo), Boldmere St. Michaels, Stratford Town, Stapenhill, Barwell, Sandwell Borough and Bolehall Swifts. Mile Oak Rovers moved to the Birmingham AFA and Alvechurch Villa joined as a new club.

Division One

West Midland Fire Service	36	25	5	6	86	35	80
Handrahan Timbers	36	22	9	5	72	44	75
Solihull Borough Reserves	36	21	5	10	95	55	68
Kenilworth Town	36	20	8	8	77	38	68
Colletts Green	36	19	8	9	76	46	65
Olton Royale	36	19	6	11	64	43	63
Sherwood Celtic	36	16	12	8	68	41	60
Shirley Town	36	16	7	13	63	65	55
Hams Hall	36	15	3	18	66	65	48
Kings Norton ex-Servicemen's Cl.	36	11	11	14	60	65	44
Southam United	36	11	11	14	45	54	44
Upton Town	36	11	11	14	49	64	44
Monica Star	36	13	2	21	52	74	41
Becketts Sporting	36	11	6	19	49	83	39
Badsey Rangers	36	10	7	19	43	61	37
Polesworth North Warwick	36	10	4	22	54	78	34
Barlestone St. Giles	36	10	3	23	58	84	33
Dudley Sports	36	7	11	18	53	84	32
Wilmcote	36	8	5	23	54	105	29

Becketts Sporting and Solihull Borough Reserves left.

Division Two

Massey Ferguson	36	30	5	1	137	27	95
Jaguar-Daimler	36	25	5	6	103	41	80
Thimblemill R.E.C.	36	24	5	7	79	31	77
Sphinx	36	23	7	6	96	49	76
GPT (Coventry)	36	21	7	8	75	49	70
Holly Lane	36	18	8	10	91	63	62
Fairfield Villa	36	16	7	13	61	38	55
Swift PP	36	14	7	15	64	54	49
Burntwood Town	36	13	7	16	61	84	46
Rugby Town	36	11	10	15	65	67	43
Archdale '73'	36	12	7	17	60	85	43
Studley BKL Reserves	36	12	5	19	57	73	41
Alvis SGL	36	10	10	16	36	56	40
Enville Athletic	36	11	5	20	59	81	38
Coleshill Town Reserves	36	9	7	20	41	81	34
Ledbury Town '84	36	8	7	21	66	100	31
Sutton Coldfield Town Reserves	36	7	10	19	53	87	31
Meir KA Reserves	36	9	2	25	46	117	29
Earlswood Town	36	5	7	24	29	96	22

Swift PP merged with Wythall Richmond of the Birmingham AFA and continued in the league as Richmond Swifts. Sutton Coldfield Town Reserves and Meir KA Reserves left.

Division Three

Albright & Wilson	30	22	4	4	91	30	70
Continental Star	30	22	2	6	99	35	68
Blackheath Electrodrives	30	21	2	7	86	38	65
Bilston Community College	30	19	5	6	96	40	62
West Midlands Police Reserves	30	18	5	7	84	48	59
Alveston	30	17	4	9	98	53	55
Mitchells & Butlers	30	16	6	8	102	57	54
Wellesbourne Reserves	30	15	7	8	86	47	52
Stapenhill Reserves	30	14	6	10	62	48	48
Ansells Reserves	30	12	5	13	58	61	41
Kenilworth Town Reserves	30	9	3	18	59	82	30
Wilmcote Reserves	30	7	7	16	34	84	28
Park Rangers	30	6	4	20	68	98	22
Enville Athletic Reserves	30	3	4	23	30	106	13
Dudley Sports Reserves	30	2	6	22	34	110	12
Barlestone St. Giles Reserves	30	1	2	27	16	166	5

Bilston Community College were promoted to Division One.
Kenilworth Town Reserves and Stapenhill Reserves left.
Cadbury Athletic joined as a new club, Cheslyn Hay and Wolverhampton Casuals Reserves joined from the WMRL, Brownhills Town joined from the Staffordshire County League (South), Studley United joined from the Stratford Alliance, Swan Sports joined from the Birmingham Works League as Birchfield Sports and Kings Heath Reserves and Moxley Rangers Reserves also joined.

1994-95

Premier Division

Northfield Town	34	27	3	4	96	38	84
Bloxwich Town	34	21	9	4	105	39	72
Wellesbourne	34	22	4	8	71	41	70
Olton Royale	34	18	5	11	74	72	59
Alvechurch Villa	34	15	11	8	66	41	56
Meir KA	34	15	8	11	73	63	53
Handrahan Timbers	34	14	9	11	62	48	51
Studley BKL	34	14	9	11	66	53	51
Shirley Town	34	13	6	15	56	68	45
West Midland Fire Service	34	11	11	12	39	45	44
Chelmsley Town	34	10	10	14	53	65	40
Kings Heath	34	10	7	17	51	69	37
Knowle	34	9	10	15	42	63	37
Coleshill Town	34	9	9	16	45	61	36
Ansells	34	10	5	19	42	64	35
Sherwood Celtic	34	9	5	20	55	81	32
Upton Town	34	7	7	20	45	68	28
Highgate United	34	6	4	24	35	97	22

Sherwood Celtic disbanded.

Division One

Massey Ferguson	32	20	10	2	73	27	70
Sphinx	32	21	5	6	72	27	68
Southam United	32	21	3	8	72	42	66
Bilston Community College	32	19	4	9	86	40	61
GPT (Coventry)	32	18	3	11	86	63	57
Jaguar-Daimler	32	16	6	10	57	43	54
Kenilworth Town	32	12	9	11	58	49	45
Hams Hall	32	13	6	13	45	51	45
Polesworth North Warwick	32	12	5	15	67	79	41
Dudley Sports	32	10	8	14	54	63	38
Colletts Green	32	10	7	15	54	65	37
Monica Star	32	8	12	12	40	51	36
Wilmcote	32	9	6	17	48	82	33
Badsey Rangers	32	8	7	17	43	64	31
Kings Norton ex-Servicemen's Cl.	32	8	7	17	50	73	31
Barlestone St. Giles	32	7	7	18	48	82	28
Thimblemill R.E.C.	32	6	3	23	40	92	21

Jaguar-Daimler moved to the Coventry Alliance and Wilmcote moved to the Stratford Alliance.
Newhall United joined from the Central Midlands League.

Division Two

Richmond Swifts	30	24	2	4	93	23	74
Alveston	30	18	5	7	58	30	59
Fairfield Villa	30	15	8	7	58	43	53
Holly Lane	30	16	4	10	81	47	52
Albright & Wilson	30	14	9	7	65	46	51
Alvis SGL	30	15	3	12	44	35	48
Rugby Town	30	14	6	10	61	57	48
Continental Star	30	14	4	12	57	47	46
Earlswood Town	30	11	10	9	54	40	43
Enville Athletic	30	12	6	12	53	56	42
Blackheath Electrodrives	30	10	8	12	43	49	38
Ledbury Town '84	30	9	3	18	54	73	30
Coleshill Town Reserves	30	8	6	16	38	85	30
Archdale '73'	30	8	4	18	42	66	28
Burntwood Town	30	6	3	21	28	80	21
Studley BKL Reserves	30	2	7	21	27	79	13

Bromsgrove Rangers joined from the Worcester & DL.

Division Three

West Midlands Police Reserves	32	24	4	4	99	35	76
Cheslyn Hay	32	23	3	6	106	48	72
Brownhills Town	32	22	6	4	86	34	72
Wolverhampton Casuals Res.	32	20	3	9	96	42	63
Mitchells & Butlers	32	17	7	8	72	48	58
Wellesbourne Reserves	32	17	6	9	73	49	57
Kings Heath Reserves	32	17	4	11	78	62	55
Studley United	32	14	8	10	72	58	50
Cadbury Athletic	32	16	1	15	58	66	49
Birchfield Sports	32	13	6	13	64	63	45
Dudley Sports Reserves	32	12	6	14	66	65	42
Ansells Reserves	32	10	6	16	58	82	36
Park Rangers	32	10	3	19	66	100	33
Enville Athletic Reserves	32	6	4	22	30	71	22
Barlestone St. Giles Reserves	32	7	0	25	50	107	21
Moxley Rangers	32	4	5	23	39	82	17
Wilmcote Reserves	32	2	4	26	32	133	10

Moxley Rangers Reserves, Wilmcote Reserves and Ansells Reserves left. Feckenham joined from the Worcester & DL, Cradley Heath joined from the Kidderminster League, Alvechurch Villa Reserves joined from the Bromsgrove & DL and Tipton Sports & Social, Birmingham Vaults, Kenilworth Wardens, Tipton Rovers, Swan Sports and Richmond Swifts Reserves also joined.

1995-96

Premier Division

Bloxwich Town	38	31	4	3	122	45	97
Sphinx	38	25	5	8	87	43	80
Massey Ferguson	38	23	8	7	77	36	77
Knowle	38	21	10	7	87	49	73
Studley BKL	38	17	11	10	93	64	62
Kings Heath	38	18	6	14	63	65	60
Meir KA	38	15	10	13	77	72	55
Wellesbourne	38	15	10	13	55	60	55
Southam United	38	13	14	11	69	63	53
Coleshill Town	38	14	9	15	76	66	51
Chelmsley Town	38	14	8	16	65	62	50
Upton Town	38	14	6	18	68	72	48
Ansells	38	12	10	16	64	81	46
Olton Royale	38	12	8	18	56	71	44
West Midland Fire Service	38	11	9	18	51	70	42
Alvechurch Villa	38	10	10	18	57	84	40
Highgate United	38	9	10	19	56	81	37
Handrahan Timbers	38	9	10	19	46	71	37
Shirley Town	38	8	8	22	51	74	32
Northfield Town	38	3	6	29	33	124	15

Upton Town moved to Worcester and changed their name to Worcester Athletico, Sphinx changed their name to Coventry Sphinx, Ansells changed their name to David Lloyd Sports and Alvechurch Villa changed their name to Alvechurch.
Bloxwich Town moved to the Midland Alliance and Olton Royale disbanded. Bolehall Swifts joined from the Midland Alliance.

Division One

Richmond Swifts	32	26	5	1	92	18	83
Kenilworth Town	32	17	10	5	75	31	61
Bilston Community College	32	18	7	7	78	41	61
Colletts Green	32	18	7	7	76	54	61
GPT (Coventry)	32	19	3	10	84	47	60
Dudley Sports	32	16	8	8	63	39	56
Alveston	32	14	7	11	63	48	49
Polesworth North Warwick	32	12	9	11	60	69	45
Newhall United	32	11	10	11	68	63	43
Monica Star	32	11	8	13	55	56	41
Holly Lane	32	9	11	12	43	53	38
Hams Hall	32	11	4	17	55	68	37
Kings Norton ex-Servicemen's Cl.	32	12	1	19	49	82	37
Thimblemill R.E.C.	32	8	4	20	38	73	28
Barlestone St. Giles	32	8	3	21	44	91	27
Fairfield Villa	32	6	4	22	27	75	22
Badsey Rangers	32	2	7	23	30	92	13

Kings Norton ex-Servicemen's Club disbanded.
Yardley joined as a new club and Leicester YMCA also joined.

Division Two

Continental Star	32	24	6	2	89	28	78
Enville Athletic	32	21	5	6	71	31	68
Brownhills Town	32	20	5	7	73	46	65
Cheslyn Hay	32	19	4	9	76	54	61
Earlswood Town	32	16	9	7	56	30	57
West Midlands Police Reserves	32	13	8	11	47	41	47
Bromsgrove Rangers	32	12	8	12	63	59	44
Ledbury Town	32	11	9	12	71	50	42
Alvis SGL	32	10	12	10	52	41	42
Coleshill Town Reserves	32	12	6	14	49	61	42
Cadbury Athletic	32	11	6	15	36	49	39
Wolverhampton Casuals Reserves	32	11	4	17	46	79	37
Blackheath Electrodrives	32	8	8	16	40	49	32
Archdale '73'	32	7	8	17	46	60	29
Burntwood Town	32	7	7	18	41	64	28
Albright & Wilson	32	6	6	20	35	81	24
Wellesbourne Reserves	32	6	5	21	33	101	23

Rugby Town disbanded in October and their record was deleted.
Bromsgrove Rangers disbanded and the Reserves of Coleshill Town,
Wellesbourne Reserves and Wolverhampton Casuals left.

Division Three

Feckenham	34	27	5	2	102	26	86
Richmond Swifts Reserves	34	25	4	5	89	29	79
Tipton Sports & Social	34	21	5	8	68	30	68
Birmingham Vaults	34	20	8	6	62	38	68
Mitchells & Butlers	34	16	9	9	74	44	57
Studley United	34	16	6	12	64	56	54
Cradley Heath	34	13	8	13	53	46	47
Kenilworth Wardens	34	13	7	14	51	56	46
Dudley Sports Reserves	34	14	3	17	48	55	45
Kings Heath Reserves	34	13	2	19	53	79	41
Enville Athletic Reserves	34	10	8	16	47	60	38
Birchfield Sports	34	10	8	16	46	71	38
Tipton Rovers	34	10	7	17	51	59	37
Swan Sports	34	10	6	18	76	85	36
Studley BKL Reserves	34	9	6	19	45	71	33
Alvechurch Villa Reserves	34	9	4	21	45	85	31
Barlestone St. Giles Reserves	34	8	7	19	35	81	31
Park Rangers	34	5	11	18	51	89	26

Park Rangers and Studley United disbanded.
Kings Heath Reserves and Tipton Rovers left.
Tipton Town Reserves and Kenilworth Town Reserves joined.

1996-97

Premier Division

Richmond Swifts	38	30	5	3	92	29	95
Meir KA	38	26	6	6	91	39	84
Coleshill Town	38	22	10	6	69	30	76
Studley BKL	38	22	6	10	100	49	72
Knowle	38	22	4	12	83	47	70
Worcester Athletico	38	20	7	11	85	60	67
Kings Heath	38	16	8	14	66	50	56
Massey Ferguson	38	15	11	12	62	61	56
David Lloyd Sports	38	14	11	13	54	57	53
Handrahan Timbers	38	15	6	17	46	54	51
Coventry Sphinx	38	14	8	16	51	74	50
Bilston Community College	38	14	7	17	83	71	49
Bolehall Swifts	38	11	14	13	62	59	47
Southam United	38	13	8	17	53	62	47
Wellesbourne	38	12	5	21	62	89	41
Kenilworth Town	38	11	8	19	49	80	41
Highgate United	38	11	3	24	55	77	36
Alvechurch	38	9	5	24	46	82	32
Shirley Town	38	7	8	23	51	94	29
West Midland Fire Service	38	4	4	30	26	122	16

Richmond Swifts moved to the Midland Alliance as Kings Norton Town.

Division One

GPT (Coventry)	34	26	3	5	91	16	81
Continental Star	34	21	8	5	91	37	71
Alveston	34	21	7	6	78	39	70
Cheslyn Hay	34	20	4	10	89	59	64
Northfield Town	34	18	7	9	68	41	61
Newhall United	34	16	10	8	82	52	58
Dudley Sports	34	17	7	10	64	42	58
Colletts Green	34	15	6	13	59	50	51
Yardley	34	16	3	15	63	55	51
Polesworth North Warwick	34	15	5	14	62	66	50
Holly Lane	34	13	9	12	50	50	48
Monica Star	34	12	8	14	59	50	44
Leicester YMCA	34	12	5	17	57	70	41
Chelmsley Town	34	10	6	18	51	66	36
Thimblemill R.E.C.	34	5	8	21	34	99	23
Barlestone St. Giles	34	5	6	23	27	98	21
Hams Hall	34	4	5	25	44	90	17
Brownhills Town	34	4	5	25	29	118	17

Yardley left.

Division Two

Feckenham	30	21	5	4	79	27	68
Fairfield Villa	30	19	5	6	72	37	62
Ledbury Town	30	17	7	6	77	42	58
Richmond Swifts Reserves	30	17	5	8	68	32	56
Tipton Sports & Social	30	14	7	9	50	35	49
Burntwood Town	30	15	4	11	47	41	49
Alvis SGL	30	13	8	9	46	37	47
Earlswood Town	30	13	6	11	58	40	45
Blackheath Electrodrives	30	12	6	12	35	38	42
Cadbury Athletic	30	11	8	11	48	39	41
West Midlands Police Reserves	30	10	8	12	42	49	38
Enville Athletic	30	10	5	15	36	48	35
Birmingham Vaults	30	7	6	17	28	68	27
Albright & Wilson	30	6	6	18	40	75	24
Badsey Rangers	30	5	5	20	22	65	20
Archdale '73'	30	2	5	23	29	104	11

Richmond Swifts Reserves changed their name to Kings Norton Town
Reserves.
Badsey Rangers left and Stourbridge College & Community joined.

Division Three

Swan Sports	22	16	2	4	55	20	50
Studley BKL Reserves	22	14	5	3	40	16	47
Mitchells & Butlers	22	13	2	7	57	36	41
Cradley Heath	22	12	4	6	46	24	40
Kenilworth Wardens	22	12	3	7	50	26	39
Tipton Town Reserves	22	10	7	5	41	29	37
Alvechurch Reserves	22	9	3	10	42	42	30
Birchfield Sports	22	7	4	11	29	48	25
Enville Athletic Reserves	22	6	3	13	29	45	21
Kenilworth Town Reserves	22	6	1	15	29	53	19
Dudley Sports Reserves	22	5	3	14	30	52	18
Barlestone St. Giles Reserves	22	2	3	17	10	67	9

Cradley Heath, Barlestone St. Giles Reserves and Enville Athletic
Reserves all left.
Wyre Forest joined from the Kidderminster League and Old Hill Town,
Handsaker, Barnt Green Spartak, Knowle Reserves, Erdington, GNP
Sports and Continental Star Reserves also joined.

1997-98

Premier Division

Worcester Athletico	40	26	12	2	111	41	90
Southam United	40	24	11	5	84	38	83
Bolehall Swifts	40	25	8	7	76	43	83
Studley BKL	40	24	4	12	79	36	76
Coleshill Town	40	21	9	10	78	38	72
GPT (Coventry)	40	20	8	12	71	46	68
Meir KA	40	20	7	13	81	58	67
David Lloyd Sports	40	19	7	14	80	66	64
Kings Heath	40	17	12	11	62	45	63
Continental Star	40	18	7	15	78	69	61
Knowle	*40*	*14*	*12*	*14*	*81*	*72*	*54*
Bilston Community College	40	15	9	16	69	76	54
Coventry Sphinx	40	15	9	16	72	78	54
Cheslyn Hay	40	14	9	17	66	86	51
Highgate United	40	12	14	14	59	54	50
Handrahan Timbers	40	11	10	19	52	53	43
Alvechurch	40	12	6	22	67	88	42
Massey Ferguson	40	12	5	23	49	73	41
Kenilworth Town	40	6	8	26	43	98	26
Dudley Sports	40	4	7	29	54	137	19
Wellesbourne	*40*	*1*	*6*	*33*	*38*	*155*	*9*

Worcester Athletico were merged into Pershore Town of the Midland Alliance.
David Lloyd Sports and Bilston Community College disbanded.

Division One

Alveston	**30**	**23**	**5**	**2**	**82**	**24**	**74**
Northfield Town	30	18	6	6	70	40	60
Feckenham	**30**	**18**	**5**	**7**	**60**	**36**	**59**
Fairfield Villa	*30*	*17*	*6*	*7*	*85*	*38*	*57*
Colletts Green	30	17	3	10	67	45	54
Polesworth North Warwick	30	15	4	11	86	62	49
Monica Star	30	12	8	10	70	53	44
Shirley Town	30	10	11	9	54	48	41
Leicester YMCA	30	11	7	12	52	60	40
Newhall United	30	11	5	14	52	51	38
Thimblemill R.E.C.	30	12	2	16	55	62	38
Chelmsley Town	30	11	3	16	50	68	36
Holly Lane	30	8	5	17	33	59	29
Barlestone St. Giles	*30*	*7*	*5*	*18*	*45*	*74*	*26*
Hams Hall	30	7	3	20	26	73	24
West Midland Fire Service	30	3	2	25	26	120	11

Monica Star moved to the Birmingham AFA, Leicester YMCA moved to the Leicestershire Senior League, Newhall United moved to the Burton & DL and Polesworth North Warwick disbanded.
Loughborough Athletic joined.

Division Two

Blackheath Electrodrives	**32**	**18**	**8**	**6**	**66**	**28**	**62**
Kings Norton Town Reserves	**32**	**18**	**8**	**6**	**79**	**45**	**62**
Alvis SGL	**32**	**16**	**11**	**5**	**70**	**35**	**59**
Stourbridge College & Community	32	18	5	9	70	50	59
Swan Sports	32	16	9	7	67	53	57
Burntwood Town	**32**	**15**	**8**	**9**	**83**	**45**	**53**
Studley BKL Reserves	**32**	**16**	**4**	**12**	**52**	**37**	**52**
Mitchells & Butlers	32	13	6	13	59	56	45
Cadbury Athletic	32	13	5	14	45	50	44
Brownhills Town	32	12	5	15	65	66	41
Ledbury Town	32	11	6	15	53	61	39
Albright & Wilson	32	9	6	17	52	64	33
Tipton Sports & Social	32	9	9	14	56	74	36
Birmingham Vaults	32	9	6	17	46	72	33
Earlswood Town	32	7	11	14	46	69	32
Enville Athletic	32	8	2	22	29	96	26
West Midlands Police Reserves	32	6	7	19	32	69	25

Albright & Wilson, Tipton Sports & Social and Swan Sports disbanded.
Birmingham Vaults changed their name to Wonder Vaults.
Mitchells & Butlers and Stourbridge College & Community left.
Mile Oak Rovers joined from the Birmingham AFA and County Sports also joined.

Division Three

Old Hill Town	**28**	**20**	**4**	**4**	**88**	**40**	**64**
Handsaker	**28**	**19**	**2**	**7**	**81**	**27**	**59**
Wyre Forest	**28**	**18**	**5**	**5**	**84**	**35**	**59**
GNP Sports	**28**	**16**	**4**	**8**	**44**	**31**	**52**
Kenilworth Wardens	**28**	**15**	**4**	**9**	**61**	**49**	**49**
Continental Star Reserves	28	15	1	12	52	49	46
Barnt Green Spartak	28	12	7	9	71	70	43
Birchfield Sports	28	12	6	10	60	69	42
Knowle Reserves	28	9	10	9	64	50	37
Erdington	28	9	6	13	62	71	33
Archdale '73'	28	9	3	16	50	69	30
Tipton Town Reserves	28	7	7	14	65	78	28
Dudley Sports Reserves	28	7	3	18	41	75	24
Alvechurch Reserves	28	5	5	18	54	95	20
Kenilworth Town Reserves	28	1	5	22	31	100	8

Alvechurch Reserves, Erdington and Birchfield Sports left.
Wilmcote Sports & Social joined from the Stratford Alliance after merging with Stratford Froth & Elbow and MCL Claines, Burman Hi-Ton, Lichfield Enots, Leamington Hibernian and the Reserves of Bustleholme, Northfield Town, Chelmsley Town and Massey Ferguson also joined.

1998-99

Premier Division

Alveston	34	21	8	5	74	32	71
Cheslyn Hay	34	18	10	6	61	42	64
Southam United	34	16	10	8	70	49	58
Kings Heath	34	17	6	11	66	51	57
Massey Ferguson	34	15	10	9	57	51	55
Meir KA	34	15	9	10	69	47	54
Studley BKL	34	14	11	9	67	43	53
GPT (Coventry)	34	15	8	11	67	65	53
Handrahan Timbers	34	14	10	10	56	47	52
Bolehall Swifts	34	13	8	13	58	48	47
Highgate United	34	13	7	14	69	59	46
Feckenham	34	10	14	10	45	42	44
Coventry Sphinx	34	12	7	15	53	64	43
Alvechurch	34	12	4	18	61	77	40
Continental Star	34	11	7	16	57	69	40
Kenilworth Town	34	8	8	18	37	67	32
Coleshill Town	34	6	6	22	46	78	24
Dudley Sports	*34*	*2*	*5*	*27*	*27*	*109*	*11*

GPT (Coventry) changed their name to Marconi (Coventry).
Nuneaton Griff joined from the Coventry Alliance.

Division One

Northfield Town	**30**	**22**	**2**	**6**	**95**	**32**	**68**
Knowle	30	20	4	6	78	33	64
Blackheath Electrodrives	**30**	**19**	**7**	**4**	**83**	**45**	**64**
Alvis SGL	30	16	3	11	69	66	51
Thimblemill R.E.C.	30	14	5	11	67	43	47
Chelmsley Town	30	15	2	13	61	58	47
Holly Lane	30	13	6	11	59	51	45
Wellesbourne	30	14	2	14	57	55	44
Shirley Town	30	12	4	14	50	74	40
Burntwood Town	30	10	6	14	70	71	36
Hams Hall	30	9	9	12	52	54	36
Studley BKL Reserves	30	10	5	15	49	58	35
Kings Norton Town Reserves	30	9	3	18	52	82	30
Loughborough Athletic	30	10	0	20	38	84	30
West Midland Fire Service	30	8	5	17	40	68	29
Colletts Green	30	5	5	20	40	86	20

Alvis SGL changed name to Alvis Oakwood Coventry and Colletts Green changed their name to Malvern Athletic.
Studley BKL Reserves left. Brookvale Athletic and Romulus joined from the Birmingham Festival Sunday League.

Division Two

Fairfield Villa	30	22	4	4	91	28	70
Brownhills Town	30	22	2	6	99	43	68
Wyre Forest	30	18	6	6	79	36	60
County Sports	30	18	6	6	75	34	60
Mile Oak Rovers	30	19	3	8	75	45	60
Old Hill Town	30	17	3	10	61	44	54
Handsaker	30	15	6	9	68	39	51
Earlswood Town	30	15	4	11	56	47	49
GNP Sports	30	13	2	15	59	73	41
West Midlands Police Reserves	30	8	12	10	48	50	36
Barlestone St. Giles	30	10	5	15	53	75	35
Cadbury Athletic	30	9	7	14	50	71	34
Kenilworth Wardens	30	8	5	17	40	69	29
Ledbury Town	30	4	2	24	42	100	14
Enville Athletic	30	3	5	22	37	101	14
Wonder Vaults	30	2	2	26	30	108	8

Ledbury Town moved to the WMRL and Wonder Vaults also left.
Polesworth North Warwick joined after re-forming.

Division Three

MCL Claines	30	22	6	2	86	30	72
Burman Hi-Ton	30	19	3	8	67	47	60
Archdale '73'	30	14	7	9	57	36	49
Bustleholme Reserves	30	13	7	10	59	58	46
Lichfield Enots	30	16	5	9	77	57	53
Leamington Hibernian	30	12	8	10	54	47	44
Continental Star Reserves	30	12	6	12	66	73	42
Knowle Reserves	30	12	5	13	55	62	41
Chelmsley Town Reserves	30	11	7	12	55	58	40
Wilmcote Sports & Social	30	11	3	16	54	54	36
Northfield Town Reserves	30	10	6	14	45	52	36
Tipton Town Reserves	30	10	6	14	56	64	36
Kenilworth Town Reserves	30	10	5	15	46	68	35
Barnt Green Spartak	30	8	10	12	57	57	34
Massey Ferguson Reserves	30	9	7	14	60	66	34
Dudley Sports Reserves	30	3	5	22	38	103	14

Dudley Sports Reserves left.
County Sports Reserves, Droitwich St. Peters, Blackheath Electrodrive Reserves, Central Ajax and West Hagley joined.

1999-2000

Premier Division

Nuneaton Griff	38	25	10	3	118	41	85
Kings Heath	38	22	10	6	79	42	76
Studley BKL	38	21	7	10	85	50	70
Marconi (Coventry)	38	20	9	9	81	51	69
Meir KA	38	18	10	10	81	48	64
Coventry Sphinx	38	18	7	13	69	47	61
Massey Ferguson	38	17	10	11	75	59	61
Cheslyn Hay	38	17	9	12	82	60	60
Feckenham	38	16	11	11	60	47	59
Alvechurch	38	17	8	13	74	77	59
Continental Star	38	14	11	13	62	75	53
Handrahan Timbers	38	15	7	16	51	61	52
Northfield Town	38	15	6	17	57	57	51
Bolehall Swifts	38	14	8	16	90	63	50
Blackheath Electrodrives	38	13	9	16	54	73	48
Southam United	38	11	8	19	64	78	41
Alveston	38	11	5	22	52	93	38
Highgate United	38	8	7	23	53	88	31
Coleshill Town	*38*	*5*	*5*	*28*	*52*	*124*	*17*
Kenilworth Town	*38*	*3*	*3*	*32*	*34*	*139*	*12*

Coleshill Town had 3 points deducted.
Marconi (Coventry) changed their name to Coventry Marconi and Blackheath Electrodrives changed their name to Blackheath Invensys.
Pershore Town joined from the Midland Alliance.

Division One

Brookvale Athletic	38	31	3	4	145	29	93
Romulus	38	28	6	4	121	44	90
Fairfield Villa	38	25	6	7	121	46	81
Mile Oak Rovers	38	23	7	8	95	60	76
County Sports	38	21	3	14	105	61	66
Brownhills Town	38	21	3	14	91	47	66
Holly Lane	38	17	10	11	79	67	61
Thimblemill R.E.C.	38	18	6	14	100	82	60
Burntwood Town	38	17	8	13	78	59	59
Shirley Town	38	17	8	13	84	90	56
Alvis Oakwood Coventry	38	15	5	18	76	78	50
Knowle	38	13	10	15	83	74	49
Hams Hall	38	13	10	15	76	79	49
Kings Norton Town Reserves	38	13	7	18	66	91	46
Loughborough Athletic	38	13	4	21	60	90	43
West Midland Fire Service	38	10	6	22	65	101	36
Dudley Sports	38	9	8	21	54	86	35
Wellesbourne	38	12	2	24	65	109	35
Malvern Athletic	*38*	*2*	*4*	*32*	*35*	*166*	*4*
Chelmsley Town	*38*	*2*	*4*	*32*	*31*	*171*	*4*

Brookvale Athletic, Shirley Town and Wellesbourne each had 3 points deducted.
Chelmsley Town and Malvern Athletic each had 6 points deducted.
Brookvale Athletic changed their name to Sutton Town.
Kings Norton Town disbanded and their Reserves resigned.
West Midland Fire Service also resigned.

Division Two

Wyre Forest	28	18	6	4	82	27	60
Polesworth North Warwick	28	17	5	6	69	35	56
Old Hill Town	28	17	4	7	72	47	55
Handsaker	28	14	8	6	70	38	50
MCL Claines	28	14	6	8	50	31	48
Kenilworth Wardens	28	12	6	10	66	51	42
Lichfield Enots	28	12	5	11	60	58	41
Barlestone St. Giles	28	11	7	10	49	52	40
West Midlands Police Reserves	28	11	6	11	53	50	39
Cadbury Athletic	28	10	7	11	53	53	37
Archdale '73'	28	9	6	13	37	58	33
Earlswood Town	28	9	6	13	36	64	33
Enville Athletic	28	6	4	18	33	62	22
Burman Hi-Ton	28	4	5	19	32	69	17
GNP Sports	28	4	3	21	24	91	15

MCL Claines, Barlestone St. Giles and GNP Sports left.
Leamington, Rugby Town and Rugby AFC joined.

Division Three

Wilmcote Sports & Social	32	27	2	3	104	27	83
County Sports Reserves	32	21	5	6	98	40	68
Bustleholme Reserves	32	16	7	9	61	52	55
Droitwich St. Peters	32	16	6	10	58	41	54
Leamington Hibernian	32	16	6	10	73	66	54
Chelmsley Town Reserves	32	16	3	13	68	48	51
Tipton Town Reserves	32	14	6	12	53	60	48
Barnt Green Spartak	32	13	8	11	84	59	47
Northfield Town Reserves	32	12	6	14	70	67	42
Blackheath Electrodrive Reserves	32	13	3	16	56	54	42
Central Ajax	32	12	6	14	66	69	42
West Hagley	32	11	8	13	57	52	41
Continental Star Reserves	32	10	7	15	72	80	37
Massey Ferguson Reserves	32	11	4	17	64	80	34
Birchfield Oaklands	32	9	7	16	51	85	34
Knowle Reserves	32	9	4	19	42	74	31
Kenilworth Town Reserves	32	1	2	29	27	150	2

Massey Ferguson Reserves and Kenilworth Town Reserves each had 3 points deducted.
Droitwich St. Peters changed their name to Droitwich Spa.
Birchfield Oaklands and the Reserves of Bustleholme, Tipton Town and Kenilworth Town left. Wilmcote Sports, Fernhill Heath Old Boys and the Reserves of Alvechurch, Cadbury Athletic, Enville Athletic, Brownhills Town, Wellesbourne, Wilmcote Sports & Social and Loughborough Athletic joined.

2000-01

Premier Division

Nuneaton Griff	40	31	4	5	93	34	97
Studley BKL	40	30	6	4	98	32	96
Romulus	40	27	7	6	79	34	88
Pershore Town	40	22	8	10	82	62	74
Coventry Sphinx	40	20	7	13	63	38	67
Meir KA	40	20	7	13	67	53	67
Alvechurch	40	21	3	16	77	64	66
Coventry Marconi	40	19	8	13	87	61	65
Kings Heath	40	15	12	13	61	53	57
Sutton Town	40	16	7	17	67	57	55
Bolehall Swifts	40	15	9	16	77	76	54
Massey Ferguson	40	15	8	17	81	81	53
Handrahan Timbers	40	12	7	21	51	69	43
Cheslyn Hay	40	11	9	20	53	71	42
Alveston	40	11	9	20	53	87	42
Feckenham	40	9	11	20	49	80	38
Blackheath Invensys	*40*	*10*	*7*	*23*	*51*	*91*	*37*
Highgate United	40	11	4	25	49	96	37
Northfield Town	*40*	*8*	*12*	*20*	*44*	*83*	*36*
Southam United	40	10	5	25	53	79	32
Continental Star	40	10	4	26	64	98	31

Southam United and Continental Star each had 3 points deducted.
Sutton Town changed their name to Grosvenor Park and Continental Star changed their name to Handsworth Continental Star.
Studley BKL moved to the Midland Alliance and West Midlands Police joined from the Midland Alliance.

Division One

Shirley Town	**36**	**23**	**5**	**8**	**104**	**47**	**74**
County Sports	**36**	**23**	**5**	**8**	**108**	**61**	**74**
Knowle	36	22	8	6	78	33	74
Coleshill Town	**36**	**20**	**5**	**11**	**72**	**56**	**65**
Brownhills Town	36	19	6	11	76	48	63
Handsaker	36	19	9	8	63	35	63
Alvis Oakwood Coventry	36	17	9	10	80	59	60
Old Hill Town	36	19	3	14	86	73	60
Thimblemill R.E.C.	36	17	7	12	88	63	58
Fairfield Villa	36	17	7	12	81	57	58
Dudley Sports	36	14	8	14	52	63	50
Polesworth North Warwick	36	11	6	19	64	74	39
Holly Lane	36	8	13	15	62	76	37
Mile Oak Rovers	36	10	7	19	59	90	37
Burntwood Town	36	9	8	19	45	81	35
Loughborough Athletic	36	10	4	22	47	85	34
Hams Hall	36	10	3	23	51	85	33
Kenilworth Town	36	10	2	24	72	121	32
Wellesbourne	*36*	*6*	*1*	*29*	*38*	*119*	*10*

Handsaker had 3 points deducted.
Loughborough Athletic changed their name to Loughborough.
Alvis Oakwood Coventry and Hams Hall left.

Division Two

Leamington	**34**	**28**	**4**	**2**	**96**	**31**	**88**
Rugby Town	**34**	**25**	**6**	**3**	**106**	**24**	**81**
Wilmcote Sports & Social	**34**	**22**	**8**	**4**	**87**	**28**	**74**
Cadbury Athletic	**34**	**21**	**6**	**7**	**71**	**34**	**69**
Archdale '73	34	19	8	7	82	43	63
Leamington Hibernian	34	18	7	9	102	76	61
Droitwich Spa	34	17	3	14	64	55	54
Enville Athletic	34	16	6	12	53	49	54
Burman Hi-Ton	34	13	6	15	59	61	45
Earlswood Town	34	11	7	16	58	73	40
Chelmsley Town	34	11	5	18	43	72	38
West Midlands Police Reserves	34	9	8	17	50	77	35
Barnt Green Spartak	34	10	5	19	46	75	35
Lichfield Enots	34	9	7	18	43	72	34
Rugby AFC	34	7	10	17	55	81	31
Kenilworth Wardens	34	7	3	24	48	94	24
Malvern Athletic	34	6	3	25	50	112	21
County Sports Reserves	34	4	4	26	61	117	16

Wyre Forest resigned when their record was:

	7	4	0	3	18	17	12

They joined the WMRL in 2001-02.
Lichfield Enots, Rugby AFC, County Sports Reserves and Malvern Athletic left. Stockingford AA joined from the Coventry Alliance.

Division Three

West Hagley	**30**	**25**	**5**	**0**	**99**	**20**	**80**
Alvechurch Reserves	30	20	4	6	85	35	64
Wilnecote Sports	**30**	**17**	**5**	**8**	**75**	**47**	**56**
Central Ajax	**30**	**17**	**4**	**9**	**76**	**43**	**55**
Fernhill Heath Old Boys	**30**	**15**	**8**	**7**	**61**	**32**	**53**
Cadbury Athletic Reserves	**30**	**13**	**4**	**13**	**47**	**43**	**43**
Northfield Town Reserves	30	12	7	11	56	53	43
Enville Athletic Reserves	30	12	6	12	55	51	42
Knowle Reserves	30	11	5	14	61	68	38
Brownhills Town Reserves	30	12	3	15	48	65	36
Wellesbourne Reserves	30	10	4	16	44	77	34
Massey Ferguson Reserves	30	8	9	13	59	72	30
Chelmsley Town Reserves	30	8	6	16	38	78	30
Blackheath Invensys Reserves	30	8	4	18	57	78	28
Continental Star Reserves	30	8	2	20	50	72	26
Wilmcote Sports & Social Reserves	30	4	4	22	31	108	16

Loughborough Athletic Reserves resigned when their record was:

	5	0	0	5	0	21	0

Brownhills Town Reserves and Massey Ferguson Reserves each had 3 points deducted. Wellesbourne Reserves were replaced by their first XI who were relegated from Division One. The Reserves of Alvechurch, Enville Athletic and Blackheath Invensys left.
Halfords joined from the Stratford Alliance, Handsworth Wesleyan Youth joined from the Birmingham A.F.A. and Littleton, Birmingham United, Droitwich Sports and the Reserves of Coleshill Town, Chasetown and Rugby Town also joined.

2001-02   Premier Division

Grosvenor Park	42	31	4	7	111	39	97
Coventry Sphinx	42	27	13	2	91	41	94
Nuneaton Griff	42	26	6	10	98	54	84
Romulus	42	22	7	13	88	59	73
Feckenham	42	20	11	11	78	64	71
Pershore Town	42	20	7	15	86	68	67
West Midlands Police	42	18	7	17	69	75	61
Coventry Marconi	42	16	12	14	74	66	60
Massey Ferguson	42	17	9	16	82	81	60
Coleshill Town	42	18	5	19	76	68	59
Shirley Town	42	18	5	19	97	102	59
Handsworth Continental Star	42	16	9	17	76	75	57
Highgate United	42	13	12	17	70	74	51
Kings Heath	42	14	9	19	61	71	51
Meir KA	42	13	11	18	64	71	50
Handrahan Timbers	42	12	13	17	49	66	49
Cheslyn Hay	42	14	6	22	51	83	48
County Sports	42	11	13	18	64	108	46
Bolehall Swifts	42	11	11	20	68	84	44
Alvechurch	42	10	10	22	58	79	40
Alveston	42	11	5	26	56	89	38
Southam United	42	8	7	27	52	102	31

County Sports merged with Fernhill Heath Old Boys (from Division Two) to form Fernhill County Sports.
Handsworth Continental Star changed name back to Continental Star.
Grosvenor Park moved to the Midland Alliance and Shirley Town left.

Division One

Rugby Town	**36**	**30**	**3**	**3**	**100**	**25**	**93**
Leamington	**36**	**28**	**6**	**2**	**107**	**30**	**90**
Knowle	36	23	8	5	91	41	77
Loughborough	36	18	8	10	77	45	62
Fairfield Villa	36	15	6	15	70	87	51
Thimblemill R.E.C.	36	15	5	16	72	69	50
Brownhills Town	36	15	5	16	70	70	50
Dudley Sports	36	14	7	15	66	55	49
Polesworth North Warwick	36	13	9	14	72	57	48
Wilmcote Sports & Social	36	13	7	16	64	68	46
Mile Oak Rovers	36	14	2	20	59	67	44
Handsaker	36	11	10	15	39	66	43
Old Hill Town	36	13	3	20	51	70	42
Blackheath Invensys	36	11	6	19	43	77	39
Northfield Town	36	9	11	16	44	64	38
Burntwood Town	36	11	4	21	45	85	37
Cadbury Athletic	36	11	3	22	47	77	36
Holly Lane	36	10	8	18	52	76	35
Kenilworth Town	36	10	5	21	56	96	35

Holly Lane had 3 points deducted.
Blackheath Invensys changed their name to Blackheath.
Mile Oak Rovers left. Bloxwich Town joined as a newly re-formed club.

Division Two

Burman Hi-Ton	30	26	1	3	96	26	79
Stockingford AA	30	23	3	4	77	28	72
Enville Athletic	30	20	8	2	91	33	68
Barnt Green Spartak	30	19	4	7	64	42	61
Central Ajax	30	15	3	12	46	40	48
Leamington Hibernian	30	13	5	12	58	51	44
Wilncote Sports	30	12	7	11	55	55	43
West Midlands Police Reserves	30	12	5	13	55	51	41
Earlswood Town	30	9	9	12	42	43	36
Droitwich Spa	30	10	3	17	46	58	33
Fernhill Heath Old Boys	30	9	5	16	50	59	32
West Hagley	30	8	8	14	40	61	32
Cadbury Athletic Reserves	30	8	4	18	46	71	28
Chelmsley Town	30	7	9	14	33	63	27
Archdale '73'	30	7	6	17	50	81	27
Kenilworth Wardens	30	1	2	27	22	109	5

Chelmsley Town had 3 points deducted.
Burman Hi-Ton changed their name to Pilkington XXX.
Fernhill Heath Old Boys merged with County Sports (from the Premier Division) and became Fernhill County Sports Reserves.
Wilncote Sports left.

Division Three

Littleton	30	26	4	0	107	24	82
Halfords	30	21	7	2	72	23	70
Handsworth Wesleyan Youth	30	17	5	8	85	62	56
Droitwich Sports	30	16	5	9	100	54	53
Coleshill Town Reserves	30	14	8	8	68	47	50
Knowle Reserves	30	15	3	12	48	50	48
Massey Ferguson Reserves	30	13	7	10	76	59	46
Chasetown Reserves	30	13	5	12	62	47	44
Northfield Town Reserves	30	12	6	12	63	56	42
Handsworth Continental Star Res.	30	11	8	11	63	55	41
Wellesbourne	30	11	5	14	58	58	38
Rugby Town Reserves	30	11	3	16	59	82	36
Brownhills Town Reserves	30	9	5	16	47	65	32
Wilmcote Sports & Social Reserves	30	7	2	21	42	88	23
Chelmsley Town Reserves	30	3	5	22	29	82	14
Birmingham United	30	1	2	27	30	157	5

Handsworth Wesleyan Youth changed their name to Handsworth United.
Chasetown replaced their Reserves with their "A" team and Droitwich Sports, Brownhills Town Reserves and Chelmsley Town Reserves left.
Newhall United joined from the Burton & District League, Inkberrow joined from the Worcester & District League, Birchfield Oaklands joined after re-forming and the Reserves of Romulus, Tipton Town and Kenilworth Town joined.

2002-03

Premier Division

Alvechurch	42	30	7	5	126	48	97
Coventry Marconi	42	29	5	8	94	37	92
Leamington	42	27	9	6	92	48	90
Bolehall Swifts	42	27	5	10	82	53	86
Romulus	42	24	5	13	107	58	77
Rugby Town	42	22	10	10	90	52	76
Coventry Sphinx	42	23	6	13	95	72	75
Fernhill County Sports	42	21	8	13	74	59	71
Highgate United	42	23	3	16	95	67	69
Meir KA	42	21	6	15	94	75	69
Castle Vale Kings Heath	42	19	6	17	86	66	63
Nuneaton Griff	42	17	3	22	66	80	54
Continental Star	42	14	9	19	86	88	51
Coleshill Town	42	13	9	20	54	68	48
Pershore Town	42	13	7	22	74	86	46
Massey Ferguson	42	13	7	22	85	112	46
Feckenham	42	12	6	24	66	85	42
West Midlands Police	42	11	9	22	56	87	42
Handrahan Timbers	42	11	8	23	57	73	41
Alveston	42	9	7	26	66	114	34
Southam United	42	7	2	33	43	162	23
Cheslyn Hay	42	4	7	31	47	145	19

Highgate United had 3 points deducted.
Kings Heath changed their name to Castle Vale Kings Heath during the season. Alvechurch moved to the Midland Alliance and Fernhill County Sports, Handrahan Timbers and Cheslyn Hay also left.
Brocton joined from the Midland League and Shifnal Town joined from the Midland Alliance.

Division One

Knowle	36	27	3	6	104	40	84
Stockingford AA	36	26	4	6	100	45	82
Pilkington XXX	36	23	5	8	92	48	74
Dudley Sports	36	24	1	11	78	47	73
Polesworth North Warwick	36	20	3	13	66	46	63
Fairfield Villa	36	18	7	11	61	53	61
Wilmcote Sports & Social	36	16	5	15	65	63	53
Northfield Town	36	15	4	17	72	71	49
Kenilworth Town	36	14	6	16	69	82	48
Blackheath	36	12	10	14	69	73	46
Loughborough	36	11	11	14	59	57	44
Thimblemill R.E.C.	36	11	10	15	69	67	43
Burntwood Town	36	11	9	16	49	69	42
Cadbury Athletic	36	11	6	19	55	72	39
Handsaker	36	11	6	19	39	64	39
Old Hill Town	36	10	8	18	70	83	38
Bloxwich Town	36	11	3	22	59	82	36
Holly Lane	36	10	4	22	54	101	34
Brownhills Town	36	5	7	24	31	98	22

Holly Lane left.

Division Two

Barnt Green Spartak	28	20	4	4	85	31	64
Littleton	28	20	1	7	78	32	61
Droitwich Spa	28	14	7	7	65	47	49
Halfords	28	14	6	8	47	36	48
Fernhill County Sports Reserves	28	11	6	11	49	44	39
Enville Athletic	28	11	9	8	34	39	39
Cadbury Athletic Reserves	28	10	8	10	54	56	38
West Midlands Police Reserves	28	10	7	11	51	58	37
Earlswood Town	28	9	8	11	38	39	35
West Hagley	28	9	8	11	37	50	35
Leamington Hibernian	28	8	8	12	45	57	32
Archdale '73'	28	9	5	14	48	70	32
Central Ajax	28	9	3	16	55	56	27
Handsworth United	28	9	4	15	43	72	22
Chelmsley Town	28	2	6	20	38	80	12

Kenilworth Wardens resigned when their record was:

	16	1	3	12	24	52	6

Central Ajax and Enville Athletic each had 3 points deducted.
Handsworth United had 9 points deducted.
Fernhill County Sports Reserves became Fernhill Heath Sports.
Halfords left and joined the Stratford Alliance.
Heather St. Johns joined from the Leicester & District League and changed their name to Heather Athletic.

Division Three

Wellesbourne	30	24	4	2	129	43	76
Newhall United	30	22	3	5	107	48	69
Tipton Town Reserves	30	19	5	6	82	52	62
Continental Star Reserves	30	17	5	8	102	53	56
Chasetown "A"	30	17	3	10	88	62	54
Massey Ferguson Reserves	30	15	3	12	95	64	48
Inkberrow	30	14	4	12	54	50	46
Romulus Reserves	30	14	2	14	58	73	44
Knowle Reserves	30	12	5	13	82	73	41
Birchfield Oaklands	30	13	1	16	81	85	40
Coleshill Town Reserves	30	12	3	15	63	67	39
Northfield Town Reserves	30	10	3	17	41	73	33
Wilmcote Sports & Social Reserves	30	7	4	19	43	104	25
Kenilworth Town Reserves	30	7	3	20	51	108	24
Birmingham United	30	5	4	21	56	105	19
Rugby Town Reserves	30	5	2	23	50	122	17

Birchfield Oaklands, Coleshill Town Reserves and Rugby Town Reserves each had 3 points deducted.
Birchfield Oaklands, Chasetown "A" and the Reserves of Romulus, Coleshill Town and Rugby Town Reserves left.
Attleborough Village joined from the Coventry Alliance, Blackheath Reserves joined from the Kidderminster League and University of Birmingham, Mile Oak Rovers, Himley Athletic and the Reserves of Feckenham, Castle Vale Kings Heath, Bolehall Swifts and Heather Athletic also joined.

2003-04
Premier Division

Romulus	40	31	2	7	128	44	95
Leamington	40	30	4	6	101	36	94
Rugby Town	40	25	5	10	80	55	80
Coventry Sphinx	40	23	8	9	74	55	77
Feckenham	40	21	8	11	79	63	71
Coventry Marconi	40	22	4	14	84	53	70
Meir KA	40	18	11	11	89	68	65
Nuneaton Griff	40	15	15	10	74	62	60
Castle Vale Kings Heath	40	17	8	15	76	72	59
Dudley Sports	40	16	9	15	84	64	57
West Midlands Police	40	16	9	15	67	78	57
Highgate United	40	15	11	14	62	52	56
Bolehall Swifts	40	16	8	16	67	78	56
Brocton	40	15	10	15	53	59	55
Pershore Town	40	10	15	15	65	83	45
Shifnal Town	40	11	10	19	44	52	43
Massey Ferguson	40	12	5	23	65	93	41
Coleshill Town	40	11	5	24	49	83	38
Continental Star	40	6	9	25	53	88	27
Southam United	40	3	6	31	33	115	15
Alveston	40	2	8	30	29	103	14

Castle Vale Kings Heath became Castle Vale KH.
Romulus moved to the Midland Alliance and Rugby Town disbanded.

Division One

Barnt Green Spartak	34	25	2	7	90	41	77
Pilkington XXX	34	21	3	10	84	52	66
Littleton	33	18	7	8	64	41	61
Polesworth North Warwick	33	17	8	8	75	46	59
Old Hill Town	34	16	7	11	69	59	55
Cadbury Athletic	34	16	5	13	70	57	53
Bloxwich Town	34	14	10	10	53	43	52
Northfield Town	33	14	8	11	79	61	50
# Knowle	33	13	9	11	56	39	48
# Wilmcote Sports & Social	34	15	4	15	49	61	49
Thimblemill R.E.C.	34	14	4	16	64	74	46
Burntwood Town	33	13	4	16	59	66	43
Fairfield Villa	34	11	6	17	44	64	39
# Stockingford AA	33	10	7	16	61	82	34
# Blackheath	34	9	7	18	40	59	34
Kenilworth Town	34	6	5	23	34	90	23
Loughborough	33	4	8	21	30	74	20

Stockingford AA had 3 points deducted.
Handsaker resigned when their record was:

	27	9	4	14	34	46	31

It was decided that other clubs' results against them would stand and that final positions would be decided on average points per game. Clubs affected are denoted with "#".
Blackheath left and Atherstone Town joined as a re-formed club.

Division Two

Wellesbourne	32	23	5	4	94	31	74
Enville Athletic	32	20	6	6	84	45	66
Newhall United	32	17	7	8	89	43	58
Earlswood Town	32	15	11	6	67	36	56
Heather Athletic	32	17	5	10	68	44	56
Archdale '73'	32	17	8	7	49	25	56
Tipton Town Reserves	32	15	9	8	71	40	54
West Hagley	32	15	8	9	44	37	53
Leamington Hibernian	32	11	6	15	63	67	39
Droitwich Spa	32	10	8	14	59	63	38
Continental Star Reserves	32	10	5	17	44	65	35
West Midlands Police Reserves	32	8	9	15	45	64	33
Handsworth United	32	9	6	17	43	74	33
Fernhill Heath Sports	32	8	9	15	48	75	30
Cadbury Athletic Reserves	32	5	10	17	42	77	25
Central Ajax	32	6	5	21	37	94	23
Chelmsley Town	32	4	7	21	38	105	19

Brownhills Town resigned when their record was:

	9	4	2	3	15	18	14

Archdale '73' and Fernhill Heath Sports each had 3 points deducted.
Fernhill Heath Sports changed their name to Nunnery Wood Sports and Central Ajax changed their name to Warwick Town.
Wellesbourne left.

Division Three

University of Birmingham	28	20	6	2	88	27	66
Castle Vale Kings Heath Res.	28	17	7	4	54	16	58
Feckenham Reserves	28	17	3	8	55	33	54
Attleborough Village	28	14	5	9	53	37	47
Mile Oak Rovers	28	13	6	9	66	43	45
Wilmcote Sports & Social Reserves	28	12	7	9	67	45	43
Inkberrow	28	10	9	9	59	59	39
Himley Athletic	28	11	8	9	69	47	38
Blackheath Reserves	28	10	5	13	37	40	35
Knowle Reserves	28	9	8	11	43	51	35
Northfield Town Reserves	28	10	3	15	44	50	33
Birmingham United	28	11	2	15	68	75	32
Bolehall Swifts Reserves	28	8	7	13	40	58	31
Heather Athletic Reserves	28	6	4	18	32	68	22
Kenilworth Town Reserves	28	2	0	26	18	144	6

Massey Ferguson Reserves resigned when their record was:

	9	1	1	7	12	40	4

Himley Athletic and Birmingham United each had 3 points deducted. Blackheath Reserves left. Coton Green joined from the Birmingham A.F.A., Droitwich Spa Reserves joined from the Worcester & District League, Shipston Excelsior joined from the Stratford-upon-Avon Alliance, Greenhill and Atherstone Town Reserves joined as new clubs and Himley Athletic Reserves also joined.

2004-05   Premier Division

Leamington	42	35	4	3	132	40	109
Coventry Sphinx	42	28	6	8	137	73	90
Coventry Marconi	42	28	4	10	111	55	88
Bloxwich Town	42	26	7	9	91	55	85
Barnt Green Spartak	42	22	11	9	93	60	77
Southam United	42	23	5	14	84	68	74
Brocton	42	18	11	13	89	61	65
Feckenham	42	19	10	13	85	78	61
Coleshill Town	42	19	4	19	80	78	61
Castle Vale KH	42	19	4	19	79	77	61
Bolehall Swifts	42	16	9	17	67	75	57
Nuneaton Griff	42	17	4	21	75	79	55
Dudley Sports	42	15	10	17	64	71	55
Meir KA	42	15	6	21	88	91	51
Pilkington XXX	42	12	11	19	75	89	47
Pershore Town	42	13	6	23	75	95	45
Shifnal Town	42	12	9	21	55	82	45
Highgate United	42	12	8	22	50	94	44
Massey Ferguson	42	13	2	27	57	88	38
Continental Star	42	10	6	26	56	108	36
Alveston	42	9	5	28	59	122	32
West Midlands Police	42	8	4	30	47	110	28

Massey Ferguson had 3 points deducted. Feckenham had 6 points deducted. Castle Vale KH changed their name to Castle Vale and Coventry Marconi changed their name to Coventry Copsewood. Leamington moved to the Midland Alliance. Bloxwich Town also left. Bridgnorth Town joined from the Midland Alliance.

Division One

Atherstone Town	34	27	5	2	108	25	86
Cadbury Athletic	34	27	2	5	103	45	83
Polesworth North Warwick	34	19	6	9	77	48	63
Littleton	34	18	7	9	64	40	61
Knowle	34	16	10	8	70	51	58
Old Hill Town	34	16	7	11	79	56	55
Northfield Town	34	16	5	13	63	62	53
Stockingford AA	34	14	6	14	66	65	48
Wilmcote Sports & Social	34	14	4	16	67	60	43
Tipton Town Reserves	34	13	7	14	63	50	43
Loughborough	34	11	8	15	60	60	41
Thimblemill R.E.C.	34	12	6	16	61	78	39
Heather Athletic	34	11	6	17	53	73	39
Newhall United	34	10	5	19	61	90	35
Burntwood Town	34	8	8	18	58	84	32
Leamington Hibernian	34	8	8	18	59	76	29
Fairfield Villa	34	8	4	22	37	82	28
Kenilworth Town	34	5	2	27	31	116	17

Wilmcote Sports & Social, Tipton Town Reserves, Thimblemill R.E.C. and Leamington Hibernian each had 3 points deducted.
Wilmcote Sports & Social changed their name to Ettington and Kenilworth Town changed their name to Kenilworth Town KH.
Old Hill Town and Tipton Town Reserves left.

Division Two

Archdale '73'	34	24	4	6	98	35	76
Handsworth United	34	23	3	8	86	33	72
University of Birmingham	34	21	6	7	79	34	69
Mile Oak Rovers	34	20	5	9	77	44	65
West Midlands Police Reserves	34	19	6	9	62	40	63
Droitwich Spa	34	17	10	7	85	45	61
West Hagley	34	18	6	10	61	44	60
Earlswood Town	34	18	3	13	48	50	57
Castle Vale KH Reserves	34	15	7	12	79	58	52
Himley Athletic	34	13	8	13	72	63	47
Chelmsley Town	34	13	6	15	56	67	45
Feckenham Reserves	34	12	7	15	61	57	43
Cadbury Athletic Reserves	34	10	5	19	51	77	35
Nunnery Wood Sports	34	9	5	20	46	61	32
Enville Athletic	34	9	4	21	61	105	31
Continental Star Reserves	34	7	4	23	47	110	25
Warwick Town	34	7	2	25	47	98	23
Attleborough Village	34	4	3	27	27	122	15

Castle Vale KH Reserves, Feckenham Reserves, Enville Athletic and Warwick Town each had 3 points deducted.
Bartley Green joined from the Birmingham A.F.A.
West Midlands Police Reserves and Attleborough Village left.

Division Three

Coton Green	25	18	5	2	56	14	59
Kenilworth Town Reserves	26	18	3	5	96	39	57
Atherstone Town Reserves	25	17	2	6	53	32	53
Knowle Reserves	25	12	7	6	59	42	43
Bolehall Swifts Reserves	26	11	6	9	55	40	39
Greenhill	26	9	8	9	39	39	35
Studley Entaco	23	10	8	5	46	46	32
Wilmcote Sports & Social Reserves	26	9	5	12	47	55	32
Droitwich Spa Reserves	26	8	5	13	37	51	29
Heather Athletic Reserves	26	7	7	12	34	50	28
Inkberrow	26	8	6	12	45	45	27
Shipston Excelsior	26	5	8	13	34	60	23
Northfield Town Reserves	26	5	4	17	27	49	19
Himley Athletic Reserves	26	3	4	19	25	91	12

Birmingham United resigned when their record was:

	10	4	1	5	17	28	13

Three of Studley Entaco's games were not played.
Studley Entaco had 6 points deducted. Inkberrow had 3 points deducted. Himley Athletic Reserves had 1 point deducted.
Studley Entaco, Inkberrow and the Reserves of Kenilworth Town, Atherstone Town and Himley Athletic left. Perrywood joined from the Worcester & District League and Wellesbourne and the Reserves of Halesowen Town, Coventry Sphinx, Barnt Green Spartak, Worcester City, Coleshill Town and Chelmsley Town also joined.

2005-06   Premier Division

Atherstone Town	42	32	7	3	131	27	103
Coventry Sphinx	42	33	4	5	150	61	103
Barnt Green Spartak	42	28	3	11	82	51	87
Feckenham	42	25	6	11	107	64	81
Bridgnorth Town	42	24	7	11	75	48	79
Bolehall Swifts	42	24	6	12	90	59	78
Shifnal Town	42	23	8	11	86	44	77
Nuneaton Griff	42	19	6	17	73	72	63
Castle Vale	42	18	8	16	73	76	62
Alveston	42	18	4	20	65	61	58
Coleshill Town	42	14	9	19	79	93	51
Brocton	42	13	10	19	56	70	49
Southam United	42	13	9	20	56	65	48
Highgate United	42	13	8	21	51	86	47
Coventry Copsewood	42	14	7	21	56	79	46
Pershore Town	42	14	3	25	63	88	45
Meir KA	42	12	9	21	55	92	45
Dudley Sports	42	11	11	20	51	71	44
Pilkington XXX	42	11	8	23	62	108	41
Massey Ferguson	42	11	5	26	46	91	38
Cadbury Athletic	42	11	8	23	68	92	37
Continental Star	42	5	6	31	51	128	21

Coventry Copsewood had 3 points deducted.
Cadbury Athletic had 4 points deducted.
Bridgnorth Town, Shifnal Town and Dudley Sports moved to the WMRL and Atherstone Town moved to the Midland Alliance.
Heath Hayes, Walsall Wood and Brereton Social joined from the WMRL.

Division One

Knowle	34	21	8	5	62	22	71
Northfield Town	34	20	9	5	84	30	69
Ettington	34	19	4	11	62	50	61
Fairfield Villa	34	18	5	11	59	43	59
Burntwood Town	34	15	6	13	57	58	51
Thimblemill R.E.C.	34	15	6	13	59	66	51
Stockingford AA	34	14	8	12	75	54	50
Polesworth North Warwick	34	14	8	12	64	49	50
Mile Oak Rovers	34	14	6	14	49	43	48
Archdale '73'	34	13	7	14	48	60	46
Handsworth United	34	14	5	15	81	77	44
Heather Athletic	34	12	8	14	45	49	44
Littleton	34	12	3	19	61	70	39
Loughborough	34	11	6	17	42	70	39
West Midlands Police	34	11	4	19	49	59	37
Leamington Hibernian	34	10	5	19	42	61	35
Newhall United	34	8	11	15	46	74	32
Kenilworth Town KH	34	8	5	21	38	88	29

Handsworth United and Newhall United each had 3 points deducted.
Handsworth United changed their name to Birmingham Academy but then left. Loughborough moved to the North Leicestershire League and Polesworth North Warwick disbanded.

Division Two

Bartley Green	26	17	7	2	67	26	58
University of Birmingham	25	16	5	4	69	24	53
Earlswood Town	26	14	7	5	47	27	49
Coton Green	26	11	9	6	47	42	42
Enville Athletic	26	11	5	10	58	54	38
Feckenham Reserves	26	12	2	12	41	43	38
Droitwich Spa	25	10	5	10	31	30	35
Cadbury Athletic Reserves	25	10	3	12	39	42	33
West Hagley	26	9	6	11	51	50	30
Continental Star Reserves	25	7	6	12	42	58	27
Castle Vale Reserves	*25*	*7*	*5*	*13*	*34*	*60*	*26*
Chelmsley Town	25	6	5	14	45	64	23
Warwick Town	25	5	7	13	35	45	22
Himley Athletic	19	3	2	14	22	63	11

West Hagley had 3 points deducted.
Himley Athletic resigned during the season but their record was allowed to stand.
Nunnery Wood Sports also resigned but their record was deleted:

	5	1	0	4	8	14	3

Castle Vale Reserves became Castle Vale JKS and West Hagley left.
Wernley Athletic joined as a new club.

Division Three

Halesowen Town Reserves	28	18	6	4	84	25	60
Coventry Sphinx Reserves	28	18	6	4	79	22	60
Perrywood	28	18	5	5	66	36	59
Barnt Green Spartak Reserves	28	17	4	7	58	41	55
Worcester City "A"	28	16	5	7	54	36	53
Greenhill	28	16	2	10	49	42	50
Coleshill Town Reserves	28	14	7	7	53	34	49
Droitwich Spa Reserves	28	11	6	11	52	62	39
Knowle Reserves	28	11	5	12	50	57	38
Shipston Excelsior	28	10	5	13	47	65	35
Heather Athletic Reserves	28	7	8	13	25	43	29
Northfield Town Reserves	28	7	4	17	43	64	25
Wellesbourne	28	3	3	22	35	88	12
Chelmsley Town Reserves	28	2	5	21	27	71	11
Ettington Reserves	28	2	9	17	38	74	15

Ettington Reserves had 6 points deducted.
Bolehall Swifts Reserves resigned when their record was:

	4	0	0	4	3	28	0

Wellesbourne and the Reserves of Halesowen Town, Barnt Green Spartak and Coleshill Town left.
BNJS Mann & Co., Studley Athletic and Dosthill Colts joined as new clubs. Kenilworth Town KH and Burntwood Town Reserves also joined.

2006-07 Premier Division

Coventry Sphinx	40	29	7	4	110	40	94
Castle Vale	40	26	7	7	103	47	85
Highgate United	40	25	9	6	90	38	81
Coleshill Town	40	23	7	10	85	43	76
Pilkington XXX	40	21	11	8	65	53	74
Southam United	40	19	7	14	64	67	64
Bolehall Swifts	40	16	12	12	81	67	60
Heath Hayes	40	17	8	15	74	70	56
Barnt Green Spartak	40	16	9	15	72	57	54
Meir KA	40	15	9	16	65	62	54
Nuneaton Griff	40	15	8	17	85	71	53
Walsall Wood	40	14	11	15	50	60	53
Massey Ferguson	40	14	6	20	56	65	48
Pershore Town	40	14	6	20	66	86	48
Brocton	40	12	9	19	51	70	45
Brereton Social	40	11	9	20	49	80	42
Cadbury Athletic	40	11	9	20	48	85	42
Feckenham	40	9	10	21	50	75	37
Continental Star	40	10	7	23	59	89	36
Coventry Copsewood	40	8	11	21	39	78	35
Alveston	40	4	10	26	37	96	22

Continental Star had 1 point deducted. Barnt Green Spartak, Heath Hayes and Highgate United each had 3 points deducted.

Division One

Bartley Green	30	20	1	9	70	31	61
Northfield Town	30	19	3	8	60	34	60
Stockingford AA	30	17	5	8	57	36	56
Fairfield Villa	30	16	4	10	61	53	52
University of Birmingham	30	13	8	9	65	36	47
Heather Athletic	30	13	7	10	53	36	46
Mile Oak Rovers	30	13	6	11	56	45	45
Knowle	30	13	6	11	50	39	45
Littleton	30	13	6	11	55	45	45
Thimblemill R.E.C.	30	12	9	9	43	39	41
Archdale '73'	30	11	6	13	53	61	39
Newhall United	30	11	6	13	49	58	36
Leamington Hibernian	30	7	9	14	31	51	30
West Midlands Police	30	7	7	16	36	58	28
Ettington	30	7	3	20	32	82	24
Burntwood Town	30	4	2	24	22	89	14

Kenilworth Town KH resigned and their record was deleted. Thimblemill R.E.C. had 4 points deducted. Newhall United had 3 points deducted.

Division Two

Wernley Athletic	24	19	2	3	98	30	59
Coton Green	24	17	4	3	62	26	55
Droitwich Spa	24	15	2	7	39	26	47
Earlswood Town	24	13	4	7	49	33	43
Coventry Sphinx Reserves	24	13	3	8	61	43	42
Chelmsley Town	24	10	4	10	49	54	34
Warwick Town	24	9	3	12	39	61	30
Continental Star Reserves	24	8	5	11	31	44	29
Cadbury Athletic Reserves	24	6	6	12	39	57	24
Feckenham Reserves	24	6	6	12	24	44	24
Worcester City "A"	24	7	2	15	43	50	23
Enville Athletic	24	6	3	15	41	60	21
Perrywood	24	3	4	17	26	73	10

Perrywood had 3 points deducted.

Division Three

Castle Vale JKS	26	17	7	2	70	28	58
Ettington Reserves	26	17	4	5	76	50	55
BNJS Mann & Co.	26	16	3	7	69	33	51
Greenhill	26	15	2	9	45	36	47
Dosthill Colts	26	12	7	7	63	46	43
Chelmsley Town Reserves	26	10	8	8	35	39	38
Droitwich Spa Reserves	26	8	12	6	28	27	36
Burntwood Town Reserves	26	9	6	11	39	41	33
Northfield Town Reserves	26	8	7	11	37	38	31
Knowle Reserves	26	8	7	11	49	55	31
Heather Athletic Reserves	26	7	6	13	36	51	24
Shipston Excelsior	26	4	8	14	36	67	20
Studley Athletic	26	5	3	18	36	76	18
Kenilworth Town KH	26	3	6	17	21	53	15

Heather Athletic Reserves had 3 points deducted.

HELLENIC LEAGUE

The Hellenic League was formed on the initiative of a referee, Norman Matthews who called a meeting in Oxford late in 1952 at which it was agreed that there was a need for a new league to operate in the area between the Western and London Leagues. It was originally intended to call the competition the Coronation League but the F.A. withdrew their approval for this title and so it was decided to adopt the name Hellenic League instead. The 16 original members were: Bicester Town, Chipping Norton Town, Didcot Town, Headington United Reserves, Pressed Steel (Oxford), and Witney Town all of whom moved from the Oxfordshire Senior League; Abingdon Town, Amersham Town and Leighton United from the Spartan League; Stokenchurch, Thatcham and Wallingford Town from the Reading & District League; Buckingham Town from the North Buckinghamshire League; Newbury Town from the Metropolitan League; Princes Risborough Town from the Aylesbury & District League and Staines Town from the Parthenon League.

Several of the published tables contained errors. Additional research has succeeded in correcting many of these, totals that still do not balance are shown below the relevant columns in italics.

1953-54

Didcot Town	30	22	4	4	107	44	48
Witney Town	30	21	0	9	123	56	42
Pressed Steel (Oxford)	30	18	6	6	89	47	42
Wallingford Town	30	20	1	9	91	64	41
Chipping Norton Town	30	17	6	7	97	49	40
Headington United Reserves	30	16	5	9	81	69	37
Buckingham Town	30	15	6	9	94	75	36
Amersham Town	30	12	5	13	68	69	29
Staines Town	30	13	3	14	60	67	29
Newbury Town	30	10	5	15	64	82	25
Abingdon Town	30	10	4	16	73	96	24
Leighton United	30	10	4	16	57	78	24
Bicester Town	30	10	3	17	72	77	23
Stokenchurch	30	10	2	18	62	94	22
Thatcham	30	7	4	19	45	79	18
Princes Risborough Town	30	0	0	30	33	160	0
					1216	*1206*	

Kidlington joined from the Oxfordshire Senior League and Rickmansworth Town joined from the Spartan League.

1954-55

Witney Town	34	23	5	6	133	60	51
Bicester Town	34	23	2	9	123	77	48
Pressed Steel (Oxford)	34	20	5	9	100	63	45
Newbury Town	34	20	2	12	110	82	42
Staines Town	34	17	5	12	88	70	39
Didcot Town	34	17	5	12	100	85	39
Thatcham	34	15	9	10	96	92	39
Chipping Norton Town	34	16	6	12	99	77	38
Stokenchurch	34	15	6	13	108	89	36
Headington United Reserves	34	17	2	15	90	79	36
Wallingford Town	34	13	4	17	99	96	30
Amersham Town	34	12	4	18	104	112	28
Rickmansworth Town	34	11	6	17	78	99	28
Kidlington	34	11	6	17	74	106	28
Buckingham Town	34	12	3	19	90	116	27
Abingdon Town	34	9	6	19	64	89	24
Princes Risborough Town	34	9	1	24	58	148	19
Leighton United	34	5	5	24	61	135	15

Leighton United moved to the South Midlands League and Dunstable Town Reserves joined from the South Midlands League.

1955-56

Headington United Reserves	34	27	2	5	128	44	56
Staines Town	34	25	4	5	110	59	54
Witney Town	34	22	4	8	126	61	48
Bicester Town	34	18	6	10	97	76	42
Dunstable Town Reserves	34	19	2	13	121	77	40
Pressed Steel (Oxford)	34	17	5	12	104	89	39
Kidlington	34	17	5	12	99	94	39
Abingdon Town	34	16	4	14	81	85	36
Didcot Town	34	15	3	16	96	91	33
Rickmansworth Town	34	14	3	17	92	94	31
Amersham Town	34	14	3	17	95	113	31
Chipping Norton Town	34	12	7	15	70	101	31
Newbury Town	34	14	2	18	86	97	30
Buckingham Town	34	13	3	18	74	128	29
Stokenchurch	34	10	7	17	79	85	27
Wallingford Town	34	7	4	23	67	104	18
Thatcham	*34*	*7*	*4*	*23*	*65*	*115*	*18*
Princes Risborough Town	*34*	*4*	*2*	*28*	*52*	*126*	*10*
					1642	1639	

Rickmansworth Town moved to the Parthenon League. Bletchley & Wipac joined from the South Midlands League and Wantage Town joined from the Swindon & District League.
Thatcham and Princes Risborough Town were relegated to a new Division One where they were joined by eight new members: Amersham Town Reserves, Aylesbury Town Corinthians (from the Aylesbury & District League), Bletchley & Wipac Reserves, RAF Halton (Apprentices), Luton Town Colts, Ruislip Town (from the Great Western Combination), Staines Town Reserves and Stokenchurch Reserves.

1956-57

Premier Division

Abingdon Town	32	22	6	4	90	42	50
Stokenchurch	32	23	3	6	114	45	49
Dunstable Town Reserves	32	20	4	8	106	53	44
Witney Town	32	19	5	8	106	58	43
Staines Town	32	20	3	9	102	64	43
Didcot Town	32	19	5	8	88	53	43
Bicester Town	32	17	5	10	88	76	39
Wantage Town	32	17	3	12	78	70	37
Newbury Town	32	10	6	16	99	89	26
Chipping Norton Town	32	11	4	17	87	104	26
Headington United Reserves	32	11	4	17	70	85	26
Kidlington	32	9	6	17	80	107	24
Buckingham Town	32	10	2	20	74	119	22
Bletchley & Wipac	32	10	2	20	45	84	22
Pressed Steel (Cowley)	32	8	4	20	54	93	20
Wallingford Town	32	6	4	22	44	102	16
Amersham Town	32	5	4	23	73	145	14
					1398	1389	

Bletchley & Wipac changed their name to Bletchley Town.
Didcot Town moved to the Metropolitan League and Buckingham Town also left.

Division One

Luton Town Colts	**18**	**16**	**1**	**1**	**103**	**15**	**33**
Aylesbury Town Corinthians	18	14	2	2	68	15	30
Ruislip Town	18	10	4	4	48	27	24
Princes Risborough Town	18	9	4	5	41	38	22
RAF Apprentices (Halton)	18	9	3	6	69	48	21
Stokenchurch Reserves	18	6	6	6	39	50	18
Thatcham	18	5	5	8	32	34	15
Staines Town Reserves	18	3	2	13	22	52	8
Amersham Town Reserves	18	2	1	15	30	107	5
Bletchley & Wipac Reserves	18	1	2	15	18	71	4
					470	457	

Bletchley & Wipac Reserves left.
Aston Clinton joined from the Marsworth League, Hanwell Corinthians joined from the South-West Middlesex League, Hazells (Aylesbury) joined from the Aylesbury & District League, Henley Town joined from the Reading & District League, Stanwell District joined from the Hounslow & District League and Pressed Steel (Cowley) Reserves also joined.

1957-58

Premier Division

Witney Town	30	22	1	7	112	54	45
Dunstable Town Reserves	30	21	2	7	117	60	44
Staines Town	30	18	7	5	100	50	43
Abingdon Town	30	18	4	8	73	46	40
Stokenchurch	30	15	6	9	72	62	36
Luton Town Colts	30	13	4	13	80	65	30
Wantage Town	30	12	4	14	68	67	28
Kidlington	30	13	2	15	84	105	28
Headington United Reserves	30	11	5	14	82	81	27
Pressed Steel (Cowley)	30	11	5	14	56	78	27
Bicester Town	30	11	3	16	73	86	25
Newbury Town	30	10	4	16	77	94	24
Chipping Norton Town	30	10	4	16	58	87	24
Amersham Town	30	8	6	16	70	94	22
Wallingford Town	30	5	9	16	52	83	19
Bletchley Town	30	8	2	20	47	110	18
					1221	1222	

Dunstable Town Reserves moved to the United Counties League and Staines Town moved to the Spartan League. Hungerford Town joined from the Swindon & District League and Yiewsley Reserves also joined.

Division One

Aylesbury Town Corinthians	26	22	2	2	123	35	46
Stanwell District	26	19	3	4	95	52	41
Hanwell Corinthians	26	17	3	6	100	41	37
Thatcham	26	15	4	7	73	48	34
Aston Clinton	26	15	4	7	101	67	34
Hazells (Aylesbury)	26	14	3	9	82	56	31
Staines Town Reserves	26	10	3	13	62	73	23
Henley Town	26	9	5	12	63	79	23
Ruislip Town	26	9	4	13	71	76	22
RAF Apprentices (Halton)	26	10	1	15	70	95	21
Stokenchurch Reserves	26	7	2	17	59	99	16
Princes Risborough Town	26	6	3	17	51	87	15
Pressed Steel (Cowley) Reserves	26	5	2	19	34	98	12
Amersham Town Reserves	26	4	1	21	54	129	9
					1038	1035	

Aylesbury Town Corinthians moved to the Great Western Combination and Staines Town Reserves and Stokenchurch Reserves also left. Abingdon United joined from the North Berkshire League and Bletchley Town Reserves also joined.

1958-59

Premier Division

Abingdon Town	30	24	3	3	113	34	51
Yiewsley Reserves	30	19	8	3	77	33	46
Witney Town	30	17	5	8	74	56	39
Bicester Town	30	15	5	10	86	71	35
Hungerford Town	30	16	2	12	92	78	34
Bletchley Town	30	13	5	12	73	68	31
Stokenchurch	30	11	8	11	80	75	30
Headington United Reserves	30	12	5	13	94	77	29
Luton Town Colts	30	12	3	15	71	67	27
Amersham Town	30	10	7	13	64	72	27
Wantage Town	30	11	5	14	66	82	27
Wallingford Town	30	9	8	13	59	66	26
Newbury Town	30	10	3	17	63	77	23
Pressed Steel (Cowley)	30	8	5	17	53	94	21
Chipping Norton Town	30	8	3	19	61	111	19
Kidlington	30	6	3	21	67	132	15

Bletchley Town moved to the Spartan League and Yiewsley Reserves also left. Thame United joined from the Oxfordshire Senior League and Swindon Town "A" also joined.

Division One

	P	W	D	L	F	A	Pts
Thatcham	24	17	2	5	108	39	36
Hanwell Corinthians	24	16	3	5	99	50	35
Henley Town	24	16	1	7	86	47	33
Princes Risborough Town	24	14	3	7	94	61	31
Hazells (Aylesbury)	24	14	3	7	86	60	31
Stanwell District	24	13	5	6	86	63	31
Abingdon United	24	10	5	9	61	57	25
RAF Apprentices (Halton)	24	10	3	11	57	55	23
Ruislip Town	24	7	5	12	50	79	19
Aston Clinton	24	8	1	15	73	96	17
Amersham Town Reserves	24	6	5	13	61	109	17
Pressed Steel (Cowley) Reserves	24	1	5	18	35	103	7
Bletchley Town Reserves	24	2	3	19	36	113	7

Aston Clinton moved to the Aylesbury & District League and Bletchley Town Reserves also left. Botley United joined from the North Berkshire League and 17 Bn. RAOC (Bicester) also joined.

1959-60

Premier Division

	P	W	D	L	F	A	Pts
Abingdon Town	32	22	6	4	96	29	50
Swindon Town "A"	32	22	2	8	95	44	46
Bicester Town	32	20	3	9	89	65	43
Luton Town Colts	32	19	3	10	100	64	41
Thatcham	32	18	4	10	92	59	40
Hungerford Town	32	17	6	9	95	81	40
Headington United Reserves	32	13	9	10	98	70	35
Witney Town	32	13	7	12	82	71	33
Stokenchurch	32	16	1	15	79	78	33
Thame United	32	14	4	14	84	76	32
Newbury Town	32	14	4	14	68	78	32
Wallingford Town	32	13	4	15	64	86	30
Pressed Steel (Cowley)	32	11	3	18	59	97	25
Amersham Town	32	9	4	19	60	93	22
Kidlington	32	9	4	19	64	106	22
Wantage Town	32	5	3	24	52	120	13
Chipping Norton Town	32	2	3	27	43	103	7

Headington United changed their name to Oxford United.
Luton Town Colts left.

Division One

	P	W	D	L	F	A	Pts
Hazells (Aylesbury)	22	17	1	4	100	33	35
17 Bn. RAOC (Bicester)	22	15	0	7	64	32	30
Botley United	22	12	5	5	73	39	29
Hanwell Corinthians	22	12	3	7	66	44	27
Henley Town	22	11	4	7	70	58	26
RAF Apprentices (Halton)	22	11	2	9	73	58	24
Princes Risborough Town	22	11	2	9	56	54	24
Stanwell District	22	9	5	8	68	52	23
Abingdon United	22	9	2	11	55	63	20
Ruislip Town	22	5	1	16	47	89	11
Amersham Town Reserves	22	3	3	16	37	105	9
Pressed Steel (Cowley) Reserves	22	2	2	18	27	109	6

Amersham Town Reserves and Pressed Steel (Cowley) Reserves left. AERE Harwell and Marston United joined from the Oxfordshire Senior League and Camberley United and Didcot Town Reserves also joined.

1960-61

Premier Division

	P	W	D	L	F	A	Pts
Bicester Town	30	24	4	2	112	43	52
Thame United	30	20	7	3	98	46	47
Hazells (Aylesbury)	30	22	2	6	129	50	46
Oxford United Reserves	30	16	3	11	89	69	35
Hungerford Town	30	15	5	10	86	68	35
Swindon Town "A"	30	14	5	11	71	69	33
Witney Town	30	12	9	9	77	72	33
Wallingford Town	30	13	5	12	94	83	31
Abingdon Town	30	13	5	12	61	60	31
Wantage Town	30	12	5	13	86	69	29
Thatcham	30	9	5	16	63	91	23
Newbury Town	30	8	5	17	53	86	21
Pressed Steel (Cowley)	30	6	7	17	54	84	19
Kidlington	30	7	3	20	51	100	17
Stokenchurch	30	6	3	21	46	116	15
Amersham Town	30	5	3	22	54	128	13
					1224	*1234*	

Amersham Town moved to the London League and Yiewsley Reserves joined.

Division One

	P	W	D	L	F	A	Pts
Chipping Norton Town	26	19	3	4	108	37	41
Camberley United	26	17	5	4	87	43	39
Abingdon United	26	16	2	8	91	52	34
Stanwell District	26	13	6	7	67	58	32
Botley United	26	14	2	10	62	45	30
Princes Risborough Town	26	13	2	11	95	83	28
Marston United	26	11	5	10	84	79	27
Hanwell Corinthians	26	10	5	11	68	69	25
Didcot Town Reserves	26	12	1	13	56	67	25
RAF Apprentices (Halton)	26	10	3	13	76	71	23
17 Bn. RAOC (Bicester)	26	8	4	14	63	96	20
Henley Town	26	7	5	14	54	76	19
Ruislip Town	26	4	3	19	34	107	11
AERE Harwell	26	5	0	21	46	108	10

Ruislip Town moved to the Great Western Combination and 17Bn. RAOC (Bicester), Camberley United and Hanwell Corinthians also left. East Hendred and Faringdon Town joined from the North Berkshire League & Lambourn Sports joined from the Swindon & District League.

1961-62   Premier Division

	P	W	D	L	F	A	Pts
Thame United	32	25	2	5	156	56	52
Yiewsley Reserves	32	20	7	5	100	37	47
Hazells (Aylesbury)	32	22	3	7	127	65	47
Swindon Town "A"	32	20	5	7	101	52	45
Bicester Town	32	19	5	8	99	62	43
Abingdon Town	32	16	7	9	78	53	39
Oxford United Reserves	32	17	5	10	75	60	39
Witney Town	32	17	3	12	86	59	37
Wantage Town	32	12	1	19	66	117	25
Pressed Steel (Cowley)	32	9	6	17	64	90	24
Chipping Norton Town	32	10	4	18	64	114	24
Stokenchurch	32	8	7	17	44	76	23
Hungerford Town	32	8	6	18	60	82	22
Newbury Town	32	9	4	19	74	102	22
Wallingford Town	32	8	4	20	61	101	20
Kidlington	32	8	2	22	54	126	18
Thatcham	32	6	5	21	51	108	17

Swindon Town "A" left.

Division One

	P	W	D	L	F	A	Pts
Botley United	22	19	1	2	85	24	39
Lambourn Sports	22	16	4	2	92	38	36
Henley Town	22	12	4	6	66	45	28
Marston United	22	12	4	6	53	38	28
RAF Apprentices (Halton)	22	9	5	8	66	65	23
East Hendred	22	9	3	10	47	50	21
Abingdon United	22	9	3	10	49	65	21
Didcot Town Reserves	22	6	4	12	35	64	16
Faringdon Town	22	7	1	14	51	61	15
Princes Risborough Town	22	6	2	14	35	55	14
Stanwell District	22	6	1	15	46	80	13
AERE Harwell	22	3	4	15	38	78	10

Stanwell District left.
Amersham Town joined from the London League, Morris Motors joined from the Oxfordshire Senior League. Newbury Town Reserves joined.

1962-63   Premier Division

	P	W	D	L	F	A	Pts
Yiewsley Reserves	30	23	4	3	96	29	50
Thame United	30	22	4	4	111	45	48
Bicester Town	30	19	3	8	91	53	41
Chipping Norton Town	30	17	5	8	74	62	39
Wallingford Town	30	15	6	9	82	53	36
Newbury Town	30	16	2	12	86	50	34
Witney Town	30	13	7	10	71	54	33
Hazells (Aylesbury)	30	14	5	11	70	57	33
Abingdon Town	30	13	6	11	64	58	32
Lambourn Sports	30	12	5	13	77	88	29
Wantage Town	30	13	3	14	57	76	29
Oxford United Reserves	30	9	3	18	53	79	21
Hungerford Town	30	7	4	19	46	95	18
Stokenchurch	30	6	3	21	56	107	15
Pressed Steel (Cowley)	30	4	5	21	32	87	13
Botley United	30	4	1	25	42	115	9

Botley United moved to the North Berkshire League.
Didcot Town joined from the Metropolitan League and Swindon Town "A" also joined.

Division One

Amersham Town	26	25	0	1	149	25	**50**
Morris Motors	26	21	2	3	86	22	**44**
Thatcham	26	21	2	3	87	32	44
Henley Town	26	14	5	7	78	51	33
Marston United	26	13	3	10	49	56	29
Kidlington	26	11	4	11	56	58	26
Newbury Town Reserves	26	10	6	10	48	51	26
Princes Risborough Town	26	7	6	13	41	61	20
Faringdon Town	26	8	3	15	54	78	19
Abingdon United	26	6	7	13	49	73	19
AERE Harwell	26	8	2	16	48	62	18
RAF Apprentices (Halton)	26	7	1	18	63	101	15
East Hendred	26	5	4	17	31	88	14
Didcot Town Reserves	26	2	3	21	31	112	7

East Hendred moved to the North Berkshire League and Didcot Town
Reserves and Newbury Town Reserves also left.

1963-64

Premier Division

Amersham Town	34	23	6	5	105	45	52
Yiewsley Reserves	34	22	4	8	106	56	48
Witney Town	34	22	3	9	124	59	47
Hazells (Aylesbury)	34	21	5	8	100	58	47
Didcot Town	34	20	3	11	88	59	43
Morris Motors	34	19	4	11	102	73	42
Swindon Town "A"	34	19	2	13	111	88	40
Bicester Town	34	18	3	13	101	95	39
Thame United	34	18	1	15	112	78	37
Wallingford Town	34	14	8	12	84	74	36
Abingdon Town	34	12	8	14	77	72	32
Chipping Norton Town	34	12	4	18	76	87	28
Lambourn Sports	34	12	2	20	80	112	26
Newbury Town	34	12	2	20	66	93	26
Oxford United Reserves	34	12	2	20	76	111	26
Hungerford Town	34	7	3	24	53	111	17
Stokenchurch	*34*	*7*	*0*	*27*	*52*	*150*	*14*
Wantage Town	*34*	*6*	*0*	*28*	*50*	*142*	*12*

Yiewsley changed name to Hillingdon Borough. Oxford United moved
their Reserves to the Football Combination and replaced them with
their "A" team.

Division One

Henley Town	18	13	4	1	59	28	30
Kidlington	18	13	3	2	67	38	29
Thatcham	18	10	4	4	44	32	24
Princes Risborough Town	18	6	4	8	44	41	16
Pressed Steel (Cowley)	18	6	4	8	34	32	16
Abingdon United	18	6	4	8	44	48	16
AERE Harwell	18	6	3	9	38	45	15
RAF Apprentices (Halton)	18	6	1	11	50	82	13
Marston United	18	4	3	11	44	58	11
Faringdon Town	18	4	2	12	41	61	10

RAF Apprentices (Halton) left.
Aylesbury Town Corinthians joined from the Great Western
Combination, Dunstable Town Reserves joined from the United
Counties League, Rivet Sports and Waddesdon both joined from the
Aylesbury & District League, Smiths Industries (Witney) and Watlington
both joined from the Oxfordshire Senior League and Oxford Co-Op
Sports also joined.

1964-65

Premier Division

Witney Town	34	24	8	2	101	44	56
Amersham Town	34	23	7	4	95	57	53
Wallingford Town	34	21	5	8	92	61	47
Thame United	34	19	6	9	99	71	44
Didcot Town	34	19	4	11	95	68	42
Oxford United "A"	34	16	5	13	100	72	37
Bicester Town	34	16	5	13	91	68	37
Hillingdon Borough Reserves	34	13	11	10	64	56	37
Hazells (Aylesbury)	34	14	8	12	75	63	36
Swindon Town "A"	34	14	6	14	87	97	34
Morris Motors	34	15	3	16	85	70	33
Newbury Town	34	12	5	17	73	89	29
Chipping Norton Town	34	13	1	20	66	85	27
Abingdon Town	34	8	6	20	61	86	22
Lambourn Sports	34	8	6	20	59	106	22
Kidlington	34	9	3	22	54	87	21
Henley Town	*34*	*8*	*4*	*22*	*57*	*108*	*20*
Hungerford Town	*34*	*5*	*5*	*24*	*54*	*120*	*15*

Division One

Thatcham	30	24	3	3	115	27	51
Waddesdon	30	20	6	4	96	40	46
Dunstable Town Reserves	30	17	7	6	86	49	41
Princes Risborough Town	30	14	6	10	80	65	34
Faringdon Town	30	15	4	11	78	76	34
Marston United	30	16	1	13	68	53	33
Aylesbury Town Corinthians	30	15	3	12	84	75	33
Wantage Town	30	14	4	12	67	60	32
Watlington	30	13	5	12	72	60	31
Abingdon United	30	12	5	13	71	59	29
Smiths Industries (Witney)	30	12	5	13	70	81	29
Pressed Steel (Cowley)	30	13	3	14	68	75	29
Rivet Works (Aylesbury)	30	11	1	16	69	88	25
Stokenchurch	30	6	3	21	66	126	15
Oxford Co-Op Sports	30	4	2	24	51	125	10
AERE Harwell	30	2	4	24	37	119	8

Dunstable Town Reserves moved to the Metropolitan League and
Oxford Co-op Sports also left.
Buckingham Athletic joined from the North Buckinghamshire League
and Aston Clinton also joined.

1965-66

Premier Division

Witney Town	34	25	4	5	134	32	54
Amersham Town	34	20	10	4	104	54	50
Wallingford Town	34	22	4	8	112	58	48
Thame United	34	20	3	11	122	67	43
Hillingdon Borough Reserves	34	20	2	12	105	66	42
Didcot Town	34	16	8	10	77	57	40
Hazells (Aylesbury)	34	15	9	10	88	75	39
Chipping Norton Town	34	15	8	11	76	62	38
Swindon Town "A"	34	16	3	15	92	78	35
Bicester Town	34	15	4	15	86	75	34
Newbury Town	34	15	2	17	70	74	32
Oxford United "A"	34	12	7	15	64	72	31
Waddesdon	34	8	8	18	68	103	24
Thatcham	34	9	6	19	63	100	24
Lambourn Sports	34	10	4	20	70	168	24
Morris Motors	34	9	5	20	58	100	23
Kidlington	*34*	*8*	*2*	*24*	*54*	*116*	*18*
Abingdon Town	*34*	*4*	*5*	*25*	*49*	*135*	*13*

Banbury United Reserves joined from the Warwickshire Combination.
Hillingdon Borough Reserves moved to the Metropolitan League.

Division One

Princes Risborough Town	30	24	3	3	92	26	51
Marston United	30	23	5	2	82	40	51
Henley Town	30	22	3	5	110	41	47
Abingdon United	30	22	2	6	111	33	46
Aston Clinton	30	15	8	7	85	68	38
Watlington	30	15	3	12	83	64	33
Smiths Industries (Witney)	30	13	7	10	75	74	33
Wantage Town	30	15	2	13	67	69	32
Buckingham Athletic	30	13	2	15	66	67	28
Hungerford Town	30	11	5	14	76	73	27
Aylesbury Town Corinthians	30	10	0	20	64	94	20
Rivet Works (Aylesbury)	30	7	5	18	63	90	19
Stokenchurch	30	5	5	20	59	104	15
AERE Harwell	30	7	1	22	49	109	15
Faringdon Town	30	5	3	22	41	112	13
Pressed Steel (Cowley)	30	3	6	21	38	97	12

Faringdon Town left.
Pinehurst joined from the Wiltshire Premier League.

1966-67

Premier Division

Witney Town	34	24	4	6	102	39	52
Hazells (Aylesbury)	34	25	2	7	109	55	52
Morris Motors	34	23	3	8	94	51	49
Banbury United Reserves	34	24	0	10	83	58	48
Didcot Town	34	18	6	10	84	65	42
Wallingford Town	34	20	1	13	78	56	41
Bicester Town	34	16	4	14	83	68	36
Swindon Town "A"	34	14	8	12	69	64	36
Thame United	34	13	9	12	73	62	35
Princes Risborough Town	34	10	11	13	70	65	31
Oxford United "A"	34	12	6	16	72	103	30
Amersham Town	34	13	3	18	75	71	29
Chipping Norton Town	34	13	3	18	78	98	29
Newbury Town	34	11	5	18	49	65	27
Waddesdon	34	8	6	20	47	93	22
Marston United	34	7	7	20	51	91	21
Lambourn Sports	34	7	4	23	54	117	18
Thatcham	34	5	4	25	42	92	14

Oxford United "A" left.

Division One

Pinehurst	30	26	2	2	160	35	54
Abingdon Town	30	20	5	5	84	36	45
Aston Clinton	30	18	6	6	76	43	42
Abingdon United	30	18	2	10	86	42	38
Hungerford Town	30	16	5	9	96	64	37
Henley Town	30	16	5	9	67	56	37
Buckingham Athletic	30	14	5	11	70	71	33
Pressed Steel (Cowley)	30	13	5	12	68	81	31
Smiths Industries (Witney)	30	11	5	14	60	84	27
Kidlington	30	9	8	13	51	62	26
Wantage Town	30	12	2	16	49	70	26
Stokenchurch	30	8	6	16	60	99	22
Watlington	30	8	6	16	41	81	22
Aylesbury Town Corinthians	30	6	6	18	56	82	18
AERE Harwell	30	2	8	20	24	72	12
Rivet Works (Aylesbury)	30	2	6	22	40	110	10

Smiths Industries (Witney) moved to the Witney & District League.
Clanfield joined from the Witney & District League.

1967-68

Premier Division

Hazells (Aylesbury)	32	21	5	6	94	50	47
Witney Town	32	21	3	8	96	53	45
Pinehurst	32	16	11	5	83	52	43
Amersham Town	32	16	7	9	91	59	39
Swindon Town "A"	32	17	4	11	72	57	38
Didcot Town	32	16	6	10	70	60	38
Wallingford Town	32	15	7	10	80	71	37
Bicester Town	32	12	10	10	73	66	34
Morris Motors	32	14	5	13	82	65	33
Thame United	32	13	7	12	83	63	33
Banbury United Reserves	32	13	7	12	57	54	33
Chipping Norton Town	32	14	5	13	59	84	33
Waddesdon	32	10	7	15	59	75	27
Newbury Town	32	9	1	22	48	102	19
Abingdon Town	32	5	7	20	46	75	17
Marston United	32	5	5	22	56	94	15
Princes Risborough Town	32	5	3	24	43	110	13
						1192	1190

Banbury United Reserves left.
Chippenham Town joined from the Wiltshire Premier League.

Division One

Henley Town	30	26	4	0	116	24	56
Aston Clinton	30	22	4	4	112	38	48
Stokenchurch	30	18	5	7	76	48	41
Thatcham	30	16	6	8	72	44	38
Buckingham Athletic	30	17	3	10	83	50	37
Clanfield	30	17	2	11	66	53	36
Abingdon United	30	15	6	9	63	54	36
Kidlington	30	14	3	13	66	69	31
Aylesbury Town Corinthians	30	11	4	15	63	90	26
Wantage Town	30	9	7	14	46	56	25
Watlington	30	9	7	14	49	62	25
Pressed Steel (Cowley)	30	11	2	17	57	89	24
Rivet Works (Aylesbury)	30	6	6	18	43	101	18
Lambourn Sports	30	8	1	21	49	74	17
Hungerford Town	30	4	3	23	43	98	11
AERE Harwell	30	3	5	22	32	86	11

Ernest Turner Sports joined from the Middlesex County League and
Oxford City Reserves also joined.

1968-69

Premier Division

Wallingford Town	32	23	2	7	105	36	48
Pinehurst	32	23	0	9	113	48	46
Morris Motors	32	21	4	7	92	43	46
Thame United	32	19	6	7	82	49	44
Chippenham Town	32	17	5	10	84	50	39
Witney Town	32	15	9	8	63	47	39
Abingdon Town	32	12	11	9	49	46	35
Newbury Town	32	14	5	13	56	69	33
Didcot Town	32	13	7	12	57	60	33
Amersham Town	32	11	7	14	64	61	29
Swindon Town "A"	32	11	7	14	59	89	29
Bicester Town	32	9	8	15	62	73	26
Hazells (Aylesbury)	32	9	7	16	52	60	25
Henley Town	32	9	7	16	44	63	25
Chipping Norton Town	32	9	6	17	59	73	24
Aston Clinton	32	4	6	22	39	113	14
Waddesdon	32	2	5	25	33	152	9

Cirencester Town joined from the Gloucestershire County League.

Division One

Oxford City Reserves	34	24	9	1	125	26	57
Buckingham Athletic	34	24	5	5	97	37	53
Clanfield	34	23	5	6	106	52	51
Ernest Turner Sports	34	23	3	8	85	45	49
Abingdon United	34	16	8	10	81	72	40
Wantage Town	34	16	7	11	69	56	39
Thatcham	34	13	12	9	66	54	38
Marston United	34	15	8	11	80	69	38
Pressed Steel (Cowley)	34	14	6	14	77	77	34
Stokenchurch	34	12	9	13	73	58	33
Rivet Works (Aylesbury)	34	13	5	16	53	64	31
Lambourn Sports	34	11	8	15	77	88	30
Kidlington	34	11	6	17	72	84	28
Hungerford Town	34	8	6	20	45	84	22
AERE Harwell	34	9	3	22	64	123	21
Watlington	34	7	5	22	42	89	19
Princes Risborough Town	34	6	6	22	50	96	18
Aylesbury Town Corinthians	34	3	5	26	34	123	11
					1296	1297	

A.C. Delco joined from the South Midlands League.

1969-70

Premier Division

Thame United	34	29	2	3	94	26	60
Witney Town	34	27	4	3	96	32	58
Abingdon Town	34	18	8	8	59	33	44
Cirencester Town	34	18	6	10	57	42	42
Wallingford Town	34	18	5	11	58	47	41
Didcot Town	34	16	5	13	54	42	37
Buckingham Athletic	34	12	13	9	45	43	37
Bicester Town	34	12	10	12	57	48	34
Chippenham Town	34	14	6	14	63	66	34
Newbury Town	34	14	6	14	41	50	34
Pinehurst	34	11	11	12	54	56	33
Morris Motors	34	11	8	15	43	49	30
Swindon Town "A"	34	10	7	17	45	57	27
Oxford City Reserves	34	11	4	19	48	63	26
Amersham Town	34	10	4	20	42	70	24
Henley Town	34	8	7	19	39	64	23
Chipping Norton Town	34	4	6	24	40	93	14
Hazells (Aylesbury)	34	4	6	24	32	86	14

Oxford City Reserves left.
Moreton Town joined from the Cheltenham League.

Division One

Clanfield	36	30	3	3	120	21	63
Wantage Town	36	24	7	5	64	32	55
Ernest Turner Sports	36	25	3	8	94	63	53
Princes Risborough Town	36	22	5	9	87	50	49
Rivet Works (Aylesbury)	36	19	4	13	77	55	42
Waddesdon	36	15	10	11	57	51	40
Thatcham	36	16	7	13	77	61	39
Watlington	36	15	9	12	61	50	39
Stokenchurch	36	16	7	13	80	68	39
Kidlington	36	16	7	13	67	63	39
A.C. Delco	36	17	5	14	57	58	39
Abingdon United	36	11	8	17	62	68	30
Hungerford Town	36	11	7	18	55	76	29
Pressed Steel (Cowley)	36	10	6	20	61	80	26
Marston United	36	9	5	22	63	107	23
AERE Harwell	36	7	8	21	58	115	22
Aylesbury Town Corinthians	36	7	6	23	54	95	20
Lambourn Sports	36	6	7	23	58	95	19
Aston Clinton	36	6	6	24	42	106	18
					1294	1314	

Fairford Town joined from the Swindon & District League.

1970-71

Premier Division

Witney Town	34	26	6	2	105	16	58
Abingdon Town	34	20	12	2	74	31	52
Wallingford Town	34	22	5	7	72	37	49
Chippenham Town	34	21	6	7	72	42	48
Clanfield	34	18	9	7	87	49	45
Bicester Town	34	13	13	8	67	48	39
Thame United	34	14	7	13	75	57	35
Didcot Town	34	12	11	11	48	51	35
Moreton Town	34	12	10	12	55	54	34
Pinehurst	34	10	12	12	54	59	32
Wantage Town	34	11	8	15	40	56	30
Cirencester Town	34	12	5	17	54	57	29
Buckingham Athletic	34	8	13	13	49	65	29
Morris Motors	34	8	11	15	45	60	27
Newbury Town	34	7	8	19	49	83	22
Henley Town	34	7	8	19	44	82	22
Swindon Town "A"	34	4	7	23	30	85	15
Amersham Town	34	3	6	25	27	115	12
		228	157	227			613

Henley Town lost their ground and so could play youth football only.
Their first XI was restarted in 1973.

Division One

Hungerford Town	38	26	8	4	130	37	60
Pressed Steel (Cowley)	38	25	9	4	111	33	59
Fairford Town	38	25	9	4	99	50	59
Chipping Norton Town	38	23	7	8	98	45	53
Ernest Turner Sports	38	24	4	10	125	53	52
Stokenchurch	38	24	3	11	86	52	51
Abingdon United	38	19	5	14	78	65	43
Waddesdon	38	18	7	13	75	71	43
Marston United	38	15	10	13	75	57	40
Kidlington	38	17	6	15	87	83	40
A.C. Delco	38	16	6	16	68	80	38
Princes Risborough Town	38	13	9	16	61	63	35
Thatcham	38	13	9	16	71	75	35
Rivet Works (Aylesbury)	38	13	7	18	63	72	33
Hazells (Aylesbury)	38	11	7	20	67	86	29
Watlington	38	11	7	20	49	73	29
Lambourn Sports	38	8	5	25	55	109	21
Aston Clinton	38	6	6	26	42	116	18
Aylesbury Town Corinthians	38	4	4	30	32	156	12
AERE Harwell	38	4	3	31	37	133	11
		315	131	314			761

Burnham joined from the Wycombe Combination while Easington Sports, Garsington, Long Wittenham, M.G. Athletic and Oxford University Press all joined from the Oxfordshire Senior League. Maidenhead Social joined from the Reading Combination.

Division One split into two sections.

1971-72

Premier Division

Witney Town	32	23	5	4	78	27	51
Abingdon Town	32	19	8	5	69	29	46
Clanfield	32	19	8	5	85	45	46
Pinehurst	32	15	11	6	51	32	41
Chippenham Town	32	15	7	10	54	49	37
Moreton Town	32	14	7	11	66	52	35
Didcot Town	32	12	10	10	44	39	34
Wallingford Town	32	12	10	10	41	39	34
Pressed Steel (Cowley)	32	12	6	14	41	43	30
Newbury Town	32	10	8	14	40	51	28
Thame United	32	11	5	16	47	63	27
Wantage Town	32	12	1	19	52	66	25
Bicester Town	32	9	6	17	47	51	24
Morris Motors	32	10	4	18	41	64	24
Hungerford Town	32	8	6	18	43	60	22
Cirencester Town	32	9	4	19	50	82	22
Buckingham Athletic	32	3	11	18	37	94	17
		544	213	117	214		543

Division One – Section A

Fairford Town	24	16	5	3	67	28	37
Burnham (1)	24	15	4	5	68	26	34
Ernest Turner Sports (1)	24	15	4	5	66	35	34
Thatcham (1)	24	11	8	5	59	37	30
Long Wittenham (1)	24	13	4	7	51	39	30
Swindon Town "A" (1)	24	12	4	8	64	39	28
Hazells (Aylesbury) (1)	24	10	5	9	36	30	25
Abingdon United (2)	24	9	5	10	43	45	23
M.G. Athletic (1)	24	9	4	11	40	41	22
Marston United (2)	24	7	7	10	41	53	21
Easington Sports (2)	24	6	8	10	40	59	20
Lambourn Sports	24	2	1	21	28	83	5
Aylesbury Town Corinthians	24	1	1	22	21	109	3

Aylesbury Town Corinthians moved to the Wycombe & District League.
Lambourn Sports moved to the North Berkshire League.

Division One – Section B

Chipping Norton Town	26	17	5	4	71	34	39
Rivet Works (Aylesbury) (1)	26	16	6	4	82	29	38
Waddesdon (1)	26	17	4	5	72	37	38
Princes Risborough Town (1)	26	13	6	7	59	36	32
Amersham Town	26	11	10	5	60	37	32
Kidlington (1)	26	13	5	8	50	35	31
Garsington (1)	26	12	2	12	62	66	26
Oxford University Press (1)	26	10	5	11	45	56	25
Watlington (2)	26	8	6	12	26	41	22
A.C. Delco (1)	26	6	8	12	42	55	20
Maidenhead Social (2)	26	8	4	14	45	60	20
Aston Clinton (2)	26	5	8	13	26	46	18
Stokenchurch (2)	26	6	2	18	35	71	14
AERE Harwell (2)	26	3	3	20	23	101	9
					698	704	

Rivet Works (Aylesbury) changed their name to Rivet Sports and
Maidenhead Social changed their name to Maidenhead Town.
Amersham Town moved to the Spartan League.

Division One clubs split between Division One and a new Division Two
for 1972-73 as shown in brackets above.

61 F.C. Luton joined Division Two from the Luton & District League and
Walcot and Wroughton both joined Division Two from the Wiltshire
League.

1972-73

Premier Division

Witney Town	32	26	4	2	100	26	56
Clanfield	32	23	5	4	81	28	51
Hungerford Town	32	18	4	10	64	42	40
Wallingford Town	32	17	6	9	64	45	40
Didcot Town	32	17	5	10	56	41	39
Abingdon Town	32	12	11	9	60	42	35
Thame United	32	10	11	11	42	46	31
Pinehurst	32	12	6	14	55	51	30
Pressed Steel (Cowley)	32	8	14	10	38	45	30
Wantage Town	32	9	9	14	42	61	27
Chippenham Town	32	8	10	14	45	64	26
Bicester Town	32	8	9	15	33	43	25
Chipping Norton Town	32	9	7	16	33	67	25
Fairford Town	32	7	10	15	36	51	24
Moreton Town	32	8	7	17	44	73	23
Morris Motors	*32*	*10*	*3*	*19*	*43*	*78*	*23*
Newbury Town	*32*	*7*	*5*	*20*	*39*	*72*	*19*

Witney Town moved to the Southern League and Chippenham Town
moved to the Western League.

Division One

Thatcham	30	21	6	3	62	16	48
Burnham	30	20	6	4	73	31	46
Ernest Turner Sports	30	18	6	6	66	37	42
Hazells (Aylesbury)	30	17	3	10	64	41	37
Waddesdon	30	17	1	12	54	46	35
Long Wittenham	30	15	3	12	52	49	33
Swindon Town "A"	30	15	2	13	65	47	32
M.G. Athletic	30	12	6	12	39	43	30
Cirencester Town	30	13	4	13	50	64	30
Oxford University Press	30	12	4	14	38	46	28
Rivet Sports	30	12	3	15	65	50	27
Kidlington	30	13	1	16	43	41	27
Princes Risborough Town	30	8	9	13	30	47	25
A.C. Delco	30	7	6	17	35	72	20
Garsington	30	4	6	20	37	77	14
Buckingham Athletic	30	1	4	25	25	101	6
					798	808	

Division Two

Walcot	20	17	2	1	78	29	36
Maidenhead Town	20	12	5	3	38	20	29
Stokenchurch	20	11	4	5	46	31	26
61 F.C. Luton	20	12	1	7	53	27	25
Wroughton	20	10	3	7	36	30	23
Easington Sports	20	10	2	8	48	35	22
Aston Clinton	20	7	2	11	30	39	16
Watlington	20	6	3	11	29	39	15
Abingdon United	20	5	3	12	27	46	13
Marston United	20	5	1	14	29	50	11
AERE Harwell	20	1	2	17	14	82	4

A.C. Delco and 61 F.C. Luton moved to the South Midlands League and
AERE Harwell moved to the North Berkshire League.
Stokenchurch disbanded having lost their ground – they reformed in
1977.
Marston United also left. Oxford City Reserves joined.

Division Two was absorbed into Division One.

1973-74

Premier Division

Moreton Town	32	22	6	4	77	29	50
Clanfield	32	21	7	4	80	17	49
Wantage Town	32	20	6	6	49	25	46
Bicester Town	32	18	4	10	59	45	40
Didcot Town	32	13	11	8	52	34	37
Thatcham	32	14	9	9	54	36	37
Abingdon Town	32	14	7	11	61	40	35
Hungerford Town	32	13	9	10	54	42	35
Chipping Norton Town	32	13	9	10	48	50	35
Pinehurst	32	11	12	9	57	43	34
Burnham	32	14	6	12	51	47	34
Wallingford Town	32	10	7	15	51	53	27
Thame United	32	10	6	16	37	51	26
Fairford Town	*32*	*8*	*4*	*20*	*46*	*75*	*20*
Pressed Steel (Cowley)	*32*	*6*	*3*	*23*	*26*	*86*	*15*
Ernest Turner Sports	32	5	4	23	30	85	14
Hazells (Aylesbury)	*32*	*5*	*0*	*27*	*26*	*100*	*10*

Thatcham changed their name to Thatcham Town.
Ernest Turner Sports left.

Division One

Cirencester Town	40	29	5	6	134	43	63
Oxford City Reserves	40	28	6	6	118	49	62
Newbury Town	40	26	9	5	113	46	61
Rivet Sports	40	24	7	9	95	44	55
Walcot	40	19	13	8	79	48	51
Maidenhead Town	40	20	11	9	73	59	51
Kidlington	40	19	10	11	75	61	48
Morris Motors	40	18	9	13	78	55	45
Easington Sports	40	19	7	14	79	60	45
Aston Clinton	40	18	8	14	76	67	44
Waddesdon	40	18	7	15	88	71	43
Long Wittenham	40	16	10	14	79	66	42
Oxford University Press	40	17	6	17	72	66	40
M.G. Athletic	40	16	7	17	65	61	39
Swindon Town "A"	40	13	8	19	83	73	34
Wroughton	40	13	5	22	54	90	31
Garsington	40	13	2	25	67	94	28
Watlington	40	9	5	26	57	112	23
Abingdon United	40	5	3	32	46	134	13
Princes Risborough Town	40	4	4	32	41	129	12
Buckingham Athletic	40	2	4	34	35	179	8
	840	346	146	348			838

Watlington changed their name to Watlington Town.
Garsington and Oxford University Press moved to the Oxfordshire
Senior League, Waddesdon moved to the South Midlands League and
Wroughton moved to the Wiltshire League.
Princes Risborough Town and Swindon Town "A" also left.

Three Points were awarded for a win from the next season.

1974-75

Premier Division

Thatcham Town	32	22	4	6	49	24	70
Moreton Town	32	21	5	6	71	26	68
Burnham	32	16	9	7	56	41	57
Clanfield	32	15	5	12	60	48	50
Newbury Town	32	15	4	13	50	46	49
Chipping Norton Town	32	14	6	12	54	40	48
Wantage Town	32	14	5	13	43	41	47
Pinehurst	32	14	5	13	35	43	47
Bicester Town	32	13	4	15	61	57	43
Wallingford Town	32	11	9	12	41	45	42
Didcot Town	32	11	6	15	46	59	39
Thame United	32	11	5	16	44	52	38
Cirencester Town	32	11	5	16	49	64	38
Hungerford Town	32	10	4	18	40	55	34
Rivet Sports	32	10	4	18	36	65	34
Oxford City Reserves	32	8	8	16	48	63	32
Abingdon Town	32	8	8	16	37	51	32

Oxford City Reserves left.
Forest Green Rovers joined from the Gloucestershire County League
and Stratford Town joined from the Midland Combination.

Division One

Maidenhead Town	26	20	4	2	69	19	64
Morris Motors	26	17	6	3	50	14	57
Easington Sports	26	14	3	9	52	33	45
Hazells (Aylesbury)	26	12	8	6	48	27	44
Kidlington	26	13	5	8	47	31	44
Aston Clinton	26	10	7	9	51	40	37
Walcot	26	9	9	8	44	40	36
Long Wittenham	26	10	6	10	50	47	36
Fairford Town	26	9	6	11	25	39	33
Pressed Steel (Cowley)	26	10	2	14	51	59	32
Watlington Town	26	8	8	10	34	45	32
Abingdon United	26	8	5	13	40	51	29
M.G. Athletic	26	3	5	18	27	66	14
Buckingham Athletic	26	1	2	23	15	92	5

Thatcham became Thatcham Town. Long Wittenham moved to the
North Berkshire League and Walcot moved to the Wiltshire League.

1975-76

Premier Division

Burnham	30	19	8	3	62	20	65
Moreton Town	30	15	9	6	52	34	54
Clanfield	30	14	10	6	47	29	52
Forest Green Rovers	30	14	10	6	82	53	52
Newbury Town	30	14	9	7	54	37	51
Chipping Norton Town	30	14	8	8	46	37	50
Hungerford Town	30	11	12	7	40	31	45
Thame United	30	11	10	9	43	44	43
Thatcham Town	30	12	7	11	36	45	43
Stratford Town	30	9	11	10	49	44	38
Wallingford Town	30	9	9	12	33	44	36
Cirencester Town	30	9	6	15	41	59	33
Pinehurst	30	8	7	15	43	50	31
Didcot Town	30	6	8	16	27	39	26
Wantage Town	30	3	11	16	29	62	20
Bicester Town	30	2	5	23	29	85	11

Division One

Abingdon Town	26	22	3	1	53	12	69
Fairford Town	26	19	4	3	52	12	61
Hazells (Aylesbury)	26	15	5	6	53	23	50
Rivet Sports	26	14	7	5	40	31	49
Abingdon United	26	11	3	12	46	45	36
Pressed Steel (Cowley)	26	11	3	12	41	56	36
Maidenhead Town	26	9	5	12	37	49	32
Morris Motors	26	7	9	10	33	32	30
Watlington Town	26	9	3	14	50	57	30
Easington Sports	26	8	5	13	43	52	29
Kidlington	26	8	4	14	37	50	28
M.G. Athletic	26	6	7	13	24	34	25
Aston Clinton	26	6	6	14	37	53	24
Buckingham Athletic	26	4	2	20	26	66	14

M.G. Athletic left. Flackwell Heath joined from the Wycombe & District
League and Garrards Athletic joined from the Wiltshire League.

1976-77

Premier Division

Moreton Town	30	22	2	6	62	25	68
Thame United	30	20	4	6	54	26	64
Burnham	30	17	10	3	67	33	61
Chipping Norton Town	30	15	10	5	60	28	55
Hungerford Town	30	13	8	9	53	35	47
Clanfield	30	12	6	12	47	52	42
Newbury Town	30	11	7	12	54	44	40
Pinehurst	30	8	14	8	44	43	38
Cirencester Town	30	10	6	14	37	62	36
Wallingford Town	30	9	7	14	33	37	34
Forest Green Rovers	30	8	9	13	44	50	33
Abingdon Town	30	8	8	14	34	42	32
Fairford Town	30	8	8	14	35	45	32
Thatcham Town	30	7	8	15	33	62	29
Stratford Town	30	7	7	16	35	65	28
Hazells (Aylesbury)	30	5	6	19	35	78	21

Burnham moved to the Athenian League and Stratford Town moved to
the Midland Combination.

Division One

Didcot Town	30	21	5	4	73	21	68
Flackwell Heath	30	20	6	4	79	31	66
Abingdon United	30	19	4	7	75	37	61
Garrards Athletic	30	18	5	7	82	38	59
Kidlington	30	16	4	10	47	33	52
Bicester Town	30	15	6	9	44	33	51
Easington Sports	30	14	4	12	60	59	46
Rivet Sports	30	12	6	12	53	49	42
Wantage Town	30	10	10	10	47	53	40
Maidenhead Town	30	10	9	11	44	45	39
Pressed Steel (Cowley)	30	11	2	17	58	65	35
Watlington Town	30	9	5	16	50	69	32
Aston Clinton	30	9	4	17	32	61	31
Morris Motors	30	6	9	15	37	60	27
Dowty Staverton	30	6	5	19	42	72	23
Buckingham Athletic	30	1	2	27	19	127	5
					842	853	

Watlington Town moved to Oxfordshire Senior League.
Lambourn Sports joined from the North Berkshire League and Ruislip
Town joined from the Middlesex League.

1977-78

Premier Division

Chipping Norton Town	30	20	6	4	73	21	66
Newbury Town	30	19	8	3	66	29	65
Hungerford Town	30	17	6	7	80	30	57
Moreton Town	30	17	4	9	54	38	55
Fairford Town	30	13	11	6	42	27	50
Thame United	30	14	8	8	51	39	50
Wallingford Town	30	14	6	10	47	41	48
Pinehurst	30	13	9	8	45	43	48
Flackwell Heath	30	13	5	12	54	37	44
Didcot Town	30	11	6	13	34	43	39
Abingdon Town	30	7	10	13	28	54	31
Forest Green Rovers	30	6	12	12	49	59	30
Clanfield	30	7	6	17	32	56	27
Abingdon United	30	5	8	17	36	66	23
Thatcham Town	*30*	*3*	*7*	*20*	*20*	*73*	*16*
Cirencester Town	*30*	*3*	*4*	*23*	*28*	*83*	*13*

Hungerford Town moved to the Isthmian League and Pinehurst moved to the Wiltshire League.

Division One

Bicester Town	**30**	**20**	**5**	**5**	**79**	**28**	**65**
Garrards Athletic	**30**	**18**	**6**	**6**	**70**	**32**	**60**
Kidlington	30	17	8	5	52	27	59
Hazells (Aylesbury)	30	16	6	8	75	39	54
Easington Sports	30	16	5	9	66	42	53
Lambourn Sports	30	15	5	10	68	57	50
Ruislip Town	30	13	7	10	64	64	46
Morris Motors	30	12	7	11	53	59	43
Maidenhead Town	30	11	9	10	49	44	42
Wantage Town	30	11	6	13	36	42	39
Rivet Sports	30	11	5	14	37	49	38
Aston Clinton	30	8	8	14	50	47	32
Pressed Steel (Cowley)	30	9	2	19	51	89	29
Dowty Staverton	30	6	9	15	45	65	27
Brackley Town	30	5	8	17	30	64	23
Buckingham Athletic	30	2	4	24	27	104	10

Northwood and Rayners Lane both joined from the Middlesex League.

Two points were awarded for a win from the next season.

1978-79

Premier Division

Newbury Town	26	14	8	4	52	31	36
Fairford Town	26	14	7	5	53	39	35
Forest Green Rovers	26	15	4	7	52	35	34
Thame United	26	15	3	8	37	26	33
Bicester Town	26	12	9	5	47	38	33
Chipping Norton Town	26	14	4	8	51	27	32
Moreton Town	26	12	7	7	42	31	31
Flackwell Heath	26	10	8	8	37	33	28
Clanfield	26	9	4	13	36	47	22
Wallingford Town	26	8	4	14	41	48	20
Abingdon Town	26	6	7	13	34	51	19
Didcot Town	26	4	9	13	33	52	17
Garrards Athletic	26	4	8	14	35	51	16
Abingdon United	26	2	4	20	24	65	8

Chipping Norton Town moved to the Midland Combination and Garrards Athletic moved to the Wiltshire League.
Worrall Hill joined from the Gloucestershire County League.

Division One

Northwood	**34**	**27**	**2**	**5**	**110**	**24**	**56**
Kidlington	**34**	**24**	**4**	**6**	**87**	**35**	**52**
Morris Motors	**34**	**22**	**6**	**6**	**86**	**34**	**50**
Maidenhead Town	34	23	2	9	72	36	48
Rivet Sports	34	17	10	7	53	38	44
Lambourn Sports	34	17	8	9	86	58	42
Hazells (Aylesbury)	34	16	8	10	62	45	40
Thatcham Town	34	15	7	12	67	56	37
Rayners Lane	34	13	7	14	63	67	33
Easington Sports	34	12	7	15	60	66	31
Cirencester Town	33	13	5	15	45	66	31
Brackley Town	34	8	14	12	42	36	30
Ruislip Town	33	10	6	17	51	64	26
Pressed Steel (Cowley)	34	8	10	16	57	76	26
Dowty Staverton	34	8	4	22	34	84	20
Aston Clinton	34	7	4	23	47	90	18
Wantage Town	34	6	5	23	45	94	17
Buckingham Athletic	34	3	3	28	28	126	9

Buckingham Athletic moved to the North Buckinghamshire League.
AFC Aldermaston joined from the Reading & District League and Milton Keynes Borough joined from the United Counties League.

1979-80

Premier Division

Bicester Town	30	19	8	3	57	25	46
Fairford Town	30	17	9	4	64	35	43
Moreton Town	30	13	10	7	54	41	36
Flackwell Heath	30	14	7	9	43	33	35
Abingdon Town	30	14	5	11	49	41	33
Forest Green Rovers	30	11	10	9	56	45	32
Northwood	30	14	4	12	55	54	32
Newbury Town	30	12	7	11	59	47	31
Didcot Town	30	12	5	13	48	41	29
Kidlington	30	11	7	12	36	40	29
Morris Motors	30	11	7	12	53	59	29
Abingdon United	30	11	6	13	38	43	28
Thame United	30	9	10	11	42	48	28
Wallingford Town	30	9	3	18	36	55	21
Clanfield	*30*	*5*	*5*	*20*	*43*	*82*	*15*
Worrall Hill	*30*	*3*	*7*	*20*	*40*	*84*	*13*

Division One

Hazells (Aylesbury)	**30**	**24**	**3**	**3**	**79**	**28**	**51**
Maidenhead Town	**30**	**23**	**2**	**5**	**95**	**28**	**48**
Lambourn Sports	30	21	6	3	91	45	48
Milton Keynes Borough	30	18	6	6	72	38	42
Brackley Town	30	19	1	10	61	44	39
Cirencester Town	30	14	5	11	57	49	33
AFC Aldermaston	30	15	3	12	58	52	33
Wantage Town	30	13	6	11	60	46	32
Thatcham Town	30	12	6	12	49	55	30
Pressed Steel (Cowley)	30	9	7	14	37	52	25
Rayners Lane	30	8	5	17	48	56	21
Easington Sports	30	7	7	16	41	72	21
Dowty Staverton	30	6	4	20	26	78	16
Rivet Sports	30	5	5	20	33	69	15
Ruislip Town	30	4	7	19	34	79	15
Aston Clinton	30	2	7	21	26	76	11

Aston Clinton moved to the Wycombe Ercol League and Ruislip Town moved to the Middlesex League.
Lydney Town joined from the Gloucestershire Northern Senior League and Viking Sports joined from the Middlesex League.

1980-81

Premier Division

Newbury Town	30	23	4	3	75	27	50
Thame United	30	17	8	5	51	22	42
Hazells (Aylesbury)	30	16	8	6	53	36	40
Moreton Town	30	15	8	7	72	35	38
Flackwell Heath	30	13	8	9	47	30	34
Abingdon Town	30	13	8	9	48	37	34
Forest Green Rovers	30	14	6	10	57	53	34
Fairford Town	30	15	2	13	47	42	32
Didcot Town	30	9	9	12	36	47	27
Maidenhead Town	30	10	5	15	42	48	25
Bicester Town	30	7	11	12	41	60	25
Northwood	30	6	10	14	37	52	22
Kidlington	30	8	6	16	32	55	22
Wallingford Town	30	8	5	17	43	73	21
Morris Motors	*30*	*7*	*6*	*17*	*36*	*57*	*20*
Abingdon United	*30*	*5*	*4*	*21*	*31*	*74*	*14*

Division One

Wantage Town	**30**	**20**	**4**	**6**	**68**	**31**	**44**
Clanfield	**30**	**16**	**12**	**2**	**67**	**32**	**44**
Cirencester Town	30	16	11	3	73	34	43
Pressed Steel (Cowley)	30	17	8	5	66	29	42
Lydney Town	30	16	5	9	60	34	37
Rayners Lane	30	15	5	10	46	36	35
Brackley Town	30	12	10	8	64	43	34
Thatcham Town	30	11	12	7	48	41	34
Milton Keynes Borough	30	14	6	10	52	49	34
Viking Sports	30	9	11	10	46	50	29
Lambourn Sports	30	11	5	14	54	67	27
AFC Aldermaston	30	9	4	17	41	70	22
Worrall Hill	30	7	5	18	36	57	19
Rivet Sports	30	6	7	17	35	72	19
Dowty Staverton	30	5	4	21	38	66	14
Easington Sports	30	1	1	28	16	99	3

Rivet Sports moved to the Wycombe Ercol Senior League.
Badminton Picksons joined from the Stroud & District League.

Goal difference replaced goal average from the next season.

1981-82

Premier Division

Forest Green Rovers	30	23	1	6	71	20	47
Moreton Town	30	13	13	4	44	32	39
Wantage Town	30	14	10	6	42	28	38
Newbury Town	30	14	8	8	62	38	36
Maidenhead Town	30	14	6	10	46	34	34
Fairford Town	30	12	10	8	41	29	34
Abingdon Town	30	13	7	10	34	32	33
Flackwell Heath	30	11	10	9	27	30	32
Thame United	30	9	10	11	40	39	28
Bicester Town	30	9	10	11	40	42	28
Wallingford Town	30	11	5	14	40	54	27
Clanfield	30	8	8	14	33	53	24
Northwood	30	9	3	18	35	47	21
Hazells (Aylesbury)	30	7	7	16	26	51	21
Didcot Town	30	5	10	15	18	40	20
Kidlington	*30*	*6*	*6*	*18*	*26*	*56*	*18*

Flackwell Heath and Newbury Town moved to the Athenian League and Forest Green Rovers moved to the Southern League.
Almondsbury Greenway and Shortwood United joined from the Gloucestershire County League.

Division One

Lambourn Sports	**30**	**21**	**4**	**5**	**65**	**30**	**46**
Abingdon United	**30**	**18**	**6**	**6**	**68**	**40**	**42**
Viking Sports	30	17	6	7	59	40	40
Milton Keynes Borough	30	17	5	8	63	36	39
Badminton Picksons	30	16	5	9	65	35	37
Brackley Town	30	15	7	8	47	29	37
Cirencester Town	30	12	10	8	54	37	34
Rayners Lane	30	14	6	10	47	35	34
Morris Motors	30	13	6	11	57	59	32
Lydney Town	30	8	15	7	38	34	31
Thatcham Town	30	11	6	13	54	53	28
Pressed Steel (Cowley)	30	6	9	15	39	50	21
Dowty Staverton	30	7	5	18	31	57	19
Worrall Hill	30	7	5	18	40	81	19
AFC Aldermaston	30	3	8	19	31	75	14
Easington Sports	30	2	3	25	21	88	7

Thatcham Town moved to the Athenian League.
Pegasus Juniors joined from the Worcester & District League and Supermarine joined from the Wiltshire League.

1982-83

Premier Division

Moreton Town	30	20	8	2	78	21	48
Almondsbury Greenway	30	18	4	8	70	37	40
Abingdon Town	30	15	9	6	59	33	39
Wallingford Town	30	17	4	9	52	42	38
Thame United	30	14	9	7	40	35	37
Didcot Town	30	14	7	9	42	33	35
Fairford Town	30	12	9	9	44	43	33
Wantage Town	30	9	13	8	41	33	31
Northwood	30	11	9	10	34	36	31
Bicester Town	30	12	6	12	36	34	30
Clanfield	30	10	6	14	41	44	26
Abingdon United	30	11	3	16	42	49	25
Maidenhead Town	30	10	3	17	36	65	23
Hazells (Aylesbury)	30	8	4	18	36	52	20
Shortwood United	*30*	*6*	*3*	*21*	*30*	*66*	*15*
Lambourn Sports	*30*	*2*	*5*	*23*	*17*	*75*	*9*

Avon Bradford joined from the Wiltshire League.

Division One

Rayners Lane	**30**	**19**	**7**	**4**	**63**	**19**	**45**
Supermarine	**30**	**17**	**11**	**2**	**50**	**21**	**45**
Pegasus Juniors	30	17	5	8	58	41	39
Cirencester Town	30	17	3	10	68	36	37
Pressed Steel (Cowley)	30	14	9	7	51	36	37
Milton Keynes Borough	30	14	4	12	61	43	32
Brackley Town	30	10	9	11	52	50	29
Morris Motors	30	12	5	13	45	51	29
Lydney Town	30	10	8	12	39	50	28
Kidlington	30	10	8	12	29	49	28
Viking Sports	30	11	5	14	45	55	27
Worrall Hill	30	11	5	14	41	58	27
Badminton Picksons	30	10	5	15	55	61	25
Easington Sports	30	9	7	14	40	54	25
AFC Aldermaston	30	6	5	19	52	82	17
Dowty Staverton	30	3	4	23	29	72	10

Brackley Town moved to the United Counties League.
Kintbury Rangers joined from the North Berkshire League, Yate Town joined from the Gloucestershire County League and Bishops Cleeve also joined.

Three Points were awarded for a win from the next season.

1983-84

Premier Division

	P	W	D	L	F	A	Pts
Almondsbury Greenway	32	23	4	5	59	19	73
Moreton Town	32	18	11	3	51	10	65
Thame United	32	19	5	8	53	30	62
Abingdon United	32	16	9	7	68	34	57
Abingdon Town	32	14	9	9	53	38	51
Rayners Lane	32	13	9	10	38	40	48
Supermarine	32	11	12	9	40	34	45
Bicester Town	32	13	6	13	37	32	45
Didcot Town	32	10	10	12	39	49	40
Wallingford Town	32	10	9	13	42	45	39
Clanfield	32	7	16	9	39	43	37
Maidenhead Town	32	8	12	12	40	44	36
Northwood	32	9	7	16	34	53	34
Fairford Town	32	7	12	13	39	57	33
Wantage Town	32	8	6	18	43	53	30
Avon Bradford	*32*	*7*	*7*	*18*	*36*	*71*	*28*
Hazells (Aylesbury)	*32*	*3*	*8*	*21*	*30*	*89*	*17*

Northwood moved to the London Spartan League.
Hounslow joined from the Southern League and Sharpness joined from the Gloucestershire County League.

Division One

	P	W	D	L	F	A	Pts
Morris Motors	**34**	**23**	**8**	**3**	**71**	**30**	**77**
Shortwood United	**34**	**21**	**5**	**8**	**74**	**39**	**68**
Yate Town	34	18	11	5	90	53	65
Bishops Cleeve	34	19	6	9	59	43	63
Pegasus Juniors	34	19	5	10	71	40	62
Milton Keynes Borough	34	18	7	9	69	47	61
Pressed Steel (Cowley)	34	16	6	12	82	44	54
Viking Sports	34	15	9	10	61	43	54
Kintbury Rangers	34	14	10	10	66	56	52
Easington Sports	34	15	7	12	59	68	52
Kidlington	34	12	8	14	64	58	44
Cirencester Town	34	11	8	15	42	50	41
AFC Aldermaston	34	9	8	17	49	63	35
Worrall Hill	34	9	6	19	64	79	33
Lambourn Sports	34	8	7	19	47	85	31
Badminton Picksons	34	7	7	20	48	85	28
Lydney Town	34	4	8	22	39	75	20
Dowty Staverton	34	4	2	28	24	121	14

Lydney Town moved to the Gloucestershire Northern Senior League and Milton Keynes Borough moved to the South Midlands League.

1984-85

Premier Division

	P	W	D	L	F	A	Pts
Shortwood United	34	22	10	2	73	30	76
Moreton Town	34	19	6	9	64	32	63
Supermarine	34	17	10	7	57	33	61
Sharpness	34	15	10	9	85	54	55
Hounslow	34	14	12	8	59	37	54
Abingdon United	34	15	8	11	59	37	53
Wantage Town	34	15	6	13	45	42	51
Fairford Town	34	13	11	10	47	43	50
Morris Motors	34	15	4	15	36	45	49
Almondsbury Greenway	34	11	14	9	32	37	47
Abingdon Town	34	12	10	12	43	44	46
Rayners Lane	34	11	10	13	47	44	43
Maidenhead Town	34	10	10	14	50	65	40
Bicester Town	34	9	12	13	42	46	39
Wallingford Town	34	7	12	15	36	48	33
Thame United	34	6	14	14	51	62	32
Didcot Town	*34*	*5*	*12*	*17*	*33*	*66*	*27*
Clanfield	*34*	*3*	*3*	*28*	*34*	*128*	*12*

Division One

	P	W	D	L	F	A	Pts
Pegasus Juniors	**32**	**23**	**7**	**2**	**89**	**31**	**76**
Yate Town	**32**	**19**	**10**	**3**	**80**	**33**	**67**
Pressed Steel (Cowley)	32	18	11	3	77	34	64
Bishops Cleeve	32	19	6	7	66	35	63
Lambourn Sports	32	17	8	7	73	47	59
Cirencester Town	32	14	7	11	53	49	49
Highworth Town	32	12	7	13	54	47	43
Kidlington	32	12	7	13	51	45	43
Avon Bradford	32	13	4	15	53	57	43
Hazells (Aylesbury)	32	11	9	12	49	50	42
Kintbury Rangers	32	9	11	12	41	55	38
Badminton Picksons	32	10	7	15	62	70	37
AFC Aldermaston	32	10	5	17	47	72	35
Viking Sports	32	8	10	14	39	54	34
Easington Sports	32	7	5	20	44	68	26
Worrall Hill	32	7	2	23	37	83	23
Dowty Staverton	32	2	6	24	34	119	12

Pressed Steel (Cowley) had 1 point deducted.
Dowty Staverton moved to the Cirencester & District League and Worrall Hill also left, eventually joining the Gloucestershire Northern Senior League.
Penhill joined from the Wiltshire League.

1985-86

Premier Division

	P	W	D	L	F	A	Pts
Sharpness	34	24	4	6	88	41	76
Shortwood United	34	23	2	9	79	43	71
Hounslow	34	20	6	8	83	44	66
Abingdon Town	34	19	8	7	60	36	65
Supermarine	34	21	2	11	56	48	65
Rayners Lane	34	18	7	9	65	48	60
Abingdon United	34	17	8	9	46	33	59
Yate Town	34	15	8	11	57	44	53
Moreton Town	34	15	8	11	51	40	53
Thame United	34	13	8	13	51	54	47
Pegasus Juniors	34	13	5	16	56	64	44
Wallingford Town	34	12	5	17	45	56	41
Fairford Town	34	8	8	18	39	49	32
Morris Motors	34	7	10	17	30	44	31
Bicester Town	34	9	3	22	46	79	30
Wantage Town	34	7	6	21	40	65	27
Almondsbury Greenway	*34*	*7*	*3*	*24*	*34*	*82*	*24*
Maidenhead Town	34	5	5	24	34	90	20

Rayners Lane had 1 point deducted.
Almondsbury Greenway changed their name to Almondsbury 85.
Maidenhead Town moved to the Chiltonian League.

Division One

	P	W	D	L	F	A	Pts
Viking Sports	**30**	**22**	**5**	**3**	**100**	**37**	**71**
Penhill	**30**	**22**	**4**	**4**	**78**	**24**	**70**
Bishops Cleeve	30	17	6	7	72	45	57
Didcot Town	30	16	7	7	78	42	55
Highworth Town	30	15	6	9	61	38	51
Kidlington	30	13	8	9	52	48	47
Clanfield	30	11	8	11	53	56	41
Hazells (Aylesbury)	30	8	12	10	38	46	36
Badminton Picksons	30	8	10	12	39	62	34
Lambourn Sports	30	8	9	13	43	56	33
Pressed Steel (Cowley)	30	9	6	15	44	62	33
Cirencester Town	30	8	8	14	52	54	32
Avon Bradford	30	6	13	11	38	62	31
Easington Sports	30	8	4	18	50	81	28
Kintbury Rangers	30	4	10	16	38	67	22
AFC Aldermaston	30	5	4	21	39	95	19

AFC Aldermaston moved to the Hampshire League and Pressed Steel (Cowley) also left.
Carterton Town joined from the Witney & District League, Chipping Norton Town joined from the Oxfordshire Senior League, Cheltenham Saracens joined from the Cheltenham & District League, Cheltenham Town Reserves joined from the Midland Combination and Purton joined from the Wiltshire League.

1986-87

Premier Division

Abingdon Town	34	26	6	2	85	27	84
Hounslow	34	25	2	7	73	42	77
Shortwood United	34	20	6	8	79	38	66
Viking Sports	34	17	4	13	67	51	55
Sharpness	34	15	6	13	72	52	51
Abingdon United	34	14	9	11	49	37	51
Morris Motors	34	11	14	9	43	40	47
Moreton Town	34	13	8	13	47	49	47
Penhill	34	12	10	12	50	49	46
Yate Town	34	11	12	11	53	46	45
Supermarine	34	12	5	17	37	51	41
Pegasus Juniors	34	10	10	14	53	56	40
Rayners Lane	34	9	12	13	35	45	39
Bicester Town	34	8	11	15	31	50	35
Fairford Town	34	9	8	17	39	77	35
Wallingford Town	34	10	4	20	42	64	34
Thame United	34	9	7	18	50	84	34
Wantage Town	*34*	*5*	*6*	*23*	*26*	*73*	*21*

Hounslow moved to the Southern League.

Division One

Bishops Cleeve	**34**	**23**	**3**	**8**	**62**	**34**	**72**
Cheltenham Town Reserves	34	21	8	5	73	32	71
Didcot Town	**34**	**19**	**8**	**7**	**71**	**36**	**65**
Clanfield	34	18	9	7	64	32	63
Kidlington	34	19	6	9	72	44	63
Purton	34	16	8	10	76	44	56
Lambourn Sports	34	15	8	11	68	55	53
Highworth Town	34	14	10	10	65	53	52
Badminton Picksons	34	12	10	12	57	66	46
Carterton Town	34	13	7	14	41	50	46
Cirencester Town	34	12	7	15	38	50	43
Easington Sports	34	12	6	16	53	69	42
Chipping Norton Town	34	9	6	19	47	66	33
Cheltenham Saracens	34	10	3	21	35	84	33
Hazells (Aylesbury)	34	7	9	18	36	55	30
Kintbury Rangers	34	7	9	18	37	60	30
Almondsbury 85	34	7	8	19	32	56	29
Avon Bradford	34	7	5	22	33	74	26

Almondsbury 85 merged with Badminton Picksons to form
Almondsbury Picksons.
Hazells (Aylesbury) moved to the Chiltonian League and The Herd
joined from the Cheltenham & District League.

1987-88

Premier Division

Yate Town	34	25	7	2	73	20	82
Abingdon Town	34	22	8	4	76	31	74
Shortwood United	34	20	8	6	78	45	68
Abingdon United	34	17	11	6	58	36	62
Didcot Town	34	13	12	9	55	47	51
Penhill	34	14	9	11	47	44	51
Sharpness	34	13	11	10	63	48	50
Fairford Town	34	12	10	12	44	38	46
Thame United	34	11	13	10	54	54	46
Bicester Town	34	12	8	14	42	43	44
Viking Sports	34	11	8	15	44	64	41
Moreton Town	34	11	5	18	41	57	38
Rayners Lane	34	9	8	17	42	64	35
Morris Motors	34	8	11	15	36	63	35
Supermarine	34	8	9	17	46	58	33
Bishops Cleeve	34	7	11	16	42	70	32
Pegasus Juniors	34	9	3	22	46	61	30
Wallingford Town	34	5	6	23	26	69	21
					913	*912*	

Abingdon Town moved to the Spartan League, Morris Motors moved to
the Oxfordshire Senior League and Thame United moved to the South
Midlands League.

Division One

Cheltenham Town Reserves	30	20	6	4	70	23	66
Wantage Town	**30**	**17**	**7**	**6**	**55**	**29**	**58**
Kintbury Rangers	**30**	**16**	**9**	**5**	**48**	**26**	**57**
Almondsbury Picksons	30	16	7	7	51	33	55
Lambourn Sports	30	15	5	10	53	52	50
Kidlington	30	13	7	10	51	45	46
Highworth Town	30	12	6	12	52	57	42
Clanfield	30	13	2	15	51	59	41
Cirencester Town	30	11	7	12	43	51	40
Carterton Town	30	10	9	11	46	54	39
Chipping Norton Town	30	8	11	11	49	45	35
Purton	30	9	8	13	40	39	35
The Herd	30	9	7	14	47	47	34
Cheltenham Saracens	30	7	4	19	22	54	25
Easington Sports	30	5	10	15	26	60	25
Avon Bradford	30	3	7	20	34	64	16

Avon Bradford moved to the Wiltshire League.
Headington Amateurs joined from the Oxfordshire Senior League and
Wootton Bassett Town joined from the Wiltshire League.

1988-89

Premier Division

Yate Town	32	26	5	1	75	16	83
Sharpness	32	21	8	3	77	31	71
Abingdon United	32	18	6	8	54	26	60
Fairford Town	32	15	7	10	45	40	52
Pegasus Juniors	32	15	6	11	60	55	51
Bicester Town	32	14	8	10	70	40	50
Moreton Town	32	12	10	10	51	47	46
Didcot Town	32	12	10	10	38	36	46
Penhill	32	13	4	15	41	36	43
Bishops Cleeve	32	12	5	15	32	54	41
Shortwood United	32	11	7	14	40	47	40
Wantage Town	32	9	9	14	42	57	36
Rayners Lane	32	8	7	17	41	60	31
Supermarine	32	8	5	19	29	57	29
Kintbury Rangers	32	6	8	18	24	51	26
Wallingford Town	*32*	*6*	*8*	*18*	*31*	*64*	*26*
Viking Sports	*32*	*6*	*7*	*19*	*28*	*61*	*25*

Penhill changed their name to Swindon Athletic.
Yate Town moved to the Southern League.
Ruislip Park and newly formed Newport AFC joined.

Division One

Almondsbury Picksons	**28**	**20**	**4**	**4**	**66**	**20**	**64**
Headington Amateurs	**28**	**19**	**5**	**4**	**49**	**19**	**62**
Lambourn Sports	28	14	7	7	53	40	49
Highworth Town	28	12	8	8	52	41	44
Wootton Bassett Town	28	11	7	10	50	40	40
Purton	28	11	7	10	37	42	40
Cheltenham Town Reserves	28	12	3	13	53	50	39
Easington Sports	28	9	12	7	41	43	39
Chipping Norton Town	28	11	6	11	45	49	39
Clanfield	28	9	8	11	49	55	35
Kidlington	28	10	5	13	41	57	35
Cheltenham Saracens	28	6	10	12	33	45	28
The Herd	28	8	4	16	44	62	28
Carterton Town	28	7	5	16	36	54	26
Cirencester Town	28	3	5	20	28	59	14

Milton United joined from the North Berkshire League.

1989-90

Premier Division

Newport AFC	34	23	6	5	71	28	75
Shortwood United	34	20	7	7	81	39	67
Abingdon United	34	20	7	7	66	33	67
Sharpness	34	16	9	9	76	59	57
Fairford Town	34	17	6	11	59	42	57
Bicester Town	34	15	11	8	43	30	56
Almondsbury Picksons	34	15	9	10	60	41	54
Kintbury Rangers	34	14	8	12	37	45	50
Pegasus Juniors	34	14	6	14	47	62	48
Swindon Athletic	34	12	11	11	48	36	47
Rayners Lane	34	12	6	16	43	45	42
Headington Amateurs	34	9	14	11	43	44	41
Moreton Town	34	11	8	15	55	65	41
Wantage Town	34	10	10	14	52	58	40
Didcot Town	34	11	6	17	54	48	39
Bishops Cleeve	34	7	9	18	33	61	30
Supermarine	*34*	*6*	*5*	*23*	*25*	*72*	*23*
Ruislip Park	34	2	6	26	32	117	12

Newport AFC moved to the Southern League, Sharpness moved to the Gloucestershire Northern Senior League and Ruislip Park also left. Banbury United and Hounslow joined from the Southern League.

Division One

Carterton Town	**30**	**24**	**4**	**2**	**72**	**16**	**76**
Milton United	**30**	**21**	**3**	**6**	**77**	**22**	**66**
Cheltenham Town Reserves	30	19	2	9	78	56	59
Kidlington	30	18	3	9	52	34	57
Chipping Norton Town	30	15	8	7	44	26	53
Purton	30	14	8	8	55	36	50
Wootton Bassett Town	30	13	8	9	52	35	47
Wallingford Town	30	9	12	9	37	37	39
Viking Sports	30	11	5	14	30	43	38
Highworth Town	30	9	7	14	44	50	34
Cirencester Town	30	8	10	12	38	53	34
Clanfield	30	7	9	14	31	57	30
Easington Sports	30	7	4	19	33	68	25
Lambourn Sports	30	5	7	18	27	60	22
The Herd	30	4	9	17	27	62	21
Cheltenham Saracens	30	3	7	20	34	76	16

The Herd changed their name to Cirencester United and Cheltenham Town Reserves left.
Cinderford Town joined from the Gloucestershire County League and North Leigh joined from the Witney & District League.

1990-91

Premier Division

Milton United	34	20	11	3	66	26	71
Fairford Town	34	22	5	7	69	38	71
Bicester Town	34	19	6	9	70	37	63
Didcot Town	34	18	8	8	65	30	62
Headington Amateurs	34	18	8	8	54	34	62
Shortwood United	34	18	5	11	77	60	59
Abingdon United	34	17	6	11	57	37	57
Banbury United	34	17	4	13	58	51	55
Hounslow	34	16	5	13	63	47	53
Almondsbury Picksons	34	13	9	12	57	58	48
Kintbury Rangers	34	12	8	14	54	57	44
Carterton Town	34	10	7	17	49	62	37
Rayners Lane	34	10	6	18	34	63	36
Bishops Cleeve	34	9	8	17	43	79	35
Pegasus Juniors	34	8	7	19	46	68	31
Swindon Athletic	34	6	10	18	31	64	28
Moreton Town	34	5	7	22	30	73	22
Wantage Town	*34*	*4*	*8*	*22*	*31*	*70*	*20*

Hounslow disbanded. Some elements of the club formed Hounslow Town '91 and joined Division One of the Middlesex County League and others took part in a merger with Feltham of the Isthmian League and joined Division Three of that league as Feltham and Hounslow Borough.

Division One

Cinderford Town	**30**	**24**	**3**	**3**	**94**	**22**	**75**
Cirencester Town	**30**	**22**	**5**	**3**	**66**	**21**	**71**
Purton	30	18	6	6	66	28	60
North Leigh	30	18	3	9	83	43	57
Wallingford Town	30	17	5	8	61	35	56
Viking Sports	30	15	10	5	53	20	55
Highworth Town	30	15	4	11	45	49	49
Wootton Bassett Town	30	11	8	11	32	36	41
Cirencester United	30	11	7	12	48	51	40
Easington Sports	30	10	7	13	52	51	37
Clanfield	30	9	8	13	43	44	35
Kidlington	30	6	8	16	36	56	26
Supermarine	30	7	5	18	29	53	26
Cheltenham Saracens	30	6	7	17	31	44	25
Chipping Norton Town	30	4	1	25	12	122	13
Lambourn Sports	30	2	3	25	27	103	9

Viking Sports moved to the Combined Counties League.
Tuffley Rovers joined from the Gloucestershire County League, Wollen Sports joined from Sunday football and Yarnton joined from the Oxfordshire Senior League.

1991-92

Premier Division

Shortwood United	34	25	4	5	83	44	79
Cirencester Town	34	23	9	2	73	23	78
Almondsbury Picksons	34	19	7	8	63	38	64
Milton United	34	18	9	7	67	44	63
Cinderford Town	34	16	9	9	57	41	57
Abingdon United	34	17	5	12	54	40	56
Didcot Town	34	16	6	12	70	48	54
Swindon Athletic	34	15	9	10	61	44	54
Bicester Town	34	12	12	10	44	42	48
Banbury United	34	14	5	15	55	55	47
Fairford Town	34	12	9	13	72	55	45
Headington Amateurs	34	10	9	15	48	59	39
Pegasus Juniors	34	11	5	18	66	68	38
Kintbury Rangers	34	9	8	17	47	59	35
Rayners Lane	34	9	8	17	50	75	35
Moreton Town	34	7	4	23	38	100	25
Carterton Town	*34*	*6*	*6*	*22*	*32*	*74*	*24*
Bishops Cleeve	*34*	*2*	*6*	*26*	*25*	*96*	*12*

Swindon Athletic merged with Supermarine from Division One to form Swindon Supermarine.

Division One

Wollen Sports	**32**	**26**	**4**	**2**	**96**	**28**	**82**
Wantage Town	**32**	**23**	**6**	**3**	**83**	**32**	**75**
Tuffley Rovers	32	20	8	4	95	34	68
North Leigh	32	20	4	8	84	38	64
Cheltenham Saracens	32	15	7	10	70	45	52
Purton	32	14	7	11	48	40	49
Chipping Norton Town	32	13	6	13	54	56	45
Highworth Town	32	11	7	14	53	54	40
Cirencester United	32	11	7	14	49	55	40
Lambourn Sports	32	11	7	14	52	74	40
Yarnton	32	11	6	15	42	60	39
Wootton Bassett Town	32	10	8	14	45	59	38
Easington Sports	32	12	0	20	42	80	36
Kidlington	32	7	9	16	48	70	30
Wallingford Town	32	8	5	19	40	78	29
Clanfield	32	5	10	17	35	66	25
Supermarine	32	3	3	26	20	87	12

1992-93

Premier Division

Wollen Sports	34	25	4	5	75	31	79
Moreton Town	34	22	4	8	79	43	70
Milton United	34	21	7	6	67	33	70
Cirencester Town	34	20	8	6	54	28	68
Cinderford Town	34	15	10	9	64	44	55
Almondsbury Picksons	34	15	7	12	62	50	52
Shortwood United	34	12	10	12	63	59	46
Swindon Supermarine	34	11	13	10	46	43	46
Bicester Town	34	12	9	13	45	45	45
Rayners Lane	34	13	4	17	53	63	43
Banbury United	34	10	10	14	50	66	40
Fairford Town	34	8	13	13	55	48	37
Headington Amateurs	34	10	6	18	40	67	36
Kintbury Rangers	34	9	8	17	35	51	35
Abingdon United	34	9	7	18	49	67	34
Wantage Town	34	8	8	18	47	70	32
Pegasus Juniors	*34*	*7*	*9*	*18*	*52*	*76*	*30*
Didcot Town	*34*	*6*	*9*	*19*	*42*	*94*	*27*

Almondsbury Picksons changed their name to Almondsbury Town

Division One

Tuffley Rovers	**30**	**25**	**2**	**3**	**90**	**24**	**77**
North Leigh	**30**	**21**	**4**	**5**	**113**	**43**	**67**
Wallingford Town	30	17	9	4	84	47	60
Lambourn Sports	30	16	6	8	73	61	54
Purton	30	17	3	10	64	53	54
Kidlington	30	13	9	8	49	41	48
Yarnton	30	12	4	14	48	60	40
Cheltenham Saracens	30	12	2	16	48	47	38
Carterton Town	30	11	4	15	58	63	37
Clanfield	30	9	10	11	47	66	37
Highworth Town	30	9	6	15	48	62	33
Wootton Bassett Town	30	8	6	16	40	53	30
Bishops Cleeve	30	9	3	18	44	76	30
Cirencester United	30	8	4	18	41	78	28
Chipping Norton Town	30	7	5	18	51	82	26
Easington Sports	30	5	5	20	34	76	20

Chipping Norton Town moved to the Oxfordshire Senior League.
Ardley United joined from the Oxfordshire Senior League, Hallen joined from the Gloucestershire County League and Letcombe joined from the Chiltonian League.

1993-94

Premier Division

Moreton Town	34	25	6	3	74	21	81
Shortwood United	34	21	6	7	66	48	69
Banbury United	34	18	9	7	74	44	63
Wantage Town	*34*	*18*	*9*	*7*	*68*	*38*	*63*
Fairford Town	34	18	7	9	76	51	61
Cinderford Town	34	17	6	11	57	39	57
Bicester Town	34	17	6	11	64	48	57
Swindon Supermarine	34	16	6	12	64	42	51
Rayners Lane	*34*	*13*	*7*	*14*	*64*	*53*	*46*
Tuffley Rovers	34	14	4	16	60	53	46
Milton United	*34*	*13*	*6*	*15*	*59*	*58*	*45*
Abingdon United	34	12	8	14	60	57	44
Cirencester Town	34	12	4	18	53	62	40
North Leigh	34	10	9	15	60	58	39
Almondsbury Town	34	10	7	17	38	61	37
Headington Amateurs	*34*	*7*	*11*	*16*	*43*	*77*	*32*
Wollen Sports	34	4	6	24	34	95	18
Kintbury Rangers	34	2	1	31	17	126	7

Swindon Supermarine had 3 points deducted.
Milton United, Rayners Lane and Wantage Town were all relegated after failing to meet ground grading requirements. Wollen Sports left. Brackley Town joined from the United Counties League.

Division One

Carterton Town	**34**	**21**	**8**	**5**	**82**	**27**	**71**
Pegasus Juniors	**34**	**21**	**6**	**7**	**86**	**44**	**69**
Highworth Town	**34**	**20**	**8**	**6**	**58**	**30**	**68**
Lambourn Sports	34	17	10	7	65	38	61
Bishops Cleeve	34	17	8	9	79	54	59
Hallen	34	16	10	8	62	50	58
Easington Sports	34	15	9	10	66	49	54
Wallingford Town	34	14	11	9	74	54	53
Wootton Bassett Town	34	15	8	11	65	57	53
Cheltenham Saracens	34	14	9	11	63	50	51
Ardley United	34	12	11	11	59	50	47
Kidlington	34	10	8	16	52	68	38
Purton	34	10	7	17	52	74	37
Cirencester United	34	8	7	19	50	81	31
Didcot Town	34	9	2	23	49	97	29
Yarnton	34	8	4	22	43	85	28
Clanfield	34	4	9	21	32	75	21
Letcombe	34	6	3	25	26	80	21

Endsleigh joined from the Gloucestershire County League.

1994-95

Premier Division

Cinderford Town	30	23	4	3	118	24	73
Fairford Town	30	21	4	5	73	25	67
Swindon Supermarine	30	16	4	10	76	44	52
North Leigh	30	15	7	8	55	39	52
Shortwood United	30	16	3	11	60	53	51
Cirencester Town	30	15	5	10	56	43	50
Tuffley Rovers	30	14	7	9	65	44	49
Banbury United	30	12	7	11	44	44	43
Pegasus Juniors	*30*	*11*	*9*	*10*	*49*	*43*	*42*
Bicester Town	30	12	6	12	70	60	40
Abingdon United	30	11	5	14	55	58	38
Almondsbury Town	30	10	7	13	49	53	37
Carterton Town	30	7	9	14	36	60	30
Brackley Town	30	7	5	18	42	80	26
Highworth Town	30	2	6	22	30	93	12
Kintbury Rangers	30	3	2	25	30	145	9

Bicester Town and Kintbury Rangers each had 2 points deducted.
Moreton Town resigned and disbanded in November and their record was expunged.
Pegasus Juniors were relegated due to problems meeting ground grading requirements.
Cinderford Town moved to the Southern League and Burnham joined from the Southern League.

Division One

Endsleigh	**38**	**28**	**8**	**2**	**88**	**27**	**92**
Milton United	38	30	1	7	114	44	91
Lambourn Sports	**38**	**28**	**5**	**5**	**131**	**42**	**89**
Hallen	38	26	4	8	91	41	82
Rayners Lane	38	21	6	11	84	46	69
Purton	38	19	9	10	70	48	66
Wantage Town	38	17	11	10	86	59	62
Kidlington	38	18	6	14	74	81	60
Wootton Bassett Town	38	18	5	15	67	68	59
Didcot Town	**38**	**16**	**8**	**14**	**77**	**62**	**56**
Easington Sports	38	16	8	14	78	68	56
Wallingford Town	38	13	7	18	70	88	46
Bishops Cleeve	38	13	6	19	84	86	45
Ardley United	38	13	6	19	78	90	45
Headington Amateurs	38	11	9	18	59	75	42
Cheltenham Saracens	38	11	8	19	67	67	41
Clanfield	38	10	2	26	48	82	32
Letcombe	38	5	6	27	32	112	21
Cirencester United	38	5	5	28	46	102	20
Yarnton	38	1	2	35	30	186	5

Didcot Town were promoted due to the quality of their ground facilities. Harrow Hill joined from the Gloucestershire County League.
Wallingford Town merged with Wallingford United of the Chiltonian League and joined that league as AFC Wallingford.

1995-96

Premier Division

Cirencester Town	34	24	8	2	69	24	80
Brackley Town	34	19	12	3	60	32	69
Lambourn Sports	34	21	5	8	71	41	68
Tuffley Rovers	34	20	7	7	78	46	67
Burnham	34	20	4	10	66	37	64
Swindon Supermarine	34	20	3	11	82	33	63
Endsleigh	34	16	7	11	56	41	55
North Leigh	34	15	4	15	66	62	49
Carterton Town	34	13	9	12	57	59	48
Abingdon United	34	13	4	17	49	55	43
Fairford Town	34	10	10	14	49	52	40
Almondsbury Town	34	10	7	17	53	54	37
Shortwood United	34	10	5	19	53	82	35
Kintbury Rangers	34	8	9	17	45	74	33
Banbury United	34	8	6	20	40	66	30
Highworth Town	34	9	3	22	36	80	30
Didcot Town	34	7	7	20	39	88	28
Bicester Town	34	6	4	24	37	80	22

Cirencester Town moved to the Southern League.

Division One

Purton	34	22	6	6	79	40	72
Wantage Town	**34**	**21**	**8**	**5**	**66**	**34**	**71**
Milton United	34	18	8	8	102	63	62
Hallen	34	16	9	9	75	49	57
Harrow Hill	34	16	9	9	57	38	57
Pegasus Juniors	34	15	7	12	76	62	52
Kidlington	34	13	9	12	73	59	48
Cheltenham Saracens	34	14	6	14	71	71	48
Ardley United	34	13	6	15	47	60	45
Wootton Bassett Town	34	12	9	13	50	64	45
Clanfield	34	9	12	13	54	61	39
Bishops Cleeve	34	10	9	15	50	65	39
Rayners Lane	34	9	11	14	51	66	38
Easington Sports	34	9	10	15	45	64	37
Headington Amateurs	34	10	5	19	51	72	35
Letcombe	34	9	8	17	38	65	35
Yarnton	34	9	6	19	45	84	33
Cirencester United	34	8	8	18	53	66	32

Rayners Lane moved to the Middlesex County League.
Ross Town joined from the Worcester & District League.

1996-97

Premier Division

Brackley Town	34	25	6	3	79	20	81
Abingdon United	34	22	5	7	57	32	71
Burnham	34	20	9	5	67	34	69
Swindon Supermarine	34	21	5	8	72	40	68
North Leigh	34	17	7	10	56	39	58
Tuffley Rovers	34	16	8	10	62	43	56
Endsleigh	34	13	11	10	49	50	50
Banbury United	34	14	5	15	51	46	47
Didcot Town	34	13	7	14	42	52	46
Carterton Town	34	12	5	17	57	57	41
Shortwood United	34	11	6	17	53	60	39
Lambourn Sports	34	10	8	16	44	53	38
Bicester Town	34	10	7	17	31	53	37
Wantage Town	34	11	4	19	36	69	37
Almondsbury Town	34	8	10	16	44	52	34
Kintbury Rangers	34	9	5	20	41	67	32
Highworth Town	34	8	5	21	40	73	29
Fairford Town	34	7	5	22	32	73	26

Brackley Town moved to the Southern League.
Lambourn Sports moved to the North Berkshire League.

Division One

Ardley United	32	24	7	1	76	21	79
Hallen	**32**	**21**	**8**	**3**	**79**	**23**	**71**
Harrow Hill	**32**	**20**	**7**	**5**	**56**	**29**	**67**
Cheltenham Saracens	32	20	5	7	75	47	65
Purton	32	19	5	8	75	36	62
Kidlington	32	19	4	9	64	33	61
Pegasus Juniors	32	18	4	10	61	29	58
Headington Amateurs	32	14	6	12	49	47	48
Ross Town	32	13	7	12	56	47	46
Cirencester United	32	12	4	16	51	56	40
Wootton Bassett Town	32	9	8	15	37	50	35
Clanfield	32	9	3	20	46	64	30
Bishops Cleeve	32	7	9	16	39	66	30
Yarnton	32	9	3	20	30	67	30
Easington Sports	32	5	5	22	34	78	20
Letcombe	32	4	4	24	26	97	16
Milton United	32	2	5	25	42	106	11

Watlington Town joined from the Oxfordshire Senior League and Cirencester Academy also joined.

1997-98

Premier Division

Swindon Supermarine	34	27	3	4	83	20	84
Endsleigh	34	26	4	4	75	24	82
Burnham	34	18	10	6	65	35	64
Banbury United	34	17	7	10	69	42	58
Almondsbury Town	34	17	4	13	51	37	55
Tuffley Rovers	34	16	7	11	57	49	55
Highworth Town	34	14	7	13	52	56	49
North Leigh	34	13	8	13	51	46	47
Fairford Town	34	13	8	13	54	53	47
Abingdon United	34	12	10	12	60	57	46
Wantage Town	34	12	4	18	45	72	40
Didcot Town	34	9	12	13	48	49	39
Carterton Town	34	9	10	15	50	57	37
Shortwood United	34	10	6	18	57	78	36
Hallen	34	9	6	19	39	57	33
Harrow Hill	34	8	7	19	38	70	31
Bicester Town	34	7	8	19	43	73	29
Kintbury Rangers	34	6	5	23	32	94	23

Endsleigh changed their name to EFC Cheltenham

Division One

Ardley United	32	23	5	4	104	36	74
Cirencester Academy	**32**	**21**	**9**	**2**	**66**	**22**	**72**
Cheltenham Saracens	32	21	6	5	71	41	69
Purton	32	18	6	8	71	44	60
Kidlington	32	16	8	8	71	49	56
Easington Sports	32	15	5	12	60	56	50
Pegasus Juniors	32	14	6	12	62	50	48
Clanfield	32	14	5	13	64	56	47
Ross Town	32	13	6	13	56	57	45
Wootton Bassett Town	32	12	6	14	67	58	42
Cirencester United	32	11	7	14	51	57	40
Bishops Cleeve	32	12	3	17	42	63	39
Watlington Town	32	11	3	18	42	59	36
Headington Amateurs	32	9	7	16	47	56	34
Letcombe	32	8	3	21	40	82	27
Milton United	32	6	4	22	37	82	22
Yarnton	32	2	3	27	29	112	9

Yarnton moved to the Oxfordshire Senior League.
Worcester College Old Boys joined from the Oxfordshire Senior League and Forest Green Rovers Reserves also joined.

1998-99

Premier Division

Burnham	36	26	6	4	88	31	84
Carterton Town	36	25	6	5	82	34	81
Highworth Town	36	21	6	9	92	47	69
Banbury United	36	20	9	7	73	33	69
North Leigh	36	18	11	7	77	44	65
EFC Cheltenham	36	17	5	14	60	36	56
Abingdon United	36	17	5	14	61	55	56
Tuffley Rovers	36	16	6	14	63	55	54
Didcot Town	36	16	5	15	58	52	53
Bicester Town	36	15	8	13	58	60	53
Cirencester Academy	36	12	11	13	42	56	47
Hallen	36	10	14	12	45	48	44
Fairford Town	36	10	10	16	42	50	40
Swindon Supermarine	36	10	9	17	41	59	39
Shortwood United	36	9	11	16	37	61	38
Almondsbury Town	36	8	7	21	47	82	31
Wantage Town	36	8	5	23	36	90	29
Kintbury Rangers	36	8	8	20	48	89	26
Harrow Hill	36	4	2	30	31	99	14

Kintbury Rangers had 6 points deducted.
Burnham moved to the Southern League. Kintbury Rangers moved to the North Berkshire League and EFC Cheltenham also left.
Brackley Town joined from the Southern League.

Division One

Pegasus Juniors	**32**	**22**	**7**	**3**	**96**	**47**	**73**
Ardley United	32	19	5	8	66	46	62
Forest Green Rovers Reserves	32	18	6	8	71	40	60
Milton United	**32**	**18**	**6**	**8**	**62**	**45**	**60**
Wootton Bassett Town	32	17	7	8	64	43	58
Ross Town	32	15	7	10	57	41	52
Letcombe	32	13	9	10	56	47	48
Cheltenham Saracens	32	13	5	14	56	61	44
Worcester College Old Boys	32	11	5	16	42	59	38
Kidlington	32	10	8	14	51	74	38
Purton	32	9	9	14	41	62	36
Bishops Cleeve	32	9	7	16	55	66	34
Easington Sports	32	8	8	16	47	56	32
Cirencester United	32	8	7	17	49	55	31
Clanfield	32	9	4	19	40	71	31
Watlington Town	32	7	9	16	49	69	30
Headington Amateurs	32	6	11	15	44	64	29

Forest Green Rovers disbanded their reserve side. Watlington Town moved to the Oxfordshire Senior League.
Old Woodstock Town and Middle Barton joined from the Oxfordshire Senior League.

1999-2000

Premier Division

Banbury United	36	29	5	2	87	22	92
Highworth Town	36	25	4	7	90	54	79
Swindon Supermarine	36	23	4	9	74	27	73
Tuffley Rovers	36	22	4	10	76	44	70
Brackley Town	36	21	6	9	66	32	69
North Leigh	36	19	7	10	81	53	64
Didcot Town	36	17	10	9	61	50	61
Abingdon United	36	17	6	13	58	55	57
Carterton Town	36	15	6	15	47	50	51
Pegasus Juniors	36	15	5	16	62	61	50
Shortwood United	36	13	10	13	54	55	49
Wantage Town	36	15	4	17	50	64	49
Hallen	36	13	7	16	55	60	46
Cirencester Academy	36	10	6	20	34	53	36
Bicester Town	36	9	5	22	42	73	32
Fairford Town	36	7	8	21	32	69	29
Almondsbury Town	36	7	5	24	42	83	26
Harrow Hill	36	7	1	28	44	96	22
Milton United	36	3	7	26	36	90	16

Banbury United moved to the Southern League and Hallen moved to the Western League. Yate Town joined from the Southern League.

Division One

Cheltenham Saracens	**28**	**23**	**2**	**3**	**61**	**20**	**71**
Ardley United	28	16	6	6	63	38	54
Wootton Bassett Town	**28**	**15**	**7**	**6**	**54**	**32**	**52**
Worcester College Old Boys	28	13	6	9	53	46	45
Bishops Cleeve	28	12	8	8	44	43	44
Middle Barton	28	12	5	11	49	45	41
Letcombe	28	11	5	12	57	45	38
Easington Sports	28	10	6	12	50	58	36
Purton	28	10	4	14	42	56	34
Ross Town	28	8	8	12	32	32	32
Old Woodstock Town	28	8	8	12	43	51	32
Kidlington	28	9	5	14	36	50	32
Cirencester United	28	10	1	17	38	50	31
Clanfield	28	6	6	16	33	58	24
Headington Amateurs	28	6	5	17	29	60	23

Division One became Division One (West), expanding to 16 clubs with the addition of three clubs: Malmesbury Victoria from the Wiltshire League and two newly formed clubs, Gloucester United and Witney Academy.

A new Division One (East) was formed by the absorption of the Chiltonian League clubs all of whose first XI's joined with the exception of Iver, Stocklake who joined the Spartan South Midlands League as Haywards Way and Taplow United. The division was made up to 17 clubs by the addition of newly formed Southall Town.

2000-01

Premier Division

Swindon Supermarine	38	29	4	5	86	29	91
Brackley Town	38	25	8	5	84	45	83
Yate Town	38	21	9	8	92	38	72
Didcot Town	38	20	12	6	57	27	72
Abingdon United	38	21	6	11	80	53	69
North Leigh	38	20	6	12	77	51	66
Cirencester Academy	38	18	5	15	70	54	59
Highworth Town	38	19	2	17	74	68	59
Fairford Town	38	17	7	14	54	45	58
Carterton Town	38	16	9	13	64	57	57
Shortwood United	38	15	11	12	62	58	56
Tuffley Rovers	38	16	6	16	54	58	54
Wootton Bassett Town	38	14	10	14	54	60	52
Bicester Town	38	14	7	17	59	67	49
Pegasus Juniors	38	12	4	22	67	96	40
Wantage Town	38	11	4	23	49	83	37
Cheltenham Saracens	38	9	5	24	31	76	32
Harrow Hill	38	5	10	23	36	80	25
Almondsbury Town	38	7	3	28	36	76	24
Milton United (Relegated D1E)	*38*	*5*	*4*	*29*	*31*	*96*	*19*

Swindon Supermarine moved to the Southern League, Western Division.

Division One (West)

Gloucester United	**30**	**26**	**3**	**1**	**119**	**15**	**81**
Bishops Cleeve	**30**	**22**	**3**	**5**	**70**	**36**	**69**
Ardley United	30	21	3	6	74	34	66
Malmesbury Victoria	30	15	5	10	65	59	50
Headington Amateurs	30	15	5	10	54	50	50
Easington Sports	30	12	6	12	55	61	42
Cirencester United	30	11	6	13	50	59	39
Middle Barton	30	9	11	10	45	47	38
Clanfield	30	8	8	14	45	58	32
Ross Town	30	9	6	15	48	54	33
Kidlington	30	7	9	14	39	50	30
Letcombe	30	7	9	14	38	61	30
Purton	30	7	9	14	46	73	30
Witney Academy	30	8	6	16	37	82	30
Old Woodstock Town	30	6	8	16	36	61	26
Worcester College Old Boys	30	5	7	18	41	69	22

Worcester College Old Boys moved to the Oxfordshire Senior League.
Hook Norton joined from the Oxfordshire Senior League, Pewsey Vale from the Western League, Winterbourne United from the Gloucestershire County League and Shrivenham from the North Berkshire League.
Chipping Norton Town joined as a newly re-formed club.

Division One (East)

	P	W	D	L	F	A	Pts
Henley Town	32	25	4	3	105	33	79
RS Basingstoke	32	17	8	7	63	37	59
Southall Town	32	15	10	7	63	44	55
Quarry Nomads	32	16	7	9	66	56	55
Eton Wick	32	16	6	10	71	50	54
Rayners Lane	32	15	7	10	77	58	52
Finchampstead	32	14	8	10	75	58	50
Harrow Hill Rovers	32	15	4	13	72	71	49
Englefield Green Rovers	32	13	6	13	75	71	45
Binfield	32	13	6	13	56	55	45
Prestwood	32	12	9	11	60	65	45
Peppard	32	9	12	11	58	65	39
Chalfont Wasps	32	11	4	17	58	75	37
Martin Baker Sports	32	7	11	14	49	61	32
Penn & Tylers Green	32	10	2	20	47	75	32
Drayton Wanderers	32	7	3	22	44	90	24
Aston Clinton	32	3	1	28	40	115	10

Harrow Hill Rovers changed their name to Hounslow Borough.
Bisley Sports joined from the Surrey County Senior League.

Division One (East)

	P	W	D	L	F	A	Pts
Finchampstead	32	20	6	6	73	40	66
Aston Clinton	32	19	7	6	76	37	64
RS Basingstoke	32	16	7	9	64	53	55
Martin Baker Sports	32	15	8	9	68	43	53
Englefield Green Rovers	32	16	4	12	64	51	52
Milton United	32	12	13	7	50	37	49
Bisley Sports	32	14	5	13	53	53	47
Prestwood	32	13	6	13	58	58	45
Penn & Tylers Green	32	12	8	12	56	50	44
Eton Wick	32	12	6	14	53	59	42
Quarry Nomads	32	12	6	14	54	74	42
Drayton Wanderers	32	11	4	17	56	86	37
Peppard	32	8	11	13	39	46	35
Binfield	32	9	7	16	44	53	34
Rayners Lane	32	8	10	14	55	66	34
Hounslow Borough	32	5	11	16	47	76	26
Chalfont Wasps	32	6	9	17	44	72	27

Peppard left and withdrew from Saturday football.
Holyport joined from the East Berkshire League.

2001-02

Premier Division

	P	W	D	L	F	A	Pts
North Leigh	42	30	8	4	97	36	98
Gloucester United	42	29	6	7	106	48	93
Yate Town	42	24	13	5	105	39	85
Abingdon United	42	24	8	10	86	51	80
Didcot Town	42	24	6	12	93	56	78
Fairford Town	42	21	10	11	72	42	73
Brackley Town	42	20	9	13	70	55	69
Tuffley Rovers	42	19	11	12	53	61	68
Shortwood United	42	20	7	15	67	66	67
Bishops Cleeve	42	19	8	15	79	51	65
Carterton Town	42	18	10	14	71	48	64
Wantage Town	42	15	10	17	67	65	55
Pegasus Juniors	42	16	5	21	65	92	53
Southall Town	42	14	9	19	55	66	51
Highworth Town	42	14	7	21	66	77	49
Henley Town	42	12	10	20	51	65	46
Cirencester Academy	42	11	11	20	61	71	44
Almondsbury Town	42	12	6	24	53	84	42
Wootton Bassett Town	42	11	9	22	39	75	42
Bicester Town	42	9	6	27	58	97	33
Harrow Hill (Relegated D1W)	*42*	*7*	*2*	*33*	*31*	*104*	*23*
Cheltenham Saracens (R D1W)	*42*	*3*	*9*	*30*	*30*	*126*	*18*

Cirencester Academy left and withdrew from Saturday football.

2002-03

Premier Division

	P	W	D	L	F	A	Pts
North Leigh	40	29	6	5	84	36	93
Yate Town	40	25	8	7	87	42	83
Carterton Town	40	22	17	1	61	29	83
Highworth Town	40	23	10	7	79	41	79
Didcot Town	40	22	6	12	77	39	72
Fairford Town	40	21	8	11	65	30	71
Brackley Town	40	18	12	10	84	42	66
Abingdon United	40	20	6	14	70	52	66
Bishops Cleeve	40	19	7	14	68	50	64
Henley Town	40	17	10	13	69	48	61
Southall Town	40	18	7	15	75	65	61
Hook Norton	40	15	13	12	67	55	58
Shortwood United	40	15	10	15	64	60	55
Tuffley Rovers	40	12	9	19	56	76	45
Wootton Bassett Town	40	10	10	20	36	70	40
Gloucester United	40	9	8	23	48	89	32
Almondsbury Town	40	8	7	25	43	77	31
Pegasus Juniors	40	8	7	25	45	108	31
Pewsey Vale	40	7	8	25	45	93	29
Bicester Town	40	5	8	27	40	99	23
Wantage Town (Relegated D1E)	*40*	*5*	*7*	*28*	*36*	*98*	*22*

Gloucester United had 3 points deducted.
Yate Town moved to the Southern League, Western Division.

Division One (West)

	P	W	D	L	F	A	Pts
Hook Norton	32	22	8	2	69	21	74
Pewsey Vale	32	20	5	7	80	39	65
Ardley United	32	18	8	6	83	51	62
Purton	32	18	4	10	63	52	58
Ross Town	32	15	10	7	56	41	55
Winterbourne United	32	15	9	8	73	41	54
Middle Barton	32	13	8	11	62	64	47
Old Woodstock Town	32	11	10	11	47	38	43
Shrivenham	32	12	6	14	57	63	42
Kidlington	32	11	8	13	36	38	41
Chipping Norton Town	32	10	7	15	49	68	37
Malmesbury Victoria	32	8	11	13	49	53	35
Easington Sports	32	9	8	15	37	54	35
Clanfield	32	7	9	16	40	61	30
Cirencester United	32	8	4	20	36	69	28
Headington Amateurs	32	6	7	19	40	79	25
Letcombe	32	3	10	19	42	87	19

Witney Academy resigned and disbanded during the season when
their record was: 19 2 6 11 24 54 12
Letcombe transferred to Division One (East).
Adderbury Park joined from the Oxfordshire Senior League,
New College Academy joined not having played in a league before,
Slimbridge Town joined from the Gloucestershire County League and
newly formed Witney United (having replaced disbanded Witney
Town) also joined.

Division One (West)

	P	W	D	L	F	A	Pts
Slimbridge	38	29	6	3	114	26	93
Chipping Norton Town	38	24	10	4	76	33	82
Purton	38	25	1	12	99	49	76
Winterbourne United	38	22	6	10	80	41	72
Ardley United	38	21	6	11	93	47	69
Old Woodstock Town	38	19	6	13	65	54	63
Kidlington	38	15	9	14	67	76	54
Headington Amateurs	38	13	13	12	72	70	52
Cheltenham Saracens	38	13	12	13	61	54	51
Easington Sports	38	15	6	17	54	67	51
Adderbury Park	38	14	8	16	70	85	50
Shrivenham	38	13	10	15	55	65	49
New College Academy	38	14	4	20	57	67	46
Malmesbury Victoria	38	12	8	18	54	64	44
Witney Town	38	9	13	16	54	74	40
Middle Barton	38	10	9	19	49	83	39
Cirencester United	38	9	10	19	49	77	37
Harrow Hill	38	10	5	23	45	78	35
Clanfield	38	9	7	22	43	82	34
Ross Town	38	7	5	26	45	110	26

New College Academy left and took their Reserves' place in the
Wiltshire League, Junior Division Two.

Division One (East)

Quarry Nomads	32	21	4	7	76	41	67
Penn & Tylers Green	32	19	6	7	63	33	60
Finchampstead	32	17	9	6	61	32	60
Rayners Lane	32	18	5	9	66	40	59
Chalfont Wasps	32	18	4	10	67	44	58
Eton Wick	32	16	9	7	72	49	57
Milton United	32	14	9	9	53	39	51
Binfield	32	14	6	12	73	46	48
Letcombe	32	11	6	15	45	53	39
Englefield Green Rovers	32	12	3	17	47	62	39
RS Basingstoke	32	10	7	15	55	64	37
Bisley Sports	32	10	7	15	43	64	37
Hounslow Borough	32	9	8	15	61	73	35
Prestwood	32	8	10	14	43	63	34
Holyport	32	10	2	20	37	78	32
Martin Baker Sports	32	4	11	17	41	74	23
Drayton Wanderers	32	5	6	21	38	86	21

Penn & Tylers Green had 3 points deducted.
Aston Clinton resigned during the season and their record at the time was deleted:

	6	0	0	6	4	18	0

They joined the Aylesbury & District League the following season.
Quarry Nomads transferred to Division One (West).
RS Basingstoke moved to the Hampshire League and Drayton Wanderers withdrew from Saturday football.
Chinnor joined from the Oxfordshire Senior League and Badshot Lea joined from the Surrey Intermediate League (West).

2003-04

Premier Division

Brackley Town	42	28	8	6	106	36	92
Southall Town	42	28	8	6	104	42	92
Bishops Cleeve	42	27	8	7	94	36	89
Slimbridge	42	26	11	5	85	29	89
Didcot Town	42	28	4	10	90	35	88
Hungerford Town	42	25	6	11	90	45	80
Carterton Town	42	22	9	11	63	45	75
North Leigh	42	21	6	15	70	51	69
Highworth Town	42	19	11	12	66	45	68
Fairford Town	42	21	8	13	74	63	68
Abingdon United	42	19	11	12	54	49	68
Chipping Norton Town	42	15	9	18	57	68	54
Tuffley Rovers	42	11	13	18	43	49	46
Bicester Town	42	11	6	25	32	64	39
Henley Town	42	11	6	25	44	82	39
Wootton Bassett Town	42	11	5	26	38	73	38
Pegasus Juniors	42	11	5	26	45	105	38
Pewsey Vale	42	10	7	25	58	99	37
Shortwood United	42	11	4	27	53	95	37
Hook Norton (Relegated D1W)	*42*	*8*	*12*	*22*	*42*	*76*	*36*
Almondsbury Town	42	10	5	27	33	86	35
Gloucester United	42	4	8	30	40	108	20

Hungerford Town had 1 point deducted. Fairford Town had 3 points deducted. Brackley Town moved to the Southern League. Gloucester United and Southall Town both disbanded.

Division One (West)

Purton	34	24	10	0	83	25	82
Ross Town	34	22	8	4	73	34	74
Shrivenham	34	22	6	6	78	26	72
Witney United	**34**	**18**	**9**	**7**	**63**	**34**	**63**
Ardley United	**34**	**17**	**10**	**7**	**68**	**46**	**61**
Easington Sports	34	12	16	6	49	40	52
Quarry Nomads	34	14	7	13	71	59	49
Old Woodstock Town	34	14	7	13	53	60	49
Winterbourne United	34	13	8	13	62	52	47
Headington Amateurs	34	12	8	14	59	66	44
Harrow Hill	34	12	6	16	45	61	42
Kidlington	34	10	11	13	66	69	41
Cheltenham Saracens	34	11	8	15	47	53	41
Malmesbury Victoria	34	11	6	17	41	52	39
Cirencester United	34	8	9	17	51	66	33
Middle Barton	34	7	5	22	34	81	26
Adderbury Park	34	5	3	26	34	95	18
Clanfield	34	3	5	26	37	95	14

Old Woodstock Town transferred to Division One (East).
Trowbridge Town joined from the Wiltshire League and Tytherington Rocks joined from the Gloucestershire County League.

Division One (East)

Wantage Town	**32**	**23**	**7**	**2**	**85**	**16**	**76**
Letcombe	32	19	10	3	60	27	67
Milton United	**32**	**16**	**11**	**5**	**71**	**45**	**59**
Eton Wick	32	15	9	8	64	45	54
Binfield	32	15	8	9	52	38	53
Rayners Lane	32	14	9	9	73	51	51
Chalfont Wasps	32	15	4	13	54	51	49
Finchampstead	32	12	9	11	54	42	45
Martin Baker Sports	32	12	3	17	49	73	39
Penn & Tylers Green	32	9	11	12	46	54	38
Chinnor	32	10	5	17	46	57	35
Bisley Sports	32	9	8	15	38	52	35
Prestwood	32	9	6	17	63	75	33
Badshot Lea	32	9	6	17	50	73	33
Englefield Green Rovers	32	8	7	17	44	76	31
Hounslow Borough	32	8	5	19	45	80	28
Holyport	32	6	8	18	42	81	26

Hounslow Borough had 1 point deducted.
Martin Baker Sports moved to the Middlesex County League. Banbury United Reserves transferred from Division One of the Reserve Section and Kintbury Rangers joined from the North Berkshire League. Wokingham & Emmbrook also joined, being a new club formed by a merger of Wokingham Town of the Isthmian League and Emmbrook Sports of the Reading League.

2004-05

Premier Division

Highworth Town	42	30	8	4	101	33	98
Didcot Town	42	31	5	6	99	21	97
Bishops Cleeve	42	25	11	6	86	30	86
Slimbridge	42	26	8	8	88	48	86
Abingdon United	42	25	9	8	88	49	84
Carterton	42	24	8	10	72	48	80
North Leigh	42	24	7	11	76	46	79
Fairford Town	42	19	5	18	62	54	62
Almondsbury Town	42	16	13	13	80	59	61
Wantage Town	42	13	16	13	52	43	55
Witney United	42	15	10	17	45	52	55
Tuffley Rovers	42	12	14	16	43	47	50
Milton United	42	14	7	21	48	67	49
Henley Town	42	14	8	20	58	79	47
Shortwood United	42	13	7	22	58	77	46
Pegasus Juniors	42	12	8	22	62	95	44
Hungerford Town	42	11	9	22	45	66	42
Ardley United	42	9	15	18	48	71	42
Chipping Norton Town	42	11	7	24	39	83	40
Bicester Town (Relegated D1E)	*42*	*8*	*4*	*30*	*38*	*103*	*28*
Wootton Bassett Town (R D1W)	*42*	*6*	*9*	*27*	*30*	*85*	*27*
Pewsey Vale (R D1W)	*42*	*6*	*8*	*28*	*42*	*104*	*26*

Didcot Town had 1 point deducted.
Henley Town had 3 points deducted.
Abingdon Town joined from the Isthmian League.

Division One (West)

Shrivenham	34	25	3	6	91	36	78
Trowbridge Town	34	24	5	5	97	38	77
Kidlington	**34**	**20**	**6**	**8**	**79**	**49**	**66**
Tytherington Rocks	34	20	4	10	91	54	64
Easington Sports	34	18	7	9	60	38	61
Cheltenham Saracens	34	18	6	10	60	45	60
Headington Amateurs	34	17	6	11	69	44	57
Harrow Hill	34	16	6	12	60	44	54
Winterbourne United	34	15	7	12	53	52	52
Clanfield	34	13	7	14	55	51	46
Hook Norton	34	12	10	12	51	56	46
Ross Town	34	11	7	16	57	54	40
Purton	34	9	8	17	39	61	35
Cirencester United	34	7	11	16	40	63	32
Quarry Nomads	34	10	1	23	61	106	31
Middle Barton	34	7	4	23	36	116	25
Malmesbury Victoria	34	7	3	24	33	80	24
Adderbury Park	34	6	1	27	47	111	19

Cricklade Town joined from the Wiltshire League.
Quarry Nomads changed their name to Oxford Quarry Nomads and transferred to Division One (East).
Adderbury Park moved to the Oxfordshire Senior League.

Division One (East)

Eton Wick	34	23	8	3	100	35	77
Kintbury Rangers	34	23	5	6	79	33	74
Penn & Tylers Green	34	23	3	8	95	51	72
Finchampstead	34	19	7	8	62	37	64
Binfield	34	16	8	10	54	35	56
Banbury United Reserves	34	16	8	10	66	68	56
Badshot Lea	34	16	4	14	75	63	52
Rayners Lane	34	15	5	14	75	56	50
Chinnor	34	12	8	14	49	47	44
Hounslow Borough	34	12	7	15	61	85	43
Wokingham & Emmbrook	34	13	3	18	50	66	42
Letcombe	34	11	7	16	53	66	40
Englefield Green Rovers	34	11	7	16	49	67	40
Old Woodstock Town	34	10	9	15	50	65	39
Holyport	34	9	7	18	44	91	34
Prestwood	34	9	4	21	50	82	31
Chalfont Wasps	34	7	7	20	50	69	28
Bisley Sports	34	6	3	25	33	79	21

Letcombe and Old Woodstock Town transferred to Division One (West).

2005-06

Premier Division

Didcot Town	40	34	3	3	124	31	105
Bishops Cleeve	40	29	5	6	108	45	92
Abingdon United	40	27	3	10	88	40	84
North Leigh	40	25	6	9	78	40	81
Slimbridge	40	24	6	10	90	45	78
Witney United	40	23	4	13	88	51	73
Carterton	40	23	3	14	73	51	72
Shrivenham	40	22	5	13	82	58	71
Wantage Town	40	19	7	14	73	70	64
Ardley United	40	18	6	16	70	63	60
Milton United	40	14	9	17	62	69	51
Highworth Town	40	13	10	17	62	72	49
Pegasus Juniors	40	12	11	17	53	74	47
Almondsbury Town	40	13	6	21	50	64	45
Shortwood United	40	12	6	22	55	79	42
Hungerford Town	40	11	8	21	31	65	41
Fairford Town	40	11	6	23	42	73	39
Abingdon Town	40	9	10	21	45	88	37
Chipping Norton Town	40	6	7	27	43	99	25
Kidlington	40	7	1	32	42	108	22
Henley Town (Relegated D1E)	*40*	*5*	*4*	*31*	*28*	*102*	*19*

Tuffley Rovers resigned from the League during season and their record at the time was deleted: 3 0 1 2 3 5 1
They took their Reserves' place in the Gloucestershire Northern Senior League the following season.
Abingdon United, Bishops Cleeve and Didcot Town moved to the Southern League.
Thame United joined from the Southern League and AFC Wallingford joined from the Combined Counties League.

Division One (West)

Winterbourne United	34	24	5	5	98	36	77
Harrow Hill	**34**	**18**	**9**	**7**	**61**	**40**	**63**
Tytherington Rocks	34	19	5	10	79	54	62
Headington Amateurs	34	18	8	8	59	39	62
Wootton Bassett Town	34	17	10	7	58	30	61
Trowbridge Town	34	17	9	8	65	44	60
Old Woodstock Town	34	16	8	10	55	46	56
Cheltenham Saracens	34	14	12	8	54	40	54
Letcombe	34	14	6	14	51	45	48
Pewsey Vale	34	13	7	14	54	51	46
Hook Norton	34	13	7	14	57	58	46
Cricklade Town	34	13	5	16	55	67	44
Malmesbury Victoria	34	11	9	14	50	56	42
Cirencester United	34	11	5	18	50	64	38
Purton	34	7	9	18	33	64	27
Easington Sports	34	6	9	19	37	71	27
Clanfield	34	5	4	25	30	74	19
Ross Town	34	5	3	26	36	103	18

Purton had 3 points deducted.
Middle Barton resigned during the season and their record at the time was deleted: 4 0 0 4 3 17 0
They joined the Oxfordshire Senior League the following season.
Headington Amateurs transferred to Division One (East).
Lydney Town joined from the Gloucestershire County League.

Division One (East)

Hounslow Borough	**34**	**23**	**4**	**7**	**99**	**45**	**73**
Bicester Town	**34**	**21**	**8**	**5**	**78**	**36**	**71**
Wokingham & Emmbrook	34	21	5	8	86	47	68
Chalfont Wasps	34	20	4	10	80	49	64
Englefield Green Rovers	34	20	4	10	73	46	64
Penn & Tylers Green	34	20	4	10	69	46	64
Bisley Sports	34	19	5	10	81	51	62
Binfield	34	19	2	13	70	44	59
Kintbury Rangers	34	18	4	12	81	48	58
Eton Wick	34	17	5	12	73	64	56
Oxford Quarry Nomads	34	14	4	16	67	81	46
Badshot Lea	34	13	6	15	81	74	45
Finchampstead	34	10	7	17	58	60	37
Holyport	34	10	4	20	58	90	34
Rayners Lane	34	11	1	22	57	90	34
Chinnor	34	5	5	24	34	82	20
Banbury United Reserves	34	4	4	26	29	108	16
Prestwood	34	1	4	29	24	137	7

Banbury United Reserves transferred to Division One (West).
Marlow United joined from the Reading League.

2006-07

Premier Division

Slimbridge	38	27	7	4	93	29	88
North Leigh	38	25	10	3	77	33	85
Hungerford Town	38	21	8	9	77	40	71
Ardley United	38	19	10	9	78	54	67
Almondsbury Town	38	19	9	10	73	44	66
Witney United	38	16	13	9	67	49	61
Milton United	38	18	6	14	73	70	60
Shortwood United	38	15	9	14	76	72	54
Kidlington	38	14	11	13	47	52	53
Shrivenham	38	16	8	14	67	59	56
Wantage Town	38	13	11	14	62	60	50
Carterton	38	13	9	16	58	61	48
Fairford Town	38	12	10	16	56	61	46
Bicester Town	38	10	15	13	59	64	45
Highworth Town	38	10	14	14	54	55	44
AFC Wallingford	38	10	8	20	37	71	38
Pegasus Juniors	38	9	7	22	45	85	34
Abingdon Town	38	6	12	20	42	80	30
Harrow Hill	38	5	9	24	36	82	24
Thame United	38	6	6	26	45	101	24

Chipping Norton Town and Hounslow Borough resigned during the season and their records were deleted.
Shrivenham had 4 points deducted.

Division One (West)

Lydney Town	34	24	6	4	72	29	78
Trowbridge Town	34	21	7	6	76	31	70
Hook Norton	34	20	6	8	62	42	66
Malmesbury Victoria	34	16	11	7	62	38	59
Tytherington Rocks	34	15	10	9	71	48	55
Cheltenham Saracens	34	14	10	10	57	45	52
Old Woodstock Town	34	12	13	9	58	54	49
Cricklade Town	34	15	4	15	51	56	49
Pewsey Vale	34	12	12	10	47	46	48
Winterbourne United	34	12	11	11	64	59	47
Wootton Bassett Town	34	14	5	15	64	62	47
Cirencester United	34	13	8	13	56	58	47
Easington Sports	34	12	9	13	72	74	45
Banbury United Reserves	34	11	6	17	55	62	39
Letcombe	34	11	6	17	54	63	39
Purton	34	6	10	18	50	79	28
Clanfield	34	4	7	23	32	70	19
Ross Town	34	1	5	28	36	123	8

Division One (East)

Bisley Sports	34	27	5	2	121	22	86
Chalfont Wasps	34	25	2	7	96	37	77
Badshot Lea	34	24	4	6	98	37	76
Kintbury Rangers	34	24	3	7	92	38	75
Rayners Lane	34	19	8	7	86	46	65
Englefield Green Rovers	34	16	6	12	53	52	54
Marlow United	34	15	6	13	65	52	51
Wokingham & Emmbrook	34	15	4	15	49	73	49
Holyport	34	15	3	16	65	64	48
Headington Amateurs	34	11	9	14	57	62	42
Binfield	34	12	5	17	52	57	41
Oxford Quarry Nomads	34	13	2	19	64	79	41
Penn & Tylers Green	34	11	7	16	65	73	40
Finchampstead	34	11	7	16	51	65	40
Chinnor	34	9	9	16	45	58	36
Henley Town	34	9	4	21	43	80	31
Prestwood	34	5	3	26	25	87	18
Eton Wick	34	1	1	32	23	168	4

DEVON COUNTY LEAGUE

The Devon County League was formed in 1992 as a league to cover the whole of Devon and provide a logical step between the various local leagues and the Western League. Its 16 founder members were: Alphington, Cullompton Rangers, Newton St. Cyres, Topsham Town and Willand Rovers from the Premier Division of the Devon & Exeter League; Buckfastleigh Rangers, Northern Telecomm (Paignton), Stoke Gabriel and Teignmouth from the Premier Division of the South Devon League; Chagford and Newton Abbot who were the top two in the First Division of the South Devon League; Elburton Villa, Ivybridge Town, Plymstock United and Weston Mill Oak Villa from the Premier Division of the Plymouth & District League while the 16th member was E.A.F. Plymouth, from Division One of the Plymouth & District League.

A few of the published tables contained errors. Additional research has succeeded in correcting all but one of these, the totals that still do not balance are shown below the relevant columns in italics.

1992-93

	P	W	D	L	F	A	P
Buckfastleigh Rangers	30	25	4	1	86	21	79
Newton Abbot	30	21	5	4	91	31	68
Northern Telecom (Paignton)	30	20	5	5	81	38	65
Weston Mill Oak Villa	30	16	6	8	57	46	54
Newton St. Cyres	30	15	7	8	61	44	52
Stoke Gabriel	30	15	7	8	62	47	52
Alphington	30	13	8	9	50	37	47
Elburton Villa	30	12	6	12	62	49	42
Willand Rovers	30	11	5	14	67	70	38
Teignmouth	30	9	8	13	52	60	35
Plymstock United	30	10	5	15	47	61	35
Chagford	30	8	4	18	38	82	28
Cullompton Rangers	30	7	4	19	33	64	25
Topsham Town	30	6	6	18	46	75	24
Ivybridge Town	30	3	6	21	34	84	15
EAF Plymouth	30	3	6	21	36	94	15

EAF Plymouth changed name to Plymouth Parkway.

1993-94

Newton Abbot	30	23	3	4	122	28	72
Stoke Gabriel	30	19	6	5	85	37	63
Plymouth Parkway	30	19	4	7	71	44	61
Weston Mill Oak Villa	30	16	7	7	71	38	55
Willand Rovers	30	16	6	8	70	58	54
Northern Telecom (Paignton)	30	16	4	10	81	54	52
Buckfastleigh Rangers	30	17	1	12	59	50	52
Plymstock United	30	14	4	12	52	51	46
Alphington	30	11	8	11	65	61	41
Elburton Villa	30	12	3	15	54	55	39
Teignmouth	30	9	4	17	46	79	31
Cullompton Rangers	30	7	7	16	49	68	28
Newton St. Cyres	30	7	5	18	38	86	26
Ivybridge Town	30	7	5	18	39	95	26
Chagford	30	6	5	19	52	70	23
Topsham Town	30	3	4	23	23	95	13
						977	969

Ottery St. Mary joined from the Western League.

1994-95

Stoke Gabriel	32	27	2	3	116	18	83
Alphington	32	23	3	6	77	35	72
Northern Telecom (Paignton)	32	17	3	12	66	57	54
Plymouth Parkway	32	15	8	9	74	54	53
Willand Rovers	32	15	7	10	72	58	52
Plymstock United	32	15	7	10	76	52	52
Weston Mill Oak Villa	32	15	7	10	74	56	52
Topsham Town	32	12	8	12	72	65	44
Cullompton Rangers	32	12	7	13	60	54	43
Chagford	32	13	6	13	53	53	42
Newton Abbot	32	10	7	15	62	69	37
Ottery St. Mary	32	10	9	13	62	81	35
Buckfastleigh Rangers	32	8	6	18	58	106	30
Teignmouth	32	9	2	21	54	89	29
Newton St. Cyres	32	6	10	16	41	82	28
Elburton Villa	32	7	7	18	45	87	25
Ivybridge Town	32	5	7	20	55	101	22

Chagford and Elburton Villa each had 3 points deducted. Ottery St. Mary had 4 points deducted. Northern Telecom (Paignton) disbanded. Budleigh Salterton joined from the Devon & Exeter League, Dartmouth United joined from the South Devon League and Plymouth Command joined from the Plymouth & District League.

1995-96

Budleigh Salterton	36	21	10	5	96	41	73
Stoke Gabriel	36	22	7	7	91	36	73
Willand Rovers	36	22	6	8	73	41	72
Dartmouth United	36	22	6	8	80	52	72
Alphington	36	19	6	11	85	46	63
Topsham Town	36	17	9	10	86	60	60
Teignmouth	36	19	3	14	93	67	60
Newton Abbot	36	16	8	12	66	55	56
Plymouth Command	36	16	6	14	68	58	54
Buckfastleigh Rangers	36	12	11	13	62	66	47
Cullompton Rangers	36	13	7	16	46	57	46
Elburton Villa	36	13	7	16	56	81	46
Plymouth Parkway	36	11	12	13	72	77	45
Plymstock United	36	12	8	16	54	63	44
Newton St. Cyres	36	9	7	20	51	89	34
Ivybridge Town	36	10	4	22	55	95	34
Weston Mill Oak Villa	36	9	6	21	57	92	33
Ottery St. Mary	36	8	6	22	43	111	30
Chagford	36	4	5	27	48	95	17

Chagford moved to the South Devon League. Appledore & Bideford AAC joined from the South-Western League and Newton Abbot Spurs joined from the South Devon League.

1996-97

	P	W	D	L	F	A	Pts
Stoke Gabriel	38	25	10	3	95	39	85
Dartmouth United	38	24	6	8	88	45	78
Willand Rovers	38	22	7	9	101	52	73
Topsham Town	38	21	9	8	87	51	72
Budleigh Salterton	38	22	4	12	82	47	70
Appledore & Bideford AAC	38	21	5	12	116	49	68
Cullompton Rangers	38	22	2	14	77	60	68
Buckfastleigh Rangers	38	18	7	13	79	61	61
Newton Abbot	38	16	12	10	77	62	60
Plymouth Parkway	38	18	4	16	88	58	58
Plymouth Command	38	17	6	15	78	62	57
Ottery St. Mary	38	15	9	14	88	78	54
Alphington	38	15	8	15	62	80	50
Newton Abbot Spurs	38	14	6	18	87	71	48
Weston Mill Oak Villa	38	12	6	20	76	87	42
Elburton Villa	38	10	7	21	59	81	37
Newton St. Cyres	38	9	6	23	54	99	33
Plymstock United	38	7	5	26	51	129	26
Ivybridge Town	38	8	1	29	52	152	25
Teignmouth	38	4	0	34	40	174	3

Alphington had 3 points deducted. Teignmouth had 9 points deducted.

1997-98

	P	W	D	L	F	A	Pts
Topsham Town	38	27	4	7	97	30	85
Cullompton Rangers	38	25	7	6	95	35	82
Newton Abbot	38	25	6	7	84	40	81
Willand Rovers	38	22	9	7	88	32	75
Stoke Gabriel	38	20	9	9	85	41	69
Appledore & Bideford AAC	38	20	6	12	94	71	66
Plymouth Command	38	19	9	10	97	77	66
Budleigh Salterton	38	19	7	12	84	66	64
Dartmouth United	38	18	9	11	82	54	63
Plymouth Parkway	38	17	11	10	87	57	62
Ottery St. Mary	38	18	6	14	72	61	60
Newton St. Cyres	38	13	7	18	63	79	46
Alphington	38	10	11	17	56	79	41
Buckfastleigh Rangers	38	11	7	20	56	85	40
Newton Abbot Spurs	38	10	7	21	63	81	37
Teignmouth	38	11	1	26	59	122	31
Elburton Villa	38	8	6	24	45	86	30
Weston Mill Oak Villa	38	9	3	26	51	98	30
Plymstock United	38	7	4	27	57	114	25
Ivybridge Town	38	6	1	31	50	157	16

Teignmouth and Ivybridge Town each had 3 points deducted.
Weston Mill Oak Villa changed their name to Vospers Oak Villa.
Appledore & Bideford AAC changed their name to Appledore.
Plymouth Parkway moved to the South-Western League.
Crediton United joined from the Western League.

1998-99

	P	W	D	L	F	A	Pts
Willand Rovers	38	28	6	4	101	33	90
Cullompton Rangers	38	26	7	5	84	40	85
Budleigh Salterton	38	25	7	6	115	47	82
Vospers Oak Villa	38	21	8	9	107	55	71
Ottery St. Mary	38	20	6	12	71	50	66
Appledore	38	18	10	10	90	57	64
Stoke Gabriel	38	16	13	9	84	62	61
Dartmouth United	38	18	7	13	75	66	61
Newton Abbot Spurs	38	17	7	14	67	70	58
Buckfastleigh Rangers	38	17	6	15	97	61	57
Crediton United	38	18	3	17	67	64	57
Topsham Town	38	14	10	14	82	66	52
Newton Abbot	38	13	12	13	57	52	51
Newton St. Cyres	38	14	8	16	62	66	50
Ivybridge Town	38	14	3	21	79	93	45
Alphington	38	10	6	22	61	100	36
Plymstock United	38	6	10	22	41	80	28
Elburton Villa	38	7	5	26	48	98	26
Plymouth Command	38	6	5	27	44	109	23
Teignmouth	38	2	1	35	40	203	7

Dartmouth United changed their name to Dartmouth.
Plymouth Command moved to the Plymouth & District League and
Teignmouth moved to the South Devon League.
Exeter Civil Service joined from the Devon & Exeter League and
Heavitree United joined from the Western League.

1999-2000

	P	W	D	L	F	A	Pts
Budleigh Salterton	38	25	6	7	102	51	81
Stoke Gabriel	38	26	2	10	92	48	80
Newton Abbot Spurs	38	23	8	7	84	45	77
Alphington	38	23	4	11	82	62	73
Vospers Oak Villa	38	23	3	12	117	70	72
Ivybridge Town	38	22	6	10	99	56	72
Willand Rovers	38	20	8	10	83	44	65
Dartmouth	38	20	5	13	95	58	65
Ottery St. Mary	38	17	13	8	80	55	64
Cullompton Rangers	38	18	4	16	95	74	58
Newton Abbot	38	17	5	16	81	71	56
Exeter Civil Service	38	15	10	13	77	76	55
Appledore	38	13	12	13	63	71	51
Plymstock United	38	12	6	20	52	69	42
Buckfastleigh Rangers	38	10	6	22	43	75	36
Topsham Town	38	9	4	25	53	89	31
Crediton United	38	7	6	25	53	117	27
Heavitree United	38	7	6	25	50	118	27
Elburton Villa	38	5	7	26	58	139	27
Newton St. Cyres	38	5	5	28	52	123	20

Willand Rovers had 3 points deducted.
Newton St. Cyres moved to the Devon & Exeter League and Buckland
Athletic joined from the Devon & Exeter League.

2000-01

	P	W	D	L	F	A	Pts
Willand Rovers	38	26	9	3	98	41	87
Buckland Athletic	38	24	5	9	107	54	77
Alphington	38	21	10	7	87	58	73
Heavitree United	38	22	5	11	97	61	71
Dartmouth	38	19	11	8	108	60	68
Vospers Oak Villa	38	20	6	12	80	61	66
Ottery St. Mary	38	20	5	13	82	57	65
Budleigh Salterton	38	19	8	11	77	60	65
Newton Abbot Spurs	38	16	12	10	89	57	60
Newton Abbot	38	17	8	13	96	58	59
Elburton Villa	38	14	8	16	59	83	50
Ivybridge Town	38	13	10	15	74	74	49
Cullompton Rangers	38	11	12	15	51	69	45
Appledore	38	12	6	20	73	87	42
Topsham Town	38	10	6	22	67	105	36
Crediton United	38	10	6	22	61	103	36
Exeter Civil Service	38	8	9	21	55	82	33
Buckfastleigh Rangers	38	9	3	26	39	118	30
Stoke Gabriel	38	7	8	23	57	93	27
Plymstock United	38	4	9	25	47	123	21

Willand Rovers moved to the Western League and Dartington Sports
joined from the South Devon League.

2001-02

	P	W	D	L	F	A	Pts
Dartmouth	38	28	7	3	125	45	91
Newton Abbot	38	25	8	5	107	45	83
Vospers Oak Villa	38	24	4	10	82	38	76
Ivybridge Town	38	23	6	9	109	59	75
Newton Abbot Spurs	38	23	1	14	74	63	70
Buckland Athletic	38	19	9	10	91	59	66
Budleigh Salterton	38	20	2	16	70	87	62
Topsham Town	38	18	7	13	95	72	58
Ottery St. Mary	38	16	7	15	76	52	55
Alphington	38	15	8	15	65	86	53
Heavitree United	38	16	4	18	71	76	52
Cullompton Rangers	38	14	7	17	64	67	49
Exeter Civil Service	38	13	9	16	60	72	48
Elburton Villa	38	14	6	18	64	82	48
Plymstock United	38	13	7	18	61	71	46
Dartington Sports	38	11	9	18	63	75	42
Stoke Gabriel	38	10	4	24	63	104	34
Crediton United	38	9	5	24	52	74	32
Appledore	38	8	7	23	57	84	27
Buckfastleigh Rangers	38	2	1	35	32	170	4

Topsham Town and Buckfastleigh Rangers each had 3 points deducted.
Buckfastleigh Rangers moved to the South Devon League and
University of Exeter joined from the Devon & Exeter League.

2002-03

Dartmouth	38	29	5	4	96	32	92
Ivybridge Town	38	26	8	4	135	55	86
Buckland Athletic	38	23	6	9	88	47	75
Vospers Oak Villa	38	21	4	13	72	57	67
Alphington	38	19	7	12	80	54	64
Newton Abbot Spurs	38	19	6	13	62	49	60
University of Exeter	38	19	3	16	85	76	60
Newton Abbot	38	16	11	11	67	57	59
Plymstock United	38	14	13	11	72	58	55
Cullompton Rangers	38	15	8	15	56	65	53
Ottery St. Mary	38	15	6	17	63	74	51
Heavitree United	38	14	6	18	71	84	48
Dartington Sports	38	13	7	18	79	70	46
Appledore	38	12	9	17	51	69	45
Elburton Villa	38	11	10	17	67	69	43
Budleigh Salterton	38	12	8	18	58	77	43
Exeter Civil Service	38	9	13	16	46	79	40
Stoke Gabriel	38	7	6	25	58	92	27
Crediton United	38	7	5	26	30	109	26
Topsham Town	38	7	3	28	29	92	24

Budleigh Salterton had 1 point deducted.
Newton Abbot Spurs had 3 points deducted.
Holsworthy joined from the South-Western League.

2003-04

Holsworthy	40	26	11	3	100	40	89
Ivybridge Town	40	25	9	6	115	49	84
Vospers Oak Villa	40	25	6	9	105	53	81
Elburton Villa	40	23	7	10	93	65	76
Dartington Sports	40	22	8	10	123	71	74
Ottery St. Mary	40	20	8	12	87	64	71
Newton Abbot	40	22	4	14	79	63	70
Buckland Athletic	40	21	6	13	86	63	69
Dartmouth	40	16	10	14	88	64	58
Crediton United	40	15	12	13	78	70	57
University of Exeter	40	17	3	20	64	63	54
Budleigh Salterton	40	13	15	12	66	69	54
Plymstock United	40	13	13	14	61	63	52
Alphington	40	12	10	18	55	73	46
Appledore	40	13	6	21	54	79	45
Cullompton Rangers	40	10	14	16	71	71	44
Stoke Gabriel	40	12	7	21	53	92	43
Newton Abbot Spurs	40	9	10	21	55	103	37
Exeter Civil Service	40	5	12	23	37	79	27
Heavitree United	40	6	5	29	50	139	23
Topsham Town	40	4	6	30	28	115	13

Ottery St. Mary had 3 points added. Topsham Town had 5 points deducted.
Topsham Town moved to the Devon & Exeter League. Heavitree United
merged with Heavitree Social Club from the Devon & Exeter League
Senior Division Three and moved to the Premier Division of the Devon
& Exeter League as Heavitree United Social Club. Teignmouth joined
from the South Devon League and St. Loyes joined from the Devon &
Exeter League.

2004-05

Teignmouth	40	30	5	5	106	44	95
Plymstock United	40	27	6	7	107	41	87
Dartmouth	40	25	6	9	90	52	81
Ivybridge Town	40	22	9	9	110	60	75
Vospers Oak Villa	40	23	4	13	95	61	72
Newton Abbot	40	20	8	12	89	52	70
Buckland Athletic	40	19	12	9	78	52	69
Dartington Sports	40	20	9	11	76	53	69
Elburton Villa	40	20	6	14	95	63	66
Budleigh Salterton	40	20	6	14	81	78	66
Newton Abbot Spurs	40	18	7	15	90	71	61
Ottery St. Mary	40	16	9	15	70	71	57
St. Loyes	40	16	5	19	65	80	53
Holsworthy	40	15	5	20	67	63	50
University of Exeter	40	13	6	21	74	85	45
Cullompton Rangers	40	11	10	19	68	89	43
Alphington	40	12	3	25	44	93	39
Appledore	40	11	3	26	59	99	36
Crediton United	40	10	5	25	52	115	35
Stoke Gabriel	40	6	0	34	49	137	18
Exeter Civil Service	40	1	6	33	27	133	6

Newton Abbot had 2 points added. Vospers Oak Villa had 1 point
deducted. Exeter Civil Service had 3 points deducted. Dartington
Sports merged with Totnes Town of the South Devon League and
continued in the Devon County League as Totnes and Dartington SC.
Exeter Civil Service moved to the Devon & Exeter League.

2005-06

Ivybridge Town	38	31	4	3	122	38	97
Plymstock United	38	23	8	7	93	41	77
Holsworthy	38	23	5	10	90	67	74
Ottery St. Mary	38	21	7	10	85	60	70
Dartmouth	38	21	7	10	79	56	70
Newton Abbot	38	20	6	12	83	49	66
Budleigh Salterton	38	20	5	13	78	59	65
Newton Abbot Spurs	38	19	7	12	75	58	64
Teignmouth	38	18	9	11	90	66	63
Totnes & Dartington SC	38	17	8	13	78	62	59
Elburton Villa	38	15	6	17	59	59	54
Crediton United	38	16	4	18	53	65	52
Buckland Athletic	38	14	6	18	63	82	48
Alphington	38	13	7	18	56	79	46
Vospers Oak Villa	38	12	7	19	68	75	43
University of Exeter	38	14	2	22	66	71	40
Cullompton Rangers	38	10	4	24	56	95	34
Appledore	38	10	2	26	45	95	32
Stoke Gabriel	38	4	6	28	42	117	18
St. Loyes	38	2	4	32	31	118	10

Elburton Villa had 3 points added. University of Exeter had 4 points
deducted. St. Loyes moved to the Devon & Exeter League.
Witheridge joined from the Devon & Exeter League.

2006-07

Dartmouth	38	27	6	5	100	36	87
Newton Abbot	38	25	6	7	85	39	81
Elburton Villa	38	25	5	8	83	48	80
Budleigh Salterton	38	24	6	8	87	47	78
Holsworthy	38	21	6	11	86	71	69
University of Exeter	38	20	7	11	83	51	67
Cullompton Rangers	38	21	3	14	91	68	66
Ivybridge Town	38	18	9	11	94	52	63
Newton Abbot Spurs	38	17	12	9	70	55	63
Ottery St. Mary	38	16	7	15	68	61	55
Witheridge	38	12	9	17	64	78	45
Buckland Athletic	38	13	5	20	57	71	44
Appledore	38	12	8	18	49	69	44
Totnes & Dartington SC	38	11	10	17	73	87	43
Crediton United	38	12	5	21	47	73	41
Plymstock United	38	11	4	23	52	78	37
Vospers Oak Villa	38	10	6	22	46	80	36
Alphington	38	10	5	23	64	76	35
Stoke Gabriel	38	8	3	27	43	99	27
Teignmouth	38	5	2	31	37	140	17

At the end of this season, the Devon County League closed down and
merged with the South-Western League to form the new South-West
Peninsula League for the 2007-08 season.